GREAT WRITERS STUD

COMMONWEALTH LITERATURE

GREAT WRITERS STUDENT LIBRARY

1. The Beginnings to 1558
2. The Renaissance Excluding Drama
3. Renaissance Drama
4. Restoration and 18th-Century Prose and Poetry Excluding Drama and the Novel
5. Restoration and 18th-Century Drama
6. The Romantic Period Excluding the Novel
7. The Victorian Period Excluding the Novel
8. The Novel to 1900
9. 20th-Century Poetry
10. 20th-Century Fiction
11. 20th-Century Drama
12. American Literature to 1900
13. 20th-Century American Literature
14. Commonwealth Literature

Editor: James Vinson
Associate Editor: D. L. Kirkpatrick

GREAT WRITERS STUDENT LIBRARY

COMMONWEALTH LITERATURE

INTRODUCTION BY
WILLIAM WALSH

© by The Macmillan Press Ltd., 1979

All rights reserved. No part of this publication may be reproduced or transmitted in any form or by any means, without permission.

First published 1979 by
THE MACMILLAN PRESS LIMITED
London and Basingstoke
Associated companies in New York, Dublin
Melbourne, Johannesburg and Madras

ISBN 0333 28356 2

CONTENTS

EDITOR'S NOTE   page vii

INTRODUCTION   1

COMMONWEALTH LITERATURE   17

NOTES ON CONTRIBUTORS   277

EDITOR'S NOTE

The entry for each writer consists of a biography, a complete list of his published books, a selected list of published bibliographies and critical studies on the writer, and a signed critical essay on his work.

In the biographies, details of education, military service, and marriage(s) are generally given before the usual chronological summary of the life of the writer; awards and honours are given last.

The Publications section is meant to include all book publications, though as a rule broadsheets, single sermons and lectures, minor pamphlets, exhibition catalogues, etc. are omitted. Under the heading Collections, we have listed the most recent collections of the complete works and those of individual genres (verse, plays, novels, stories, and letters); only those collections which have some editorial authority and were issued after the writer's death are listed; on-going editions are indicated by a dash after the date of publication; often a general selection from the writer's works or a selection from the works in the individual genres listed above is included.

Titles are given in modern spelling, though the essayists were allowed to use original spelling for titles and quotations; often the titles are "short." The date given is that of the first book publication, which often followed the first periodical or anthology publication by some time; we have listed the actual year of publication, often different from that given on the title-page. No attempt has been made to indicate which works were published anonymously or pseudonymously, or which works of fiction were published in more than one volume. We have listed plays which were produced but not published, but only since 1700; librettos and musical plays are listed along with the other plays; no attempt has been made to list lost or unverified plays. Reprints of books (including facsimile editions) and revivals of plays are not listed unless a revision or change of title is involved. The most recent edited version of individual works is included if it supersedes the collected edition cited.

In the essays, short references to critical remarks refer to items cited in the Publications section or in the Reading List. Introductions, memoirs, editorial matter, etc. in works cited in the Publications section are not repeated in the Reading List.

INTRODUCTION

The purpose of this volume is to provide the reader with the appropriate facts and critical guidance in what will be still to many the relatively new, or even unknown, field of Commonwealth literature. Literary studies in English are dominated by the immensely rich achievement of English literature through the centuries, and by the current movement of writing in Britain and the United States. (It would be more appropriate, certainly in England, to invert the order of interest and to say dominated by writing first in the United States and secondly in Britain.) Commonwealth literature itself is of course a term of art. The Commonwealth is an increasingly impalpable and metaphysical conception. Even to define it would require a practised lawyer, and to point to where it exists, an accomplished politician. Here one is concerned with writing in English outside Britain and the United States. Which writers have made a significant use of the resources of the language to embody their experience and view of life? Which of them are of more than local importance? Which of them, judged by appropriate standards, have added to the canon of literature in English and realised in a creative way capacities implicit in the language? One harps constantly on the language because the existence of a work of literature depends not on the writer alone but also on the degree of maturity the language it is written in has reached, just as its complexity and fineness depends on the range of resources within the language. One thing will certainly become clear from the work of the writers considered in this book, namely the amazing capacity of the English language to express an immense span of sensibility, whether West Indian, Canadian, Australian, African, New Zealand, or Indian, a testimony not just to the gifts of the individual writers but to the genius of the language itself. All these writers write in English but they do not, of course, think of themselves, nor are they to be thought of, as Commonwealth writers, which would make as much sense as UNESCO writers or Esperanto writers. They feel themselves to be Australians or New Zealanders or Canadians, writing against a particular historical and national context, not contributors to an amorphous Commonwealth. It is the English language in which they are united, not the Commonwealth. Nevertheless, the term is convenient and represents in a reasonably uncontentious way a fact of history and substance about the tradition and the art of these writers.

The shared language brings up at once the central paradox of Commonwealth literature, namely the coexistence in it of the literatures of English-speaking nations and of those in which English is only a second, or learnt, language. The two most extraordinary cases of this are those of India and Africa. Indeed, it is an Indian, Buddhadeva Bose, who has given, even if unsympathetically, an accurate analysis of the predicament of writers writing in English out of an alien experience with no constant, inward, and organic connection with English as a living language (from *Modern Indian Poetry in English*, edited by P. Lal, 1969):

> The best of Indian-English verse belongs to the nineteenth century, when Indians came nearest to "speaking, thinking and dreaming in English." In authenticity of diction and feeling Sri Aurobindo far outshines the others, but Toru Dutt's charming pastiche still holds some interest. As for the present-day "Indo-Anglians," they are earnest and not without talent, but it is difficult to see how they can develop as poets in a language which they have learnt from books and seldom hear spoken in the streets or even in their own homes, and whose two great sources lie beyond the seven seas. A poet must have the right to change and recreate language, and this no foreigner can ever acquire. As late as 1937, Yeats reminded Indian writers that "no man can think or write with music and vigour except in his

mother tongue"; to the great majority of Indians this admonition was unnecessary, but the intrepid few who left it unheeded do not yet realise that "Indo-Anglian" poetry is a blind alley, lined with curio shops, leading nowhere.

There is a certain unanswerable truth hidden in Bose's observations, but, however irresistible the case made by Bose is, there is no *a priori* truth or dogma in literature. There is no doubt that there have been poets in India and Africa who have written what are by any standards poems in English of genuine merit and authentic individuality. Let me name only from India Kamala Das, Nissim Ezekiel, Arvind Krishna Mehrotra, R. Parathasarathy, Gieve Patel, A. K. Ramanujan; or from Africa Gabriel Okara, Christopher Okigbo, Michael Echeruo, Wole Soyinka, J. P. Clark, Kewsi Brew. One of these, Nissim Ezekiel, whose poetry is intellectually complex and fastidious in diction, has made with his own poetry a sufficient reply. He has also retorted to Bose's strictures (in the same volume) in a more explicit fashion:

> The tone and implied attitudes of Mr. Buddhadeva Bose's article are distasteful to me.... He begins, for example, by pretending to be surprised that "Indians should ever have tried to write verse in English." What is so surprising about it? Is Mr. Bose completely devoid of a sense of history? Does it not occur to him that since English was introduced as a medium of higher education in India, some Indians *naturally* took to writing verse in it, just as other Indians wrote political commentaries, philosophical essays, sociological surveys, economic studies, and so on? Historical situations create cultural consequences.... To write poetry in English because one cannot write it in any other language is surely not a despicable decision.

"Historical situations create cultural consequences." Indeed they do, whether in the absent-minded and oppressive British Empire or in the more calculated and weightless Commonwealth. It was indeed natural that Canada, Australia, and New Zealand should develop as they have done from the late eighteenth century and the detritus of an exhausted Augustan literary idiom. In Australia this idiom was blended with the sweetness of Walter Scott, as it was in Canada where it followed first Romantic and then Tennysonian models. The literary life of Canada, Australia, and New Zealand in its earliest stages showed novelists and poets using on the material of their own life instruments of vision devised elsewhere for quite different purposes. In each of the three countries the effort was to assimilate the new experience to the old, whether that was English, Irish, or Scottish. A. J. M. Smith described the two aims of the earliest Canadian poets, whether French or English, in *The Oxford Book of Canadian Verse* (1960):

> One group has made an effort to express whatever is unique or local in Canadian life, while the other has concentrated on what it has in common with life everywhere. The poets of the first group sought to discover something distinctively and especially "Canadian" and thus come to terms with what was new in the natural, social, and political environment in which they found themselves or which they helped to create; the others made an effort to escape the limitations of provincialism or colonialism by entering into the universal civilizing culture of ideas. The first group was more homely, more natural, and sometimes more original, but it lacked, until the twentieth century, the technical proficiency necessary for real success. The danger for the second group was to be merely literary.

In Australia the manipulation of Australian material to make it conform to an English sensibility – for example, in *The Recollections of Geoffry Hamlyn* (1859) by Henry Kingsley – was succeeded by a phase characterised by the substitution of Dickens for Scott as the primary English influence on the novel. We see this, for example, in *For the Term of His*

Natural Life (1874) by Marcus Clarke. It led in Australia to the effort to establish a genuinely Australian character and tone in its literature and the effort accurately to draw the contours of the true Australian voice and powerfully to respond to an Australian scene, unmisted by English importation. In Australia a great part in this transformation was played by the group of writers formed around a handful of literary periodicals, the most important of which was the *Bulletin,* whose passion was for an exclusively Australian Australia. This group of writers played an important part in the long preparation of a separate Australian identity.

The development of the early literature of New Zealand rehearses the progress we see both in Australia and Canada, that is, it begins with the literature of observation, travel, and history, in which the actual terrain and the mode of life is seen through European eyes. New Zealand, for example, was frequently taken as a testing ground for the theory of the Noble Savage. It was an English woman, Lady Barker, who first communicated a genuine sense of the realities of New Zealand life. Her work is unfatigued by current cliché, and the fine instrument of an acute perception. The range of New Zealand experience became articulate in a group of women novelists, Edith Searle Grossman, Alice F. Webb, Blanche Baughan, and Jane Mander. These writers attempted and sometimes succeeded in discovering a distinguished New Zealand voice and had come to a point where they were capable of seeing New Zealand life unrefracted through an alien haze. This development was brought to a much higher point of maturity by a group of writers in the 1930's, of which the theorists were the critic and moralist M. H. Holcroft and the poet Allen Curnow, who wrote (in *The Penguin Book of New Zealand Verse,* 1960) that the "individual talent" should take its place in the historical "tradition" of New Zealand: "whatever is true vision belongs, here, uniquely to the islands of New Zealand. The best of our verse is marked or moulded everywhere by peculiar pressures – pressures arising from the isolation of the country, its physical character, and its history."

In Canada, a more positive effort than in New Zealand, a less truculent one than in Australia, to arrive at the same kind of thing, the development of a separate Canadian tradition, was one of the consequences of the work of the post-Confederation poets, Lampman, Roberts, Crawford, Carman, and Scott. Their work, particularly that of Lampman and Scott, had an intrinsic merit and distinct historical significance in that it helped to articulate, in a way which could be used in the future, a Canadian tradition. Such a tradition had been inaugurated in the history of the American Francis Parkman, of theologians like Henry Alline, of philosophers like Thomas McCulloch, and these poets gave it the richness and density of art – the first literary and local expression of the Canadian spirit. Both in Canada and Australia the most important literary work was in the poetry and the novel. The drama led a feeble and hardly separate existence.

In India in the nineteenth century a considerable quantity of significant writing had certainly appeared in English but of an abstract and discursive kind. It had a strong Victorian philosophy and much of it had to do with communicating Western ideas in pursuit of the effort to reform Hindu thought and to bring into it a stricter ethic and a more scientific habit of thought. This was a tradition inaugurated by Ram Mohan Roy, sustained by Vivekananda, and still represented in the modern world by Nirad C. Chaudhuri. The fact that these writers worked in English was a large, though implicit, recognition of the fact and influence of British civilization in India. The effort of all these writers and particularly of Chaudhuri, whose *The Autobiography of an Unknown Indian* (1951) is probably the greatest example of this kind of non-fictional literary work written in a language other than the mother-tongue, was to bring a questioning Western mind into touch with an Indian tradition and sensibility. All these writers found the concepts, principles, usages, and styles which they wished to bring into Indian life not in the cramped civilization of British India but in the immensely more inclusive source of the English language and its literature. It was not till the 1930's and later that the novel in English really began its separate and impressive Indian existence. There are now a considerable number of these writers but they all have in common the genuine novelist's impulse to illustrate, to be specific and concrete and embodied. They are genuine novelists for whom fiction is an end in itself and not a means of communicating other kinds of truth. They range from Mulk Raj Anand, who is passionately concerned with the villages, with poverty, with the cruelties of caste and social injustice, to Raja Rao whose work is profoundly philosophical or metaphysical. It is as concrete as Mulk Raj Anand who is concerned with the inner life, or as subtle as the translucent, sensitive, and Chekhov-like work of R. K. Narayan. Narayan beautifully illustrates the use of a language bred in one tradition and history to be the instrument of a vision derived from a totally different one. His is a concentrated and limiting art, concerned with modest unself-confident and over-conscious heroes of the middle class. His novels are varied, but one sees a common pattern which traces the development of spiritual maturity among the young, in a setting of marvellously authentic Indian life.

If the literature of Canada, Australia, and New Zealand started at the end of the eighteenth and the beginning of the nineteenth centuries, the literature of the West Indies is essentially a creation of the twentieth century. There are, according to George Lamming (in *The Pleasure of Exile,* 1960), three important events in British Caribbean history. "The first event is the discovery.... The next event is the abolition of slavery and the arrival of the East – India and China – in the Caribbean Sea.... The third important event ... is the discovery of the novel by West Indians as a way of investigating and projecting the inner experience of the West Indian community." The West Indian community is the product of a society descended from European landlords, functionaries, and traders, African slaves, Indentured Indians, from Chinese and others, the scope of whose origin and sufferings matches the virtuosity of the language which is its voice. George Lamming believes that it is the life of the West Indian peasant which is the centre of the West Indian experience, and it is their success in giving a voice to this silent richness that makes him admire Mittelholzer, Samuel Selvon, and Roger Mais, whose work is shot through and through with the urgency of peasant life. But this is perhaps to exclude one of the greatest of West Indian writers, V. S. Naipaul, a detached critic of West Indian society. His combination of peasant sagacity and cultivated elegance has produced a distinctively individual fiction which is also strongly representative of the complex society of the West Indies. Some of the hostility shown to Naipaul in his native land may be attributable to an aristocratic flinching from what he sees as the common brutality of so much human life, something which in his later work has become almost a Swiftian and obsessive distaste. Nevertheless, Naipaul has himself most skilfully engaged with some of the main themes of West Indian fiction, with, for example, the vitality of folk life, with the irrationality of folk life, particularly in the half-institutionalised form it takes in the West Indies, and, finally, with what is perhaps the deepest and most painful theme in West Indian fiction, the agony and pride of race. Wounded racial feeling at a profound spiritual level is a strong impulse and staple motif of much West Indian writing, in Vic Reid's *New Day* (1949) and *The Leopard* (1958) for example, and in some of the most impressive fiction of George Lamming himself.

Commonwealth literature in India began to assume its own character in the 1930's, in the West Indies in the later 1950's, and in Africa in the 1960's. In Africa, its most impressive talent is shown in the novel and the play, particularly in the novels of Chinua Achebe and the drama of Wole Soyinka. Historical circumstances again account for the English connection of these writers, but not for the remarkable quality of the achieved work. Chinua Achebe, who works from a near-Renaissance impulse to teach by entertaining, is much concerned with the growth and decline of Ibo civilisation, a world which is masculine, coherent, and, in a sense, Greek. The classical Ibo world embodied in his fiction is rounded and intricate, and in correspondence with a great range of human impulses, embodying both the aristocratic and democratic principles. It is a life lived by a clan of equals which yet allows for the exceptional man. Later novels show how external forces, of Christianity and the British administrative system, invade and infect this poised and fragile synthesis. The talent of Wole Soyinka has the fullness and substance of Achebe's, but is more richly and elaborately orchestrated. He has, too, like Achebe, a profound feeling for peasant life, but has a much more sophisticated literary culture, and a very worried and anxious contemporary consciousness. Soyinka's drama is embedded in religious myth, enlivened by a magnificently muscular vernacular idiom and humour, and expressed in a language of great power and range.

In neither of these writers, so close is the expression to the experience, do we find that linguistic strain displayed when experiences nourished by one stratum of experience and history are expressed in a language from another. This is a fundamental friction we see in the work, for example, of John Pepper Clark, in which an African content is frequently at odds with the English idiom. As it seems to me we do also, for example, in the work of the East African poet Okot p'Bitek, or in the curious combination of film script, best-seller, and market pamphlet practised by Cyprian Ekwensi. That so much African and West Indian fiction should be in English is the result no doubt of the writer's desire to use Western categories of analysis and dissection and the rich English mode of expression on his unique African experience, as much as a desire to build up an international audience. The number of these novelists increases yearly. Many of these writers are at home in a complicated language, and some of them, chiefly for reasons of education, find it impossible not to write in English. This would be truer, I judge, of the Indian novelists than of the African. Wole Soyinka, for example, has indicated a willingness to write in an indigenous national language should one become possible and acceptable. But R. K. Narayan, who has made an Indian sensibility at home in English art, once said that he felt no linguistic strain and that for him English was always the natural language to write in. When Narayan was in England in 1968 I asked him in a radio conversation (23 February) whether he found it any strain to write in English. His reply will interest the reader:

> Until you mentioned another tongue I never had any idea that I was writing in another tongue. My whole education has been in English from the primary school, and most of my reading has been in the English language. The language and literature of this country flourished in the Indian soil until lately. It still remains a language of the intelligentsia. But English has been with us for over a century and a half. I am particularly fond of the language. I was never aware that I was using a different, a foreign, language when I wrote in English, because it came to me very easily. I can't explain how. English is a very adaptable language. And it's so transparent it can take on the tint of any country.

No doubt there will be other R. K. Narayans and Chinua Achebes living the same double life and coming to a similar resolution. In their distinctly difficult conditions they will at any rate have one supreme advantage, the use of a language of such capacity and range that no reach of human experience is beyond it.

I have referred to some of the historical circumstances in the development of Commonwealth literature, to the fundamental "given" of the English language, and to some characteristic themes and their various expressions in different parts of the globe. And it is true that none of these literatures could have developed without their special connection with the English literary tradition, and without the vast potency of the English language. Moreover, one has to recognise the special difficulties of writers in countries where there exist no adequate audience, no range of publishers and journals and critics, and whose governments, while finding the English language a useful technological and diplomatic tool, look on literature as a frivolous luxury. But as well as these there is the essential requirement of individual talent and I want now to turn to that handful of writers in the Commonwealth who seem, as critics in this volume will say, to have made substantial and even major contributions to literature in English in the modern world.

From India one would be bound to take R. K. Narayan. He writes of the middle class, his own class, the members of which are neither too well off not to be worried about money and position, nor de-humanized by absolute need. His hero is usually modest, sensitive, ardent, wry about himself, and sufficiently conscious to have an active inner life and to grope towards some existence independent of the family. The family is the immediate context in which he operates, and his novels are remarkable for the delicacy and precision of the family relations treated – that of son and parents, and brother and brother in *The Bachelor of Arts* (1937); of husband and wife, and father and daughter in *The English Teacher* (1945); of father and son in *The Financial Expert* (1952); of grandmother and grandson in *Waiting for the Mahatma* (1955).

The firmly delineated town, therefore, is the outer circle of the action; within it is the subtler and more wavering ring of the family; and at the centre of that stands, or rather flinches, the Narayan hero, a tentative, spiritually sensitive, appealingly limited character, in whom modesty is a positive force, whether he be the leathery old proprietor of a tiny industry like Jagan in *The Vendor of Sweets* (1967), or the converted con-man Raju in *The Guide* (1958; apologetically converted, note, in spite of himself), or the nervous editor of the press on Market Road, Nataraj, in *The Man-Eater of Malgudi* (1961). The characteristic Narayan figure always has the capacity to be surprised by the turn of events. His individuality has a certain formlessness, a lack of finish, indeed, as though the definition of his personality depended upon the play of external influences – which of course in India, with the immense weight of inherited tradition, it so frequently does. This quality of the incompleteness in the person means the further capacity not just to be startled by what happens but to be at least in part reconstituted by it. The procedure in a Narayan novel is almost invariably a renovation or reforming of character in response to the encouragement or provocation of events, which is never, however, total enough to be revolutionary but sufficient to make a new bend in the flow of continuity. If this is how the process appears to the observer, it shows itself to the protagonist as his effort to achieve a more explicit and articulate sense of self.

Narayan's novels are comedies of sadness, calling up the name of Chekhov rather than anything in English literature, as Graham Greene pointed out in his introduction to *The Bachelor of Arts*. The sadness comes from the painful experience of dismantling the routine self, which, the context being Indian, seems less a private possession than something distilled by powerful and ancient conventions, and secondly the reconstitution of another personality. The comedy arises from the sometimes bumbling, sometimes desperate, sometimes absurd exploration of different experience in the search for a new and, it may be, an exquisitely inappropriate role. The complex theme of Narayan's serious comedies, then, is – one must not balk at the word in an Indian context – the rebirth of self and the process of its pregnancy or education, the set of conditions in which it takes place. His characters occupy a universe of which the substantial features are both the flux of being and the plurality of being. Things flow, an infinite variety of things, of men and manners, relations and women, avocations and degrees, joys, disappointments, and disasters. To the author this is the nature of reality, to the characters what they will, perhaps, with a moderate kind of happiness, finally accommodate themselves to. This complicated cargo is carried on an English style which is limpid, simple, calm, and unaffected, natural in its run and tone, and beautifully measured to its purposes. It has neither the American purr of the combustion engine nor the thick marmalade quality of British English, and it communicates with complete ease a different, an Indian sensibility.

If I move from India on a natural route to the West Indies, I should produce the names of V. S. Naipaul and Derek Walcott. Naipaul's earliest novels suggest that he is the possessor of a delicate, attractive talent, at once gentle and mischievous, feeling and unsentimental. And Naipaul's gift clearly is all of this. But there are, both in *Miguel Street* (1959) and *The Mystic Masseur* (1957), hints of deeper resonances, insinuations of less tractable disasters. There is a kind of sadness folded into the quick lines of the sketches in *Miguel Street*. It is unemphatic and never despairing because neither author nor characters take up any indignant stance about what happens to them. They accept it. And they do so because of a conviction, or if that is too explicit and articulate, because of a profound attitude or a posture in the bones and nerves, that one part of being human is simply hopelessness, and another part is practising a ritual to make that tolerable. There is an image of this cool tragic sense even in the tumultuously farcical career of Ganesh the Mystic Masseur in the death of his father.

It is a driving need to establish both for others and themselves their human necessity which initiates and sustains *A House for Mr. Biswas* (1961), Naipaul's largest, most generous and inclusive work. "How terrible it would have been," Mr. Biswas reflects as he lies dying in his mortgaged house. "How terrible it would have been, at this time, to be without it: to have died among the Tulsis, amid the squalor of that large, disintegrating and indifferent family; to have left Shama and the children among them, in one room; worse, to have lived without even attempting to lay claim to one's portion of the earth; to have lived and died as one had been born, unnecessary and unaccommodated."

In Naipaul's work we see an independent and fastidious talent fully engaged and brilliantly successful: in the treatment of the second-hand violated colonial and post-colonial society; in the understanding of the psychology of the sensitive young, appalled by the sight others have of their secret life; in the rendering of political and social ideas, not as untethered formulations but living activities; in the evocation of place and physical context – the London light, the cocoa valleys, houses, weather, hotels – all, we often feel, so much more constant, so much more faithful to themselves than devious, impotently treacherous man; in the general composition and suppleness of tone and the scope of concretely realized experience; and above all in the penetration and vitality with which he develops his central, constitutive theme – one of profound human meaning – an exploration of the ways in which the conscious individual in a given society establishes modes of mediation between himself and his experience.

Derek Walcott is the finest, the most complete, of the West Indian poets. His early work, like that of many other contemporary poets, is derivative from seventeenth-century English poets, from Eliot, and from Auden. But these models are being used by a talent capable of ripening into its own unique self: and when one remembers how much Walcott had *not* the benefit of, in what immediate poetic context he had to construct a voice for his sensibility, his achievement, and one's admiration for his tense integrity, are very high indeed. His temptation was to slide into the satin smoothness admired by an earlier generation and made more enticing in his case by a cultivated love of the English language and its history. His achievement was to construct an idiom and rhythm which were in touch with traditional resources in the language while they established connections with the modern world in general and the West Indian situation in particular. His best poems bring a personal compassion to bear on more impersonal considerations, as in "Ruins of a Great House."

His range embraces the near-clinical analysis of the relations of separating lovers in the febrile "A Care-free Passion"; the quarrel of the African and the European in the West Indian blood; the magnificent Victorian dignity of an ancient West Indian lady, Mabel Rawlins, together with the civilized sobriety and the clear moral tone implied in her vocabulary and address. We have in the intrinsic and difficult music of such a poem as "A Letter from Brooklyn," an indication of the distance Walcott's poetry has come from its early external euphony. His poetry is now one of a deeper and strengthened experience, of a more personal and ravaged attachment to his own art and his West Indian world.

Wole Soyinka is an impressive poet and a novelist too, but it is in his plays that his gifts are most fully realized. He is much preoccupied with the mystery of time. The treatment of the theme of time in his plays persuades us that a society which has failed in an objective and progressive way to come to terms with time may well succeed in dealing with it in another way. When history is contracted to the span of memory between a grandfather and grandson and historical testimony to immediately existing and transient artefacts, then it is possible in thought and word for time to be distorted, contracted, or collapsed altogether. Which is just what Wole Soyinka does to the dimension of time in *A Dance of the Forests* (1960). Time in such a society is even more a mental construct than it is in those loaded with external historical evidence. But this is only a neutral and contextual condition of the dramatist's success. A more intimate and active means for managing time is a language sanctioned by the living belief of a people, with range, vitality, and sufficient resource to be equal to every layer of experience.

The Lion and the Jewel (1959) is a near-Roman comedy of a goatish ancient out-bluffing women of several generations and accomplishing in an off-hand way an intricate and difficult seduction. The action here is strict and nimble, the verse harder and thinner, the design very clear and unblurred. Neither Lakunle the schoolteacher, a most unhefty Leftie, the beautiful, simple Sidi, nor the cunning crone Sadiku, standing for a cerebral future, an unintelligible present, and a passively conventional past, respectively, is any match for the disillusioned and energetic conservatism of Baroka, the "Bale," or ruler and priest: "I do not hate progress, only its nature/Which makes all roofs and faces look the same."

The Road (1965) imposes the discipline of *The Lion and the Jewel* on the poetry of *A Dance of the Forests*. The play is set along a road, the road from life to death; the cast is a superbly seedy gang, including the driver of a passenger-truck No Danger No Delay; his passenger-tout and driver's mate, Samson, a mixture of Enobarbus and Mosca; a Captain of Thugs called Say Tokyo Kid; and a splendidly pliable policemen, Particulars Joe; and brooding over all with menacing benevolence, Professor, proprietor of the driver's haven (AKSIDENT STORE – ALL PART AVAILEBUL), a dismissed lay-reader but also the oppressively strange death-in-life figure. Everyone in the play is the servant, or agent, or priest, or student of death. The road itself is ruled by Ogun, the god of war and death and roads. Road accidents, which Professor, the missionary of death, helps to arrange by removing road signs from dangerous points of the road, are Ogun's High Masses. The theme of the work is life conceived of as a movement towards dissolution; the action of the play is an arrest of time at the point where man is dissolving into the under-world. This bleak and difficult subject is enriched by a mulch of religious myth, Yoruba custom and tradition, and indigenous cosmology, and enlivened by a vernacular idiom and a humour which is by turns wild, grim, and despairing. The imagination is peremptory, potent, fertile; the intrinsic logic of the play is Yoruba in its myth, Western in its dramatic categories; the use of the language, in the intuitive feel for its grain and phrasing, is triumphantly English.

Katherine Mansfield was a writer who succeeded in her best work, in "Prelude" and "At the Bay," for example, in raising a whole world on the slim basis of half a dozen members of a provincial New Zealand family. She was able quite unportentously to suggest the human universality implicit in the Wellington household. Taking over a new house is itself an instance of the way in which domestic commonplace becomes more largely significant since it is a natural extension of the human impulse to turn impersonal things in the direction of humanity. The conditions of success required by Katherine Mansfield for making the brilliantly pictured particular expressive of substantial human nature were the creative action of memory working in a setting with which she was intimate without strain, a set of characters in whom lurked all the actualities of her own past, and a nest of relationships which were rich and ancient but also thronging with possibilities of development and contrast; and as well as these, a general sense (not by any means present in most of her stories), the sense that Beryl has intermittently in "Prelude" – that "life is rich and mysterious and good...." The goodness comes from the coherence of value and attitude which supports the life of the family and its society; the richness from the emotionally grounded and significantly interesting and worthwhile life its different members live, in which variety is sustained by the strength of the family union; the mysteriousness from the writer's power to reproduce the radiant and inexplicable in human experience. In these New Zealand stories Katherine Mansfield's sympathetic imagination is controlled by a gift for allowing freedom to the subject so that an extraordinary sureness of touch goes with a remarkable absence of manipulation or forcing of the material.

Katherine Mansfield's stories are complex, subtly woven organisms, making their points by a blend of implication, imagery, contrasting half-tones, and the manoeuvring of distinct but chiming voices, each voice and each viewpoint melting without grating into the next. They use, in fact, a poetic technique with the characteristic of such, a capacity to stay transparently faithful to the author's vision and also to take on colour, whether it be subdued or strong, perfectly fitted to the theme at any given moment.

The two major figures in Australian literature are A. D. Hope, the poet, and Patrick White, the novelist. Hope turned to the seventeenth century for the style made up of the passionate subtleties and the intellectual sensuousness of the metaphysical poets and the masculine, ironic force of Dryden. *Why* the seventeenth century should be looked to as the source has to do with the congruence between Hope's own poetic nature and the adult, ardent, almost mathematically reasoning habit of the metaphysicals: a balance further modified by another, the symmetry between Hope and his admired Dryden's gift of sensitive manliness, his way of being at once independent and level with his experience, however intricate; and modified yet again by Hope's sympathetic understanding of Dryden's skill in calling upon a range of poetic resonance within a strictly defining, disciplining pattern. Nor should we overlook the fact that Hope had to make his choice of exemplar at a particular time and from within a certain literary tradition — not only the wider one grounded on the English language and the English literary tradition but within the local Australian one based on the altered language of his own country. It could not be a purely personal choice, although it had to be primarily a personal one, answering to the need felt in the poet's own nerves. The poet as poet is not engaged in any explicit mission to renovate a literary tradition. But of course he is involved in such an undertaking, and the more significant he is as a poet, the more profound is his involvement. Hope's "conservatism" in fact is truly radical. His poetry had to be freed from the influence of home, from a tradition still too much domesticated within the nineteenth century in which British gentility and blandness were curiously reinforced in their parochialism by an unambitious, and suspicious, Australian matiness. The seventeenth century, so different, so remote from the nineteenth century in its inclusiveness and in the very assurance of its scepticism, to which poets in Britain earlier directed their attention, could be the same cleansing, tonic influence for Australia: above all if the connection were to be made by an Australian poet.

Hope is a remarkable poet, the most distinguished his country has produced. His very positive literary character is both grainily individual and strongly in the main Western literary tradition. It is, it is clear, the central tradition he adheres to: accretions, whether modish or cliqueish, he has no use, and indeed considerable scorn, for. The lucidity and correctness which he is at pains to develop in his work are qualities he admires from artistic conviction, as a humanist opposed both to romantic haze and conventional trends. But they also testify to a profound cultivation of spirit, a certain wholeness and the harmony of nature, as they do too to a fine independence of literary fashion.

Patrick White is so different a writer, or so much himself as a writer, that he requires of any reader, and perhaps particularly of the British reader, an unusual steadiness of application. Genuine and stubborn difficulties have to be faced before the reader is at home in a fiction in which the idiom is often opaque and the narrative conducted through choking thickets of imagery. As well as the perplexities provoked by the manner there are those provided by the character of the time and space in which most of Patrick White's work is located. It is not the more extended past, the nineteenth century as in *Voss* (1957), which is hard for the reader to grasp, but, oddly, the nearer past — say from 1914 to 1939 — the period from which so many of White's characters take their habits and assumptions. The sensibility of that time, possibly because of its relative nearness, because it is something we ourselves have shed, seems almost totally gone and bafflingly hard for a contemporary British reader to grasp with spontaneous understanding. Then there is the mystery of Australian space, that beautiful and positive emptiness, which envelops the community and overwhelms the individual. Difficulties of access, however, in the long run diminish, even if they never disappear; and certainly they come to seem less important against the reader's increasing conviction that he is in the presence of a true creative power. It is a power which derives its strength from inner resources. It is free of "cleverness" and remarkably unaffected by fashion. It has great ease and flow — not facility — of conception, a kind of creative insouciance, which finds subjects and themes both urgent and permanent, lying waiting to be exposed in situations of the seediest simplicity and among characters of quite humdrum mediocrity.

Patrick White is a sumptuously prodigal artist, loving the pure creative play or flourish. Yet by the end of the first movement of *Voss* a considerable amount of the work of the novel has been completed and the rest set in train. The dowdy town and the easy country around it, against which the harshness of the desert will be measured, are clearly in the reader's mind; the decent average of the population against which the ferociously extreme nature of the

German explorer, Voss, can be tested has been established; the relationship of Voss and Laura has been initiated, a relationship which, since they never meet again, is carried on in the imagination of each and opened up to the reader by their correspondence. The members of the expedition have been sketched with just the right degree of definition to mark them off as separate persons and yet to keep them united in a single party. And all the preliminary work on the gigantic figure of Voss is carried firmly through.

In the second phase of the novel two lines of narrative are sustained. In one the expedition is conducted through more and more difficult, and finally brutal, country towards its disastrous end; in the other the relationship of Voss and Laura is developed in a series of meditations and (unreceived) letters. The two worlds of actuality and possibility are kept in touch and the latter, it is suggested, offers in the end a chance of redemption to the former. There is a passage at one point in the journey in which this touching of two orders of existence is itself used as an image of the land: "Over all this scene, which was more a shimmer than the architecture of landscape, palpitated extraordinary butterflies. Nothing had been seen yet to compare with their colours, opening and closing, opening and closing. Indeed, by the addition of this pair of hinges, the world of semblance communicated with the world of dream." Not only in the architecture of landscape but also in the architecture of people the two worlds of semblance and dream communicate with each other.

In the third part of *Voss* there occur some lines which make an apt epigraph for *Riders in the Chariot* (1961). "It was his niece, Laura Trevelyan, who had caused Mr. Bonner's world of substance to quake." The upheaval of the substantial world is the great shaping activity working through *Riders in the Chariot*. The novel follows the favored White pattern – a strong central conception, development by means of a biographical method, and an endless multiplication of palpable detail. The world of substance made to quake in the novel includes not only the thick, resistant one of common life and convention but other and odder worlds too: the world of a crazy specimen of the decayed Australian gentry, the world of an unpretentious working woman, the world of a persecuted German Jew, the world of an uprooted aborigine. In addition each of the characters in whom these worlds are defined and examined gives access to one species of a fourfold variety of experience: experience of the natural world, of plants and animals through Miss Hare's nearly non-human instinct for otherness; of integral, simple goodness in Mrs. Godbold, the East Anglian immigrant; of the profoundest religious experience in Himmelfarb, the saintly survivor of the Nazi camps; and of art through the painting of Dubbo, the tubercular half-caste. The four lives, their separate worlds and different orders of experience connect, or are violently knotted together, in the small, dry, dusty town of Sarsaparilla. The range, the imaginative scope, is extraordinary, and the control of the varied material has that unstressed ease which comes from a total inward familiarity.

What causes the world of substance to quake is the possession by each of the quartet of a special direct, nondiscursive apprehension of realities which the world of substance either does not recognize at all or recognizes as dangerous and deserving of destruction. This faculty or organ of consciousness is independent of experience in that it is in some sense a quality of genius, a gift, but it is not at all freakish, not attached to the character like an extra limb or head. It makes its presence felt gradually like any other function of the personality, and it speaks through the articulation of the characters' lives and in the idiom of action. The consciousness – of which the chariot is the symbol – resides in each of the four, Miss Hare, Mrs. Godbold, Dubbo, and Himmelfarb, in a form appropriate to the experience of each. But it has, too, qualities in common. This gift of insight is secret, kept and nourished in privacy; and it is recognized only by those who themselves possess it. Suffering is a necessary condition of its development. Only suffering can reduce the person to that state of painfully earned simplicity which is the essential preparation for a clarified consciousness. Again it invariably provokes persecution, whether it is persecution in the home by a companion or in the factory by workmates or more monstrously in Hitler's Germany by virtually the whole of a society.

Patrick White belongs to a line of novelists whose art embodies a concentrated and dazzling vision of man. Such writers are not manipulators of plot or cultivators of a sensibility or critics of manners or chroniclers of a period. Their art is initiated by their vision, and its form is determined more by a force from within than by any extrinsic scaffolding. It is somewhere between imaginative power and authenticity and crispness of detail that Patrick White's work is imperfect, in the area where architectural capacity and taste are required. The failure is not in the generating concept nor in the worked-out detail – in neither the idea nor the vocabulary, that is – but somewhere between, in what one might call the syntactical structure. *Voss* and *Riders in the Chariot* certainly answer this account I believe: impressive in the constructive idea, superb in the palpable concreteness, but apt on occasion to offer an imposed and gratuitous symbolism in place of organic design. It shows us insistently the ravaged harshness of Patrick White's reading of human reality. Communities lust to persecute anyone or anything beyond the average. In the family the old torture the young, the young savage the old; outside it men and women are locked together in malice. At the same time we are aware, though more obliquely, less positively, in *The Eye of the Storm* (1973) than in *The Tree of Man* (1955), *Riders in the Chariot,* or *The Solid Mandala* (1966), of the flow of love, of the possibility of illumination, of the conditions under which something rich and healing could be constructed. It takes a talent of a rare order to keep the two themes in place and in proportion.

In 1965 the late Douglas Grant, reviewing Carl F. Klinck's *Literary History of Canada* (in *The Journal of Commonwealth Literature*), ventured to write:

> Klinck is properly quite unabashed by the utter mediocrity of the majority of the writers brought under discussion.... Canadian literature must contain more writers not worth the grading than any other literature in existence; a literature that cannot offer the reader even one great writer in compensation for the hundreds of nonentities that would pour through any sieve coarser than *Literary History of Canada.*

I don't believe it is possible to hold such a view any more. Canadian literature in English, deriving from a complex cultural situation, has at the back of it two major literatures and the pressure of the giant to the south. It has produced in the last twenty years an immense range of poets touching every shade of sensibility. Probably the two best, and most representative, of those poets are A. M. Klein and Earle Birney. The fact that they should both be poets has a certain significance in that Canada seems to be the one Commonwealth country in which the poetry is at least equal if not superior to the prose.

"The poetry of Abraham Moses Klein springs from the roots of a consciousness where Hebrew and legal lore have become strangely and exotically intermingled with Shakespeare and T. S. Eliot," as Leon Edel remarks (in *A. M. Klein,* edited by Tom Marshall, 1970). Klein is one of the few serious Canadian writers untroubled by the problem of identity and free of its attendant, modish hysteria about alienation. His work has in it all the richness, the inclusiveness, of the Jewish character and mind, the product of an ancient, sophisticated, oppressed, and still living tradition. At the same time he is alert to the several nuances of contemporary Canadian life, and the marriage of a suffering but essential serenity with a nervous and accurate response makes for a poetry which is altogether independent but also splendidly central.

The inclusiveness and centrality of Klein's poetry correspond to the complexity of his nature and in particular to the two-fold strain in it, the tough and the tender, the stony and the tolerant. The double impulse and the double idiom are lissomly exercised in "*In re* Solomon Warshawer," but they come to their full power in *The Second Scroll* (1951) and *The Rocking Chair* (1948). There is a direct connection between the pared and harsher diction of some parts of "Solomon Warshawer" and the severity and abstinence of the manner of *The Rocking Chair,* another between the rhetoric of lamentation in the Jewish voice in the same poem and the layered, antique but passionate formality of the novella *The Second Scroll.*

The Rocking Chair, Klein's final appearance as a poet, apart from the verse in *The Second*

Scroll, and his first volume of poems to be published in Canada, came out in 1948. In the achieved poems an imagination charged with history and a consciousness clarified by an ancient coherence are brought to bear on persons, places, things, processes, conditions, saltily, stingingly, fresh and Canadian. The past in the poet is locked with the present in the object. The effect is to produce a reality which has both roundness and depth. Each clean surface is backed by a thick supporting texture of allusion and reference from history, literature, traditional assumption, and racial memory and luminous Jewish reverence for the life of the word and the book, an unbroken order of human experience.

The other poet, whose art seems both in resource and character decidedly more indigenous, is Earle Birney. The paradox of Birney's nature is the combination within a single temperament of warmth, of the impulse for communion, with the bleak recognition of man's final isolation. Indeed, Birney's is almost a specification of Coleridge's idea of the structure of human personality. It is "an instinct of our human nature to pass out of self – i.e. the image or complex cycle of images ... which is the perpetual representative of our Inviduum, and by all unreflecting minds confounded and identified with it.... Not to suffer any form to pass into me and become a usurping self" (*Inquiring Spirit,* edited by Kathleen Coburn, 1951). The consequence of this mental form, uniting the outgoing and the reserved, in Birney's poetry is that his most intense relationships are not with the known and named individual but with anonymous members of a class. There is little in his poetry, for example, of the intricate ecstasy and the complex despair of individual love.

Birney's poetry, like some of the best contemporary verse, has quite dispensed with any Victorian sense of strait-laced *genres*. His humour, graven-faced and gravelled-voiced as it is, is both joyful and sane. His poems have nothing abstractly or specifically comic about them. These are not comic poems, and the comic is simply a constituent of the vision and the poetry. It is because he evokes the actual with such presence and authenticity that what is comic in it – and the alert eye can always discern it – strikes one as just and irresistible. He appreciates very well his own disadvantages. He is simply the looker-in, the man with the tongue half locked in the cell of his own language, as he remarks in "Cartagena de Indias." He realizes that he is in a minority of one in a world in which there are two races:

> we human citizens
> who are poor but have things to sell
> and you   from outer space
> unreasonable   our one tourist
> but plainly able to buy

He suffers the rough justice the weak can perform on the strong, some pushing and cheating, some subdued revenge. But he has his advantages too, an eye for the suggestive shape, a feeling for what is common even to two races so utterly divided as the indigenous and the tourist, and an ear with a musician's communicating precision.

The aim of the studies that follow is to bring home to us how many writers outside Britain and the United States have realized in a creative way, particularly in the twentieth century, capacities implicit in the language, while they simultaneously embodied the exact tone and the peculiar idiom of personal and national experiences. Many of these are serious writers, all are genuinely representative. Some are more important representatively than intrinsically. I have been at pains to insist on what they have in common, the resources of the English language. But one cannot overlook the great differences in context in which these writers operate. Patrick White, for example, writes straight from the heart of the British tradition, even though it may be given his own national modification and even though he may do it at immense physical distance; Kenneth Slessor, A. D. Hope and James McAuley, all Australian poets, have in common the will to open up access to human and poetic resources outside those bequeathed to Australia by a parochial nineteenth-century culture. R. K. Narayan works against the background of his own powerful and very different civilization and in a second language learnt at school; Mulk Raj Anand writes out of a feeling for the deprived and a grasp of the social structure of his society, whereas Raja Rao, a poetic and metaphysical novelist, is concerned to express in fiction a meditation on the nature of existence; Chinua Achebe also writes in a second language but against a much more strongly oral tradition; John Pepper Clark, who comes from the Ijaw country of the Niger delta, draws strongly on the tradition of Ekine drama, whereas Amos Tutuola, a writer so immersed in an ancient *Africanité* that general ideas are anathema to him, transmits directly the oral tales of the Yoruba people, packed with ghosts, "deads," and monsters; George Lamming brilliantly articulates a consciousness grounded in the peasantry; Wilson Harris writes from a sensibility which aspires to a condition of mysticism; the Canadian Morley Callaghan works under the influence, and suffers the pressure, of both English and American literature, and is one in whom honesty in reporting has been raised to the level of sensitive perception; the same is true of the New Zealander Frank Sargeson who adds to this power an ear alert to the exact pitch and run of New Zealand speech; much of the best work of Katherine Mansfield and V. S. Naipaul was actually composed in England although the life it deals with may belong to remote and different worlds. But to be aware of this work is an extension of consciousness; it gives intimate access to a universe of varied experience, and it extends our understanding of the human faculty.

READING LIST

1. Bibliographies, handbooks, etc.

Rhodenizer, Vernon B., *Handbook of Australian Literature*, 1930.
Miller, E. Morris, *Australian Literature from Its Beginnings: A Bibliography*, 2 vols., 1940; revised edition by Frederick T. Macartney, 1956.
Ingamells, R. C., *Handbook of Australian Literature*, 1949.
Canton, E. B., *A Bibliography of West Indian Literature 1900–57*, 1957.
Watters, Reginald E., *A Check List of Canadian Literature and Background Materials 1628–1950*, 1959; revised edition, 1966.
Burns, J. A. S., *A Century of New Zealand Novels: A Bibliography of the Period 1861–1960*, 1961.
Who's Who of Indian Writers, 1965.
Jahn, Jahnheinz, *A Bibliography of New African Literature*, 1965.
Storey, Norah, editor, *The Oxford Companion to Canadian History and Literature*, 1967; Supplement, 1973.
Parcsy, P., *A New Bibliography of African Literature*, 1969.
Johnston, Grahame, *Annals of Australian Literature*, 1970.
The Brock Bibliography of Published Canadian Stage Plays in English 1900–1972, 1972; First Supplement, 1973.
Gnarowski, Michael, *A Concise Bibliography of English-Canadian Literature*, 1973.
Pichanick, J., A. J. Chennells, and L. B. Rix, editors, *Rhodesian Literature in English: A Bibliography (1890–1974/5)*, 1977.

2. General Histories

Nathan, Manfred, *South African Literature*, 1925.
Smith, Elizabeth M., *A History of New Zealand Fiction from 1862 to the Present Time*, 1939.

Roderick, Colin, *The Australian Novel*, 1945.
Pacey, Desmond, *Creative Writing in Canada*, 1952; revised edition, 1962.
McCormick, Eric Hall, *New Zealand Literature*, 1953.
Miller, G. M., and Howard Sergeant, *A Critical Survey of South African Poetry in English*, 1957.
Tennant, Kylie, *The Development of the Australian Novel*, 1958.
Green, H. M., *A History of Australian Literature*, 2 vols., 1961.
Iyengar, K. R. Srinivasa, *Indian Writing in English*, 1962.
Narasimhaiah, C. D., editor, *An Introduction to Australian Literature*, 1965.
Klinck, Carl F., editor, *Literary History of Canada: Canadian Literature in English*, 1965; revised edition, 3 vols., 1976.
Stevens, Joan, *The New Zealand Novel 1860–1965*, 1966.
Taiwo, O., *An Introduction to West African Literature*, 1967.
Stevens, Joan, *New Zealand Short Stories: A Survey*, 1967.
Van Sertima, Ivan, *Caribbean Writers*, 1968.
Ramchand, Kenneth, *The West African Novel and Its Background*, 1970.
Green, H. G., and G. Sylvestre, *A Century of Canadian Literature*, 1970.
Walsh, William, *Commonwealth Literature*, 1970.
King, Bruce A., editor, *Introduction to Nigerian Literature*, 1971.
Wilkes, G. A., and J. C. Reid, *The Literature of Australia and New Zealand*, 1971.
Mukherjee, Meenakshi, *The Twice-Born Fiction* (Indian fiction), 1971.
Palmer, Eustace, *An Introduction to the African Novel*, 1972.
Rees, Leslie, *The Making of Australian Drama: An Historical and Critical Survey from the 1830's to the 1970's*, 1973.
Smith, A. J. M., *The Colonial Century: English-Canadian Writing Before Confederation*, 1973.
Smith, A. J. M., *The Canadian Century: English-Canadian Writings since Confederation*, 1973.
Hemenway, S. I., *The Novel of India*, 2 vols., 1975.
McAuley, James, *A Map of Australian Verse*, 1976.
Larson, C. R., *The Novel in the Third World*, 1976.
Dawes, Neville, *Prolegomena to Caribbean Literature*, 1977.
Williams, H. M., *Indo-Anglian Literature 1800–1970: A Survey*, 1977.

3. Topics, themes, short periods, etc.
Brown, E. K., *On Canadian Poetry*, 1943.
Buckley, Vincent, *Essays on Poetry, Mainly Australian*, 1957.
Smith, A. J. M., editor, *Masks of Fiction: Canadian Critics on Canadian Prose*, 1961.
Smith, A. J. M., editor, *Masks of Poetry: Canadian Critics on Canadian Verse*, 1962.
Coulthard, G. R., *Race and Colour in Caribbean Literature*, 1962.
Holcroft, M. H., *Islands of Innocence: The Childhood Theme in New Zealand Fiction*, 1964.
Dutton, Geoffrey, editor, *The Literature of Australia*, 1964.
Wright, Judith, *Preoccupations in Australian Poetry*, 1965.
Wilson, Edmund, *O Canada: An American's Notes on Canadian Culture*, 1965.
Hope, A. D., *The Cave and the Spring: Essays on Poetry*, 1965.
Smithyman, Kendrick, *A Way of Saying: A Study of New Zealand Poetry*, 1965.
Press, John, editor, *Commonwealth Literature*, 1965.
Murray-Smith, Stephen, editor, *An Overland Muster* (on Australian literature), 1965.
Baxter, James K., *Aspects of Poetry in New Zealand*, 1967.
Elliott, Brian, *The Landscape of Australian Poetry*, 1967.
Semmler, Clement, editor, *Twentieth-Century Australian Literary Criticism*, 1967.
Narasimhaiah, C. D., *Fiction and the Reading Public in India*, 1967.
Beier, Ulli, editor, *Introduction to African Literature: An Anthology of Critical Writings from Black Orpheus*, 1967.

James, Louis, *The Islands in Between* (on Caribbean literature), 1968.
Laurence, Margaret, *Long Drums and Cannons: Nigerian Dramatists and Novelists*, 1968.
Lal, P., *The Concept of an Indian Literature: Six Essays*, 1968.
Rhodes, H. Winston, *New Zealand Fiction since 1945*, 1968.
Moore, Gerald, *The Chosen Tongue*, 1969.
Jones, D. G., *Butterfly on Rock: A Study of Themes and Images in Canadian Literature*, 1970.
McAuley, James, *The Personal Element in Australian Poetry*, 1970.
Walsh, William, *A Manifold Voice*, 1970.
Woodcock, George, *Odysseus Ever Returning: Essays on Canadian Writers and Writing*, 1970.
Roscoe, A., *Mother Is Gold: A Study in West African Literature*, 1971.
Clark, John Pepper, *The Example of Shakespeare: Critical Essays in African Literature*, 1971.
Argyle, Barry, *An Introduction to the Australian Novel 1830–1930*, 1971.
Kiernan, Brian, *Images of Society and Nature: Seven Essays on Australian Novels*, 1971.
Frye, Northrop, *The Bush Garden: Essays on the Canadian Imagination*, 1971.
Heywood, Christopher, *Perspectives on African Literature*, 1971.
New, W. H., editor, *Dramatists in Canada*, 1972.
New, W. H., *Articulating West: Essays on Purpose and Form in Modern Canadian Literature*, 1972.
Mason, Bruce, *New Zealand Drama: A Parade of Forms and a History*, 1972.
Harrex, S. C., *The Modern Indian Novel in English*, 1972.
Ngugi, James, *Homecomings: Essays on African and Caribbean Literature, Culture, and Politics*, 1972.
"Contemporary Indian Poetry in English" issue of *Quest*, January–February 1972.
Rao, A. V. Krishna, *The Indo-Anglian Novel and the Changing Tradition*, 1972.
Smith, A. J. M., *Towards a View of Canadian Letters: Selected Essays 1928–1972*, 1973.
Walsh, William, editor, *Readings in Commonwealth Literature*, 1973.
Killam, G. D., editor, *African Writers on African Writing*, 1973.
King, Bruce A., editor, *Literature of the World in English*, 1974.
Woodcock, George, editor, *Poets and Critics*, 1974.
New, W. H., editor, *Among Worlds: An Introduction to Modern Commonwealth and South African Fiction*, 1975.
Keesing, Nancy, editor, *Australian Postwar Novelists: Selected Critical Essays*, 1975.
Stewart, Douglas, *The Broad Stream*, 1975.
Burns, D. R., *The Direction of Australian Fiction 1920–1974*, 1975.
Hankin, Cherry, editor, *Critical Essays on the New Zealand Novel*, 1976.
Naik, M. K., S. K. Desai, and G. S. Amur, editors, *Critical Essays on Indian Writing in English*, 1977.
Ferres, John H., and Martin Tucker, editors, *Modern Commonwealth Literature*, 1977.
Harrex, S. C., *The Fire and the Offering: The English Language Novel of India 1935–70*, 1977.
Moss, J., *Sex and Violence in the Canadian Novel*, 1977
Narasimhaiah, C. D., editor, *Awakened Conscience: Studies in Commonwealth Literature*, 1978.
Mohan, Ramesh, editor, *Indian Writing in English*, 1978.
Parker, Kenneth, *The South African Novel in English: Essays in Criticism and Society*, 1978.
Jones, E. D., editor, *African Literature Today: Prospect and Retrospect*, 1979.
Core, George, editor, "Commonwealth Literature" issue of *Sewanee Review*, Spring 1979.

4. Anthologies of Primary works
Smith, A. J. M., editor, *The Book of Canadian Poetry*, 1943; revised edition, 1948, 1957.
Davin, Dan, editor, *New Zealand Short Stories*, 1953; second series edited by C. K. Stead, 1966.

Wright, Judith, editor, *A Book of Australian Verse*, 1956; revised edition, 1968.
Chapman, R., and J. Bennett, editors, *An Anthology of New Zealand Verse*, 1956.
Butler, Guy, editor, *A Book of South African Verse*, 1959.
Smith, A. J. M., editor, *The Oxford Book of Canadian Verse: In English and French*, 1960; revised edition, 1965.
Curnow, Allen, editor, *The Penguin Book of New Zealand Verse*, 1960.
Weaver, R., editor, *Canadian Short Stories*, 1960; second series, 1968.
Moore, Gerald, editor, *Seven African Writers*, 1962.
Moore, Geoffrey, and Ulli Beier, editors, *Modern Poetry from Africa*, 1963; revised edition, 1968.
James, Brian, editor, *Australian Short Stories*, second series, 1963.
Moore, T. Inglis, and Douglas Stewart, editors, *Poetry in Australia*, 2 vols., 1964.
Wilson, M. T., editor, *Poetry of Mid-Century 1940–60* (Canadian verse), 1964.
Komey, Ellis, and Ezekiel Mphahlele, editors, *Modern African Stories*, 1964.
Ward, Russel, editor, *The Penguin Book of Australian Ballads*, 1964.
Brent, P. L., editor, *Young Commonwealth Poets '65*, 1965.
Doyle, Charles, editor, *Recent Poetry in New Zealand*, 1965.
Hosain, Shahid, editor, *First Voices: Six Poets from Pakistan*, 1965.
Salkey, Andrew, editor, *Stories from the Caribbean*, 1965; as *Island Voices*, 1970.
Figueroa, John, editor, *Caribbean Voices: An Anthology of West Indian Poetry*, 2 vols., 1966–70.
Mphahlele, Ezekiel, editor, *African Writing Today*, 1967.
Sergeant, Howard, editor, *Commonwealth Poems of Today*, 1967.
Stewart, Douglas, and Beatrice Davis, editors, *Short Stories of Australia*, 2 vols., 1967.
Nwoga, Donatus Ibe, editor, *West African Verse*, 1967.
Smith, A. J. M., editor, *Modern Canadian Verse: In English and French*, 1967.
Cope, Jack, and Uys Krige, editors, *The Penguin Book of South African Verse*, 1968.
Sergeant, Howard, editor, *New Voices of the Commonwealth*, 1968.
Higham, Charles, editor, *Australian Writing Today*, 1968.
Dathorne, O. R., and Willfried Feuser, editors, *Africa in Prose*, 1969.
Lal, P., editor, *Modern Indian Poetry in English*, 1969.
Richler, Mordecai, editor, *Canadian Writing Today*, 1970.
O'Sullivan, Vincent, editor, *An Anthology of Twentieth-Century New Zealand Poetry*, 1970; revised edition, 1976.
Rutherford, Anna, and Donald Hannah, editors, *Commonwealth Short Stories*, 1971.
Ramchand, Kenneth, and C. Gray, editors, *West Indian Poetry*, 1971.
Salkey, Andrew, editor, *Breaklight: An Anthology of Caribbean Poetry*, 1971.
Stewart, Douglas, editor, *The Wide Brown Land: A New Selection of Australian Verse*, 1971.
Okpaku, J., editor, *Contemporary African Drama: A Critical Anthology*, 1971.
Heseltine, H., editor, *The Penguin Book of Australian Verse*, 1972.
Alphonso-Karkala, J. B., editor, *An Anthology of Indian Literature*, 1972.
Nandy, Pritish, editor, *Indian Poetry in English 1947–72*, 1972.
Natwar-Singh, R., editor, *Stories from India*, 1972.
Kalman, R., editor, *A Collection of Canadian Plays*, 5 vols., 1973–77.
Smith, A. J. M., editor, *The Canadian Experience: A Brief Survey of English-Canadian Prose*, 1974.
Jussawalla, Adil, editor, *New Writings in India*, 1974.
Grant, Peter, and Finley Martin, editors, *New Atlantic Writing*, 1975.
Parthasarathy, R., editor, *Ten Twentieth-Century Indian Poets*, 1976.
Newlove, John, editor, *Canadian Poetry: The Modern Era*, 1977.
Sander, Reinhard W., editor, *From Trinidad: An Anthology of Early West Indian Writing*, 1977.

ABRAHAMS, Peter (Henry). South African. Born in Vrededorp, near Johannesburg, 19 March 1919. Educated at Church of England mission schools in South Africa. Married 1) Dorothy Pennington in 1942 (divorced, 1948); 2) Daphne Elizabeth Miller in 1948, one son and two daughters. Worked in South Africa as a kitchen helper, porter and clerk, also as an editor in Durban; seaman, 1939–41; settled in England, 1941–56, and lived in France, 1948–50; regular contributor to *The Observer*, London, and the *Herald Tribune*, New York and Paris, 1952–64; emigrated to Jamaica, 1956: Editor, *West Indian Economist*, and Controller, "West Indian News" program, Jamaica, 1958–62. Lives in St. Andrews, Jamaica.

PUBLICATIONS

Fiction

Dark Testament (stories). 1942.
Song of the City. 1945.
Mine Boy. 1946.
The Path of Thunder. 1948.
Wild Conquest. 1950.
A Wreath for Udomo. 1956.
A Night of Their Own. 1965.
This Island Now. 1966.

Verse

A Blackman Speaks of Freedom! Poems. 1938(?).
Here, Friend. N.d.

Other

Return to Goli (reportage). 1953.
Tell Freedom: Memories of Africa. 1954.
Jamaica: An Island Mosaic. 1957.
The World of Mankind, with others. 1962.

Reading List: *Abrahams* by Michael Wade, 1972.

*   *   *

Peter Abrahams has spent more of his life outside South Africa than in it (he left there in 1939 when he was twenty years of age) but the impact of the South African system on him in his formative years has been such that with one exception all his work has been set in Africa and deals with racial conflict, oppression, economic injustice, and social and political deprivation. The one exception is *This Island Now*, which is set in Jamaica. It is easy to see why Peter Abrahams chose Jamaica, for, given the conditions which exist there, he is able to explore the same themes which concern him and show them at work in a slightly different setting.

His most successful writing is to be found in his non-fiction, particularly in his autobiography, *Tell Freedom*. Here he describes his early life in South Africa, the frustrations and humiliations he suffered, and the growing disillusionment until he reached the decision that he must leave. What adds an extra dimension to this work is "the portrait of the artist as a young man" flavour which it possesses. The incompatability of art and apartheid was a major factor in his choice of exile.

His fiction deals with familiar South African themes: the boy who leaves the village for the town (*Mine Boy*), the dilemma of the coloured (*The Path of Thunder*). He moves away from the expected in *Wild Conquest*, which deals with the Great Trek and the clash between the Boers and the Matabele, and in *A Wreath for Udomo*, which is set in a fictitious African state in 1956 (Ghana comes most readily to mind).

Abrahams never makes facile judgements, the truth is rarely simple. For example, Boer and Matabele alike are criticized in *Wild Conquest*, and in *A Wreath for Udomo* there are no easy solutions to the dilemmas facing the leader of a newly independent African state. Abrahams's greatest weakness lies in his depiction of character. They lack psychological depth and tend to become romanticized mouth-pieces for Abrahams's ideas. It is almost certain that his reputation as an artist is likely to decrease and his main interest will be as a phenomenon of literary history.

—Anna Rutherford

ACHEBE, Chinua. Nigerian. Born Albert Chinualumogu in Ogidi, East Central State, 16 November 1930. Educated at the Government College, Umuahia, 1944–47; University College, Ibadan, 1948–53, B.A. (London) 1953. Married Christie Okoli in 1961; two sons and two daughters. Talks Producer, Lagos, 1954–57, Controller, Enugu, 1958–61, and Director, Lagos, 1961–66, Nigerian Broadcasting Corporation; Co-Founder, with Christopher Okigbo, and Chairman, Citadel Books Ltd., Enugu, 1967. Since 1967, Senior Research Fellow, University of Nigeria, Nsukka. Visiting Professor, University of Massachusetts, Amherst, 1972–73, University of Connecticut, Storrs, 1975. Founding Editor, Heinemann African Writers series, 1962–72, and since 1970 Director, Heinemann Educational Books (Nigeria) Ltd., and Nwankwo-Ifejika Ltd., publishers, Enugu. Since 1971, Editor, *Okike*, a Nigerian journal of new writing. Travelled to the United States, with Gabriel Okara and Cyprian Ekwensi, to seek help for Biafra, 1969. Member, University of Lagos Council, 1966; Chairman, Society of Nigerian Authors, 1966. Since 1971, Member of the East Central State Library Board. Recipient: Margaret Wrong Memorial Prize, 1959; Nigerian National Trophy, 1960; Rockefeller Fellowship, 1960; UNESCO Fellowship, 1963; Commonwealth Poetry Prize, 1973; Neil Gunn International Fellowship, 1974. D.Litt.: University of Stirling, Scotland, 1974; University of Southampton, Hampshire, 1974. Honorary Fellow, Modern Language Association of America, 1974; Fellow, Ghana Association of Writers, 1975. Lives in Nigeria.

PUBLICATIONS

Fiction

Things Fall Apart. 1958.
No Longer at Ease. 1960.

The Sacrificial Egg and Other Stories. 1962.
Arrow of God. 1964.
A Man of the People. 1966.
Girls at War (stories). 1972.

Verse

Beware Soul-Brother and Other Poems. 1971; revised edition, 1972.
Christmas in Biafra and Other Poems. 1973.

Other

Chike and the River (juvenile). 1966.
How the Leopard Got His Claws (juvenile). 1972.
Morning Yet on Creation Day. 1975.
In Person: Achebe, Awooner, and Soyinka at the University of Washington. 1975.

Editor, *The Insider: Stories of War and Peace from Nigeria.* 1971.

Bibliography: in *Africana Library Journal,* Spring 1970.

Reading List: *The Novels of Achebe* by G. D. Killam, 1969; *Achebe* by Arthur Ravenscroft, 1969; *Achebe* by David Carroll, 1970; *Achebe* edited by Bernth Lindfors and C. L. Innes, 1978.

* * *

Chinua Achebe published four novels between 1958 and 1966, but since that time has turned to short stories and poetry. The turbulent history of Nigeria in the last ten years may explain this shift, especially as Achebe is an Ibo and thus sadly involved in the Biafran war. Some of Achebe's novels, while they are obviously relevant to the confused situation in Nigeria today, are also impressive records of Nigeria's past.

In *Things Fall Apart,* perhaps his most impressive work, Achebe describes the fall of Okonkwo, a tribal chieftain unable to accommodate himself to the new values brought in by English missionaries. While Achebe is careful not to take sides in the conflict between African and European values, the tragedy of Okonkwo is such that we are sympathetic to his side, especially as the African code of behaviour is shown to be more fluid than that of the missionaries. It is Okonkwo's failure to recognize this fluidity which causes his downfall. In *No Longer at Ease,* we see Okonkwo's grandson Obi, living in the 1950's, in a similar dilemma as he tries to reconcile the claims of his African tribe and the lessons he has learnt in Europe. *No Longer at Ease,* a slight work, shows Obi's decline into corruption, a decline never satisfactorily explained. In *Arrow of God,* Achebe returns to the past, this time to the 1920's when Nigerian tribal life has to accommodate itself to the colonial administration. Both Ezeulu, the tribal priest, and Winterbottom, the Colonial administrator, fail because they try to impose their own rigid deterministic philosophy on an intransigent world. In *A Man of the People,* we have the familiar conflict between the virtuous but priggish narrator Odih and the corrupt but charming politician Nanga as they struggle for power in a newly independent state. Corruption wins, and the conclusion of the novel is a pessimistic one. Achebe is a little uncertain in his use of the first person narrative in the last novel, but all his novels are stylistically effective, especially in the use of dialogue, where the subtle variation of stately African phrases, their slightly absurd literal translations, pidgin English, and the formal English of administrators and missionaries serve to point the conflicts he is describing.

—T. J. Winnifrith

ANAND, Mulk Raj. Indian. Born in Peshawar, 12 December 1905. Educated at Khalsa College, Amritsar; Punjab University, 1921–24, B.A. (honours) 1924; University College, University of London, 1926–29; Cambridge University, 1929–30; League of Nations School of Intellectual Cooperation, Geneva, 1930–32. Married 1) the actress Kathleen Van Gelder in 1939 (divorced, 1948); 2) the dancer Shirin Vajifdar in 1950, one daughter. Lecturer, School of Intellectual Cooperation, Summer 1930, and Workers Educational Association, London, intermittently 1932–45; has also taught at the universities of Punjab, of Banares, Varanasai, and of Rajasthan, Jaipur, 1948–66: Tagore Professor of Literature and Fine Art, University of Punjab, 1963–66; Visiting Professor, Institute of Advanced Studies, Simla, 1967–68. Fine Art Chairman, Lalit Kala Akademi (National Academy of Art), New Delhi, 1965–70. Since 1946, Editor of *Marg* magazine, Bombay. Since 1970, President of the Lokayata Trust, for creating a community and cultural centre in Hauz Khas village, New Delhi. Recipient: Leverhulme Fellowship, 1940–42; World Peace Council prize, 1952; Padma Bhushan, India, 1968. Member, Indian Academy of Letters. Lives in Bombay.

PUBLICATIONS

Fiction

The Lost Child and Other Stories. 1934.
Untouchable. 1935.
Coolie. 1936; revised edition, 1972.
Two Leaves and a Bud. 1937.
The Village. 1939.
Lament on the Death of a Master of Arts. 1939.
Across the Black Waters. 1940.
The Sword and the Sickle. 1942.
The Barber's Trade Union and Other Stories. 1944.
The Big Heart. 1945.
The Tractor and the Corn Goddess and Other Stories. 1947.
Seven Summers: The Story of an Indian Childhood. 1951.
The Private Life of an Indian Prince. 1953; revised edition, 1970.
Reflections on the Golden Bed (stories). 1954.
The Road. 1962.
The Old Woman and the Cow. 1963.
Death of a Hero. 1964.
The Power of Darkness. 1966.
Morning Face. 1968.

Play

India Speaks (produced 1943).

Other

Persian Painting. 1930.
Curries and Other Indian Dishes. 1932.
The Golden Breath: Studies in Five Poets of the New India. 1933.
The Hindu View of Art. 1933; revised edition, 1957.
Apology for Heroism: An Essay in Search of a Faith. 1934.
Letters on India. 1942.
Indian Fairy Tales: Retold (juvenile). 1946.
On Education. 1947.
The Bride's Book of Beauty, with K. N. Hutheesing. 1947.
The Story of India (juvenile). 1948.
The King Emperor's English; or, The Role of the English Language in the Free India. 1948.
Lines Written to an Indian Air: Essays. 1949.
Indian Theatre. 1950.
The Story of Man (juvenile). 1954.
More Indian Fairy Tales (juvenile). 1956.
Kama Kala: Some Notes on the Philososphical Basis of Hindu Erotic Sculpture. 1958.
India in Colour. 1959.
Homage to Khajuraho, with Stella Kramrisch. 1960.
Is There a Contemporary Indian Civilisation? 1963.
The Volcano: Lectures on the Painting of Rabindranath Tagore. 1968.
Annals of Childhood. 1968.
Ajunta, photographs by R. R. Bhurdwaj. 1971.
Seven Summers. 1972.

Editor, *Marx and Engels on India.* 1933.
Editor, with Iqbal Singh, *Indian Short Stories.* 1947.
Editor, *Introduction to Indian Art*, by A. K. Coomaraswamy. 1956.
Editor, *Experiments: Contemporary Indian Short Stories.* 1968.

Reading List: *Anand: A Critical Essay*, 1948, and *The Lotus and the Elephant*, 1954, both by Jack Lindsay; *An Ideal of Man in Anand's Novels* by D. Riemenschneider, 1969; *Anand: The Man and the Novelist* by Margaret Berry, 1970; *Anand: A Study of His Fiction in Humanist Perspective* by G. S. Gupta, 1975; *So Many Freedoms: A Study of the Major Fiction of Anand* by Saros Cowasgee, 1978.

*   *   *

Mulk Raj Anand is the most controversial of the Indian writers writing in English, and, along with R. K. Narayan, the best known.

He is a socially committed writer, and, though he denies the influence of Marx on his writing (he calls himself a rational humanist), there can be little doubt that his writing is to a certain extent influenced by Marxist theories. An advocate of equality and universal brotherhood, he believes in man's latent goodness which will triumph over evil given the right conditions. And it is socialism alone which can provide the right conditions for man's total development.

Anand's characters invariably fall into three classes: the victims, who are usually the protagonists; the oppressors, those who oppose change and progress; and the good men. Under the last category fall the social workers, the labour leaders, all those who believe in progress and can see how modern science can improve the lot of the sufferers and help bring about the equality of all men. One feels in all his work his deep compassion for others and his understanding of, to quote his own words, "the dignity of weakness of others."

Anand is a prolific writer; apart from some twenty works of fiction he has written an almost equal number of works of non-fiction on subjects which range from Persian painting to Indian food. He has also begun a seven-volume autobiography. His best work is the fiction produced in the 1930's and 1940's, *Untouchable*, *Coolie*, the trilogy *The Village*, *Across the Black Waters*, and *The Sword and the Sickle*, and *The Private Life of an Indian Prince* (written in 1948 though not published until 1953).

Most socially committed novelists have a tendency towards didacticism; the artist becomes the propagandist, style is sacrificed for the message. Anand does not escape these failings; Bonamy Dobrée once criticized him for substituting "emotions for criticism," but in the above mentioned works he avoids most of the pitfalls. They are his most successful attempts at combining the role of artist and social critic.

—Anna Rutherford

ATWOOD, Margaret (Eleanor). Canadian. Born in Ottawa, Ontario, 18 November 1939. Educated at Victoria College, University of Toronto, B.A. 1961; Radcliffe College, Cambridge, Massachusetts, A.M. 1962; Harvard University, Cambridge, Massachusetts. Lecturer in English, University of British Columbia, Vancouver, 1964–65; Instructor in English, Sir George Williams University, Montreal, 1967–68. Recipient: E. J. Pratt Medal, 1961; President's Medal, University of Western Ontario, 1966; Governor-General's Award, 1967; Centennial Commission prize, 1967. Lives in Ontario.

PUBLICATIONS

Verse

Double Persephone. 1961.
The Circle Game. 1964; revised edition, 1966.
Talismans for Children. 1965.
Kaleidoscopes: Baroque. 1965.
Speeches for Doctor Frankenstein. 1966.
The Animals in That Country. 1968.
Five Modern Canadian Poets, with others, edited by Eli Mandel. 1970.
The Journals of Susanna Moodie: Poems. 1970.
Procedures for Underground. 1970.
Power Politics. 1971.
You Are Happy. 1974.
Selected Poems. 1976.

Fiction

The Edible Woman. 1969.
Surfacing. 1972.
Lady Oracle. 1976.

Other

Survival: A Thematic Guide to Canadian Literature. 1972.

Reading List: "The Poetry of Atwood" by John Wilson Foster, in *Canadian Literature* Autumn 1977.

*   *   *

Margaret Atwood's poetry succeeds not by masterly technique or style but by a peculiar and highly individual force of content, by exciting transformations whereby the identities of Canadian pioneers, of forest animals, Indians, the wilderness, women, and Canada itself conduct strange traffic with one another. These identities flesh out in multiple guise the root formula of Atwood's poetry. In most of her work, Atwood concerns herself with the self's inhabitation of spaces and forms, and the metamorphoses entailed therein. In her world, extinction and obsolescence are illusory, for life is a constant process of re-formation. Metaphor, simile, and personification in her verse might therefore just as easily be explained in terms of zoomorphism, anthropomorphism, and totemism as in terms of poetic convention. The self is eternally divided in its attitude to the forms and spaces it inhabits, simultaneously needing, fearing, desiring, and despising them. Hence the paranoid and schizophrenic motifs of the poetry.

Atwood's many Canadian admirers regard her as being deeply involved, at a time of cultural resurgence in Canada, with the problematic identity of her country, and to an extent this is true. As though aware of belonging to a minority culture on the North American continent, Atwood has in her poetry, particularly *The Circle Game, The Animals in That Country, Procedures for Underground,* and, above all, *The Journals of Susanna Moodie,* re-enacted her pioneer ancestors' experience in early Canada. But the metaphoric possibilities of pioneering are what interest Atwood.

Animals, for example, abound in her poetry as they did in the world of the pioneer, but they frequently embody the timeless dreads of the poet and her speakers. They are also the heraldic and mythic animals of the red men whom the settlers confronted and who still pre-empt white Canadians. The wilderness still beckons and forbids Canadians, as the novel *Surfacing* and the poetry demonstrate; it represents the interior and dangerous landscape of the mind as well as the primordiality to which all must in the end revert, as the briefly resurrected Susanna Moodie explains: "at the last/judgement we will all be trees."

Atwood's verse transformation of Mrs. Moodie's nineteenth-century pioneer journals (e.g., *Roughing It in the Bush*) is her finest volume of poetry, and offers pioneering as one extended metaphor for contemporary women's questioning of the traditional roles laid down by men for them to play. *Power Politics* explores sexual identity and relationships by means of the different metaphor of politics. Yet another and more original metaphor is the Circe episode of the *Odyssey* in the "Circe/Mud Poems" sequence of *You Are Happy,* in which the themes of pioneering, Canada and womanhood are connected.

Atwood is a prolific poet and novelist (occasionally hasty, one might feel) who seems, like her speakers, both to desire and fear escape from form. Her verse avoids rhyme and merely flirts with stanzaic pattern. Her basic unit is not the line (sense is fractured into an abundance of short lines) but the insight, and this in turn relies on the terse shock of metaphor. Yet the bones of older forms show appropriately through, to provide an uneasy counterpoint to her themes.

—John Wilson Foster

AVISON, Margaret (Kirkland). Canadian. Born in Galt, Ontario, 23 April 1918. Educated at the University of Toronto, B.A. 1940. Recipient: Guggenheim Fellowship, 1956; Governor-General's Award, 1961. Lives in Toronto.

PUBLICATIONS

Verse

Winter Sun. 1960.
The Dumbfounding. 1966.

Other

The Research Compendium, with Albert Rose. 1964.

Reading List: *Avison* by E. H. Redekop, 1970.

*   *   *

Throughout her life, Margaret Avison has been concerned with the nature of imaginative perception. She writes of the transcendental nature of reality, about the ability of the "optic heart" to see beyond the surfaces of things. Like many Canadian poets, she has a strong sense of the physical landscape, of earth, rock, water, of city streets and buildings which support or overwhelm man, but a close, often undefinable and dangerous, relationship links man to the world in which he lives. In many of the shorter poems of her first book, *Winter Sun,* she depicts, with acuteness and compassion, the modern city, sometimes in extraordinary vignettes, sometimes in sequences of brief scenes or images. Strange and sudden interlockings of external and internal landscapes occur; her landscape becomes multiple, an everywhere inhabited by the mind of the poet, an always in which past and present collide.

Avison believes that the forms of language, words themselves, are threatened by our inability to see things freshly. So the "deciphering heart" must take the confusion in speech between the ancient and the new and resolve it into a new imaginative order. She does this in her own language, crossing the often rigid boundaries between our newest technologies and our lagging perceptions of history, between the secular and sacred imaginations, between given poetic forms and new structures of words. In her longer poems, she moves freely back and forth between centuries and places, creating pieces of a jigsaw world which the reader must put together. The reader, in fact, must behave much like her persona of the artist, "at once Hansel and Gretel," plunging into the forests and seas of the imagination, for her diction is terse and economical, sometimes arcane, her syntax often convoluted, and her images always dense.

In the context of other contemporary poetry, some of Avison's most remarkable poems are the explicitly Christian poems in *The Dumbfounding*. Here she writes in the traditions of Donne, Herbert, and Hopkins, drawing ideas and sometimes language from each, and creating poems that are deeply personal expressions of the poet's relation to God. Many of them, although at first sight somewhat remote from the poems in *Winter Sun*, are about ways of perceiving reality, spiritual exercises of the optic heart. In poem after poem, she imagines the vision of rebirth, the moment when, like her swimmer, man recognizes the existence of the whirlpool and enters the black pit, or when Christ transcends the defining lines drawn by man. The recognition of this moment of love is for her "the dumbfounding." In a poem arising out of the first landing by man on the moon, she continues to express this "now" as the moment beyond the technical data of the moon mission – that epiphanic, dumbfounding perception of reality.

Avison's poems are both immediately recognizable and profoundly strange, because her perspectives of common, ordinary things are always unexpected. She communicates in all her poetry a strong sense of historical continuity, but the contemporary world of dams, TV, space flight, napalm, and fission is always at hand, waiting for the encounter with imagination, waiting for judgment.

—E. H. Redekop

BAUGHAN, Blanche (Edith). New Zealander. Born in Putney, London, in 1870; emigrated to New Zealand, 1900. Educated at Brighton High School, Sussex; Royal Holloway College, University of London, B.A. Social worker, prominent in penal reform: Honorary Secretary, and Vice-President, 1928, Howard League for Penal Reform. *Died in August 1958.*

PUBLICATIONS

Verse

Verses. 1898.
Reuben and Other Poems. 1903.
Shingle-Short and Other Verses. 1908.
Hope. 1916(?).
Poems from the Port Hills. 1923.

Other

The Finest Walk in the World (on the Milford Track). 1909; revised edition, 1926.
Snow Kings of the Southern Alps. 1910.

Uncanny Country: The Thermal Country of New Zealand. 1911.
Brown Bread from a Colonial Oven, Being Sketches of Up-Country Life in New Zealand. 1912.
Forest and Ice. 1913.
A River of Pictures and Peace (on Wanganui River). 1913.
The Summit Road: Its Scenery, Botany, and Geology, with Leonard Cockayne and Robert Speight. 1914.
Studies in New Zealand Scenery. 1916; revised edition, as *Glimpses of New Zealand Scenery,* 1922.
Akaroa. 1919.
Arthur's Pass and Otira Gorge. 1925.
Mt. Egmont. 1929.
People in Prison, with F. A. de la Mare. 1936.

* * *

Blanche Baughan's essential writing is in *Reuben and Other Poems, Shingle-Short and Other Verses,* and her by no means negligible prose sketches (rather of people, like her verse, than places) *Brown Bread from a Colonial Oven.* Her "gift" died after illness in 1910 – "I did not desert it, it deserted me." Through nearly six decades following she became a pioneer of prison reform and was involved with Indian thought. Of one anthologised poem in *Shingle-Short,* New Zealand's leading poet, an uncompromising critic, Allen Curnow, writes: "But nothing about this time compares with Blanche Baughan's 'A Bush Section,' written within a few years of her arrival in 1900. No earlier New Zealand poem exhibits such unabashed truth to its subject....It is the best New Zealand poem before Mason and how different in kind!" Here is its "burned-off" landscape:

> ... the opposite rampart of ridges
> Bristles against the sky, all the tawny, tumultuous landscape
> Is stuck, and prickled, and spiked with standing black and grey splinters....

Its child protagonist is: "Here, to this rough and raw prospect, these black-blocks of Being assign'd –" and so:

> Standing, small and alone:
> Bright Promise on Poverty's threshold!
> What art thou? Where hast thou come from?
> How far, how far! wilt thou go?

"Reuben" masters Wordsworthian blank verse and Crabbe-like realism; other poems in that book echo, say, Christina Rossetti or are increasingly colloquial ("The Old Place"); some use cantering dactyls and fourteeners reminiscent of Australiana.

With some unevenness *Shingle-Short* shows her full strength. The title character is mentally handicapped; outcasts and isolates (compare Patrick White's *The Burnt Ones*) recur; yet (as in *Brown Bread*) a dominant theme is the prevailing colonial work ethic. Her chief mode is dramatic monologue; tone, language, topics are for the most part sophisticatedly demotic; generally these pages may recall Browning, the Christina Rossetti of "Goblin Market," or numerous analogues in comparable North America, say, Lanier or James Whitcomb Riley (as *Brown Bread* may suggest Sarah Orne Jewett). "Maui's Fish" is a stunning free verse rendering of that legend. "The Paddock" is a long "cantata" in many styles and voices, a patch-work quilt most authentically colonial (her titles are revealing!) on colonial dilemmas of youth and age and place; a Maori component is, again, in rhetorical free verse; there are passages of brilliance in this unjustly neglected work.

In *Brown Bread* a "foreigner" expostulates: "Oh you live so bad, you do live so bad!" Our author comments: "Art comes at all times scantly to the back-blocks; and with what hope can Literature appeal to brains exhausted already by the exhaustion of the body?" Miss Baughan's contemporaries – Satchell in fiction, Jessie Mackay in poetry – lack either her single-minded *esthetic* commitment or ability, yet she has been "out of step" both with her own and later generations. In breadth and consistency of technical achievement, and in themes and strategies alike, Miss Baughan both far surpasses her predecessors and has no peer until the generations of R. A. K. Mason and Robin Hyde. The new ground on which she stands is precisely that where Maui's envious elders slither and fall, the ground, slippery and changing, of truth to emergent New Zealand consciousness.

—Peter Alcock

BAXTER, James K(eir). New Zealander. Born in Dunedin, 29 June 1926; son of the writer Archibald Baxter. Educated at Quaker schools in New Zealand and England; Otago University, Dunedin; Victoria University, Wellington, B.A. 1952. Married Jacqueline Sturm in 1948; two children. Worked as a labourer, journalist, and school-teacher. Editor, *Numbers* magazine, Wellington, 1954–60. Spent 5 months in India studying school publications, 1958; started commune in Jerusalem (a Maori community on the Wanganui River), 1969. Recipient: Unesco grant, 1958; Robert Burns Fellowship, Otago University, 1966, 1967. *Died 22 October 1972.*

PUBLICATIONS

Verse

> *Beyond the Palisade: Poems.* 1944.
> *Blow, Wind of Fruitfulness.* 1948.
> *Hart Crane.* 1948.
> *Rapunzel: A Fantasia for Six Voices.* 1948.
> *Charm for Hilary.* 1949.
> *Poems Unpleasant*, with Louis Johnson and Anton Vogt. 1952.
> *The Fallen House: Poems.* 1953.
> *Lament for Barney Flanagan.* 1954.
> *Traveller's Litany.* 1955.
> *The Night Shift: Poems of Aspects of Love*, with others. 1957.
> *The Iron Breadboard: Studies in New Zealand Writing* (verse parodies). 1957.
> *In Fires of No Return: Poems.* 1958.
> *Chosen Poems, 1958.* 1958.
> *Ballad of Calvary Street.* 1960.
> *Howrah Bridge and Other Poems.* 1961.
> *Poems.* 1964.
> *Pig Island Letters.* 1966.
> *A Death Song for M. Mouldybroke.* 1967.
> *A Small Ode on Mixed Flatting: Elicited by the Decision of the Otago University Authorities to Forbid This Practice among Students.* 1967.

The Lion Skin: Poems. 1967.
A Bucket of Blood for a Dollar: A Conversation Between Uncle Sam and the Rt. Hon. Keith Holyoake, Prime Minister of New Zealand. 1968.
The Rock Woman: Selected Poems. 1969.
Ballad of the Stonegut Sugar Works. 1969.
Jerusalem Sonnets: Poems for Colin Durning. 1970.
The Junkies and the Fuzz. 1970.
Jerusalem Daybook (poetry and prose journal). 1971.
Jerusalem Blues (2). 1971.
Autumn Testament (poetry and prose journal). 1972.
Four God Songs. 1972.
Letter to Peter Olds. 1972.
Runes. 1973.
The Labyrinth: Some Uncollected Poems, 1944–1972. 1974.
The Bone Chanter: Unpublished Poems 1945–1972. 1977.
The Holy Life and Death of Concrete Grady: Various Uncollected and Unpublished Poems, edited by J. E. Weir. 1977.

Plays

Jack Winter's Dream (broadcast 1958). In *The Wide Open Cage and Jack Winter's Dream,* 1959.
The Wide Open Cage (produced 1959). In *The Wide Open Cage and Jack Winter's Dream,* 1959.
The Wide Open Cage and Jack Winter's Dream: Two Plays. 1959.
The Spots of the Leopard (produced 1963).
The Band Rotunda (produced 1967). In *The Devil and Mr. Mulcahy and The Band Rotunda,* 1971.
The Sore-Footed Man, based on *Philoctetes* by Euripides (produced 1967). In *The Sore-Footed Man and The Temptations of Oedipus,* 1971.
The Bureaucrat (produced 1967).
The Devil and Mr. Mulcahy (produced 1967). In *The Devil and Mr. Mulcahy and The Band Rotunda,* 1971.
Mr. O'Dwyer's Dancing Party (produced 1968).
The Day Flanagan Died (produced 1969).
The Temptations of Oedipus (produced 1970). In *The Sore-Footed Man and The Temptations of Oedipus,* 1971.
The Devil and Mr Mulcahy and The Band Rotunda. 1971.
The Sore-Footed Man and The Temptations of Oedipus. 1971.

Radio Play: *Jack Winter's Dream,* 1958.

Other

Recent Trends in New Zealand Poetry. 1951.
The Fire and the Anvil: Notes on Modern Poetry. 1955; revised edition, 1960.
Oil (primary school bulletin). 1957.
The Coaster (primary school bulletin). 1959.
The Trawler (primary school bulletin). 1961.
New Zealand in Colour, photographs by Kenneth and Jean Bigwood. 1961.
The Old Earth Closet: A Tribute to Regional Poetry. 1965.
Aspects of Poetry in New Zealand. 1967.

The Man on the Horse (lectures). 1967.
The Flowering Cross: Pastoral Articles. 1969.
The Six Faces of Love: Lenten Lectures. 1972.
A Walking Stick for an Old Man. 1972.

Reading List: *The Poetry of Baxter* by J. E. Weir, 1970; *Baxter* by Charles Doyle, 1976; *Baxter* by Vincent O'Sullivan, 1976.

* * *

At his best one of the finest English-language poets of the past thirty years, James K. Baxter is the one New Zealand poet of undeniable international reputation. Although he died in his mid-forties, his literary career lasted for over thirty years. Its fruits were many volumes of poems, a number of plays, works of literary commentary or criticism, essays on religious topics, and a small amount of fiction (he was a fine exponent of the parable).

With publication of his first book, *Beyond the Palisade*, when he was eighteen, Baxter at once became a figure of note in New Zealand letters. Within a few years, he already occupied a central position in the literary scene, so that his booklet, *Recent Trends in New Zealand Poetry*, a beautifully condensed commentary, was from the first accepted as authoritative. Alongside his literary reputation, Baxter quickly began to build one as a maverick and a bohemian. When, late in the 1940's, he moved to Wellington and began his long friendship and collaboration with Louis Johnson, they became the focus of the "romantic" element in New Zealand writing, which found its centre in Wellington for the next dozen years or so.

Throughout the 1950's Baxter produced a prolific variety of poems, plays, stories, and criticism, work which ranged from makeshift to brilliant. With Johnson and Charles Doyle (and, latterly, others) he edited the characteristically erratic periodical *Numbers*, then the only alternative to the few "establishment" periodicals such as *Landfall*.

1958 was a crucial moment in Baxter's career. Until then, his adult life had been a strange compound of Christian concern and rip-roaring bohemianism. That year he stayed for a long spell in the Trappist monastery at Kopua, Hawke's Bay, and was converted to Roman Catholicism. At the same time, his superb collection *In Fires of No Return* drew upon the work of his whole career to that point. *Howrah Bridge and Other Poems* followed in 1961 and was composed of new poems plus fine pieces ranging back to the 1940's; but Baxter's talent as a poet for a time seemed to lose focus. It was typical of Baxter that he made little or no effort to become known outside his own country; untypical as he was, he was very deeply a New Zealander, though anguished at his country's unspiritual puritanism.

After a low-energy period, Baxter's career gathered momentum again when he was awarded a Burns Fellowship at the University of Otago. Writing in the *Dominion* on 23 October 1965, Louis Johnson suggested that "the Burns scholarship may well mark a turning-point in his career" and this proved to be the case in remarkable ways. First, it produced what many consider to be Baxter's best verse collection, *Pig Island Letters*, a book in which he learned from, and transcended, the unlikely twin influences of Lawrence Durrell and Robert Lowell. Besides the critical-autobiographical pieces of *The Man on the Horse* and *Aspects of Poetry in New Zealand*, those years in Dunedin witnessed the flowering of Baxter's career as a playwright. During 1967 and 1968, Patric Carey at the Globe Theatre produced seven Baxter plays, including all the most important. Although secondary to the poetry, those plays make it a reasonable claim that, besides being the country's foremost poet, Baxter is the most productive and interesting New Zealand playwright up to the present.

The Dunedin years also led him more deeply into religious and social concerns. After a period of catechetical work in the city, he went into solitude for some months at Jerusalem (Hiruharama), a tiny religious settlement on the Wanganui River. Later he founded a commune there for troubled youths and social drop-outs, and he was also the moving spirit in setting up doss-houses in both Auckland and Wellington. These ventures, pursued in a

Franciscan spirit, including a vow of poverty, took much of his energy, but the commitment also carried over into his vocation as a poet and this period witnessed a further remarkable shift in the development of his writing, especially in the Jerusalem writings, *Jerusalem Sonnets*, *Jerusalem Daybook*, and *Autumn Testament*. He developed a very personal "sonnet" form, in fluid pentameter couplets, and, particularly in *Jerusalem Daybook*, made effective use of an amalgam of prose and verse. Baxter was also important in his community as a man. His best poems have a natural incandescence which partly derives from his being permeated from boyhood with the finest poetry of the British tradition, but which also comes from a human commitment based on religion. New Zealand is a relatively successful social welfare state, secular in spirit. Baxter, notably, brought to it a strong religious consciousness. A literary talent with a touch of genius was deepened and strengthened by the religious element in his character. That this did not escape the notice of his fellow-countrymen is evident from the crowds which thronged to his funeral and memorial services. Baxter's legacy to his country is a double one, a substantial amount of first-rate writing, especially poems, and the example of a man able to carry the spiritual life as far as it can go.

—Charles Doyle

BENNETT, Louise. Jamaican. Educated at primary and secondary schools in Jamaica; Royal Academy of Dramatic Art, London (British Council Scholarship). Worked with the BBC (West Indies Section) as resident artist, 1945–46, 1950–53, and with repertory companies in Coventry, Huddersfield, and Amersham. Returned to Jamaica, 1955: Drama Specialist with the Jamaica Social Welfare Commission, 1955–60; Lecturer in drama and Jamaican folklore, Extra-Mural Department, University of the West Indies, Kingston, 1959–61. Represented Jamaica at the Royal Commonwealth Arts Festival in Britain, 1965. Has lectured in the United States and the United Kingdom on Jamaican music and folklore. Recipient: Silver Musgrave Medal, Institute of Jamaica. M.B.E. (Member, Order of the British Empire). Lives in Jamaica.

PUBLICATIONS

Verse

Dialect Verses. 1940.
Jamaican Dialect Verses. 1942; expanded version, 1951.
Jamaican Humour in Dialect. 1943.
Miss Lulu Sez. 1948.
Anancy Stories and Dialect Verse, with others. 1950.
Laugh with Louise: A Potpourri of Jamaican Folklore, Stories, Songs, Verses. 1960.
Jamaica Labrish. 1966.

Reading List: Introduction by Rex Nettlefold to *Jamaica Labrish*, 1966.

* * *

Afters years of popularity Louise Bennett is now attracting the attention of the critic and scholarly researcher. This belated attention is partly in response to Bennett's formidable merits as a poet, but it also reflects the current interest in Afro-Caribbean folk arts (music, songs, dances, folktales) – not simply as sources for writers and folklorists, but more importantly as significant art forms in their own right. And as a poet whose art has always been based on oral performance and rooted in Jamaican folk idioms, Bennett fully exploits the potentiality of folk arts in the Caribbean. Indeed her themes repeatedly emphasize both the oral nature of her poetry and her own role as a performer. Moreover her language and the loquacious characters in her poems dramatize the political, emotional, and cultural significance of the spoken word among Jamaica's poor and unlettered classes.

Conversely her unlettered but robust folk often ridicule the literate middle-class world of the printed word, not because they reject literacy and middle-class values as such, but because Bennett questions the tendency, in some quarters, to elevate the European values inherent in standard English literacy at the expense of the experience represented by the folk idiom and its Afro-Caribbean cultural milieu. For that cultural milieu results from a complex cultural synthesis of African, European, and New World sources which is in danger of being ignored or minimized by a narrowly literate value system. Bennett's techniques (particularly her choice of language and the oral nature of her poetry) are therefore integral to her vision as an artist. These techniques enable her to immerse her audience in the experience of the folk, affirming in the process that that experience is central rather than peripheral to a Jamaican (and West Indian) consciousness.

This cultural immersion is aided by another Bennett technique: she never allows her authorial voice to obtrude upon the theme of any work, and this is a constant in her work, notwithstanding the authoritarian, even overbearing, voice which discourses on a variety of topics in her poetry. The voice we hear belongs to the persona of the moment, whether it is a politician, a trades unionist, a loyal Black colonial, or a spirited anti-colonialist. And on the whole her poetry relies upon the unfettered self-description of her characters rather than upon some comprehensive definition or overview by the author herself. Hence although Bennett the poet says nothing directly about the status and experience of women, her work represents the most thorough exploration of the woman's experience in the Caribbean. Nearly all of her poems are presented through the eyes – and energetic voices – of women, and in the process they reveal a wide variety of women's attitudes towards men, themselves, and society as a whole. In their vocal self-expressiveness Bennett's women emerge as a rather diverse lot – militant, conventional, strong, or weak. They are therefore representations of Bennett's special kind of poetic truth – a relentless realism that confronts her audience with society and its people as they are and as they express their diverse selves in their oral modes.

—Lloyd W. Brown

BETHELL, Mary Ursula. New Zealander. Born in Surrey, England, 6 October 1874. Educated in England and New Zealand; studied music and painting. Social worker in London and Scotland, 1898–1902; returned to New Zealand permanently in 1919, and settled in Canterbury. *Died 15 January 1945.*

PUBLICATIONS

Verse

From a Garden in the Antipodes. 1929.
The Glad Returning and Other Poems. 1932.
The Haunted Gallery and Other Poems. 1932.
Time and Place. 1936.
Day and Night: Poems 1924–1934. 1939.
Collected Poems. 1950.

Reading List: *Bethell* by M. M. Holcroft, 1975.

*   *   *

Almost all of Mary Ursula Bethell's verse was written (though not published) during a single period of sustained creative activity from 1924 to 1934, between her fiftieth and sixtieth years. Her late flowering began when, after a lifetime spent moving back and forth between England (where she was born) and New Zealand (where she had spent her childhood), she finally settled permanently in New Zealand. With her beloved companion Effie Pollen she moved into a house on the Cashmere Hills overlooking the city of Christchurch, with the Pacific coast of the South Island curving away to the north and east and the Canterbury plains stretching away to the mountains of the Southern Alps in the north and west, as described in "Southerly Sunday":

> The great south wind has covered with cloud the whole of the river-plain,
> soft white ocean of foaming mist, blotting out, billowing
>
> fast to the east, where Pacific main surges on vaster bed.
> But here, on the hills, south wind unvapoured encounters the sunshine,
> lacing and interlocking, the invisible effervescence
> you almost hear, and the laughter of light and air at play overhead.
>
> Seabirds fly free; see the sharp flash of their underwings!
> and high lifted up to the north, the mountains, the mighty, the white ones
> rising sheer from the cloudy sea, light-crowned, established.

Her productive phase ended when Miss Pollen died in 1934 and the house and garden on the hills was vacated. Little was added to her work in the last decade of her life beyond a sequence of annual anniversary poems, written to commemorate the friend whom she considered the "only begetter" of her verse.

Her first book, *From a Garden in the Antipodes*, consists of brief, unpretentious, apparently mundane but deceptively simple poems recording the trivia of a gardener's chores and observations through the seasonal cycle from one autumn to another. Digging, planting, weeding, planning, watching shrubs and plants sprout and bloom, reporting changes in the weather and the view – such is the substance of these modest, prosaic but delightful verses. Beyond the simple surface, however, are wider implications, as suggested by the phrase "garden of exile, garden of my pilgrimage" from an unpublished poem. Ursula Bethell felt herself to be a transplanted Englishwoman for whom her garden (and her poetry which she tends to identify with it) was both a reminder of her exile and a compensation for it. To some degree she stands for all New Zealanders, colonists all, gardening the antipodes. The garden is also her pilgrimage, her way to God. She was a deeply religious woman, and her garden poems were her means of localising the transcendent truths of her religion, though the religious meaning is seldom pointed directly as it is almost invariably in her later volumes.

In *Time and Place* and *Day and Night* the symbolism is more explicit and the message more manifestly Christian. The final stanza of "Southerly Sunday," for example, points the religious meaning of the preceding landscape description (quoted above):

> This sparkling day is the Lord's day. Let us be glad and rejoice in it;
> for he cometh, he cometh to judge and redeem his beautiful universe,
> and holds in his hands all worlds, all men, the quick and the dead.

Time and Place is organised according to the sequence of the seasons, *Day and Night* according to the diurnal cycle, thereby underlining the theme of death and resurrection which is central to her work. The religious poems tend on the whole to be less spontaneous than the garden poems, and are occasionally overwrought both emotionally and technically. When the natural occasion, however, is sufficiently realised to sustain the supernatural meanings attributed to it, Ursula Bethell achieves poems of considerable beauty and force.

—Peter Simpson

BIRNEY, Earle. Canadian. Born in Calgary, Alberta, 13 May 1904. Educated at the University of British Columbia, Vancouver, B.A. 1926; University of Toronto, M.A. 1927, Ph.D. 1936; University of California, Berkeley, 1927–30; Queen Mary College, London, 1934–35. Served in the Canadian Army, in the reserves, 1940–41, and on active duty, 1942–45; Major-in-Charge, Personnel Selection, Belgium and Holland, 1944–45. Married Esther Bull in 1940; one child. Instructor in English, University of Utah, Salt Lake City, 1930–34; Lecturer, later Assistant Professor of English, University of Toronto, 1936–42; Supervisor, European Foreign Language Broadcasts, Radio Canada, Montreal, 1945–46; Professor of Medieval English Literature, 1946–63, and Professor and Chairman of the Department of Creative Writing, 1963–65, University of British Columbia; Writer-in-Residence, University of Toronto, 1965–67, and University of Waterloo, Ontario, 1967–68; Regents Professor in Creative Writing, University of California at Irvine, 1968. Since 1968, free-lance writer and lecturer. Literary Editor, *Canadian Forum*, Toronto, 1936–40; Editor, *Canadian Poetry Magazine*, Edmonton, 1946–48; Editor, *Prism International*, Vancouver, 1964–65; Advisory Editor, *New: American and Canadian Poetry*, Trumansburg, New York, 1966–70. Recipient: Governor-General's Award, 1943, 1946; Stephen Leacock Medal, 1950; Borestone Mountain Poetry Award, 1951; Canadian Government Overseas Fellowship, 1953, Service Medal, 1970; Lorne Pierce Medal, 1953; President's Medal, University of Western Ontario, 1954; Nuffield Fellowship, 1958; Canada Council Senior Arts Grant, 1962, 1974, Medal, 1968, Special Fellowship, 1968, and Travel Grant, 1971, 1974. LL.D.: University of Alberta, Edmonton, 1965. Fellow, Royal Society of Canada, 1954. Lives in Toronto.

PUBLICATIONS

Verse

David and Other Poems. 1942.
Now Is the Time. 1945.
Strait of Anian: Selected Poems. 1948.
Trial of a City and Other Verse. 1952.
Ice Cod Bell or Stone. 1962.
Near False Creek Mouth. 1964.
Selected Poems 1940–1966. 1966.
Memory No Servant. 1968.
Poems. 1969.
Pnomes, Jukollages and Other Stunzas. 1969.
Rag and Bone Shop. 1971.
Five Modern Canadian Poets, with others, edited by Eli Mandel. 1970.
Four Parts Sand: Concrete Poems, with others. 1972.
Bear on the Delhi Road. 1973.
What's So Big about Green? 1973.
Collected Poems. 2 vols., 1974.

Play

The Damnation of Vancouver: A Comedy in Seven Episodes (broadcast, 1952). *In Trial of a City,* 1952; revised version (produced 1957), in *Selected Poems,* 1966.

Radio Play: *The Damnation of Vancouver,* 1952.

Fiction

Turvey: A Military Picaresque. 1949.
Down the Long Table. 1955.

Other

The Creative Writer. 1966.
The Cow Jumped over the Moon: The Writing and Reading of Poetry. 1972.

Editor, *Twentieth Century Canadian Poetry.* 1953.
Editor, *Record of Service in the Second World War.* 1955.
Editor, with others, *New Voices.* 1956.
Editor, with Margerie Lowry, *Selected Poems of Malcoim Lowry.* 1962.
Editor, with Margerie Lowry, *Lunar Caustic,* by Malcolm Lowry. 1963.

Bibliography: in *West Coast Review,* October 1970.

Reading List: *Birney* by Richard Robillard, 1971; *Birney* by Frank Davey, 1971; *Birney* edited by Bruce Nesbitt, 1974.

*   *   *

Earle Birney is almost certainly the most distinguished of living Canadian poets. Even in his earliest verse we can see his essential poetic qualifications, a gift for cut and graven detail, a flowing empathy, and a natural rhythm in which the breathing meets the sense to produce an evolving, living line. Impressive miniatures of these powers are "Slug in Woods" and "Aluroid."

Landscape is a traditional theme in Canadian poetry, a fact which is hardly surprising in a country so physically overwhelming and so variously beautiful as Canada, where even today life is intimately harnessed to the rhythms of the climate and the seasons. Some of the most notable members of Birney's Canadian scene are "Atlantic Door," "Maritime Faces," "Dusk on the Bay," "Hands," "North of Superior," "Ellesmere Land, I," "North Star West," "The Ebb Begins from Dream," "Winter Saturday," "Holiday in the Foothills," "Bushed," "Images in Place of Logging," "David," an energetic narrative poem about climbing, and reminiscent of those "action" poems of the 1930's in England, is less successfully realised, perhaps spoilt by moralising, as is another well-known poem, "November Walk by False Creek Mouth." But the successful poems of this kind compose a poetic geography of Canada, defining its bone, frame, moods, and treacheries. Birney evokes in each of these poems of landscape the natural world in process: the verbs are continuous, there is a sense of stirring molecular activity implicit in the stoniest, harshest landscape, the mountains are weathering, the rooms lighting, the dampness steams. At the same time, something enduring in the country matches something stubborn in the poet. Birney's sensibility has, indeed, a hard and cobbled quality, a strength which does not forbid sensitivity and delicate registration but which sustains and toughens them. It is a note which we find in that slim, perfectly articulated poem, "Ellesmere Land, I."

What is clear from these poems and many others is a central fact of human existence for Birney: that man exists in a state of stoic detachment from the supporting earth, from his neighbours, from everything. In the candid and occasionally tetchy preface to his *Selected Poems 1940–1966* he explains that the poems are not so much efforts to bridge the gap as recognitions of the fact:

> That I go on so stubbornly to publish my incantations,
> in a world which may not last long enough to read them,
> and has shown little need for them so far, might be
> construed as mere vanity, or again as proof that the
> outer me is as abnormally compulsive as the inner. I
> prefer to believe, rather, that my poems are the best
> proof I can print of my humanness, signals out of the
> loneliness into which all of us are born and in which
> we die, affirmations of kinship with the other wayfarers....

Just so: and man is joined to man not by his effort, and its necessary failure, to cross over to his neighbour or his lover, but by the acknowledgment of a common predicament.

Buoyant and balanced: this phrase aptly describes his work at large. About its buoyancy one can say that the poet's natural sense of rhythm, itself the development of a profound human instinct, has been educated over fifty years of severe professional practice to such a pitch of intuitive taste, as to be utterly responsive to the needs of the poetry, and completely clean of any involuntarily deposited sludge or accidental silt. The medium has become an instrument. The same is true of the self. By unremitting application, by the most disinterested discipline, Birney's nature has been scraped and scrubbed free of affectation, presupposition, prejudice, so that it appears in the poetry of these last years in its authentically individual, true, worn state.

Buoyancy, not bounce, the product of discipline and a certain ease and confidence of character, itself the hard-won consequence of a life spent in the service of poetry and the mind, enables Birney in his poems, particularly in those of travel, to see a situation squarely with no distorting squint of preconception, without the patronage of self-indulgent pity or defensive guiltiness. He deals with it solely out of his own resources and purely on its own merits. There is, then, a balance or proportion between subject and object, a wholeness and unity in the former recognising the fullness and complexity of the latter. A Birney poem is never just the evocation of a scene. It always has an intellectual and moral structure. In all his poems of place, place itself aspires to support, or even to be, an event.

—William Walsh

BOLDREWOOD, Rolf. Pseudonym for Thomas Alexander Browne. Australian. Born in London, England, 6 August 1826; emigrated to Australia 1831. Educated at O'Connell Street Dame School, Sydney; W. T. Cape's private academy, Sydney; Sydney College, 1835–41; tutored by Rev. David Boyd, Melbourne. Married Margaret Maria Riley in 1861; five daughters and four sons. Pioneer squatter (i.e., grazier), 1844–63 in the western district of Victoria; sheepfarmer and Justice of Peace in Narrandera, New South Wales, 1864–69; gave up farming 1869; Police Magistrate, Gulgong, New South Wales, 1871; Goldfield's Commissioner, 1872, and later District Coroner, Gulgong, until 1881; Police Magistrate, Dubbo, New South Wales, 1881–84, and Armidale, New South Wales, 1884; Chairman, Land Licensing Board, Albury, New South Wales, 1885–87, and Police Magistrate and Mining Warden, Albury, 1887–95; settled in Melbourne, 1895. *Died 11 March 1915.*

PUBLICATIONS

Collections

The Portable Boldrewood, edited by Alan Brissenden. 1978.

Fiction

Ups and Downs: A Story of Australian Life. 1878; as *The Squatter's Dream*, 1890.
Robbery under Arms: A Story of Life and Adventure in the Bush and in the Goldfields of Australia. 1888; revised edition, 1889.
The Miner's Right: A Tale of the Australian Goldfields. 1890.
A Colonial Reformer. 1890.
A Sydney-Side Saxon. 1891.
Nevermore. 1892.
A Modern Buccaneer. 1894.
The Sphinx of Eaglehawk: A Tale of Old Bendigo. 1895.
The Crooked Stick; or, Pollie's Probation. 1895.
The Sealskin Cloak. 1896.
My Run Home. 1897.
Plain Living: A Bush Idyll. 1898.
A Romance of Canvas Town and Other Stories. 1898.

"War to the Knife"; or, Tangata Maori. 1899.
Babes in the Bush. 1899.
In Bad Company and Other Stories. 1901.
The Ghost Camp; or, The Avengers. 1902.
The Last Chance: A Tale of the Golden West. 1905.

Other

S. W. Silver's Australian Grazier's Guide. 2 vols., 1879–81.
Old Melbourne Memories. 1884; revised edition, 1886; edited by C. E. Sayers, 1969.

Bibliography: *Boldrewood: An Annotated Bibliography, Checklist, and Chronology* by Keast Burke, 1956.

Reading List: *Boldrewood* by T. Inglis Moore, 1968; *Boldrewood* by Alan Brissenden, 1972.

* * *

T. A. Browne began writing (as Rolf Boldrewood) in middle life to supplement a depleted income and repay debts to relatives, drawing on his experience as a squatter and his unbounded admiration for the novels of Scott. Most of his work was first printed in weekly periodicals (12 of his 16 novels originally appeared as serials). His good-natured attitude to life was expressed in six pastoral romances and ten adventure stories; material for several of these – the best are *The Miner's Right* and *Nevermore* – derived from his life on the goldfields.

Browne often fictionalized historical events with success, especially in *Robbery under Arms*, an exciting tale of bushrangers which has remained popular. Its hero, Captain Starlight, and the Marstons – old Ben, an ex-convict, and his sons Dick and Jim – steal cattle, rob a bank, raid homesteads, and hold up a rich gold escort. Though generally successful, the outlaws plan to escape to America. On their way to take ship from Queensland, they are betrayed. Starlight and Jim are shot dead, and Dick, the teller of the tale, is condemned to hang. Dick's sentence is commuted, and, on his release, he marries the faithful Grace Storefield and they take up a new life on a cattle station.

The novel succeeds where others by Browne fail because its structure is tight but varied and the action is depicted vividly. Most of all, through choosing an ill-educated colonial as his narrator, Browne was able to restrain his usually weak, florid style. He was the first to use the Australian vernacular in this way for a novel, and the first to present Australian-born colonials as main characters. The Marstons are a foil for the noble Englishman Starlight, a dashing Byronic figure who is a master of manners, wit, and disguise. Important historically, the novel is also good reading. Others, e.g., *A Colonial Reformer*, *A Sydney-Side Saxon*, and a volume of reminiscences, *Old Melbourne Memories*, have value more as sources of social history than as lively writing.

Politically conservative, Browne disagreed with the nationalistic mood of Australia in the 1890's and refused to write for its chief voice, the *Bulletin*. He was patriotic, but ambiguously so, lauding the colonial life with its opportunities for wealth and its physical excellence, while firmly believing a noble lineage and an ancestral home to be ultimately desirable. His most vigorous characters are the native-born men and women of *Robbery under Arms*; his most vivid writing is in the descriptions, seen through Dick Marston's eyes, of the Australian bush and the gang's exploits. While the novel lacks the depth of vision of Marcus Clarke's *For the Term of His Natural Life* and the consistency of Henry Kingsley's *Geoffry Hamlyn*, it is more distinctively Australian than either in its depiction of the relationship between the young colonials and the immigrant landowners, in the swinging gusto of its narration, and particularly in its language.

—Alan Brissenden

BOYD, Martin (à Beckett). Australian. Born in Lucerne, Switzerland, of Australian parents, 10 June 1893; grew up in Melbourne. Educated at Trinity Grammar School, Kew, Victoria; St. John's Theological College, Melbourne; trained as an architect, but never practised. Served as a Lieutenant in The Buffs Regiment, 1916; Observer, Royal Flying Corps, 1917; Pilot, Royal Air Force, 1918. Settled in London, 1919; member of a religious community for a time; thereafter a full-time writer; reviewer for the *Times Literary Supplement*, London, 1931–40; returned to Australia briefly, 1948, came back to England, then settled in Rome. Also a painter: one-man shows, Cambridge, 1964, Melbourne, 1967. Recipient: Australian Literary Society Gold Medal, 1928, 1956. *Died 3 June 1972.*

PUBLICATIONS

Fiction

Love Gods. 1925.
Brangane: A Memoir. 1926; as *The Aristocrat: A Memoir,* 1927.
The Montforts. 1928; as *Madeleine Heritage,* 1928; revised edition, 1963.
Scandal of Spring. 1934.
The Lemon Farm. 1935.
The Picnic. 1937.
Night of the Party. 1938.
Nuns in Jeopardy. 1940.
Lucinda Brayford. 1946.
Such Pleasure. 1949; as *Bridget Malwyn,* 1949.
The Cardboard Crown. 1952.
A Difficult Young Man. 1955.
Outbreak of Love. 1957.
When Blackbirds Sing. 1962.
The Teatime of Love: The Clarification of Miss Stilby. 1969.

Verse

Retrospect. 1920.

Other

The Painted Princess: A Fairy Story (juvenile).   1936.
A Single Flame (autobiography).   1939.
Much Else in Italy: A Subjective Travel Book.   1958.
Day of My Delight (autobiography).   1965.
Why They Walk Out: An Essay in Seven Parts.   1970.

Bibliography: *Boyd* by Brenda Niall, 1978.

Reading List: *Boyd* by Kathleen Fitzpatrick, 1963; *Boyd* by Brenda Niall, 1974.

*   *   *

In Martin Boyd many literary impulses meet, but the last impression is old-fashioned. There is a *pot-pourri* fragrance in his writing, but it is a fragrance of spice, not of sentiment. His professed concern was for what he called artistic truth; but it is doubtful if he could have conceived of that without a humanizing abundance of romantic humour. Humour is with him crossed with both sympathy and criticism: he is in effect an ironist.

In him many loyalties conflict; but if there were no contradictions there would be less life and vigour in the irony. His first family inheritance was the old, basic colonial conflict: were the Australians Englishmen in exile, a stockbroker-professional-Government House aristocracy, or were they mental republicans articulating the new world? Boyd himself was capable of varying moods, as an Australian Englishman, as aesthete and sceptic, snob and anti-snob, fantasist and realist. As an artist he trusts more than most to spontaneity and intuition, believing that the imagination when truly excited cannot go seriously wrong. On the whole his style justified that trust, though his books have a certain amiable sprawl – especially the collective Langton chronicle, which, being discursively conceived, is perhaps a little too leisurely. His shorter novels are well-made; the more ambitious tend to be overburdened with material (*The Montforts, Lucinda Brayford*) or to be architecturally shaky, however full of attractive nooks and crannies. In the case of the Langton series, it is the family material itself that holds the work in proportion.

Apart from structural considerations Boyd's style is highly personal. A man of strong and at times obstinate opinions, not incapable of bias and prejudice if touched on a sensitive spot (he would hear no good, for instance, of Winston Churchill), he nevertheless possessed a humour which invariably distinguished his best writing. Perhaps, like Joseph Furphy (with whom he had little else in common), he could be called a humourist in the tradition of Sterne, Steele, or Goldsmith – or his own à Beckett great-uncle who edited *Punch*. He approves the eighteenth-century virtues, detests the eighteenth-century sins (hypocrisy, false dealing, rapacity), as well as colonial philistinism or any form of artistic insincerity. To read him as he intends, one must be able to distinguish between iniquities and peccadilloes. Austin's scandalous life with Hetty, for example, monstrous as Aunt Mildred thinks it, is not condemned because it is passionate and human; but Mildred's ("Aunt Mildew's") mean opinion is, because it is arid and insensitive. Dominic's riding his horse into the house is merely a brave and bold defiance of cold, dead convention; but Dominic's allowing the horse to die of neglect is a black mark against him. And Wolfie is condemned not for the adultery involved in sleeping with the floozy who is the "subject" of his beautiful musical tone-poems, but for being coarse enough to leave his socks on in bed.

These values may seem odd in a Melbourne context, but their conservatism is attractive and enlivening. It is one of the ways in which Boyd contrives to convey in his novels a pervading sense of continuity, something piquant in the survival of the half-forgotten past into the not-yet-too-clearly-defined present. So in effect it happens that time is always a cogent factor in Martin Boyd's imaginative world: time, that is, as a present experience, never merely as mere historical order or sequence. The essence of Boyd is imagination, sympathy, and humanity. The books have certain wandering weaknesses, but they never lack life. The truth that he sought − artistic truth − is the major cause of their never-failing warmth.

—Brian Elliott

BRATHWAITE, Edward. Barbadian. Born in Bridgetown, Barbados, 11 May 1930. Educated at Harrison College, Barbados; Pembroke College, Cambridge (Barbados Scholar), 1950–54, B.A. (honours) in history 1953, Cert. Ed. 1954; University of Sussex, Brighton, 1965–68, D.Phil. 1968. Married Doris Monica Welcome in 1960; one son. Education Officer, Ministry of Education, Ghana, 1955–62; Tutor, University of the West Indies Extra Mural Department, St. Lucia, 1962–63. Lecturer, 1963–72, and since 1972 Senior Lecturer in History, University of the West Indies, Kingston. Plebiscite Officer in the Trans-Volta Togoland, United Nations, 1956–57. Founding Secretary, Caribbean Artists Movement, 1966. Since 1970, Editor, *Savacou* magazine, Mona. Recipient: Arts Council of Great Britain bursary, 1967; Camden Arts Festival prize, London, 1967; Cholmondeley Award, 1970; Guggenheim Fellowship, 1972; City of Nairobi Fellowship, 1972; Bussa Award, 1973. Lives in Kingston, Jamaica.

PUBLICATIONS

Verse

Rights of Passage. 1967; *Masks,* 1968; *Islands,* 1969; combined version, as *The Arrivants,* 1973.
Other Exiles. 1975.
Mother Poem. 1977.

Plays

Four Plays for Primary Schools (produced 1961–62). 1964.
Odale's Choice (produced 1962). 1967.

Other

The People Who Came, 1–3 (textbooks). 3 vols., 1968–72.
Folk Culture of the Slaves in Jamaica. 1970.
The Development of Creole Society in Jamaica. 1971.
Caribbean Man in Space and Time. 1974.
Contradictory Omens: Cultural Diversity and Integration in the Caribbean. 1974.

Editor, *Iouanaloa: Recent Writing from St. Lucia.* 1963.

Bibliography: in *Savacou Bibliographical Series 2,* 1973.

* * *

Edward Brathwaite has emerged as one of the major writers in contemporary West Indian literature. His trilogy *Rights of Passage, Masks,* and *Islands* (reprinted as *The Arrivants*) is an epic of sorts on Black West Indian history and culture. Much of his present reputation rests on that trilogy, although he has published other poetry, and his scholarly writing has established him as a West Indian historian. Paradoxically, however, Brathwaite's reputation as a poet-historian of the "Black diaspora" sometimes has the effect of minimizing rather than illuminating his full achievements as a poet. The point is not, of course, that the themes of Black ethnicity are themselves insignificant. Indeed the opposite is the truth, a truth that needs to be repeatedly emphasized in light of the fact that ethnic and national consciousness has historically been an underdeveloped aspect of West Indian life. And, accordingly, writers like Brathwaite have had a significant impact on their Caribbean readership because their ethnic themes appeal to a cultural consciousness that has only assumed mass proportions since the achievement of nationhood. Brathwaite's appeal as an ethnic poet is in itself an interesting reflection on the belated nature of the ethnic awakening.

Indeed, the intensity with which Brathwaite has been received in some quarters has tended to limit perception and analysis of his less obtrusive but crucial emphasis on the complex texture of West Indian history and identity. That texture reflects the distinctive intermingling of African, European, and American elements that is characteristic of West Indian society. For like the equally distinguished Derek Walcott (St. Lucia) with whom he is more often contrasted than compared, Brathwaite really perceives and describes the West Indies as a synthesis of diverse cultural traditions. *Islands,* for example, reflects the contributions of Western religion and literature, just as much as the symbols of Akan culture pervade the language and vision of *Masks.* And on the whole the techniques and themes of the trilogy are an example as well as explication of this Afro-Caribbean diversity.

There is also a danger of approaching Brathwaite, in strictly thematic terms, as a compiler of historical statements about the West Indian experience rather than as a complex artist whose crucial cultural themes are interwoven with a sophisticated awareness of the nature of his own art as poet. In fact his poetry is not only socially descriptive but also introspective in that it explores the function of the poetic imagination itself and by extension the implications of the artist's identity. The quest themes of the trilogy are illustrative here. In one sense they reinforce a sense of cultural and historical continuities, or movements, as we move with Brathwaite's composite cultural archetypes from the Caribbean to North America and back (*Rights of Passage*), to West Africa (*Masks*) and back to the Caribbean (*Islands*). But in another sense this cultural quest is an allegory, dramatizing the nature and function of the artist's imagination: art is a journey through time and space, analogous to and at the same time inseparable from memory itself — the memory of the poet as individual artist, the imaginative memory of all artists like himself (the Black musician, for example) and the collective memory of the poet's people as it is manifested in their songs, dances, and other folk art forms. Moreover, as an act of memory the artistic imagination imitates the cycles of time itself, imitating and exemplifying the manner in which the mind simultaneously anticipates the future and recreates the past in the present: the Akan sounds of welcome in *Masks,* for example, greet the West Indian visitor returning to West African roots but they simultaneously evoke the earlier, unsuspecting offer of hospitality to the seventeenth-century slavetrader. Brathwaite is therefore a poet-historian both on the basis of his vision of cultural history and in light of the manner in which his poetic imagination imitates perceived patterns of time and history.

—Lloyd W. Brown

BRENNAN, Christopher (John). Australian. Born in Sydney, New South Wales, 1 November 1870. Educated at Riverview School, Sydney; University of Sydney, M.A. 1892; studied philosophy and classics at the University of Berlin (travelling scholarship), 1892–94. Married Anna Elizabeth Werth in 1897 (divorced, 1925); two sons. Assistant Librarian, rising to Chief Cataloguer, Sydney Public Library, 1897–1908; joined the Modern Languages Department, University of Sydney, 1908: Lecturer in French and German, 1908–1920; Associate Professor of German and Comparative Literature, 1920–25; schoolteacher, 1926–32. Recipient: Commonwealth Literary Fund pension. *Died 7 October 1932.*

PUBLICATIONS

Collections

The Verse, The Prose, edited by A. R. Chisholm and J. J. Quinn.   2 vols., 1960–62.

Verse

XVIII Poems, Being the First Collection of Verse and Prose.   1897.
XXI Poems (1893–1897): Towards the Source.   1897.
Poems 1913.   1914.
A Chant of Doom and Other Verses.   1918.
Twenty-Three Poems.   1928.

Play

A Mask, with John Le Gay Brereton, Jr. (produced 1913).   1913.

Other

Editor, with G. G. Nicholson, *Passages for Translation into French and German.*   1914.

Bibliography: *Brennan: A Comprehensive Bibliography* by Walter Stone and Hugh Anderson, 1959.

Reading List: *Brennan* by H. M. Green, 1939; *Brennan: The Man and His Poetry,* 1946, and *A Study of Brennan's "A Forest of Night,"* 1970, both by A. R. Chisholm; *New Perspectives on Brennan's Poetry* by G. A. Wilkes, 1952; *Brennan* by James McAuley, 1973.

*   *   *

Christopher Brennan, a legend still in Australian literature, belonged, like Herman Melville in *Clarel* and Walter Pater in *Marius the Epicurean* to that numerous company of 19th-century writers who, finding belief too difficult, found unbelief even more difficult, and so embarked on an impossible quest for certainties. Writing of the doctrine of correspondences, Brennan said in an essay on Nineteenth Century Literature (1904): "What spiritual fact needs is corroboration, and of corroboration it can never have enough." His verse traces the inner history of an unremitting search, as elusive as the alchemists' dream, for corroboration, for intellectual confirmation of faith.

Brennan was a devout Catholic, of Irish parentage, who as a young university student abandoned his intention to become a priest and became estranged from the practice of his faith. This loss of commitment is likely to have affected him more deeply than he admitted, and it is possible he tried to internalize his vocation, first as a philosopher, then as a poet, seeking a religion without a personal god. Keats's *Endymion* seems to have initiated him into the poet's perennial quest, and it is possible that he came into contact with esoteric ideas before he left Sydney, perhaps by reading Maitland's novels, or by associating with Spiritualists, or through hints in Pater. When he arrived in Berlin and became aware of the French Symbolist movement, he found Mallarmé's theory and practice of poetry immensely congenial to him, though the cast of his mind and his style in prose and verse belong much more to the German tradition than to the French. As a technician Brennan is indeed a mosaic of the Victorians, and, through the Victorians, an inheritor of Miltonic eloquence. His chief affinities, he said later in life, were Mallarmé and Coventry Patmore! More important, Brennan was above all a scholar-poet; he was indeed one of Australia's most brilliant classical scholars, whose theories about the manuscripts of Aeschylus attracted the attention of Jowett, and have since been vindicated. On this foundation and on that of a wide knowledge of German, Italian and French, he pursued his studies in German theosophy, Jewish mysticism, and Eastern gnosticism, while his personal and professional life began to crumble around him, and in the end he returned, with enriched understanding of the common human predicament, to the simple pieties of his youth, "*naturaliter Christiana.*" In an essay on Mallarmé he spoke of throwing the mystics overboard and returning to the visible world: "Our daily bread, if we are satisfied with it, will prove richer than we thought."

Brennan's reputation rests principally on *Poems 1913*, though "Fifteen Poems," circulated in typescript and published after his death as "The Burden of Tyre," is of great interest in foreshadowing the complexities of his Eden symbol, to be fully explored in the main work.

Brennan is the one Australian poet who practised what Arnold would have recognised as "the grand style," and, though it was going out of fashion when he wrote and is quite obsolete now, it could be argued that no other would have served his theme quite so well, even though it lays him open to charges of using archaic poetic diction, occasional Victorian lushness or Pre-Raphaelite sweetness, and syntactically convoluted paragraphs.

It is divided into five sections or "movements," for if, as has been claimed, *Poems 1913* is a *livre composé*, it is so in a musical rather than a purely literary sense. "Towards the Source" is the first step on the journey towards the innermost self, through the agency of love and marriage. Though, as in the poems as a whole, the autobiographical element is strong, it would be unwise to ignore esoteric interpretations of "nuptial exchanges," especially in view of the alchemical references scattered throughout. "The Forest of Night" is the most sustained and powerful attempt to penetrate to the depths of the unconscious, and the brooding and majestic figure of Lilith, "mournful until we find her fair," is one of the most compelling symbols in modern English verse of the mysterious, terrible, yet fascinating womb of becoming, of the Void in which all possibilities wait for being, where "gods and stars and songs and souls of men/are the sparse jewels in her scattered hair." The third movement, "The Wanderer," returns us to the conscious world with its ever-present conflict between social and individual man, between the longing for security and the urge to explore, symbolised in contrasting images of window and hearth, of winds and sea. Questing is accepted as an end in itself, necessary to continuing life, and courage is its moral imperative. The two final sections, "Pauca Mea" and "Epilogues," in turn agonised and defiant, culminate not in capitulation, but in the quiet wisdom of "1908," which offers staff and scrip for the journey. In spite of Brennan's deep involvement with the French symbolists and the legacy of Hegel and Novalis, it is conceivable that he drew his theories of poetry from earlier sources, from Augustine's "Rhetoric of Silence," for example, with its vision of the world as a divine poem which man had to learn, while in the flesh, to read, in the expectation of encountering its meaning in the spirit, face to face. The notion of the "grand man" may also have come to him, not from Swedenborg, but more directly from Origen.

As a poet, Brennan is still, as he was in his lifetime, isolated from the main tradition of Australian poetry. His is the work of a man struggling with a great internal solitude, and in it he accuses not only himself, but his society and his civilisation of a "total dereliction from the human path, the human dream" and sees mankind, perhaps, as a fellow-poet saw him: "a star in exile, unconstellated at the south," alienated from his true self as the image of God.

—Dorothy Green

BROWNE, Thomas Alexander. See **BOLDREWOOD, Rolf.**

BUTLER, (Frederick) Guy. South African. Born in Cradock, Cape Province, 21 January 1918. Educated at a local high school; Rhodes University, Grahamstown, M.A. 1939; Brasenose College, Oxford, M.A. 1947. Served during World War II in the Middle East, Italy, and the United Kingdom. Married Jean Murray Satchwell in 1940; three sons, one daughter. Lecturer in English, University of the Witwatersrand, Johannesburg, 1948–50. Since 1952, Professor of English, Rhodes University, Grahamstown. Editor, with Ruth Harnett, *New Coin* poetry quarterly, Grahamstown. D.Litt.: University of Natal, Durban, 1968. Lives in Grahamstown.

PUBLICATIONS

Verse

Stranger to Europe. 1952; augmented edition, 1960.
South of the Zambezi: Poems from South Africa. 1966.
On First Seeing Florence. 1968.
Selected Poems. 1975.
Ballads and Songs. 1977.

Plays

The Dam (produced 1953). 1953.
The Dove Returns (produced 1956). 1956.
Take Root or Die (produced 1966). 1970.
Cape Charade (produced 1968). 1968.

Other

An Aspect of Tragedy. 1953.
The Republic of the Arts. 1964.

Editor, *A Book of South African Verse.* 1959.
Editor, *When Boys Were Men.* 1969.
Editor, *The 1820 Settlers.* 1974.

* * *

When Guy Butler was serving as a soldier in Italy he carried his paintings with him in a shell-case, hoping to return to his native South Africa with a pictorial record of his European experiences. His poems and plays reflect a life-long attempt to contrast what Europe and Africa mean to him. In "Cape Coloured Batman" Butler finds himself on the "terraced groves of Tuscany," contemplating the pathetic fusion of Europe and Africa in the shape of the despised half-caste. But in "Servant Girl" he is aware of his distance from true African culture:

> [She is] singing a song which seems more integral
> With rain-rinsed sky and sandstone hill
> Than any cadence wrung
> From my taut tongue.

Butler's descriptive talent enables him to present sympathetically the African ritualistic killing of an ox, or, in "Isibongo of Matiwane," a legendary warrior:

> Matiwane, royal, wearing the blood-red feathers of the lourie,
> his eyes red, red his lips from drinking the blood of strong men,
> moves over the earth with the speed of a startled gnu.

Sometimes, as in "The Underdogs," Butler is sharply satirical about White South Africa:

> "Lord, save the shining Christian culture
> Of White South Africa!" Then squat
> Heroically behind clean Vickers guns
> Jabbering death in our innocent hands.

But a more characterisitc attitude is the positive desire, as expressed in the long poem, "Home Thoughts," to "civilize my semi-barbarous land" by the meeting and mating of European clarity (Apollo) and African primitive instinct (Black Dionysus).

Guy Butler's range is wide. He can recount family anecdotes in a simple, but moving, manner; recall poignantly the ironies of war; or paint for us his Cradock Mountains in lines both detailed and lyrical. Varied though his style is, it is always verbally inventive (a train whistle "drove a long spear through/The unexpecting stillness") and rich with a painter's vision. It can adapt itself to many poetic strands – social satire, elegy, narrative, or religious meditation. His stylistic flexibility succeeds outstandingly in the long poem *On First Seeing Florence*, a masterly evocation of personal experiences leading to profound metaphysical intuitions.

His major plays, *The Dam* and *The Dove Returns*, are verse dramas on South African themes. *The Dam* is an anguished, but not despairing, symbolic play about personal destinies within a multi-racial society, written in a verse which modulates remarkably from colloquial idiom to impassioned utterance.

Guy Butler's achievement, in poems and plays, has been to look profoundly and honestly at South African life today, and to write about it with sensitive clarity in an original style which avoids eccentricities.

—Dennis Davison

CALLAGHAN, Morley (Edward). Canadian. Born in Toronto, Ontario, 22 September 1903. Educated at St. Michael's College, University of Toronto, B.A. 1925; Osgoode Hall Law School, Toronto, LL.B. 1928; admitted to the Ontario Bar, 1928. Worked with the Royal Canadian Navy on assignment for the National Film Board during World War II; travelled across Canada as Chairman of the radio forum "Of Things to Come," 1944. Married Lorette Florence Dee in 1929; two sons. Worked on the Toronto *Star* while a student; full-time writer since 1928; lived in Paris, 1928–29. Recipient: Governor-General's Award, 1952; Lorne Pierce Medal, 1960; Canada Council Medal, 1966; Molson Prize, 1969; Royal Bank of Canada Award, 1970. LL.D.: University of Western Ontario, London, 1965. Lives in Toronto.

PUBLICATIONS

Fiction

Strange Fugitive. 1928.
A Native Argosy. 1929.
It's Never Over. 1930.
A Broken Journey. 1932.
Such Is My Beloved. 1934.
They Shall Inherit the Earth. 1935.
Now That April's Here and Other Stories. 1936.
More Joy in Heaven. 1937.
The Varsity Story. 1948.
The Loved and the Lost. 1951.
Stories. 2 vols., 1959–67.
The Many Colored Coat. 1960.
A Passion in Rome. 1961.
An Autumn Penitent. 1973.
A Fine and Private Place. 1975.
Close to the Sun Again. 1977.

Plays

Turn Again Home (produced 1940; as *Going Home,* produced 1950).
To Tell the Truth (produced 1949).

Other

No Man's Meat. 1931.
Luke Baldwin's Vow (juvenile). 1948.
That Summer in Paris: Memories of Tangled Friendships with Hemingway, Fitzgerald, and Some Others. 1963.
Winter. 1974.

Reading List: *Callaghan* by Victor Hoar, 1969; *The Style of Innocence: A Study of Hemingway and Callaghan* by Fraser Sutherland, 1972.

* * *

Morley Callaghan's achievement has moved in a majestically cyclic manner, from an early period of gauche apprentice work to a time when he found his true talent in the superb short stories and tense moralistic novellas that led Edmund Wilson to liken him, perhaps over-generously, to Chekhov and Turgenev. This was during the 1930's. From the 1950's through the early 1970's, Callaghan strove to turn himself from a writer of sparse *récits* into a novelist in the full-figured nineteenth-century manner, and failed. Finally, in 1977, at the age of 74 with a novella entitled *Close to the Sun Again*, he returned to the manner of those sparse fictions he wrote forty years ago, and the result was success and renewal.

Callaghan has written very little that is not fiction. During the years when he found it hard to earn a living by fiction, he appeared on quiz shows and did other radio work in preference to becoming involved in journalism and teaching, as most other Canadian writers did in his time. But he did write two plays, which had short runs but were never published, and among his best books is the fragment of autobiography, *That Summer in Paris*, which appeared during one of his fallow periods, and which told of the period in the late 1920's when he spent eight months in the French capital, associating with Hemingway, whom he had known when they both worked for the Toronto *Star*, Joyce, and Fitzgerald.

That Summer in Paris is not only an evocative memoir, written with a laconic vividness characteristic of Callaghan at his best. It is also interesting as the only book setting out his aim of writing a direct and non-metaphorical prose that will show things as they are and put no literary screen between the reader and the characters. It was a theory similar to Orwell's idea of "prose like a window pane," but, like most such dogmas, it was carried out only imperfectly in practice, for even the sparsest of Callaghan's novels tends to be dominated by a symbolic structure in which the towers of the Catholic church, which plays so potent a role in his imagination, are notably present at crucial times.

Though it provided unhappy glimpses of his literary heroes, the period described in *That Summer in Paris* was a crucial one in Callaghan's development, which is perhaps why he remembered it so vividly. He had already published a novel, *Strange Fugitive*, about a weak man's involvement through vanity in a gangland where he is destroyed, and had written *It's Never Over* about the effects on a man's family and friends of his execution for murder. These novels, and also *A Broken Journey* were gauche, tentative, and implausible, and it seemed as though Callaghan – whose bittersweet ironical tales had appeared in *Native Argosy* – was essentially a short story writer.

Then, in the mid-1930's, he turned to a quite different kind of novel. He was certainly affected by the tragic circumstances of the depression, but the books he produced were moral parables rather than political tracts, and gained great strength from the fact that Callaghan evidently knew what he wanted to attain and was in full command of the means he needed. In the three novels of this time – *Such Is My Beloved* (about a priest who helps prostitutes), *They Shall Inherit the Earth* (about a son who lets his father be ruined because of a false suspicion of murder) and *More Joy in Heaven* (about a reformed criminal destroyed by former associations) – the characters move, through the curious limbo of suspended existence that the depression created for so many people, towards their almost classic fates. The biblical titles are only half ironical; though Callaghan rejected conventional morality in action, he did not reject Christian charity as such, and indeed suggested that it might in the end be superior to the revolutionary doctrines some of his characters project. In each of the novels there is a leading character who acts with personal integrity and is destroyed by the conventional morality of society and its institutions.

In his trio of post-World War II books – *The Loved and the Lost*, *The Many Colored Coat*, and *A Passion in Rome* – he attempted a lusher, decorated style, and adopted the more complex form of the classic realist novel. But he used the equipment of a writer of short stories and novellas, with a consequent corruption of style, an offending of credibility. Both *The Loved and the Lost* and *A Passion in Rome* fail in the unity of conception and force of moral passion that distinguished such books as *They Shall Inherit the Earth*. *The Many Colored Coat* comes nearer the 1930's novels, at least in spirit, but it is too long and over-written for its simple theme. In 1975 Callaghan reached the end of this long phase in his career by producing an almost autobiographical novel, *A Fine and Public Place*, about an unjustly neglected novelist; it is really a kind of *apologia pro vita sua*, and a somewhat embarrassing one in its lack of emotional control.

In 1977 Callaghan finally broke away from his attempt to become a realist novelist, and, in a splendid novella, *Close to the Sun Again*, worked out in concise form and vibrant prose a tale of amnesia and recollection at the point of death. A powerful tycoon is the central figure, and the main theme is the idea that the will to power only develops among men when their natural impulses are suppressed and their personal defeats come to dominate them. Touch a powerful man and you find an emotional cripple. It is a remarkable book for a man in his seventies to have written, and a fine instance of the resilience of the creative urge.

—George Woodcock

CAMPBELL, Alistair (Te Ariki). New Zealander. Born in Rarotonga, Cook Islands, 25 June 1925; emigrated to New Zealand in 1933. Educated at Otago Boys' High School, Dunedin; Victoria University of Wellington, B.A. in Latin and English. Married 1) the poet Fleur Adcock (divorced), two sons; 2) Meg Anderson in 1958, three children. Editor, Department of Education School Publications Branch, Wellington, 1955–72. Since 1972, Senior Editor, New Zealand Council for Educational Research, Wellington. Lives in Wellington.

PUBLICATIONS

Verse

Mine Eyes Dazzle: Poems 1947–49. 1950; revised edition, 1951, 1956.
Sanctuary of Spirits. 1963.
Wild Honey. 1964.
Blue Rain. 1967.

Drinking Horn. 1971.
Walk the Black Path. 1971.
Kapiti: Selected Poems, 1947–71. 1972.
Dreams, Yellow Lions. 1975.

Plays

When the Bough Breaks (produced 1970). 1970.

Radio Plays: *The Homecoming; The Proprietor; The Suicide; The Wairau Incident.*

Television Documentaries: *Island of Spirits,* 1973; *Like You I'm Trapped,* 1975.

Other

The Fruit Farm (juvenile). 1953.
The Happy Summer (juvenile). 1961.
New Zealand: A Book for Children. 1967.
Maori Legends. 1969.

Reading List: essay by James Bertram, in *Comment,* January–February 1965; "Campbell's *Mine Eyes Dazzle:* An Anatomy of Success" by David Gunby, in *Landfall,* March 1969; "Campbell's *Sanctuary of Spirits:* The Historical and Cultural Context" by F. M. McKay, in *Landfall,* June 1978.

* * *

Alistair Campbell's first book, *Mine Eyes Dazzle,* laid out as his territory the natural world. The descriptions of nature are notable for an animism which gives them a primitive strength and which is perhaps to be accounted for by Campbell's part-Polynesian background. The volume announced him as a Romantic poet who had learnt much from Yeats, though Campbell's concern has always been to explore feeling rather than ideas. His Romanticism is deepened by an empathy with Maori culture in which the spoken arts are highly poetical and a good deal of imagery is drawn from nature. One of the best of these early poems is "The Elegy," in memory of a fellow-student killed while climbing in the Southern Alps. As James K. Baxter wrote, in this poem "mountain, gorge, tree, and river become protagonists in the drama." The mysterious poem "The Return," peopled by strange figures on a beach, "Plant gods, tree gods, gods of the middle world," for some readers expresses a kind of race memory of the early Polynesian migrations.

The vividness of Campbell's evocation of the landscape is matched by the strong physicality of his love poetry, with its truly pagan delight in youth and beauty. Campbell's poetry is rooted in this world and he is the least metaphysical of New Zealand poets.

Sanctuary of Spirits is a lyrical sequence based on the history of the great pre-colonial Maori fighting-chief Te Rauparaha. To his theme Campbell brought a realism made possible by his capacity to enter into the actualities of an oral culture and to acclimatise the style of Maori oratory into English verse. The allusive method of the sequence allowed Campbell to compress into a brief compass the rich and complex history of the chief who has been called the Maori Napoleon. Success with Maori themes has evaded most previous New Zealand poets; by showing how they might be handled Campbell has reclaimed a valuable territory for New Zealand poetry.

Campbell's early poems were written in tight forms inherited from Yeats. More recently he has loosened his style. This has allowed him to develop the talent for creating moods he demonstrated in earlier poems like "At a Fishing Settlement" and "Hut Near Desolated Pines," where every detail establishes that feeling of sadness and loneliness which Campbell's verse often conveys. He is not a prolific poet, but he has established himself as one of the best lyric writers New Zealand has produced.

—F. M. McKay

CARMAN, (William) Bliss. Canadian. Born in Fredericton, New Brunswick, 15 April 1861. Educated at Fredericton Collegiate School, 1872–78; University of New Brunswick, Fredericton, 1878–81, B.A. 1881, M.A. 1884; University of Edinburgh, 1882–83; Harvard University, Cambridge, Massachusetts, 1886–87. Became associated with Mary Perry King in 1897; lived with the King family in Haines Falls, New York, and New Canaan, Connecticut, 1897–1929. Taught at Fredericton Collegiate School, 1883–84; studied law with the firm of James Douglas Hazen, Fredericton, 1884–86; private tutor, 1885; Literary Editor, New York *Independent*, 1890–92; Staff Member, *Current Literature*, New York, 1892, and *Cosmopolitan*, New York, 1894; Editor, *The Chapbook*, Cambridge, Massachusetts, 1894; Staff Member, *Atlantic Monthly*, Boston, 1895; Columnist, Boston *Transcript*, 1895–1900; Reader, Small Maynard and Company, publishers, Boston, 1897–1903; Editor, *The Literary World*, 1905; Staff Member, *Gentleman's Journal*, 1909; part-time advertising writer, 1909–19; made lecture tours of Canada in the 1920's. Recipient: Lorne Pierce Gold Medal, 1929; Poetry Society of America Award. LL.D.: University of New Brunswick, 1906; Litt.D.: Trinity College, Hartford, Connecticut. Corresponding Member, Royal Society of Canada, 1925. *Died 8 June 1929.*

PUBLICATIONS

Collections

Selected Poems, edited by Lorne Pierce. 1954.

Verse

Low Tide on Grand-Pré. 1889(?).
Low Tide on Grand-Pré: A Book of Lyrics. 1893; revised edition, 1894.
Saint Kavin: A Ballad. 1894.
Songs from Vagabondia, with Richard Hovey. 1894; *More Songs*, 1896; *Last Songs*, 1901.
Behind the Arras: A Book of the Unseen. 1895.
A Seamark: A Threnody for Robert Louis Stevenson. 1895.
Ballads of Lost Haven: A Book of the Sea. 1897.
By the Aurelian Wall and Other Elegies. 1898.
The Green Book of the Bards. 1898.
A Winter Holiday. 1899.

The Vengeance of Noel Brassard: A Tale of the Acadian Expulsion. 1899.
Christmas Eve at S. Kavin's. 1901.
Ballads and Lyrics. 1902.
Coronation Ode. 1902; revised edition, 1902.
Pipes of Pan Number One, From the Book of Myths. 1902; revised edition, 1904; *Number Two, From the Green Book of the Bards,* 1903; *Number Three: Songs of the Sea Children,* 1904; *Number Four: Songs from a Northern Garden,* 1904; *Number Five, From the Book of Valentines,* 1905; complete version, 1906.
Sappho: Lyrics. 1902.
The Word at St. Kavin's. 1903.
A Vision of Sappho. 1903.
Sappho: One Hundred Lyrics. 1904.
Poems. 2 vols., 1904.
The Princess of the Tower, The Wise Men from the East, and To the Winged Victory. 1906.
The Gate of Peace. 1907.
The Rough Rider and Other Poems. 1909.
A Painter's Holiday and Other Poems. 1911.
Echoes from Vagabondia. 1912.
Album of Six Songs, by Henri Duparc, music by Debussy. 1914.
April Airs: A Book of New England Lyrics. 1916.
Four Sonnets. 1916.
The Man of the Marne and Other Poems, with Mary Perry King. 1918.
Later Poems. 1921.
Ballads and Lyrics. 1923.
Far Horizons. 1925.
Wild Garden. 1929.
Sanctuary: Sunshine House Sonnets. 1929.
The Music of Earth. 1931.
Poems. 1931.
Youth in the Air. 1932.
To a Chickadee (Sierra Madre Mountains, California). 1933.
A Little Child's Prayer. 1939.

Plays

The Daughters of Dawn: A Lyrical Pageant or Series of Historical Scenes, with Mary Perry King. 1913.
Earth Deities and Other Rhythmic Masques (includes *Children of the Year, Dance Diurnal, Pas de Trois*), with Mary Perry King. 1914.

Other

The Kinship of Nature. 1903.
The Friendship of Art. 1904.
The Poetry of Life. 1905.
The Making of Personality, with Mary Perry King. 1908.
James Whitcomb Riley: An Essay. 1918.
Talks on Poetry and Life (lectures), edited by Blanche Hume. 1926.
Bliss Carman's Scrap-Book, edited by Lorne Pierce. 1931.

Editor, *The World's Best Poetry.* 10 vols., 1904.

Editor, with Lorne Pierce, *Our Canadian Literature: Representative Verse.* 1922.
Editor, *The Oxford Book of American Verse.* 1927.

Reading List: *Carman* by Julian Hawthorne, 1929; *Carman and the Literary Currents and Influences of His Times* by James Cappon, 1930; *Carman: A Portrait* by Muriel Miller, 1935; *Carman: Bibliography, Letters, Fugitive Pieces and Other Data* by William Inglis Morse, 1941; *Carman* by Donald G. Stevens, 1966.

* * *

There was a time, two or three decades ago, when Bliss Carman was the best-known of Canadian poets, with a reputation that extended throughout the English-reading world. Yet it is evident, now his vogue has declined, that Carman was the least interesting of the company of poets in which literary history places him. He began to write and publish as one of the small group that emerged in the early 1880's in Fredericton under the leadership of his cousin Charles G. D. Roberts. Later his fame became national, even for a brief period international. He is remembered now as one of the Confederation poets, the men born in the same decade as the dominion of Canada and whose work came to maturity in the final years of the nineteenth century.

Carman began with the kind of sensitive evocation of Canadian landscape and rural life that all the members of his group attempted, but there are few among the poems he produced so prolifically in the 1890's and the early years of this century that show either the precise observation of nature and of human occupations that characterized the rural poems of Charles G. D. Roberts or the taut and craftsmanly adaptation of romantic styles to Canadian themes shown by Archibald Lampman, another Confederation poet. The dreamy resonance of even Carman's best poems, like the famous *Low Tide on Grand Pré*, tends to be marred by thinness of feeling, by a weakening vagueness of imagery and statement:

> And that we took into our hands
> Spirit of life or subtler thing –
> Breathed on us there and loosed the bands
> Of death, and taught us, whispering,
> The secret of some wonder-thing.

Carman soon fell under the influence of Whitman and W. E. Henley, and in books like *Songs from Vagabondia* he tried to develop a poetry of the manly life and the open road, but lost himself in a kind of meretricious heartiness, as in poems like "Lord of My Heart's Elation."

> Bear out, bear out, bear onward
> This mortal soul alone,
> To selfhood or oblivion
> Incredibly thine own....

Yet Carman's influence was by no means wholly negative, for, like the other Confederation poets, he helped to teach Canadian writers that the substance of poetry lay in giving expression to their own life and their own world and not in attempting, as the versifiers of the pioneer past had done, to recreate the poetry of England in an alien land.

—George Woodcock

CLARK, John Pepper. Nigerian. Born in Kiagbolo, 6 April 1935. Educated at Warri Government College, Ughelli, 1948–54; University of Ibadan, 1955–60, B. A. (honours) in English 1960; Princeton University, New Jersey (Parvin Fellowship), 1962–63; University of Ibadan (Institute of African Studies Research Fellowship, 1961–64). Married; has one daughter. Nigerian Government Information Officer, 1960–61; Head of Features and Editorial Writer, *Daily Express*, Lagos, 1961–62. Founding Editor, *The Horn* magazine, Ibadan. Since 1964, Member of the English Department, and currently Professor of English, University of Lagos. Founding Member, Society of Nigerian Authors. Lives in Lagos.

PUBLICATIONS

Verse

Poems. 1962.
A Reed in the Tide: A Selecton of Poems. 1965.
Casualties: Poems 1966–1968. 1970.

Plays

Song of a Goat (produced 1961). 1961.
Three Plays: Song of a Goat, The Raft, The Masquerade. 1964.
The Masquerade (produced 1965). In *Three Plays*, 1964.
The Raft (broadcast 1966). In *Three Plays*, 1964.
Ozidi. 1966.

Screenplays (documentaries): *The Ozidi of Atazi; The Ghost Town.*

Radio Play: *The Raft*, 1966.

Other

America, Their America 1964.
Example of Shakespeare: Critical Essays on African Literature. 1970.

* * *

John Pepper Clark says about himself in the introduction to *A Reed in the Tide* that he is "a cultural mulatto." In this way he draws attention to the fact that his outlook is the result of a synthesis of two different cultures, the traditional Nigerian and the modern Western. This is reflected in his authorship which deals with traditional Ijaw myths as well as the modern American way of life which he criticizes from the point of view of an outsider, bringing an African sensibility to bear on the excesses of modern society. On the other hand his choice of the English language is deliberate, born of the desire to reach as many people as possible.

Clark is playwright, poet and prose writer. *Three Plays* contains *Song of a Goat, The Masquerade,* and *The Raft*. The first two plays deal with the tragic events that befall a family in the Niger river delta as a result of an initial crime against the gods. The plays move with a relentless inevitability towards final death and destruction, and the prevailing atmosphere of doom as well as a dramatic use of a chorus show Clark's debt to classical Greek drama. The subject matter, however, is firmly rooted in traditional tales from the Niger delta. *The Raft* is about a group of fishermen set adrift on a raft on the Niger drawing towards their final destruction in the whirlpools at the mouth of the river. The play explores the psychology of the fishermen, but it is also capable of an allegorical interpretation dealing with the Biafran war and Nigerian unity. In *Ozidi* Clark returns to the traditional Ijaw myth. *Ozidi* is based on an Ijaw saga, which took seven days to tell and was accompanied by music and mime. In all the plays the language is very poetic and imaginative, rich in metaphors which are often surprisingly fresh and which show Clark's ability as a poet.

A Reed in the Tide is a collection of occasional poems, varied in aspect and theme (visual images, moral reflections, myths), written in free verse, often deliberately echoing Dylan Thomas or W. H. Auden. The poem "Night Rain," describing a heavy tropical downpour in the wet and swampy Niger delta stands out as an excellent example of successful nature poetry about exotic places.

Casualties deals with the Biafran war. Clark was very close to the events and had an inside knowledge which is denied the ordinary reader, and the collection is therefore heavily glossed and cannot be read without an intimate knowledge of the movements of the war.

As a prose writer Clark has chosen "straight reporting" as his medium for his criticism of America in *America, Their America*. The criticism is flamboyant and often idiosyncratic.

From his writings Clark emerges as a person with strong beliefs, tempered with a compassion and tenderness which appear mainly in his poetry.

—Kirsten Holst Petersen

CLARKE, Marcus (Andrew Hislop). English. Born in Kensington, London, 24 April 1846. Educated at Cholmeley Grammar School, Highgate, London, 1858–62. Married Marion Dunn in 1869; six children. Emigrated to Australia, 1863: worked in a Melbourne bank, 1863–65; lived at an agricultural station on the Wimmera River, to learn farming, 1865–67; abandoned intention to become a farmer, and went to Melbourne: contributor to *The Age*, and Columnist ("Peripatetic Philosopher"), *Australasian*, 1867–70; Owner and Editor, *Colonial Monthly*, 1868–69; Editor, *Australian Journal*, 1870; Secretary to the Trustees, 1870, Sub-Librarian, 1873, and Assistant Librarian, 1876–81, Melbourne Public Library; Columnist ("Atticus"), *Leader*, from 1877; declared insolvent in 1874 and 1881. A Founder, The Yorick Club, 1868. *Died 2 August 1881.*

PUBLICATIONS

Collections

A Clarke Reader, edited by Bill Wannan. 1963.
(Selections), edited by Michael Wilding. 1976.

Fiction

Long Odds. 1869; as *Heavy Odds,* 1896.

Holiday Peak and Other Tales. 1873.
His Natural Life. 1874; as *For the Term of His Natural Life,* 1885; edited by Stephen Murray-Smith, 1970.
'Twixt Shadow and Shine: An Australian Story of Christmas. 1875.
Four Stories High. 1877.
The Man with the Oblong Box. 1878.
The Mystery of Major Molineaux, and Human Repetends. 1881.
The Conscientious Stranger: A Bullocktown Idyll. 1881.
Sensational Tales. 1886.
Chidiock Tichbourne; or, The Catholic Conspiracy. 1893.
Australian Tales. 1896.

Plays

Goody Two Shoes and Little Boy Blue. 1870.
Twinkle, Twinkle, Little Star; or, Harlequin Jack Frost, Little Tom Tucker, and the Old Woman That Lived in a Shoe. 1873.
Reverses. 1876.
Alfred the Great, with H. Keiley. 1876.
The Happy Land, from the play *The Wicked World* by W. S. Gilbert (produced 1880).

Other pantomimes, with R. P. Whitworth.

Other

The Peripatetic Philosopher. 1869.
Old Tales of a Young Country. 1871.
The Future Australian Race. 1877.
Civilization Without Delusion. 1880.
What Is Religion? A Controversy. 1895.
Stories of Australia in the Early Days. 1897.
Colonial City: High and Low Life: Selected Journalism. edited by L. T. Hergenhan. 1972.

Editor, *History of the Continent of Australia and the Island of Tasmania (1787–1870).* 1877.
Editor, *We 5: A Book for the Season.* 1879.
Editor, *Poems,* by Adam Lindsay Gordon. 1887.

Reading List: *Clarke* by Brian Elliott, 1858; *Clarke* by Michael Wilding, 1978.

* * *

As Brian Elliott says, "Marcus Clarke was the most facile, most gifted, most charming writer in Australia in his day and generation." In his journalism, he captured the spirit of the times with vividness and immediacy. With laconic ambivalence and wit, he simultaneously deprecated and exalted many elements of the Australian character, such as contempt for culture and authority. In the process he lowered his own standards of taste at the same time as he raised the standards of Australian journalism. Much of his work from the *Argus* and other papers remains uncollected.

Clarke, like Dickens, first published his tales and novels in the papers to which he contributed and which he sometimes edited. His *Old Tales of a Young Country*, mainly published in the *Australasian* at earlier dates, are admittedly compilations from pamphlets, books, and government records, but he has endowed them with such literary quality and creative insight that they have become the focal source for most of the highlights of colonial Australian history: the landing of the First Fleet in Sydney Cove, the destiny of the swell-mob pickpocket George Barrington, William Huckley's survival among the aborigines for thirty-two years, Captain Bligh and the Rum Rebellion, Michael Howe's activities as a bush-ranger, Jorgenson's checkered career from King of Iceland to prisoner in Van Diemen's Land, the make-up of early newspapers, the life of the settlers, the closing of Macquarie Harbour as a penal settlement, mutinies, shipwrecks, land speculation, and much more.

Clarke's novel *Long Odds*, first printed in the *Colonial Monthly*, is a fast-paced melodrama, not entirely unmotivated, involving a young Australian in London; but it is for *His Natural Life*, rewritten and drastically abridged from the *Australian Journal* version and reprinted dozens of times under the title of *For the Term of His Natural Life*, that he is chiefly remembered. A psychological romance with elements of the macabre – cannibalism and torture – the work emphasizes the brutal effect of the convict system upon the human spirit. Its virtue, despite the exaggerations of unnatural punishments, is Clarke's fidelity to the theme of the progressive degeneration of an innocent human being subjected to barbaric cruelty, which gradually destroys all glimmerings of hope, turns his mind into a hard shell of sullen obduracy, goads him into perverse rebellion, and, finally, drives him to the brink of insanity. The work is more of a requiem than a classic, the last word which can be said about an unjust system which had been buried years before and which Clarke himself (in "Port Arthur Visited, 1870") admitted had "only the smell of it left." Still Clarke's concern was not with the already obsolete system of transportation of felons, but, on a humanistic level, like Hugo and Dostoevsky, with the forces of good and evil embroiling his central characters in a "tempest of the soul."

Clarke also wrote for the Australian theatre – largely pantomimes, translations, and adaptations – to supplement his income; but these works are negligible. As Brian Elliott concludes, "It is as a colonial journalist and the writer of one book that Marcus Clarke has a claim to the remembered."

—Wesley D. Sweetser

COURAGE, James (Francis). New Zealander. Born in Amberley, Canterbury, New Zealand, 9 February 1903. Educated at Christ's College, Christchurch; St. John's College, Oxford. Lived in England 1923 until his death. *Died 5 October 1963.*

PUBLICATIONS

Fiction

One House. 1933.
The Fifth Child. 1948.

Desire Without Content. 1950.
Fires in the Distance. 1952.
The Young Have Secrets. 1954.
The Call Home. 1956.
A Way of Love. 1959.
A Visit to Penmorten. 1961.
Such Separate Creatures: Stories, edited by Charles Brasch. 1973.

Play

Private History (produced 1938).

* * *

Although James Courage had aspired to a literary vocation from the time he was an undergraduate at Oxford, his work seldom reached the public (and made no great impression when it did) until he was in his forties. It was with the publication of his second novel, *The Fifth Child*, that he found his most fertile setting – the Canterbury farmland of New Zealand where he had grown up. An unusually large autobiographical element was to be present in all that he subsequently wrote.

The distinguishing mark of the five New Zealand novels is the exploration of disharmonies between an imported set of English middle-class refinements and a colonial bluffness and practicality. Such a conflict is characteristic of a much earlier phase of New Zealand's social history, and it is to be remembered that Courage lived in England from 1923 until his death. Though his novels were appearing well after such poets as A. R. D. Fairburn, Allen Curnow, Charles Brasch and Denis Glover, and such novelists as Robin Hyde, John Mulgan, John Lee, Frank Sargeson, and Dan Davin, had founded a distinctly New Zealand literature, Courage appears unwilling or unable to contribute to this development. By the time his own work began, the New Zealand society he remembers had passed away and the fictional models he works from had been locally supplanted. But the conflict he examines, though it is historically outdated, retains some symbolic force in the study of marital and family strife; for the English gentility is embodied in an unhappy wife, and the colonial crudeness in her husband. A son, often named Walter in the novels and stories, is vulnerably placed between these parents, and the loving allegiance to the mother is matched by a crippling hostility towards the father. A refuge from parental discord is found in the placid wisdom of a grandmother whose acceptance of her new country is graceful and complete.

The Fifth Child, Desire Without Content, and *Fires in the Distance* are all studies in family strife and sexual perplexity for which, as in *The Call Home*, there may be a happy resolution that tends towards the romantic and wishful. Courage is always professionally competent, having learned much from his reading of Forster and Lawrence, particularly in emulating, sometimes a little ineptly, their symbolic use of scene or object.

The Young Have Secrets is usually regarded as Courage's most successful novel. The centre of experience is placed in a ten-year-old boy who, as a boarder in Christchurch, is a puzzled trespasser in adult lives, particularly in their love intrigues. There is a well-drawn range of characters, some of them comic, and a striking representation of place and period (1914) is achieved.

The last two novels have English settings. *A Way of Love* is an ironic, honest and compassionate study of homosexual society; and *A Visit to Penmorten* traces, rather superficially, the recovery of its hero from an Oedipal trauma.

Thirty-two of Courage's short stories survive, and the fifteen of them that have been collected provide a compendious representation of his work in both its New Zealand and its English settings.

—R. A. Copland

CRAWFORD, Isabella Valancy. Canadian. Born in Dublin, Ireland, 25 December 1850; emigrated to Canada, 1858. Lived in Paisley, Lakefield, Peterborough, Ontario, and in Toronto, after c. 1876. *Died 12 February 1887.*

PUBLICATIONS

Collections

Collected Poems, edited by J. W. Garvin. 1905.
Selected Stories, edited by Penny Petrone. 1975.

Verse

Old Spookses' Pass, Malcolm's Katie, and Other Poems. 1884.
Hugh and Ion, edited by Glenn Clever. 1977.

Reading List: *Crawford* by Amelia B. Garvin, 1923; "Crawford" by James Reaney, in *Our Living Tradition*, edited by R. G. McDougall, 1959; "The Hunters Twain" by Dorothy Livesay, in *Canadian Literature 55*, Winter 1973.

* * *

The life of Isabella Valancy Crawford is the most obscure of all the 19th-century Canadian writers of prose or poetry. How she came to write in such a wide variety of styles and on such a range of subject matter when she was relatively isolated from the literary life of the period is a matter of wonderment. After the death of her doctor father in Peterborough, Ontario, the writer must have persuaded her mother that Toronto, the publishing centre of English Canada, was the place where she could best eke out a living.

In Toronto, she wrote a quantity of occasional verse for the local papers, a number of serialized novels and novellas for Frank Leslie's New York publications, and articles for *The Fireside Weekly* and, probably, Dickens's journal *All the Year Round*. In 1886, she became the first local writer to have a novel, *The Little Bacchante; or, Some Black Sheep*, serialized in the Toronto *Evening Globe*. It was called "vastly superior to the ordinary run of newspaper fiction," but for the most part Crawford's prose followed the fashion of the *feuilletons* of the day. It was formula fiction, romantic-gothic, flowery, melodramatic. Yet there are indications that the young woman possessed an ability to write realistically concerning pioneer life in Canada.

Crawford published one book of poetry at her own expense, *Old Spookses' Pass, Malcolm's Katie, and Other Poems*. For this she received scant recognition in her life-time, but increasing respect and delight from twentieth-century critics. She was one of those Victorian poets for whom Tennyson was the guide and idol. But in her long poems "Malcolm's Katie" and "Old Spookses' Pass" she displayed a remarkable flair for narrative, and for combining plot, theme, and characterization with an exuberant and arresting use of wilderness imagery. She lived at the beginning of our time in Canada, and saw, with remarkable vision, what paths we might take.

—Dorothy Livesay

CURNOW, Allen. New Zealander. Born in Timaru, 17 June 1911. Educated at Christchurch Boys High School, 1924–28; University of New Zealand, Canterbury, 1929–30, and Auckland, 1931–38, B.A. 1938; St. John's College (Anglican theological), Auckland, 1931–33. Married 1) Elizabeth J. LeCren in 1936; 2) Jenifer Mary Tole in 1965; three children. Cadet Journalist, *Sun*, Christchurch, 1929–30; Reporter and Sub-Editor, 1935–48, and Drama Critic, 1945–47, *The Press*, Christchurch; Member of the News and Sub-Editorial Staff, *News Chronicle*, London, 1949. Lecturer, 1951–53, Senior Lecturer, 1954–66, and since 1967 Associate Professor of English, University of Auckland. Recipient: New Zealand State Literary Fund travel award, 1949; Carnegie grant, 1950; New Zealand University Research Committee grant, 1957, 1966; Jessie Mackay Memorial Prize, 1957, 1962; Institute of Contemporary Arts Fellowship, Washington, D.C., 1961; Whittall Fund award, Library of Congress, 1966; New Zealand Poetry Award, 1975. Litt.D.: University of New Zealand, Auckland, 1966; University of Canterbury, Christchurch, 1975. Lives in Auckland.

PUBLICATIONS

Verse

Valley of Decision. 1933.
Another Argo, with Denis Glover and A. R. D. Fairburn. 1935.
Three Poems. 1935.
Enemies: Poems 1934–1936. 1937.
Not in Narrow Seas. 1939.
Recent Poems, with others. 1941.
Island and Time. 1941.
Verses, 1941–1942. 1942.
Sailing or Drowning. 1943.
Jack Without Magic. 1946.
At Dead Low Water, and Sonnets. 1949.
Poems 1947–1957. 1957.

A Small Room with Large Windows: Selected Poems. 1962.
Whim Wham Land. 1967.
Trees, Effigies, Moving Objects: A Sequence of 18 Poems. 1972.
An Abominable Temper and Other Poems. 1973.
Collected Poems 1933–1973. 1974.

Plays

The Axe: A Verse Tragedy (produced 1948). 1949.
Moon Section (produced 1959).
The Overseas Expert (broadcast 1961). In *Four Plays*, 1972.
Doctor Pom (produced 1964).
The Duke's Miracle (broadcast 1967). In *Four Plays*, 1972.
Resident of Nowhere (broadcast 1969). In *Four Plays*, 1972.
Four Plays (includes *The Axe, The Overseas Expert, The Duke's Miracle, Resident of Nowhere*). 1972.

Radio Plays: *The Overseas Expert*, 1961; *The Duke's Miracle*, 1967; *Resident of Nowhere*, 1969.

Other

Editor, *A Book of New Zealand Verse, 1923–1945.* 1945; revised edition, 1951.
Editor, *The Penguin Book of New Zealand Verse.* 1960.

Reading List: "Curnow's Poetry (Notes Towards a Criticism)" by C. K. Stead, in *Landfall*, March 1963; "Curnow's *The Axe*" by A. Krishna Sarma, in *The Achievement of Christopher Fry and Other Essays*, 1970.

* * *

Allen Curnow is the New Zealand poet who has been most closely associated with the pursuit, common to all emergent societies, of a national identity. His sense of the complex possibilities of language as personality, individual and national, made him one of the outstanding poets of his time and place.

Self-scrutiny and a sense of identity are urgent, perhaps primary, objectives in any small and isolated community where Allen Tate's sense of the word regionalism may be applied. Curnow's major subject has been what he called the imaginative discovery of New Zealand, and his most "major" poetry came in the years when he led the search. His later poetry, technically even more accomplished, is characterised by a search for what Kendrick Smithyman (in an essay in *Essays on New Zealand Literature*, edited by Wystan Curnow, 1962) called the "true voice of feeling."

Smithyman's own favoured definition for poetry, a way of saying, is perhaps too limiting a term for Curnow. Consistently doctrinaire, though courteously argumentative rather than abrasive, he is always conscious of the isolation not only of his country but of the poet himself in the community generally indifferent or even hostile to the linguistic and moral aspects of aesthetics which the poet is the first to record. His life and his poetry show him consistently rejecting the ivory tower and the easy assumption that poets write only for other poets. For many years in fact, he wrote a weekly verse column for an Auckland newspaper, commenting on current events, and he has written verse broadsheets attacking local philistinism. Curnow's efforts to activate his ideas in the community appear on a different level in his plays, but it is perhaps best to consider them as complex, well-articulated presentations of themes accessible in his poems.

Island and Time, *At Dead Low Water*, and *A Small Room with Large Windows* are his best collections of verse. They include highly wrought meditative poems, mostly short, in a voice that sounds mannered without being idiosyncratic or exhibitionistic. No single poem can be taken as representative of a poetic career as long as Curnow's or of an *oeuvre* in which every poem is a carefully achieved entity, but the verbal precision and concentration are well demonstrated by the opening lines of "The Eye Is More or Less Satisfied with Seeing" (from *Poems 1949–57*):

> Wholehearted he can't move
> From where he is, nor love
>
> Wholehearted that place,
> Indigene janus-face,
>
> Half mocking half,
> Neither caring to laugh.
>
> Does true or false sun rise?
> Do both half eyes tell lies?

Curnow's voice is uniquely his own. Stylistic and other debts do show up in his poetry, but he never seems imitative. Such influences as do show themselves indicate a firmly eclectic collector's instinct. He has Eliot's concern for tradition and for a literate Europeanism. More conspicuously though, in view of his efforts towards an imaginative discovery of his region's identity, his work does show graftings from American poetry of the 1930's and 1940's, especially the poets of the American South.

C. K. Stead has made the point that the perspectives in Curnow's poems are simultaneously physical, local realities and moral, intellectual, and emotional landscapes. Imaginative self-discovery integrates the two. That kind of concern uses poetic devices as it absorbs influences, without attitudinising, without falling into a single idiom as many poets more ready with words than Curnow have done. His grappling with words and realities alike is slow, earnest, and scrupulous. Curnow is one of the three or four life-size – to use his own term – writers New Zealand has produced.

—Andrew Gurr

DAVIES, Robertson. Canadian. Born in Thamesville, Ontario, 28 August 1913. Educated at Upper Canada College, Toronto; Queen's University, Kingston, Ontario; Balliol College, Oxford, 1936–38, B.Litt. 1938. Married Brenda Mathews in 1940; three children. Teacher and actor, Old Vic Theatre School and Repertory Company, London, 1938–40; Literary Editor, *Saturday Night*, Toronto, 1940–42; Editor and Publisher, *Examiner*, Peterborough, Ontario, 1942–63. Since 1960, Professor of English, and since 1962, Master of Massey College, University of Toronto. Formerly, Governor, Stratford Shakespeare Festival, Ontario; Member, Board of Trustees, National Arts Centre. Recipient: Dominion Drama Festival Louis Jouvet Prize, for directing, 1949; Leacock Medal, 1955; Lorne Pierce Medal, 1961; Governor-General's Award, 1973. LL.D.: University of Alberta, Edmonton, 1957;

Queen's University, 1962; University of Manitoba, Winnipeg, 1972; D.Litt.: McMaster University, Hamilton, Ontario, 1959; University of Windsor, Ontario, 1971; York University, Toronto, 1973; Memorial University of Newfoundland, St. John's, 1974; University of Western Ontario, London, 1974; McGill University, Montreal, 1974; Trent University, Peterborough, Ontario, 1974; D.C.L.: Bishop's University, Lennoxville, Quebec, 1967; D.C.V.: University of Calgary, Alberta, 1975. Fellow, Royal Society of Canada, 1967. C.C. (Companion, Order of Canada), 1972. Lives in Toronto.

PUBLICATIONS

Fiction

Tempest-Tost. 1951.
Leaven of Malice. 1954.
A Mixture of Frailties. 1958.
Fifth Business. 1970.
The Manticore. 1972.
World of Wonders. 1975.

Plays

Overlaid (produced 1947). In *Eros at Breakfast and Other Plays*, 1949.
Voice of the People (produced 1948). In *Eros at Breakfast and Other Plays*, 1949.
At the Gates of the Righteous (produced 1948). In *Eros at Breakfast and Other Plays*, 1949.
Hope Deferred (produced 1948). In *Eros at Breakfast and Other Plays*, 1949.
Fortune My Foe (televised; produced 1948). 1949.
Eros at Breakfast (produced 1948). In *Eros at Breakfast and Other Plays*, 1949.
Eros at Breakfast and Other Plays. 1949.
At My Heart's Core (produced 1950). 1950.
King Phoenix (produced 1950). In *Hunting Stuart and Other Plays*, 1972.
A Masque of Aesop (produced 1952). 1952.
A Jig for the Gypsy (broadcast; produced 1954). 1954.
Hunting Stuart (produced 1955). In *Hunting Stuart and Other Plays*, 1972.
Love and Libel; or, The Ogre of the Provincial World, from his novel *Leaven of Malice* (produced 1960).
A Masque of Mr. Punch (produced 1962). 1963.
Hunting Stuart and Other Plays (includes *King Phoenix* and *General Confession*). 1972.
Question Time (produced 1975). 1975.

Radio Plays: *A Jig for the Gypsy*, and others.

Television Plays: *Fortune My Foe, Brothers in the Black Art*, and others.

Other

Shakespeare's Boy Actors. 1939.
Shakespeare for Young Players: A Junior Course. 1942.
The Diary of Samuel Marchbanks (essays). 1947.

The Table Talk of Samuel Marchbanks (essays). 1949.
Renown at Stratford: A Record of the Shakespeare Festival in Canada, 1953, with Tyrone Guthrie and Grant MacDonald. 1953.
Twice Have the Trumpets Sounded: A Record of the Stratford Shakespearean Festival in Canada, 1954, with Tyrone Guthrie. 1954.
Thrice the Brinded Cat Hath Mew'd: A Record of the Stratford Shakespearean Festival in Canada, 1955, with Tyrone Guthrie. 1955.
A Voice from the Attic. 1960.
The Personal Art: Reading to Good Purpose. 1961.
Samuel Marchbanks' Almanack. 1967.
Stephen Leacock: Feast of Stephen. 1970.
The Revels History of Drama in English, vol. 7, with others. 1975.
One Half of Davies: Provocative Pronouncements on a Wide Range of Topics. 1978.

* * *

Critics have attempted to read into Robertson Davies's writings a high-flying ambition to construct a parable of the conflict with "the hideous and pervasive forces of materialism." Writing of his own work Davies used Jung's phrase "the Search for the Self" to describe the theme which is central to his novels and to most of his plays. Such pomposities, whether they are expressed by others or by himself, serve only to undervalue Davies by endowing him with the very pretentiousness which from the beginning of his literary career he has set out to destroy. Davies is, in truth, a comic author of considerable skill, conservative in his literary manner but determined to use the sharp edge of satire to reform or to destroy the provincialism which is the prime goal of Canadian society.

His fiction is a small part of his work. He is a sound scholar, a wise critic, a prolific playwright and an elegant essayist, but in these forms only the satirical newspaper columns written in the late 1940's (and collected as *The Diary of Samuel Marchbanks* and *The Table Talk of Samuel Marchbanks*) promised from Davies something more than might come from any other cosmopolitan academic.

Marchbanks, unhesitatingly Canadian and yet unashamedly a twentieth-century successor to Samuel Johnson, applied his caustic fury to the pettiness of life in Canada. For the Salterton trilogy which followed Davies forsook the tradition of Johnson and took over the mantle of Anthony Trollope. Davies's Barchester is Kingston, Ontario, thinly disguised as Salterton. *Tempest-Tost*, the first in the series, is an uproarious travesty of Shakespeare's play. The subsequent novels, *Leaven of Malice* and *A Mixture of Frailties*, are in purpose more solemn and in achievement less satirically brisk, but Davies does not lose his skill in devising romance so that it will serve his purpose as a commentator on Canadian culture.

His second triology also has its origins in small-town Ontario. But Davies's ambitions have become extravagant, and their fulfilment only just short of complete. A snowball thrown by Percy Boyd Staunton at his friend Dunstan Ramsay hits instead the Baptist minister's pregnant wife and so her child, Magnus Eisengrim, is born eighty days too soon: from that simple beginning develops three novels of rare power. *The Fifth Business* belongs primarily to Ramsay, rational and determined, *The Manticore* to Staunton, the man of instinct, and *World of Wonders* to the magician Eisengrim. But the distinctive emphasis in each book is little more than a device, a platform from which Davies can range the world of reality, the world of ideas and the other-world of illusion. The theatre, Canada, Passchendaele, circus-life, Switzerland, love, Jungian psychology, London, teaching, myth, the international film industry: there is no logical progression for the catalogue of Davies's concerns in a triology which is at times elegant, often comic and always admirably bold.

—J. E. Morpurgo

DAVIN, Dan(iel Marcus). New Zealander. Born in Invercargill, New Zealand, 1 September 1913. Educated at Marist Brothers School, Invercargill; Sacred Heart College, Auckland; Otago University, Dunedin, M.A. 1936; Balliol College, Oxford (Rhodes Scholar), 1936–39, B.A. 1939, M.A. 1945. Served in the Royal Warwickshire Regiment, 1939–40, and in the New Zealand Division, 1940–45: Major; mentioned in despatches; M.B.E. (Member, Order of the British Empire), 1945. Married Winifred Gonley in 1939; three daughters. Junior Assistant Secretary, 1946–48, and Assistant Secretary, 1948–69, Clarendon Press, Oxford. Since 1970, Deputy Secretary to the Delegates, and since 1974, Director of the Academic Division, Oxford University Press. Fellow of Balliol College, 1965. Fellow of the Royal Society of Arts. Lives in Oxford.

PUBLICATIONS

Fiction

Cliffs of Fall. 1945.
The Gorse Blooms Pale (stories). 1947.
For the Rest of Our Lives. 1947.
Roads from Home. 1949.
The Sullen Bell. 1956.
No Remittance. 1959.
Not Here, Not Now. 1970.
Brides of Price. 1972.
Breathing Spaces (stories). 1975.

Other

An Introduction to English Literature, with John Mulgan. 1947.
Crete. 1953.
Writing in New Zealand: The New Zealand Novel, with W. K. Davin. 1956.
Katherine Mansfield in Her Letters. 1959.
Closing Times (memoirs). 1975.

Editor, *New Zealand Short Stories.* 1953.
Editor, *Selected Stories,* by Katherine Mansfield. 1953.
Editor, *English Short Stories of Today: Second Series.* 1958.

Reading List: "Davin: Novelist of Exile" by James Bertram, in *Meanjin 32,* June 1973; "Davin's *Roads from Home*" by H. Winston Rhodes, in *Critical Essays on the New Zealand Novel* edited by Cherry Hankin, 1976; Introduction by Lawrence Jones to *Roads from Home,* 1976.

* * *

When he published three novels and a volume of short stories in the first four years following World War II, Dan Davin established himself as the leading New Zealand novelist of his generation. Since then, his devotion to a difficult profession and his continued expatriation have kept him from consolidating that position (he has noted that "the expatriate writer lives on a diminishing capital of deeply felt knowledge"). However, with his gifts as provincial historian, sceptical philosopher, and psychological moralist, he has made a significant contribution to New Zealand fiction.

As a provincial historian with a critical but loving eye, he has captured the Irish Catholic enclave within the Southland community in the 1920's and 1930's, seen against a sharply realised physical background of Invercargill and the surrounding countryside. The Connolly family, of many of the stories in *The Gorse Blooms Pale* and *Breathing Spaces*, and the Hogan family, of *Roads from Home*, most fully exemplify this provincial sub-culture. Richard Kane, in *No Remittance*, provides an outside perspective on it, for he, a charming English scoundrel, marries into it, and the body of the novel is made up of his retrospective account of his struggles with it and absorption into it over a period of fifty years.

In his other novels, Davin shows his Southland characters taking various "roads from home." The shortest road is that to Dunedin and the University of Otago, where the heroes of *Cliffs of Fall* and *Not Here, Not Now* receive their intellectual and sexual initiations and do battle with puritanism in its Scottish Presbyterian rather than its Irish Catholic form. A longer road takes the characters of some of the short stories and of *For the Rest of Our Lives* to the Mediterranean theatre of World War II, where they become part of a special and temporary community of men, the New Zealand Division, whose structure and mores Davin observes as closely as he had those of Irish Southland. For those who survive that journey, the road goes on to England. *The Sullen Bell* pictures expatriate New Zealanders in London trying to start life anew after the intensity and the losses of the war. *Brides of Price* looks at Oxford from the standpoint of a New Zealander long established there, and then brings the hero on a return visit to New Zealand (as do several stories in *Breathing Spaces*).

If the provincial historian in Davin has defined a social environment, the philosopher has defined a larger metaphysical environment. A sceptical, naturalistic philosophy underlies the books and becomes explicit in the meditations of the characters and the author, a vision of man in an indifferent natural universe from which he is estranged by his consciousness but to which he is subject. Man's plight is evident in the sexual impulse which shows us that "we are still creatures of the force that dragged us from the protoplasm to humanity," in the inevitable erosion of all joy and accomplishment by time, and in "the inescapable and unacceptable fact of death."

Davin has said that "for the novelist the web should be important only because it is indispensable to the struggle of the spider and the fly," and in his fiction both the metaphysical and the social webs are there to form the environment against which his characters define themselves. The psychological moralist in Davin focuses on the attempts of those characters to come to terms with nature, society, and a self "that could not exist without other selves" but "could never quite extend to them the priority and autonomy which it instinctively claimed for itself." The stories about childhood and adolescence in Invercargill show the young protagonists awakening to the nature and complexity of self and world. The Southland and Dunedin novels show their young men struggling against the "subtle web of obligation" woven by family and others who would limit their full development of themselves. In *Cliffs of Fall*, Mark Burke, melodramatically Dostoevskian, destroys himself when he attempts to assert his superiority to nature and community by killing his pregnant girl. In *Roads from Home*, John and Ned Hogan are caught in dilemmas in which they painfully realize that their needs inevitably conflict with the needs of others. In *Not Here, Not Now*, Martin Cody tries to reconcile love and ambition, having to face the costs to family, fiancée, and self of his determined drive for a Rhodes Scholarship and the opportunity to develop his talents.

The other novels explore more mature characters' attempts to accomodate themselves to a complex and imperfect world. Such an accomodation requires that one be sceptical and without illusions, but not cynical or despairing. In *For the Rest of Our Lives*, Tony Brandon is destroyed, but Frank Fahey and To O'Dwyer achieve at least an armed truce with existence. In *The Sullen Bell*, Hugh Egan moves beyond despair to a positive acceptance, while Adam Mahon in *Brides of Price*, who has come to believe in nothing "except how complex everything was," arrives at an unexpectedly satisfactory accommodation.

Davin's problem as novelist has been how to bring the social historian, the philosopher, and the psychological moralist together in a structure that is both inclusive and coherent. He has succeeded fully only within the more limited scope of such stories as "Saturday Night" and "The Quiet One." All of the novels are flawed, for in *Cliffs of Fall*, *Roads from Home*, and *The Sullen Bell* melodramatic plotting brings unity at the expense of complexity (the too-neat plotting of *Brides of Price* is carried out more playfully), while *For the Rest of Our Lives*, *No Remittance*, and *Not Here, Not Now* achieve a chronicle-like inclusiveness at the expense of formal coherence. However, in all of the novels there are individual scenes and entire sequences in which Davin brings his gifts together, setting fully developed characters within a convincing social environment, the whole given depth and universality by the philosophic meditations.

—Lawrence Jones

DAVIS, Arthur Hoey. See **RUDD, Steele.**

de la ROCHE, Mazo (Louise). Canadian. Born in Newmarket, Ontario, 15 January 1879. Educated at schools in Galt, Ontario, and Toronto; Parkdale Collegiate Institute, Toronto; University of Toronto. Had two adopted daughters. Full-time writer from childhood; lived in Windsor, England, 1929–39; thereafter lived in Toronto. Recipient: Lorne Pierce Medal, 1938; University of Alberta University National Award Medal, 1951. Litt.D.: University of Toronto, 1954. *Died 12 July 1961.*

PUBLICATIONS

Fiction

Explorers of the Dawn (stories). 1922.
Possession. 1923.
Delight. 1926.
Jalna. 1927.
Whiteoaks of Jalna. 1929; as *Whiteoaks*, 1929.
Finch's Fortune. 1931.
Lark Ascending. 1932.
The Thunder of New Wings. 1932.
The Master of Jalna. 1933.
Beside a Norman Tower. 1934.
Young Renny (Jalna – 1906). 1935.
Whiteoak Harvest. 1936.

Growth of a Man. 1938.
The Sacred Bullock and Other Stories of Animals. 1939.
Whiteoak Heritage. 1940.
Wakefield's Course. 1941.
The Two Saplings. 1942.
The Building of Jalna. 1944.
Return to Jalna. 1946.
Mary Wakefield. 1949.
Renny's Daughter. 1951.
A Boy in the House and Other Stories. 1952.
The Whiteoak Brothers: Jalna – 1923. 1953.
Variable Winds at Jalna. 1954.
Centenary at Jalna. 1958.
Morning at Jalna. 1960.

Plays

Low Life (produced 1925). 1925.
Come True (produced 1927).
The Return of the Emigrant (produced 1928). 1929.
Whiteoaks, from her own novel (produced 1936). 1936.
The Mistress of Jalna (produced 1951).

Other

Portrait of a Dog. 1930.
The Very House. 1937.
Quebec, Historic Seaport. 1944.
The Song of Lambert (juvenile). 1955.
Ringing the Changes: An Autobiography. 1957.
Bill and Coo (juvenile). 1958.

Reading List: *de la Roche* by Ronald Hambleton, 1966; *de la Roche* by George Hendrick, 1970.

* * *

Mazo de la Roche became a best selling novelist at the age of 48, when her *Jalna* won the first *Atlantic Monthly*-Little Brown prize of $10,000 in 1927. Supported by a wide-ranging American advertising campaign, the novel sold 100,000 copies in three months. To satisfy the demands of a public that expanded to her native Canada and Europe, Miss de la Roche eventually wrote 15 sequels, the last appearing a few months before her death in 1961. By that time, her publishers estimated that nearly nine million hard-cover copies of the *Jalna* novels had been sold.

Miss de la Roche had been a professional writer for twenty-five years when *Jalna* was published, her first story appearing in *Munsey's Magazine* in 1902. A collection of short stories and two novels had been published, but her literary earnings were meager before *Jalna*; and though nineteen non-Jalna books were eventually printed they owe nearly all their success to her Jalna reputation. Many are accounts of children and animals, fiction and non-fiction; this work is neither negligible nor very distinguished.

The Jalna novels are more remarkable for their popular appeal than for their literary merit.

Jalna and its first two sequels were respectfully received, however. American reviewers in such magazines as the *Nation* and the *Bookman* were impressed by the lively characters and lovely scenery of Southern Ontario. As the sequels multiplied, the Whiteoaks of Jalna were compared to Galsworthy's Forsytes – but it became clear that there was no social significance in Miss de la Roche's fiction. The real ingredients were Dickensian characters, somewhat larger than life-size, sensuous details more romantic than real, and erotic behavior that readers accepted as evidence of virility and strong passions. Her Whiteoak family were English colonial landed gentry, and there was a snob appeal in this escape fiction. Six of the novels examined the family history before the original *Jalna*, which took place in the 1920's. This allowed the author to bring back the lustiest Whiteoak, Adeline, who had dominated *Jalna* in her hundredth year and had died playing backgammon in *Whiteoaks of Jalna*. The family squabbled over her money in *Finch's Fortune*. Thereafter Mazo de la Roche's readers lived with her in a Whiteoak world that preserved in fantasy English colonial life and traditions – at Jalna.

Ringing the Changes: An Autobiography is disappointing in its account of the novelist's creative life and inaccurate in its factual information. The two books on Mazo de la Roche published in the decade following her death agree that she had moved her actual birth date forward six years. More significant are the affirmations of her strong emotional attachment to her cousin and life-long companion, Caroline Clement, and to her father, William Roche. But the chief interest in *Ringing the Changes* is the author's account of "the Play," sometimes called "the Game" – the dream world Mazo de la Roche invented as a child and shared with Caroline Clement. Although "the Play" has been compared to the Angria and Gondal fantasies of the Brontë sisters, even by Miss de la Roche, the characters and episodes of "the Play" were preserved only in the memories of the two girls. *Explorers of the Dawn* was a "marketing" of material from "the Play," according to Ronald Hambleton. To George Hendrick its chief significance is that it "supplied her with overwrought fictional material and kept her an emotional adolescent all her life."

—Clarence A. Glasrud

DOBSON, Rosemary (de Brissac). Australian. Born in Sydney, New South Wales, 18 June 1920; grand-daughter of the poet Austin Dobson. Educated at Frensham, Mittagong, New South Wales; University of Sydney; studied art. Married A. T. Bolton in 1951; one daughter, two sons. Recipient: Myer Award, 1966. Lives in Canberra.

PUBLICATIONS

Verse

In a Convex Mirror. 1944.
The Ship of Ice and Other Poems. 1948.
Child with a Cockatoo and Other Poems. 1955.
(Poems). 1963.
Cock Crow: Poems. 1965.

Rosemary Dobson Reads from Her Own Work (with recording). 1970.
Collected Poems. 1973.
Greek Coins. 1977.

Other

Focus on Ray Crooke. 1971.

Editor, *Australia, Land of Colour, Through the Eyes of Australian Painters.* 1962.
Editor, *Songs for All Seasons: 100 Poems for Young People.* 1967.

Reading List: "Dobson: A Portrait in a Mirror" by A. D. Hope, in *Quadrant*, July–August 1972; "The Poetry of Dobson" by James McAuley, in *Australian Literary Studies*, May 1973.

*   *   *

A detachment in Rosemary Dobson's poetry, a high-bred reserve, as well as a reticence in publishing it, has tended to cause her work to be overlooked by the general public. Its fine craftsmanship, its formal elegance, its lack of obvious emotional appeal are not to the taste of this technicolour age. It is true that in the early poems in *In a Convex Mirror* one can perhaps detect here and there a genuine inhibitedness, a fear of feeling, in "Foreshore," "The Dove," or "The Rider." The very title of the book suggests remoteness and detachment: a convex mirror causes objects to look smaller and farther away than they are, though it sharpens their outlines and gives them a curious, brilliant patina. This sheen is characteristic of the work as a whole, and lends a certain distinction to the poems independent of their general success. The poems written in the 1940's, like so many Australian poems of that period, were concerned with the metaphysics of time but it is not certain that the author was merely following a fashion. She is the granddaughter of the Victorian poet and essayist Austin Dobson, and it may have been his poem "The Paradox of Time" which first interested her in the notion of time standing still while humanity moves on. This idea attracts her to great pictures, for example, about which she has written so often and so acutely: their power to hold a given moment forever, as well as their power to lift the commonplace to an otherworldly dimension. Her fullest treatment of the time theme is the long dramatic poem "The Ship of Ice," the title-poem in a book which also contains the masterly sequence "The Devil and the Angel," a series of sharp, dramatic, Browningesque sketches in which lyricism, wit, and humour combine to convey a metaphysical idea. In these poems, the Devil and the Archangel Michael meet various figures who are about to die to invite them to make a final decision on which direction they wish to take – to Heaven or to Hell. The poems point up not only the difference between the two angels, but the subtle similarities between them, especially in the last poems where we find them subject to flattery from a poet. One of the most interesting is the encounter with a scarecrow in a summer field, who refuses to choose at all. He prefers life as an inanimate object in a world of natural objects to eternal, spiritual life – ironic praise of the visible world.

Child with a Cockatoo contains many poems about paintings, including the beautiful "The Bystander" and "Detail from an Annunciation by Crivelli." More traditional in form than Auden's they are, like his "Musée des Beaux Arts," points of departure for individual meditations. More of the poems in this volume, however, are concerned with personal experience, especially the experience of motherhood. One, "Cock Crow," conveys poignantly the difficulties of being at once daughter, mother, and poet. Some pieces are influenced by medieval ballads and have an eerie, legendary, magical quality entirely their own, for example, the haunting "The Stepdaughter":

> She went to the well for water,
> More beautiful than morning,
> Than sweet, clear running water
> And humble as the day.
> She fetched for her sister
> And carried for her mother,
> And the flame on the hearth-stone
> Spoke to her "Stay."

This book contains a few poems which herald Rosemary Dobson's interest in Greek themes. *Greek Coins*, which she has also illustrated, is inspired by J. G. Frazer's and Peter Levi's translations of Pausanias's *Guide to Greece*. These four-line "coin-sized" poems are as exquisitely evocative as epigrams from the *Greek Anthology* itself.

—Dorothy Green

DOMETT, Alfred. English. Born in Camberwell Grove, Surrey, 20 May 1811. Educated at St. John's College, Cambridge, 1829–33; Middle Temple, London, 1835–41; called to the Bar, 1841. Married Mrs. Mary George in 1856. A friend of Robert Browning from c. 1840; emigrated to New Zealand, 1842: Editor of the *Nelson Examiner*, 1844–46; Member of the New Zealand Legislative Council, 1846; Colonial Secretary for New Munster, 1848; Civil Secretary for the colony of New Zealand, 1851; Commissioner of Crown Lands and Magistrate of Hawke's Bay, 1853–56; Member of the New Zealand Parliament for Nelson, 1855–63; Commissioner of Crown Lands, Nelson, 1856; Member, Provincial Council for Nelson, 1857–63; Prime Minister of New Zealand, 1862–63; Secretary for Crown Lands, Legislative Councillor, and Commissioner of Old Lands Claims, 1864; Registrar-General of Land, 1865; Administrator of Confiscated Lands, 1870; retired from New Zealand politics and returned to England, 1871. C.M.G. (Companion, Order of St. Michael and St. George), 1880. *Died 2 November 1887.*

PUBLICATIONS

Verse

Poems. 1833.
Venice. 1839.
Ranolf and Amohia: A South-Sea Day Dream. 1872; revised edition, 2 vols., 1883.
Flotsam and Jetsam: Rhymes Old and New. 1877.
It Was the Calm and Silent Night: A Christmas Hymn. 1884.

Other

Narrative of the Wairoan Massacre. 1843.
Petition to the House of Commons for the Recall of Governor Fitzroy. 1845.
Diary 1872–85, edited by E. A. Horsman. 1953.
Canadian Journal, edited by E. A. Horsman and Lillian Rea Benson. 1955.

Reading List: *Robert Browning and Domett* by Frederic G. Kenyon, 1906.

* * *

Alfred Domett is more notable as a New Zealand statesman and friend of Robert Browning, who immortalized him in "Waring" (1842) and "The Guardian Angel" (1855), than as a poet in his own right. Prior to his emigration, Domett's major publication was *Poems* (1833). Largely experimental, the contents consist of translations, occasional verse, unfinished poems, untitled poems, and comic verse, written mainly in quatrians, though some are in couplets and two are Petrarchan sonnets. They display a certain limited competence, but are lacking in versatility and originality. Two (Untitled, pp. 73–75 and "Long Ago," pp. 78–85) are distinctly derived from Wordsworth's "Ode: Intimations of Immortality." Domett later contributed a few poems to *Blackwood's Magazine,* one of which, "A Christmas Hymn (Old Style, 1837)," has been frequently reprinted and is included in *The Oxford Book of Victorian Verse* (1913). Written in ten-line stanzas – two quatrains and a refrain – it is an imaginative projection to the time of Christ's birth, capturing the unsuspecting and quiet moment preceding a miraculous event which is to change the way of life forever.

During Domett's nearly thirty years in New Zealand, he published little other than official, legal, and political exposition; but doubtless he had nearly completed his long narrative poem *Ranolf and Amohia* which appeared the year after his return. It is a philosophical romance with the usual colonial overtones of the period – the white man's burden of bringing light and wisdom to the untutored savage – but, unlike Kipling, Domett finds a ground for the figurative East and West to meet in the common belief in an eternal spirit, an intelligent First Cause. The union is symbolized by the ultimate marriage, via difficulties and doubt, of Ranolf, a sailor-adventurer, and Amohia, daughter of a Maori king. The essentially British view is gradually meliorated by the wild natural setting and native legend and song until, through an act of faith alone, the union is consummated. A tribute to Browning as "Subtlest Assertor of the Soul in Song! –" is interjected. Domett in his *Diary* says that Tennyson afforded *Ranolf and Amohia* faint praise, but the work was revised in 1883.

In 1877, Domett published a random collection of poems, *Flotsam and Jetsam,* written before and after his New Zealand tenure and dedicated to Robert Browning, "A mighty poet and a subtle-souled psychologist." Much more versatile in verse form and meter than his 1833 *Poems,* the first part contains many works inspired by his travels in the United States, Canada, and Europe. Nature, however, is not used as a central theme, but rather as a simile suggesting some fleeting emotion or human characteristic. Also notable is his witty defense in "Lines Sent to Robert Browning, 1841, on a Certain Critique on *Pippa Passes.*" Among the poems in the second part, written in his later years, are an elegy on Livingstone; a previously unpublished proem to *Ranolf and Amohia*; a tribute to Milton entitled "Cripple-gate"; "A Christmas Hymn (New Style, 1875)," which takes cognizance of the growth of science, but expresses the faith that it will one day show the spirit-realm; and, finally, a remarkable poem on St. Paul's which marvellously captures the soul-expanding spirit of the cathedral.

Domett was not a great poet, but he was good enough to recognize that his major talents lay elsewhere.

—Wesley D. Sweetser

DUGGAN, Eileen (May). New Zealander. Born in Tua Marina, 21 May 1894. Educated at Marlborough Girls' High School; Victoria University College, M.A. (honours) in history 1918. Teacher, Dannevirke High School, St. Patrick's College; Lecturer in History, Victoria University College. Recipient: Royal Society of Literature Honarary Fellowship, 1943. O.B.E. (Officer, Order of the British Empire). *Died in 1972.*

PUBLICATIONS

Verse

Poems. 1921.
New Zealand Bird Songs. 1929.
Poems. 1937.
New Zealand Poems. 1940.
More Poems. 1951.

Other

Editor, *Letters from the North Solomons,* by Emmet McHardy. 1935.

Reading List: *Duggan* by F. M. McKay, 1977.

* * *

Eileen Duggan was the first New Zealand poet to establish an international reputation. Her background – the daughter of Irish immigrants and a childhood coloured by tales of famine, rack rents, and evictions – gives her verse its direction. She came to see that the restlessness of exile, experienced through identification with the dispossessed Irish, could be resolved only in New Zealand. This realisation is the basis of her search for a national identity, later a preoccupation of the poets of the 1930's. Her nationalism is apparent in her themes, imagery, and turns of expression. The landscape, in particular that of the Marlborough province, is closely observed and memorably expressed in many lines. In a poem such as "The Tides Run up the Wairau" personal emotion is firmly located in New Zealand. Duggan's interest in Maori themes is part of her nationalism, and she is a pioneer in marrying Maori words and phrases to the natural movement of English verse.

The sense of disinheritance experienced in New Zealand by Katherine Mansfield, Robin Hyde, and others of Duggan's generation took in her case a second and a deeper channel in a ceaseless and growing aspiration for the divine. Her religious faith is grounded in our humanity; "the mystic is no refuge if it forsake the human." "Contrast" presents through the images of the shepherds and the magi the rational and the intuitive approach to belief. In the many poems that explore the dark ways of providence, Duggan's faith is that of the shepherds who instinctively abandon themselves to the incomprehensible mystery of divine love.

The best of her early poems have the qualities of good Georgian verse, simplicity, warmth, and moral innocence. They have, too, clarity, technical skill, and appreciation of the countryside, the unnoticed, and the ordinary. Notable among her early verse is folk-poetry such as the ballad "The Bushfeller" and a striking evocation of childhood, "Twilight." Her later work goes beyond her Georgian origins to find an individual expression in an alert, imaginative, and deeply thoughtful poetry. In her final volume her verse has a greater reach and concentration. Her imagination is possessed by a cosmic vision forced on her by the events of World War II, which like many others she saw as threatening the collapse of civilisation. The didactic nature of many of these poems comes from her diagnosis that bewilderment was the real danger of the time, and that when mankind is bewildered it can be "baffled or hectored to its spiritual ruin." In a time of disillusionment, even despair, she wrote optimistic poetry whose characteristic utterance is affirmation.

—F. M. McKay

DUGGAN, Maurice (Noel). New Zealander. Born in Auckland, 25 November 1922. Educated at the University of Auckland. Married Barbara Platts in 1945; one child. Worked in advertising from 1961: with J. English Wright (Advertising) Ltd., Auckland, 1965 until his death. Recipient: Hubert Church Memorial Award, 1957; Esther Glen Award, 1959; Katherine Mansfield Award, 1959; Robert Burns Fellowship, Otago University, 1960; New Zealand Literary Fund Scholarship, 1966; Freda Buckland Award, 1970. *Died in January 1975.*

PUBLICATIONS

Fiction (stories)

Immanuel's Land. 1956.
New Authors: Short Story 1, with others. 1961.
Summer in the Gravel Pit. 1965.
O'Leary's Orchard and Other Stories. 1970.

Other

Falter Tom and the Water Boy (juvenile). 1957.
The Fabulous McFanes and Other Children's Stories. 1974.

* * *

Of his own work, Maurice Duggan modestly wrote, "The output has been small, and I must take what confidence I can from what seem to me small successful things." However, those "small successful things" include some of the finest short stories and novellas ever written in New Zealand, and show the kind of development associated with a major writer.

That development was partially stylistic, a move towards complexity. Such early stories as "A Small Story" (1951) are exercises in controlled simplicity, written, as Duggan said, on the assumption that "If it was to be strong, it had to be simple." In the later novellas and long stories the style becomes more allusive, figurative, dense, as it attempts to evoke the consciousness of complex central characters, for each of whom there is an appropriate idiom – the sad imagist poetry of "Blues for Miss Laverty" (1960), the Beckett-like ravings of Riley in "Riley's Handbook" (1961), the self-conscious raciness of Buster O'Leary in "Along

Rideout Road That Summer" (1963), the wry wit of "O'Leary's Orchard" (1967), the elliptical mode of "An Appetite for Flowers" (1967).

The developing style was at the service of a developing moral vision, an imaginative vision that takes us "through the looking-glass, through the superficial fascinations of the mirror-image, past the deceitful gaze to the concentration of the puzzle" so that "the map of the way of our going and of our being may begin to be exposed," in the words of the writer Ben McGoldrick in "The Magsman Miscellany" (published in *Islands*, Winter 1975). That vision focuses on the attempts of the self to find an accommodation with an absurd world in which human relations are both the only possible source of value and the most frequent cause of pain. The early stories present primarily the experience of children and adolescents in a puzzling world of unhappy homes (in the stories of the Lenihan family) and unjust adult authority (in the stories dealing with a Catholic boarding school). The later stories concentrate on adults – the disastrous Lenihan marriage (in "The Deposition" and "The Departure"), the lonely spinster denied any significant human contact ("Blues for Miss Laverty"), the rootless male cutting himself off from life in the fear of commitment ("The Wits of Willie Graves"). All these characters show the difficulty of knowing, without illusions, not only the external world but also the self, for the psyche is "simply the expressive instrument of one's secret desires, wishes made in darkness below the level of consciousness, a repository of half-thoughts and unconscious gestures." If Tryphena Price (in "For the Love of Rupert") and Buster O'Leary show the danger of acting on illusions, the older O'Leary (in "O'Leary's Orchard") and Hilda Preeble (in "An Appetite for Flowers") show the difficulty and pain of moving beyond them without constructing a defence of cynicism. In Duggan's world, life is always painful, not least for those who see most.

—Lawrence Jones

DUTTON, Geoffrey (Piers Henry). Australian. Born in Anlaby, South Australia, 2 August 1922. Educated at Geelong Grammar School, Victoria, 1932–39; University of Adelaide, 1940–41; Magdalen College, Oxford, 1946–49, B.A. 1949. Served in the Royal Australian Air Force, 1941–45: Flight Lieutenant. Married Ninette Trott in 1944; three sons, one daughter. Senior Lecturer in English, University of Adelaide, 1954–62; Visiting Lecturer in Australian Literature, University of Leeds (Commonwealth Fellow), 1960; Visiting Professor of English, Kansas State University, Manhattan, 1962. Editor, Penguin Australia, Melbourne, 1961–65. Since 1965, Editorial Director, Sun Books, Melbourne. Co-Founder, *Australian Letters*, Adelaide, 1957, and *Australian Book Review*, Kensington Park, 1962. Member, Australian Council for the Arts, 1968–70, and Commonwealth Literary Fund Advisory Board, 1972–73; Member, Australian Literature Board, 1972–74. Lives in South Australia.

PUBLICATIONS

Verse

Nightflight and Sunrise. 1945.

Antipodes in Shoes. 1955.
Flowers and Fury. 1963.
On My Island: Poems for Children. 1967.
Poems Soft and Loud. 1968.
Findings and Keepings: Selected Poems 1940–70. 1970.
New Poems to 1972. 1972.

Fiction

The Mortal and the Marble. 1950.
Andy. 1968.
Tamara. 1970.
Queen Emma of the South Seas. 1976.

Other

A Long Way South (travel). 1953.
Africa in Black and White. 1956.
States of the Union (travel). 1958.
Founder of a City: The Life of William Light. 1960.
Patrick White. 1961.
Walt Whitman. 1961.
Paintings of S. T. Gill. 1962.
Russell Drysdale (art criticism). 1962.
Tisi and the Yabby (juvenile). 1965.
Seal Bay (juvenile). 1966.
The Hero as Murderer: The Life of Edward John Eyre, Australian Explorer and Governor of Jamaica, 1815–1901. 1967.
Tisi and the Pageant (juvenile). 1968.
Australia's Censorship Crisis. 1970.
Australia's Last Explorer: Ernest Giles. 1970.
Australia since the Camera: 1901–14. 1971.
From Federation to War. 1972.
White on Black: The Australian Aborigine Portrayed in Art. 1974.

Editor, *The Literature of Australia.* 1964; revised edition, 1976.
Editor, *Australia and the Monarchy.* 1966.
Editor, *Modern Australian Writing.* 1966.
Editor, with Max Harris, *The Vital Decade: 10 Years of Australian Art and Letters.* 1968.
Editor, with Max Harris, *Sir Henry Bjelke, Don Baby, and Friends.* 1971.

Translator, with Igor Mezhakoff-Koriakin, *Bratsk Station,* by Yevgeny Yevtushenko. 1966.
Translator, with Igor Mazhakoff-Koriakin, *Fever,* by Bella Akhmadulina. 1968.
Translator, with Eleanor Jackman, *Kazan University and Other New Poems,* by Yevgeny Yevtushenko. 1973.

* * *

Wartime air-force experience has had a seminal effect on Geoffrey Dutton's poetry – not so much in subject matter as in its lasting synthesis into a perspective of aerial vision: the lone pilot among the clouds pondering the meaning of existence, the freshness and intensity of his perceptions of the world below enriched by a grateful return to base. Thus we find in Dutton's work a rare marriage of delicate observation and abstract discourse. Expectations of breath-taking vistas, or what he wryly calls "high octane/illusions of freedom," are thwarted by the apocalyptic vision of his early work: "the end uncertain and the past dissolved," "the future groping and the memory slain." Many of his poems give the impression of being specifically addressed, for in the face of this uncertainty, hope lies in the discovery of a meaningful realationship.

The threat of solitude haunts his poetry. "Abandoned Airstrip" poses the attractions of a dingo's freedom against innate fears of isolation: "Lacking lions and wars, our country bred/ In us a fear of loneliness instead." Love and affection, an obvious counterforce, are accordingly given considerable attention, and the wide range of treatments testifies to the variety found in his work. In "Night Fishing" the elaboration of a conceit in a manner reminiscent of the Metaphysicals climaxes with the duality of analogy fused into images of profound tranquillity, the lovers

> Exposed in their ghostly nakedness ...
> Welcome or terrible as they share
> In and around her in his arms the sea.

At the other extreme, the sustained treatment of love manifest in the day-to-day occurrences of a living relationship recalls Williams, particularly in the reverence towards flowers and the disarming fidelity of "Let's risk being obvious in happiness" – complexity is not an end in itself.

Dutton's talent for evocation is well seen in the travel poetry: an English landscape sheltering from industrialization; the "dark centre" of the Danube; a derelict aerodrome in France, when a skylark mockingly alights on a rotting disembowelled aircraft whose "shattered instruments measure the speed of rust"; and the outstanding poem sequence "A Russian Journey" which subtly exposes the blurred vision of conditioning meeting reality – austerity is not compensated by "Remembering the blood that tyranny wrings."

A study of Whitman inspired in the 1960's what Dutton has called "a more complex human response to my own country." Though there is evidence of Whitman's dramatic soliloquizing and a new sense of responsibility brought about by the re-orientation ("Land, that I love, lying all open to me ... I will protect you, I have promised that"), the catalogue is for the most part avoided – there are other ways of conveying vastness. By stressing the elemental in all his descriptions, Dutton can be both comprehensive and express a sense of unity in the imposing massiveness of his subject: "And the winter sun is filling all the ranges/With the blue smoke of the flameless fires of light."

Yet travel has given his Whitmanesque bravura a Jamesian awareness of cultural ambiguity, a "torrent of comparative values" that is also explored in greater detail in the novels (increasingly occupying his attention). Critical of the British legacy, he nevertheless concedes "No style grows out of nothingness"; and, while resenting the "shrivelled sacred umbilical cord" from Mother England, he links it to the bestially mature "hairy bellies" of the uncivilised colonists. Dutton sees Australia's innocent potentiality in the young; their ignorance leads him to treasure "the gift of suffering" and those insights peculiar to the travelling sensibility of a cultural and continental aviator, a heightened awareness with which to seek out contentment in the poetry.

—Garth Clucas

EKWENSI, Cyprian. Nigerian. Born in Minna, Northern Nigeria, 26 September 1921. Educated at Government College, Ibadan; Achimota College, Ghana; School of Forestry, Ibadan; Higher College, Yaba; Chelsea School of Pharmacy, University of London. Married to Eunice Anyiwo; five children. Lecturer in Biology, Chemistry and English, Igbodi College, Lagos, 1947–49; Lecturer in Pharmacognosy and Pharmaceutics, School of Pharmacy, Lagos, 1949–56; Pharmacist, Nigerian Medical Service, 1956; Head of Features, Nigerian Broadcasting Corporation, 1957–61; Director of Information, Federal Ministry of Information, Lagos, 1961–66. Since 1966, Director of Information Services in Enugu. Travelled to the United States, with Chinua Achebe and Gabriel Okara, to seek help for Biafra, 1969. Chairman, East Central State Library Board, Enugu, 1971; Member, Nigerian Arts Council. Recipient: Dag Hammarskjöld International Award, 1968. Lives in Enugu.

PUBLICATIONS

Fiction

People of the City. 1954.
Jagua Nana. 1961.
Burning Grass: A Story of the Fulani of Northern Nigeria. 1962.
Beautiful Feathers. 1963.
The Rainmaker and Other Stories. 1965.
Lokotown and Other Stories. 1966.
Iska. 1966.
Restless City, and Christmas Gold. 1975.
Survive the Peace. 1976.

Other (juvenile)

When Love Whispers. 1947.
Ikolo the Wrestler and Other Ibo Tales. 1947.
The Leopard's Claw. 1950.
The Drummer Boy. 1960.
The Passport of Mallam Ilia. 1960.
Yaba Roundabout Murder. 1962.
An African Night's Entertainment: A Tale of Vengeance. 1962.
The Great Elephant-Bird. 1965.
Trouble in Form Six. 1966.
The Boa Suitor. 1966.
Juju Rock. 1966.
Coal Camp Boy. 1973.
Samankwe in the Strange Forest. 1973.
The Rainbow-Tinted Scarf and Other Stories. 1975.
Samankwe and the Highway Robbers. 1975.

Reading List: *Ekwensi* by Ernest Emenyonu, 1974.

* * *

Cyprian Ekwensi is a prolific writer who covers many genres, novels, short stories, folklore collections, children's stories, and newspaper articles. He is a very popular novelist who writes for the masses.

His literary career started in 1947 when he published the novella *When Love Whispers*. It formed part of the Onitsha Market Literature which flourished after the second World War. Written for and by the newly literate urban masses this literature concerned itself with the problems of adapting to a westernized way of life in the melting-pots of the fast-expanding towns in southern Nigeria. Subjects like romantic love, the generation gap, how to get on in life, and how to avoid the pitfalls of drink and prostitutes were prevalent in this popular literature.

Ekwensi is rooted in this culture, and, although he has written about the life of Fulani cattle-raisers in the North, he is mainly thought of as a writer of city life. His major novels, *People of the City*, *Jagua Nana*, and *Beautiful Feathers*, are all concerned with the problems of surviving in a big city. Ekwensi has an ambiguous attitude to his subject. On the one hand he is a moralist trying to warn people of the dangers of the city – the bars with their prostitutes, the corrupt politicians and businessmen, the con-men and thieves, the deceitful friends. Ekwensi's city is a jungle in which everybody is on his own, fighting everybody else for survival. On the other hand, Ekwensi is obviously fascinated by the city, particularly its more seedy aspects. This is most obvious in *Jagua Nana*. The main character, Jagua Nana, is a magnificent but ageing prostitute who can still trap men in her favourite haunt, the nightclub "Tropicana"; however, she prefers a young school teacher, Freddy, whom she supports only to be replaced by a younger and more respectable woman.

The books are flawed by contradictions, inconsistencies, improbabilities, heavy sentimentalizing, shallow characterization, and a cliché-ridden English which places Ekwensi squarely among the writers of popular literature, but his historical importance is considerable.

—Kirsten Holst Petersen

FAIRBURN, A(rthur) R(ex) D(ugard). New Zealander. Born in Auckland, 2 February 1904. Educated at Parnell Primary School, Auckland; Auckland Grammar School, 1918–20. Served in the New Zealand Army, 1943. Married Jocelyn Mays in 1931; one son, three daughters. Clerk, New Zealand Insurance Company, Auckland, 1920–26; Labourer, free-lance writer, and part-time teacher, 1926–30; came to London, 1930, and lived in Wiltshire, 1931–32; Spokesman for the radical writers of the Phoenix group, Auckland, 1932–33; held various relief jobs in New Zealand, 1932–34; Assistant Secretary, and Editor of *Farming First* magazine, Auckland Farmer's Union, 1934–42; radio scriptwriter, Auckland, 1943–46; produced and designed fabrics, 1946–47; Tutor in English, 1947–54, and Lecturer, Elam School of Fine Arts, 1954–57, Auckland University College. *Died 25 March 1957.*

PUBLICATIONS

Collections

Collected Poems, edited by Denis Glover. 1966.
The Woman Problem and Other Prose, edited by Denis Glover and Geoffrey Fairburn. 1967.

Verse

He Shall Not Rise. 1930.
The County. 1931.
Another Argo, with Allen Curnow and Denis Glover. 1935.
Dominion. 1938.
Recent Poems, with others, 1941.
Poems 1929–1941. 1943.
The Rakehelly Man and Other Verses. 1946.
Three Poems. 1952.
Strange Rendezvous: Poems 1929–1941, with Additions. 1953.
The Disadvantages of Being Dead and Other Sharp Verses, edited by Denis Glover. 1958.
Poetry Harbinger, with Denis Glover. 1958.

Fiction

The Sky Is a Limpet (A Pollytickle Parrotty), also Four (4) Stories, or Moral Feebles. 1939.

Other

A Discussion on Communism Between Fairburn and S. W. Scott. 1936.
Who Said Red Ruin? 1938.
Hands Off the Tom Tom. 1944.
We New Zealanders: An Informal Essay. 1944.
How to Ride a Bicycle in Seventeen Lovely Colours. 1947.
Crisis in the Wine Industry. 1948.
R. M. S. Rangitoto. 1949.

Bibliography: *Fairburn: A Bibliography* by Olive Johnson, 1958.

Reading List: *Fairburn* by W. S. Broughton, 1968.

*   *   *

A. R. D. Fairburn's poetic development may be seen as a paradigm for the New Zealand writers of his generation. Allen Curnow has described their "common line of development" in these terms: "A mostly personal lyric impulse in the first place changed early to more or less direct lyric argument in which assertions about New Zealand itself ... became a dominant theme." Later these poets returned to "more personal and universal themes, lest their discovery of New Zealand should end in isolation." After a ritual pilgrimage "Home" to England exposed him to the reality of English life in 1930, Fairburn repudiated his limply derivative early verse. His first book, *He Shall Not Rise*, ended with a poem (from which the title was taken) that, in effect, disowned its own contents. Georgianism, he wrote after returning to New Zealand, was "another string which tripped up the feet of New Zealand poets." Instead they must embrace "the anarchy of life in a new country." Fairburn attempted this in *Dominion*, an ambitious portrait of New Zealand in the depression years, a poem which, in the words of one contemporary, decided "the struggle for poetry in New Zealand – rata blossoms v. reality, spooju v. style." Ranging from intemperate Poundian tirades to Wordsworthian celebrations of Nature, *Dominion* is an uneven but vigorous survey of the history and institutions, the land and the people of New Zealand. Fairburn is most effective and original when the lyrical and satirical modes merge, as in "Conversation in the Bush":

> "Observe the young and tender frond
> Of this punga: shaped and curved
> like the scroll of a fiddle: fit instrument
> to play archaic tunes."
>   "I see
> the shape of a coiled spring."

Here accurate natural description is made to serve wider purposes; from the speakers' difference of opinion over the shape of a fern leaf can be inferred contrasting aesthetic and political attitudes to the national crisis of the time.

After the thirties Fairburn turned away from national issues. His longer poems became more personal in emphasis (*Three Poems*), his satire more occasional, more amusing, but unfortunately, much slighter. *The Rakehelly Man* contains the best of his comic verse, immensely enjoyable if seldom of permanent interest. Much more of his creative energy went into lyric poetry, the best of which was collected in *Strange Rendezvous*. In his first book Fairburn had written of "the peace/and the forgetting/of the instant of love;/and the flat calm of death," and these traditional themes remain his central preoccupations; but his style matured into a flexible and distinctive idiom, combining a lovely relaxed movement with vividly particular sensations, as in "The Cave":

> We climbed down, and crossed over the sand,
> and there were islands floating in the wind-whipped blue,
> and clouds and islands trembling in your eyes.

Out of the conflict between sexual love on the one hand and time and death on the other Fairburn wrote several lyrics of great intensity ("The Cave," "Tapu," "A Farewell"), but perhaps his most distinctive poem, one of the few in which he achieved total integration of his complex nature, was "Full Fathom Five," both an Arnoldian exploration of the conflict of imagination and reality and an oblique self portrait:

> And eventually and tragically finding he could not drown
> he submitted himself to the judgment of the desert
> and was devoured by man-eating ants
> with a rainbow of silence branching from his lips.

—Peter Simpson

FINLAYSON, Roderick (David). New Zealander. Born in Auckland, 26 April 1904. Educated at the Ponsonby School; Seddon Memorial Technical College, 1918–21; School of Architecture, University of Auckland, 1922–24. Married Ruth Evelyn Taylor in 1936; three daughters and three sons. Architectural draftsman, 1922–28; printing-room assistant, Auckland City Council, 1958–66. Recipient: New Zealand Centennial Prize, 1940. Lives in Manurewa, New Zealand.

PUBLICATIONS

Fiction

Brown Man's Burden (stories). 1938.
Sweet Beulah Land (stories). 1942.
Tidal Creek. 1948.
The Schooner Came to Atia. 1953.
Brown Man's Burden and Later Stories, edited by Bill Pearson. 1973.
Other Lovers (novellas). 1976.

Other

Our Life in This Land (essay). 1940.
The Coming of the Maori. 1955.
The Coming of the Pakeha. 1956.
The Golden Years. 1956.
The Return of the Fugitives. 1957.
Changes in the Pakeha. 1958.
The Maoris of New Zealand, with Joan Smith. 1959.
The New Harvest. 1960.
The Springing Fern (juvenile). 1965.
D'Arcy Cresswell: His Life and Works. 1972.

Reading List: "The Maori and Literature 1938–1965," in *Essays in New Zealand Literature* edited by Wystan Curnow, 1973, and "Attitudes to the Maori in Some Pakeha Fiction," both by Bill Pearson, in *Fretful Sleepers and Other Essays,* 1974; "Narrative Stance in the Early Short Stories of Finlayson" by John Muirhead, in *World Literature Written in English 14,* April 1975.

*   *   *

Roderick Finlayson is a writer with a social thesis that is articulated not only in his fiction, but also in polemical essays – notably *Our Life in This Land.* For the terms of the thesis Finlayson was indebted to the New Zealand poet and sometime visionary D'Arcy Cresswell, whose prose works are a rejection of the scientific spirit of modern society. Finlayson's advocacy of Cresswell's doctrine is apparent in his 1972 study *D'Arcy Cresswell.* But Finlayson drew primarily from his own experience of New Zealand life, particularly during the galvanic years of the depression.

The depression expelled him from the urban white middle class and prompted his reappraisal of its values. Searching for the cause of social collapse, Finlayson eventually "identified the villain as our ruthlessly technological and acquisitive society. Others called it capitalism." He found an alternative creed among the rural Maoris and European subsistence farmers to whom he then turned. He called it the "poetic ideal": "a life dependent on the forces and powers of Nature." When based on a harmonious relationship with the earth, work could be creative, no longer an unwilling enslavement to machines; men would be freed from economic competition, and a sense of community could flourish. Yet already Finlayson recognised the collapse of this ideal with the insinuation of the profit motive into the countryside.

Finlayson's first short stories, published in *Brown Man's Burden* and *Sweet Beulah Land*, observe the decline of the Maori ideal. His was a new insight into Maori experience, eschewing previous literary stereotypes of noble primitive or comically stupid rascal. As Finlayson acknowledges, "no one had touched the life of men and women of flesh and blood in the confusing period between two worlds" – that of the ancient tribal ways, now dying, and that of a painful coercion by the dominant European ethos. The stories explore the tragic and comic ironies of this situation. Such themes are illustrative of Finlayson's social thesis, but he was able to avoid the admonitory tone that marks his essays. Finlayson had a natural affinity with the Maoris, and it enabled him to record their experience as they felt it. This was achieved technically by a narrative style modelled on the Sicilian stories of Giovanni Verga. The author creates a narrative voice that shares the simple dialect of his peasant protagonists, so that the story can be told without apparent authorial intrusion.

That narrative discipline is not always attained in the stories with European themes to which Finlayson turned, in *Sweet Beulah Land* and subsequently; in these stories, the social thesis sometimes obstructs the imaginative realisation of life. Finlayson's intention is too didactic: characters become flat victims or oppressors, without the ambiguity of his Maori protagonists. If this is often so of the European short stories, however, Finlayson's novels largely avoid the tendency to polemic. Beneath the comic and anecdotal surface of *Tidal Creek*, the poetic ideal is made flesh in the peasant figure of Uncle Ted. There is considerable power, too, in Finlayson's treatment of the passionate puritan Hartman, in *The Schooner Came to Atia*, although the energy of this novel is partly dissipated by Finlayson's introduction of an anti-colonialist theme. Similar personal and social crises are better integrated in "Jim and Miri," the most successful of the three novellas published as *Other Lovers*.

Overall, Finlayson's work represents a problem in New Zealand fiction at large: it stems from a recognition of reality so alarming that its expression is often polemical rather than suggestive of its themes. But where Finlayson's sympathy provides a conduit for his imagination to work, as in the Maori stories, his moral awareness is held in check and his art becomes a subtle recreation of life. It is to these stories, republished in *Brown Man's Burden and Later Stories*, that the reader will return.

—John Muirhead

FitzGERALD, Robert D(avid). Australian. Born in Hunters Hill, New South Wales, 22 February 1902. Educated at Sydney Grammar School; Sydney University, 1920–21; Fellow, Institute of Surveyors. Married Marjorie-Claire Harris in 1931; four children. Surveyor, FitzGerald and Blair, 1926–30; Native Lands Commission Surveyor, Fiji, 1931–36;

Municipal Surveyor, 1936–39; Surveyor, Australian Department of the Interior, 1939–65, now retired. Visiting Lecturer, University of Texas, Austin, 1963. Recipient: Australian Sesqui-Centenary Poetry Prize, 1938; Australian Literature Society Gold Medal, 1938; Grace Leven Prize, 1952, 1959, 1962; Fulbright grant, 1963; Encyclopedia Britannica Award, 1965. O.B.E. (Officer, Order of the British Empire), 1951. Lives in Hunters Hill, New South Wales.

PUBLICATIONS

Verse

The Greater Apollo. 1927.
To Meet the Sun. 1929.
Moonlight Acre. 1938.
Heemskerck Shoals. 1949.
Between Two Tides. 1952.
This Night's Orbit. 1953.
The Wind at Your Door. 1959.
Southmost Twelve. 1962.
Of Some Country: 27 Poems. 1963.
(Poems). 1963.
Forty Years' Poems. 1965.
Product. 1978.

Other

The Elements of Poetry. 1963.
Of Places and Poetry. 1976.

Editor, *Australian Poetry 1942.* 1942.
Editor, *(Poems),* By Mary Gilmore. 1963.
Editor, *The Letters of Hugh McCrae.* 1970.

Reading List: *Six Australian Poets* by T. Inglis Moore, 1942; *FitzGerald* by A. Grove Day, 1973.

*　*　*

Robert D. FitzGerald is the only Australian poet of any real importance whose work can be described as deliberately and consistently philosophical (as distinct from mystical or theosophical), one of the few whose verse generates a continual intellectual excitement, sensuously expressed. In his first two books, *The Greater Apollo* and *To Meet the Sun,* FitzGerald, using metaphor as a scientist uses hypothesis, is already tossing up philosophical ideas: determinism, as in "Meeting"; freewill, as in "Calm"; and concepts of change, endurance, and eternality, as in the sequence "The Greater Apollo." His interest in the last three questions places him in the tradition of Brennan and the 19th-century Romantics of Germany and France, an interest which his family connections may have fostered. A more direct impulse towards exploring these ideas was the reading of A. N. Whitehead's *Science and the Modern World,* with its base of Bergsonian thought, though it would be wrong to assume that FitzGerald is mere versified Whitehead. The analysis of the nature of continuity itself is, indeed, FitzGerald's permanent theme, and the phrase "diamond waterfalls" an early metaphor for it.

Moonlight Acre shows an increasing confidence and craftsmanship, a more idiosyncratic style, probably based on Browning. There is a growing preoccupation with concepts of freedom and a willingness to challenge accepted conventions, as in "Exile," a poem which should be compared with "Law-breakers," written during the Vietnam war thirty years later. The cragginess of the diction and the occasionally tortuous syntax in the longer poems in this book are evidence not of an absence of a lyrical sense, but of the inherent difficulty of the subject matter. FitzGerald can be simple and sensuous if he wants to, as the love-poems and the verses about some of his Fijian encounters indicate.

With "The Hidden Bole," a long elegy on the death of Pavlova, however, FitzGerald reaches his full stature, displaying both intellectual toughness and a lyric sweetness far less characteristic of him. The poem explores the nature of beauty, with its inseparable element of transience; the use of Pavlova's dancing as an image of its perfection parallels Whitehead's statement that "the only endurances are structures of activity." The fusion of the ballet image, with Pavlova as its centre, and the image of the sacred banyan tree with its "hidden bole," the symbol of life, is not accomplished without some strain, but the vigour and excitement of the poem are enough to carry us over the rough place; the last two stanzas, which bring the focus of attention back to Pavlova herself, are an exquisite evocation of the dancer:

> Eyes, were you drunk or blind
> not knowing her steps, although you watched their thief,
> the wind's toe-pointing leaf,
> not seeing her chase the pebbled river?
> She is the prisoned sunshine that became
> delicate contour of escaping fire;
> she is the snowflake blown upon the flame—
> song and the melting wraith of song's desire.

The use of images as hypotheses to be successively eliminated in analysing concepts is employed also in "Essay on Memory." It is an impressive, if not wholly successful poem, and certainly the most interesting of the attempts to provide the country with "a usable past." "Heemskerck Shoals and "Face of the Waters" and "Fifth Day" (from the volume *This Night's Orbit*) are far more accomplished pieces, the first expressing the paradox that the practical man is often the truest dreamer, the second on the agony of "striving to be" and of "not-being," the third on the impossibility of writing history, using the trial of Warren Hastings as an instance: "history hooks/the observer into the foreground as he looks...."

FitzGerald's most ambitious poem is *Between Two Tides*, though his most disturbing one, morally, is perhaps *The Wind at Your Door*, on a convict theme. *Between Two Tides* has for its subject the struggle for power between two Tongan chiefs, a vehicle for the argument that events present "straws" for man's choosing, that it is his duty to choose, and that by choosing he is able to determine the nature of the "straws" themselves. Human life is the indefinable moment between two tides when man is able to assert his "thusness" through his choosing. The poem is slow-moving but compellingly structured as a series of dissolving views: Finau's tale, filtered through several intermediaries to the poet, who becomes the omniscient narrator interpreting for the reader. In this poem FitzGerald makes use of the early experience of his life in Fiji, which had been working in him for many years below the surface. Unfamiliar setting and exotic characters provide the distancing necessary to an economical working out of the theme, and the result is the first really powerful narrative poem in Australian literature. The interconnections between what men are and the institutions they create are developed perhaps with greater human sympathy and humility in *The Wind at Your Door*. History, the past within us becoming the present and shaping the future, is one of FitzGerald's life-long preoccupations; in it he seems to discern, in spite of relapses into savagery, some secret "force towards order," though he is no facile optimist. His profession, surveying, has been a discernible influence on his work, and so has the Irish component in his ancestry, while his long sojourn in the Fijian Islands gives a mysterious dimension to his work, a perspective that marks him off from his contemporaries, some of whom seem culture-bound in comparison.

Besides his books of verse, FitzGerald has edited a selection of Mary Gilmore's poems, and a selection of the letters of Hugh McCrae. He has also published a book of criticism, *The Elements of Poetry*, robust, sensitive and individual. *Of Places and Poetry* is a collection of family reminiscences, portraits, literary explorations, and essays on the theory and practice of verse. Some of his sketches of literary personalities are illuminating and reasonably objective; his poetic theory is his own and strongly held, if not particularly stimulating, but there is a curious naivety about his prose style which is absent from his verse. Poetry is his native element.

—Dorothy Green

FRAME, Janet (Paterson). New Zealander. Born in Dunedin, 28 August 1924. Educated at Oamaru North School; Waitaki Girls' High School; Otago University Teachers Training College, Dunedin. Recipient: Church Memorial Award, 1951, 1954; New Zealand Literary Fund Award, 1960; New Zealand Scholarship in Letters, 1964; Robert Burns Fellowship, Otago University, 1965. Lives in Dunedin.

PUBLICATIONS

Fiction

The Lagoon: Stories. 1951; revised edition, as *The Lagoon and Other Stories*, 1961.
Owls Do Cry. 1957.
Faces in the Water. 1961.
The Edge of the Alphabet. 1962.
The Reservoir: Stories and Sketches. 1963.
Snowman, Snowman: Fables and Fantasies. 1963.
Scented Gardens for the Blind. 1963.
The Adaptable Man. 1965.
The Reservoir and Other Stories. 1966.
A State of Siege. 1966.
The Rainbirds. 1968; as *Yellow Flowers in the Antipodean Room*, 1969.
Intensive Care. 1970.
Daughter Buffalo. 1972.

Verse

The Pocket Mirror. 1967.

Other

Mona Minim and the Smell of the Sun (juvenile). 1969.

Reading List: *An Inward Sun: The Novels of Frame*, 1971, and *Frame*, 1977, both by J. A. Downie; "Preludes and Parables" by H. Winston Rhodes, in *Landfall 102*, 1973.

*   *   *

Janet Frame's best-liked novel, certainly in her own country, is her first, *Owls Do Cry*, a strongly autobiographical account of childhood in a small, rural New Zealand town. But before writing this she dealt with similar experiences in her first collection of short stories, *The Lagoon*, which presents several recollections of an idyllic childhood threatened, like her own, by bereavement and pain. Two of her sisters were drowned in separate accidents during her own girlhood; these tragedies are given to the Withers family of *Owls Do Cry*, becoming conflated in the burning of the oldest child, Francie, a tragedy which comes to symbolize the extinction of innocence and imagination by adult society. A parallel tragedy, linked to this by images, occurs later when Daphne, the second Withers child, is given a leucotomy after being forced into a mental hospital when her only "illness" is possession of a vividly lyrical imagination.

Some of the unresolved themes of this novel are treated in her next two, *Faces in the Water* and *The Edge of the Alphabet*, which complete a trilogy devoted to the Withers family. In *Faces in the Water*, Daphne, concealed behind the name of Istina Mavet, is a young woman who has entered a mental hospital after long periods of confusion and unhappiness. The novel is a descent into hell, and carries Istina from a ward of near-normal patients through others to a ward full of wild, deranged figures. Her recovery and eventual discharge have echoes of Orpheus's quest for Eurydice. These echoes occur again in *The Edge of the Alphabet*, the story of the journey to England made by Toby, the doltish son of the Withers family, who is seeking both his ancestry and the chance to write a novel. His failure to do either is balanced by the success of his friend, Zoe Bryce, in creating a small sculpture, a forest made of silver paper, that symbolizes the imaginative world both characters have found so difficult to capture in words.

The fugitive nature of written words becomes the dominant subject of Janet Frame's next two novels, *Scented Gardens for the Blind* and *The Adaptable Man*. H. Winston Rhodes has pointed to the parabolic relationship of all her stories of this period, collected in *The Reservoir* and *Snowman, Snowman*, to her other fiction; he refers particularly to the metaphor of blindness in her stories and its importance in the fourth novel, which deals with humans' refusal to see the harsh light of reality, and their preference for the scented gardens of civilization. The novel's three narrators are revealed finally to have been one, an ancient mute in a mental hospital; the incoherent grunts with which she ends the work suggest some return to a primitive communion and lead to the linguistic concerns of *The Adaptable Man*, a novel concerned again with a quest for a new language that will heal humans instead of dividing them. The only one of her novels to be set entirely in England, this work shows great control, confidence, and maturity, and may well come to be regarded as her finest and most significant work. Its theme of adaptability has evolutionary and linguistic implications alike, and the historical perspective of the novel gives her writing new dignity and compassion. In addition, it continues her concern with the form and techniques of writing, issues which she dextrously makes the subject of the novel.

A State of Siege and *The Rainbirds* have the simple directness of the parabolic form they use; the first concerns a spinster schoolteacher who retires to a cottage on an island in the north of New Zealand to learn to paint authentically but finds herself besieged by her imagination and memory instead, and is destroyed; the second is about an undistinguished immigrant from England who is knocked over by a car in a New Zealand town, deemed dead but comes to life again in hospital, and finds that his family and friends shun him as if he were diseased, that his job has been taken by someone else, and finally that actual death will be his only reward.

Intensive Care and *Daughter Buffalo* are products of periods spent at writers' colonies in the U.S.A. during the protests against the Vietnam War. *Intensive Care* is a substantial work, partly retrospective and partly visionary, which examines New Zealand's obsession with war and the kind of society this obsession produces; its final section is a nightmare vision of New Zealand as Vietnam, swarming with American soldiers who are to execute all local inhabitants whose imagination and intellect make them unusual and hence suspect. *Daughter Buffalo* is a slighter work, set almost entirely in New York, and is a kind of dialogue between Edelman, an American-Jewish doctor who specializes in studying death, and Turnlung, an elderly New Zealand writer whose interests are much the same. The earlier ruse of revealing a novel to have been written by a single figure occurs here, but by the time this is shown the book has comprehensively surveyed modern man's obsession with death, not simply in the U.S.A. but in New Zealand as well, and, by implication, throughout the world.

It is this wide range of significance that most distinguishes Janet Frame's best writing, which develops from personal concerns to a general compassion for human suffering and the kind of ignorance that prevents people from developing into whole human beings. It is distinguished, too, by her advocacy of a language charged with imagination and insight as an anodyne for these problems. Her occasional tendencies toward obsessiveness and obscurity are far outweighed by these distinctive qualities.

—Patrick Evans

FUGARD, Athol. South African. Born in Middleburg, Cape Province, 11 June 1932. Educated at Port Elizabeth Technical College; Cape Town University, 1950–53. Married Sheila Meiring in 1955; one daughter. Worked as a seaman, journalist, and stage manager; since 1959, actor, director, playwright; Director, Serpent Players, Port Elizabeth, since 1965; Co-Founder, The Space experimental theatre, Cape Town, 1972. Recipient: Obie Award, 1971. Lives in Port Elizabeth.

PUBLICATIONS

Plays

Nongogo (produced 1957). In *Dimetos and Two Early Plays*, 1977.
No-Good Friday (produced 1958). In *Dimetos and Two Early Plays*, 1977.
The Blood Knot (produced 1961). 1963.
Hello and Goodbye (produced 1965). 1966.
People Are Living There (produced 1968). 1969.
The Occupation, in *Ten One Act Plays*, edited by Cosmo Pieterse. 1968.
Boesman and Lena (produced 1969). 1969.
Statements after an Arrest under the Immorality Act (produced 1972). In *Statements*, 1974.

Sizwe Bansi Is Dead, with John Kani and Winston Ntshona (produced 1972). In *Statements*, 1974.
The Coat, with *The Third Degree* by Don MacLennan. 1973.
The Island, with John Kani and Winston Ntshona (produced 1974). In *Statements*, 1974.
Statements: Two Workshop Productions Devised by Fugard, John Kani and Winston Ntshona, Sizwe Bansi Is Dead and The Island, and a New Play, Statments after an Arrest under the Immorality Act. 1974.
Dimetos (produced 1975). In *Dimetos and Two Early Plays*, 1977.
Botticelli (produced 1976).
Dimetos and Two Early Plays. 1977.
The Guest (screenplay). 1977.

Screenplays: *Boesman and Lena*, 1972; *The Guest at Steenkampskraal*, 1977.

Television Play: *Mille Miglia*, 1968.

*   *   *

Athol Fugard has emerged as the major South African dramatist. His particular strength lies in a unique combination of a specific social protest and a universal concern with the human condition. Each of his plays deals with one or several aspects of apartheid, and they all carry a strong condemnation of its inhumanity – *Statements after an Arrest under the Immorality Act* is concerned with the immorality act and *The Island* with prison conditions on Robben Island. To that extent his plays fall under the heading of protest literature, but the protest is in each case widened out to include comments and reflections on aspects of human nature, in particular on the problem of identity.

In this as well as in his use of the Open Space theatre technique (theatre of the mind) Fugard owes much to Samuel Beckett. This is most obvious in *Boesman and Lena*, which has strong overtones of *Waiting for Godot*. The set of apartheid laws dealt with in this play are the ones designed to prevent squatting on South African-owned land by homeless migratory workers. Thus the coloured couple Boesman and Lena wake up one morning to find that bulldozers have arrived to destroy their shack, and they wander off in search of somewhere to sleep for the night. Boesman takes his frustrations out on Lena and beats her. In his excessive emotional cruelty he is a convincing psychological portrait of a victim of a cruel society. Lena on the other hand is beset by the problem of her identity. Stranded on featureless mudflats where they spend the night she is disorientated in time and space and she sees the clue to her identity in recognition by others, "Another pair of eyes," to acknowledge her existence. She establishes a relationship with a dog and a dying old African, but even this meagre contact is destroyed by Boesman who chases the dog away and kills the old man, thus forcing them to flee from the law, the system, and themselves.

In *Sizwe Bansi Is Dead* the problem of identity is further exacerbated by the pass laws. A black migratory worker Robert Swelinzima is "endorsed out" of Johannesburg, i.e., sent back to his homeland because his passbook is out of order. He is naive and honest, and therefore helpless in the maze of South African pass laws, but his smart city friend persuades him to steal the identity-card from the body of a dead man they find lying in the street. Robert thus changes his identity and becomes Sizwe Bansi. This creates great confusion in his mind, and he makes a bid to maintain his name because to him it carries his dignity and human worth mainly in his role as a husband and father. He is, however, persuaded to change his mind by his cynical friend who has become totally disillusioned: he has realized that as black men in South Africa they have no dignity to preserve, and the struggle to simply maintain life must take priority over concerns with dignity and identity.

These problems are, however, not confined to the blacks in South Africa; in *Hello and Goodbye* Fugard explores the effect of Calvinism and the resulting Boer morality on the poor section of the white community. Hester and her brother Johnnie search through their late father's belongings looking for a sum of money they think he has received as compensation for the loss of his leg while working on the railway. They are both prisoners of their society; Hester is a prostitute, and her brother is drawing near to madness as a result of the loneliness he feels as a result of the father's death. The search for the compensation becomes a search for a memory of just one act of love or kindness to compensate for the coldness and sterility of their Boer upbringing. Needless to say they do not find it: Hester returns to her life as a prostitute devoid of all illusions of love, and Johnnie takes the final step into madness and assumes the father's identity because it provides him with a past and thereby an identity. "I'm a man with a story," he says. Thus their attempts to establish an identity through memory are thwarted.

The Blood Knot explores what in the world of today can only be termed a myth – that all men are brothers, we are all descendants of Adam and share a universal mother. Morrie and Zachariah share the same mother but not father: Zachariah is black, and Morrie light enough to pass for a white. The entire action of the play takes place in a one-room shack in the Non-White location of Korsten, near Port Elizabeth. On the realistic level it is Zach's home which is now being shared by Morrie, while on the symbolic level it is a microcosm of South Africa. Zach, who is illiterate, has acquired a penpal whom Morrie writes to; from her letters it becomes obvious that she is white, and this polarizes them into black and white attitudes. Prompted by this event they explore their roles in a series of games. They leave behind their identities and in suspended time act out the archetypal roles of black and white, forcing each other into extreme caricature. The play acting is stopped by the ringing of an alarm clock, bringing them back to time, history, and reality. The games they play perform a psychological function. Insofar as they force each other into their stereotyped roles and compel each other to see themselves as black or white society sees them, they are in effect acting as Freudian analysts on each other, exposing their neuroses and hopefully, through exposure, curing them. Fugard does not, however, offer this as a solution to the South African problem. He is merely reflecting on the situation, and his preoccupation with role playing and identity problems is a logical result of a situation where – in his own words – "people have lost their faces and have become just literally the colour of their skins."

—Kirsten Holst Petersen

FURPHY, Joseph. Pseudonym: Tom Collins. Australian. Born at Yering Station, near Yarra Glen, Victoria, 26 September 1843. Educated at home, and at schools in Kangaroo Ground and Kyneton. Married Leonie Germain in 1867; two sons and one daughter. Farmer, later teamster in northern Victoria; bullock-driver in Riverina for about seven years; worked in his brother's foundry at Shepparton, 1884–1904; contributor to the *Bulletin* from 1889; lived in Fremantle, Western Australia, 1905 until his death. *Died 13 September 1912.*

PUBLICATIONS

Fiction

Such Is Life, Being Certain Extracts from the Diary of Tom Collins. 1903; abridged and edited by Vance Palmer, 1937.

Rigby's Romance. 1921; complete version, 1946.
The Buln-Buln and the Brolga. 1948.

Verse

Poems, edited by Kate Baker. 1916.

Bibliography: *Furphy: An Annotated Bibliography* by Walter W. Stone, 1955.

Reading List: *Furphy: The Legend of the Man and His Book* by Miles Franklin, 1944: *Furphy* by John Barnes, 1963.

*   *   *

No Australian novelist of the nineteenth century is held in higher esteem today than Joseph Furphy, who wrote under the pseudonym of Tom Collins. Yet his *Such Is Life,* not published until 1903, had only a small devoted following until towards the end of World War II when, with increasing frequency, his name became linked to Henry Lawson's as one of the founders of a native literary tradition.

Apart from some poems and stories, Furphy's writing was contained in the original manuscript of *Such Is Life* which he sent to A. G. Stephens of the *Bulletin* in 1897. This manuscript, which drew on his experiences as a bullock driver in the Riverina and his voluminous reading, became through excisions and revisions *Such Is Life, Rigby's Romance* (serialized in 1905, but first complete book publication in 1946) and *The Buln-Buln and the Brolga.*

Such Is Life was taken to be mainly a work of reminiscence for the first forty years after publication, until the critical climate for its recognition as a novel with a fictional view of life developed. Furphy's love of literature, and especially his affection for Fielding and Sterne, inspired him to narrative playfulness and stylistic parody. In the post war period, these characteristics answered to critical interests in self-conscious fictionalizing, experiments with points of view, and form as a means of perception. The novel's strengths are sufficiently diverse for it to answer to future critical demands. It is an encyclopaedic study of provincial life as a microcosm focusing universal issues, as well as a comic demonstration of the vanity of philosophic speculation on such issues. Furphy's literary erudition, at times pedantic, combines with a forceful vernacular realism to make the work unique – and irreducible to critical formulae.

Furphy held nationalistic and social attitudes similar to those of his contemporary Henry Lawson, and described his original manuscript as having "temper, democratic; bias, offensively Australian." Like Lawson, he was concerned to discover a form that would express the reality he had observed, and to reject the romantic conventions that he felt falsified life. *Such Is Life* purports to be a recollection of the comic picaro Tom Collins as he randomly turns up entries in his diary for 1883: it seems a realistically unstructured collection of sketches, remembered conversations (in various dialects), tales, and incessant philosophical reflections from Collins – some in interior monologue, some in direct address to the reader. Collins seizes every opportunity to ridicule "romance" and the conventions he associates with popular fiction, especially melodramatic plot. Henry Kingsley's *Geoffry Hamlyn,* the classic "colonial romance," is his favourite target. Art, though, has its revenge, because a maze of relationships and intricate coincidences lie beneath the apparently random surface, undetected or unacknowledged by Collins.

The Buln-Buln and the Brolga and *Rigby's Romance* were both expanded from discarded chapters of *Such Is Life.* The first highlights Furphy's parody of prevailing literary clichés, and provides a very good introduction to his work. Its antagonists, Fred Falkland-Pritchard and Barefoot Bob, compete to tell the tallest tale. As their names suggest, they draw on different traditions – that of the literary romance and that of the oral yarn. As narrator, Tom Collins provides a background of humorous realism through his recollection of childhood in a country town. As with some of Lawson's work, there are correspondences with what Mark Twain and other western humorists had been doing in America. *Rigby's Romance* emphasizes Furphy's interest in social theory. Structurally it consists of exemplary tales told during a protracted discussion of socialism around a camp-fire. Once it is appreciated that the American Rigby will evade his chance of romance through theorizing to Collins and others, the book can be appreciated for its polysyllabic humour and its sly engagement with the ideals of Christian Socialism.

—Brian Kiernan

GHOSE, Manmohan. Indian. Born in Bhagalpore, 19 January 1869; lived in England from age 10. Educated at Manchester Grammar School; St. Paul's School, London; Christ Church, Oxford, 1887–90, B.A. 1890. Married Malati Bannerjee in 1898 (died, 1918), two daughters. Returned to India, 1894: taught at Patna and Dacca colleges; Professor of English, Presidency College, Calcutta, 1902–21. *Died 5 January 1924.*

PUBLICATIONS

Collections

Selected Poems, edited by P. Lal. 1969.
Selected Poems, edited by Lotika Ghose 1974.

Verse

Love-Songs and Elegies. 1898.
Songs of Love and Death, edited by Laurence Binyon. 1926.

* * *

Though Manmohan Ghose was born in India, he lived in England from the age of 10 until he was 25. English thus became his first language (Laurence Binyon says that when he returned to India in 1894 he had to relearn Bengali, his mother tongue), and the English tradition of verse became *his* tradition.

Ghose's early poetry in the booklet *Love-Songs and Elegies*, and much of his later work as well, should be seen in the late Victorian context, and not in the Anglo-Indian tradition. Like his friends Binyon and Stephen Phillips, he wrote elegantly, and on a high technical level, of the English landscape, of London, of the melancholy and other emotions associated with the 1890's Thus, from "London":

> Can I talk with leaves, or fall in love with breezes?
> Beautiful boughs, your shade not a human pang appeases.
> This is London. I lie, and twine in the roots of things.

or from "On His Twentieth Birthday":

> Lightly leaves he behind all the sad faces of home;
> Never again, perchance, to perceive them; lost in the tempest,
> Or on some tropic shore dying in fever and pain!

or from "April" (a late work):

> April delicious
>   Young, sunny maiden,
>   Arch, gusty, capricious,
>   With fresh flowers laden

Binyon urged him to write on Indian themes, but even after he returned to India Ghose continued to write of English Aprils rather than Indian seasons, of Greek and Christian mythology rather than Indian legends and history. He *did* write an Indian "mystery play," "Nollo and Damayanti," based on a story from the Sanskrit epic the *Mahabharata*, but his major works, unfinished and unpublished at his death, were "Perseus – The Gorgon-Slayer" and "Adam Alarmed in Paradise: A Lyric Epic."

—George Walsh

GILMORE, Mary (Jean). Australian. Born in Cotta Walla, near Goulburn, New South Wales, 16 August 1865. Pupil-teacher in Cootamundra, Albury, and Wagga. Married William Alexander Gilmore in 1897 (separated, 1911); one son. Taught in Silverton, 1888–89, and in Sydney, 1890; relief worker during maritime strike, 1890; emigrated to utopian colony "New Australia," Cosme, Paraguay, 1896: teacher, and Editor of *Cosme Evening Notes*; returned to Australia, 1902: farmer in Casterton, Victoria, 1902–11; settled in Sydney, 1911; Founding Editor of the women's page, *The Worker*, Sydney, 1908–30; Columnist, *Tribune* (communist newspaper), 1952–62. Founding Executive Member, Australian Workers Union (first woman member). D.B.E. (Dame Commander, Order of the British Empire), 1937. *Died 3 December 1962.*

PUBLICATIONS

Collections

(Poems), edited by Robert D. FitzGerald. 1963.
Gilmore: A Tribute, edited by D. Cusack and others. 1965.

Verse

> *Marri'd and Other Verses.* 1910.
> *The Tale of Tiddley Winks.* 1917.
> *The Passionate Heart.* 1918.
> *The Tilted Cart: A Book of Recitations.* 1925.
> *The Wild Swan.* 1930.
> *The Rue Tree.* 1931.
> *Under the Wilgas.* 1932.
> *Battlefields.* 1939.
> *The Disinherited.* 1941.
> *Pro Patria Australia and Other Poems.* 1945.
> *Selected Verse.* 1948; revised edition, 1969.
> *All Souls.* 1954.
> *Fourteen Men.* 1954.

Other

> *Hound of the Road.* 1922.
> *Old Days, Old Ways: A Book of Recollections.* 1934.
> *More Recollections.* 1935.

Bibliography: in *Gilmore: A Tribute*, 1965.

Reading List: *Gilmore* by Sylvia Lawson, 1966; *Three Radicals* by W. H. Wilde, 1969.

*   *   *

Mary Gilmore's long life spanned more than half of Australia's whole history and encompassed the most dramatic and significant events in its struggle for recognition as a nation: gold-rushes, the great strikes of the 1890's leading to the formation of the Labour Party and the consolidation of industrial unionism, Federation, the first World War and Gallipoli, the Depression, the second World War and the Pacific War, and the economic expansion of the cheap oil decades. Mary Gilmore's prose and poetry, her sixty years as a working journalist, reflect all these changes, as well as her personal response to them. This response never wavered from the religious and idealistic principles on which her moral attitudes rested: the principles of the brotherhood of man and of the Christian ethic as revealed towards the end of *Matthew* 25. In accordance with these principles, she extended the meaning of brotherhood to cover the long-forgotten convicts who helped found the country and the dispossessed Aboriginals, at a time when there were few people to see good in either. "Old Botany Bay" and "The Myall in Prison" express the tragedy of both.

Mary Gilmore was of Scottish descent, and her hearing was early attuned to the great ballads, the Bible, and the timeless hymns and psalms of her ancestors. In addition, there was in her a genuine streak of Celtic mysticism, or at least of the "feyness" common to so many Scotchwomen, added to an element of gnomic wisdom, and her work in consequence conveys a curious impression of being spoken by a tribal Wise Woman. All of it is distinguished by a warm, simple, and sincere humanity. In common with the balladists, she has a strength and vitality unusual in women poets. Like most of the balladists, she is a poet of the people and knows their struggles from the inside, not as a spectator. Her verse comes as naturally as song to a bird; she writes with the same unselfconsciousness as would attend the making of bread, and both activities are part of the unity of her personality. Like her contemporary Hugh McCrae, she thinks naturally in images, which are not, unlike McCrae's, merely the result of observation, but are bound up indissolubly with some mental state, mood, or idea:

> Nurse no long grief,
> Lest the heart flower no more;
> Grief builds no barns; its plough
> Rusts at the door.

But a simple, natural style does not always achieve such timeless perfection and Mary Gilmore's art has the defects of its qualities. A reluctance to realise the need for self-criticism, for whatever reason, sometimes results in vagueness, in the commonplace, in facile emotional self-indulgence. Nevertheless the wide range of her subjects and her sympathies, her intelligence and sensitivity, her vigour and individuality, the sense that in reading her we are listening to the voice of a race give her a place of first importance in Australian literature. She speaks in addition for women, not for Australian women alone, though she does that, but for womankind, though she was no feminist: one of the best of her poems is the early "Evesong." Yet some of the best and the strongest come from her last book, *Fourteen Men*, published in her 90th year, in which all her gifts and her preoccupations are as vital as ever: her awareness of the natural world, her sympathy with humble people, her religious faith, her empathy with Aboriginals, her interest in world affairs, especially in peace movements, her wisdom and her passion and her sense of mystery. The risk is that she may be underrated: it is rarely pointed out, for instance, how much is owed to her example by Judith Wright.

Mary Gilmore wrote three books of essays and recollections, besides her books of verse: *Hound of the Road, Old Days, Old Ways*, and *More Recollections*. These have the same qualities as her verse and bring the era in which she grew up vividly to life. Some of her best work, however, may still lie buried in *The Worker*, the women's page of which she edited for more than twenty years. Other journalistic articles wait for discovery in Argentina newspapers, to which she contributed after the New Australia experiment in Paraguay came to an end.

—Dorothy Green

GLOVER, Denis (James Matthews). New Zealander. Born in Dunedin, 10 December 1912. Educated at Auckland Grammar School; Christ's College; Canterbury University College, A.B. Served as an officer in the Royal Navy during World War II: Distinguished Service Cross. Married 1) Mary Granville in 1936, one son; 2) Lyn Cameron in 1972. Taught English at Canterbury University, 1936–38, and typography at the Technical Correspondence Institute, Christchurch. Founder, Caxton Press, Christchurch, 1936; joined Pegasus Press, 1953, and Wingfield Press, 1955. Formerly, Journalist, *The Press*, Christchurch. Former President, New Zealand P.E.N. and Friends of the Turnbull Library, Wellington; Member of the Canterbury University Council, and of the New Zealand State Literary Fund Committee. Recipient: Jessie Mackay Award, 1960. Lives in Wellington.

PUBLICATIONS

Verse

Short Reflection on the Present State of Literature in This Country. 1935.
Another Argo, with Allen Curnow and A. R. D. Fairburn. 1935.
Thistledown. 1935.
Six Easy Ways of Dodging Debt Collectors. 1936.
A Caxton Miscellany, with others. 1937.
The Arraignment of Paris. 1937.
Thirteen Poems. 1939.
Cold Tongue. 1940.
Recent Poems, with others. 1941.
The Wind and the Sand: Poems 1933–44. 1945.
Summer Flowers. 1945.
Sings Harry and Other Poems. 1951.
Arawata Bill: A Sequence of Poems. 1953.
Since Then. 1957.
Poetry Harbinger, with A. R. D. Fairburn. 1958.
Enter Without Knocking: Selected Poems. 1964; revised edition, 1972.
Sharp Edge Up: Verses and Satires. 1968.
Myself When Young. 1970.
To a Particular Woman. 1970.
Diary to a Woman. 1971.
Dancing to My Tune. 1974.
Wellington Harbour. 1974.

Plays

Screenplays: *The Coaster,* 1951; *Mick Stimson,* with John Lang, 1972.

Radio Play: *They Sometimes Float at Sea,* 1970.

Fiction

3 Short Stories. 1936.

Other

Till the Star Speaks. 1939.
D Day. 1944.
A Clutch of Authors and a Clot. 1960.
Hot Water Sailor. 1962.
Glover's Bedside Book. 1963.

Editor, with Ian Milner, *New Poems.* 1934.
Editor, *The Disadvantages of Being Dead and Other Sharp Verses.* by A. R. D. Fairburn. 1958.
Editor, *Cross Currents,* by Merrill Moore. 1961.
Editor, *Collected Poems,* by A. R. D. Fairburn. 1966.

Editor, with Geoffrey Fairburn, *The Woman Problem and Other Prose*, by A. R. D. Fairburn. 1967.

* * *

Denis Glover, naval Commander, boxing blue, poet, publisher, printer, "looking rather like Mr. Punch in naval uniform" (John Lehmann, 1941) has been a minor kind of colonial/Renaissance man. All which helps establish his very distinctive poetic tone, although in parenthesis one might note his admirable wartime prose in *Penguin New Writing* (notably "It Was D-Day"), and his eminently readable autobiography *Hot Water Sailor*. His poetry begins, part Georgian, part Audenesque, in the middle 1930's when that "shock of recognition" of the Depression ignited so much local creativity. He also, with developing elegance, printed and published (under the imprint Caxton Press) his own verse, along with much other significant poetry, fiction, and critical prose, through the next crucial and formative decade.

Early verse presents the dignity of labour ("The Road Builders") and lyric response to landscape ("Holiday Piece"); his very first Caxton Press book, incidentally, with that sharp, irreverent and dangerous wit he still displays, is titled *Six Easy Ways of Dodging Debt Collectors*, with the explanation "Called on the outside, because of the difficulty of selling verse, *Six Easy Ways....*" In *Recent Poems* he moves into his stride with, perhaps most notably, the memorable ballad "The Magpies" with its lyric opening, "When Tom and Elizabeth took the farm/The bracken made their bed," but lamentable conclusion:

> The farm's still there, Mortgage corporations
> Couldn't give it away.
> And *Quardle oodle ardle wardle doodle*
> The magpies say.

The same volume sustains his impudent wit ("Thoughts on Cremation"); *The Wind and the Sand* not only promotes his St. Exupéry-like romanticism but adds themes of nostalgia and mortality and that marine sensibility he alone brings to New Zealand verse.

In my view, *Sings Harry* is his best single volume. This contains "A Note to Lili Kraus" where he articulates a representative local fear of feeling: "Lili, emotion leaves me quite dismayed:/If I'm on fire I call the fire-brigade." Alastair Campbell ("Glover and Georgianism," *Comment 21*) has shown it is through "Harry" (possibly copying Yeats) that Glover finds an emotionally liberating persona. Harry, like his subsequent fellows, 'Wata Bill and Mick Stimson, is that true colonial archetype, a rural male loner. From "Sings Harry to an Old Guitar":

> These songs will not stand –
> The wind and the sand will smother.
>
> Not I but another
> Will make songs worth the bother:
>   The rimu or kauri be,
>   I'm but the cabbage tree

and from "Sings Harry in the Wind-Break":

> From the cliff-top a boy
> Felt that great motion
> And pupil to the horizon's eye
> Grew wide with vision,

and from "Themes":

> What shall we sing? sings Harry.
>
> Sing all things sweet or harsh upon
> These islands in the Pacific sun,
> The mountains whitened endlessly
> And the white horses of the winter sea.

His subsequent *Arawata Bill*, though ingenious and admired, seems too contrived and rhythmically stiff to create quite the same niche for a wandering prospector. Only perhaps in "Towards Banks Peninsula: Mick Stimson" (*Since Then*) does a similar warmth, more tranquil, infuse his lines: this poem should possibly be linked with "Towards Banks Peninsula: Peraki" (*Poetry Harbinger*) as part of that poetry of the sea prominent in his later work.

—Peter Alcock

GORDIMER, Nadine. South African. Born in Springs, Transvaal, 20 November 1923. Educated at the Convent School, and the University of the Witwatersrand, Johannesburg. Married 1) G. Gavron in 1949; 2) Reinhold Cassirer in 1954; one son and one daughter. Visiting Lecturer, Institute of Contemporary Arts, Washington, D.C., 1961, Harvard University, Cambridge, Massachusetts, 1969, Princeton University, New Jersey, 1969, Northwestern University, Evanston, Illinois, 1969, and the University of Michigan, Ann Arbor, 1970; Adjunct Professor of Writing, Columbia University, New York, 1971. Recipient: Smith Literary Award, 1961; Thomas Pringle Award, 1969; Black Memorial Prize, 1972; Booker Prize, 1974; Grand Aigle d'Or Prize, France, 1975; CNA Literary Award, 1975. Lives in Johannesburg.

PUBLICATIONS

Fiction

Face to Face: Short Stories. 1949.
The Soft Voice of the Serpent and Other Stories. 1952.
The Lying Days. 1953.
Six Feet of the Country (stories). 1956.
A World of Strangers. 1958.
Friday's Footprint and Other Stories. 1960.
Occasion for Loving. 1963.
Not for Publication and Other Stories. 1965.
The Late Bourgeois World. 1966.
A Guest of Honour. 1970.

Livingstone's Companions: Stories. 1971.
The Conservationist. 1974.
Selected Stories. 1975.
Some Monday for Sure (stories). 1976.

Other

On the Mines, with David Goldblatt. 1973.
The Black Interpreters (literary criticism). 1973.

Editor, with Lionel Abrahams, *South African Writing Today.* 1967.

Bibliography: *Gordimer, Novelist and Short Story Writer: A Bibliography of Her Works* by Racilia Jilian Nell, 1964.

Reading List: *Gordimer* by Robert F. Haugh, 1974; *Gordimer* by Michael Wade, 1978.

* * *

Nadine Gordimer is one of the foremost fiction-writers in South Africa. Her short stories and novels capture the stresses and ironies of life in that authoritarian, segregated society. Although her fiction deals mainly with the lives of English-speaking whites, she is one of the few South African writers who creates equally convincing sketches of black Africans, Asians, and Afrikaners.

Her writing is closely involved with politics yet seldom explicitly political. Not only is she a hauntingly accurate recorder of the sclerotic effects of white domination, but also the pre-eminent portraitist of white, English-speaking middle-class life. Gordimer both knows that society intimately and remains detached from it in her writing. This element of detachment has resulted in her being unjustly considered cold by some critics. But the accuracy and detail of her observations are moulded by a profoundly sympathetic intelligence. Gordimer seldom recreates for their own sake the quirks of comfortable, provincial, white, South African society. In her novels and short stories the relentless accuracy of detail is almost invariably tied to an emotional reaction: a sense of loss, of impotence, and – rarely – of vitality or courage.

It is because Gordimer deals so closely with individuals in observed situations that politics form a menacing background to almost all her writing. As she remarked in an interview with Alan Ross in the *London Magazine* (May 1965): "whites among themselves are shaped by their peculiar position, just as black people are by theirs. I write about their private selves; often, even in the most private situations, they are what they are because their lives are regulated and their mores formed by the political situation."

The emphases in the private lives of Nadine Gordimer's fictional characters change with the age. One can trace the deterioration in the South African political situation throughout her writing career of more than thirty years. The short stories in particular illustrate the growing powerlessness of the "decent," "liberal" white minority.

In the early volumes, many tales reveal the grotesque inequalities inherent in white supremacy. Both blacks and whites are portrayed as helpless victims of a brutally stratified society: "civilised" whites are capable of little more than token sympathy for their black servants; the private tragedies of blacks rarely perturb more than the surface of a bland, decorous white world. In *Not for Publication* and *Livingstone's Companions* the atmosphere has changed. There are still marvellously evocative accounts of the slightly bewildered social antics of an increasingly outdated, isolated white culture. But the growth of the police state in the later stories brings with it a relentless ossifying of liberal responses, a steady cheapening of defiant gestures, and an inexorable dwindling of determined political opposition from black and white. The short stories are not uniformly bleak, however. Nadine Gordimer frequently builds a personal tale around a fleeting but sharply focused moment of revelation or insight. These concise evocations of the vital, the ephemeral, or the corrosive element in various relationships give a range to her writing far beyond that of the social themes for which she is best known.

Her novels follow the same pattern of development as her short stories. *The Lying Days* describes the struggle of the heroine to break free, first from the taboos of the mining community in which she grows up, and second from the facile group of intellectual whites with whom she later mixes in Johannesburg. She encounters racial violence and a feeling of impotence after the Afrikaner Nationalist victory of 1948, but decides not to run away from her disillusion and guilt.

This beautifully observed *bildungsroman* is Nadine Gordimer's most optimistic book. Disillusion itself and the increasingly fragmented nature of life in a segregated society are the pressing themes of her later novels. In *A World of Strangers* a visiting Englishman tries unsuccessfully to move both in affluent white Johannesburg and in the fast, illicit world of the black townships. Real contact between the two is, however, impossible. *Occasion for Loving* records the corrosive effects of a love affair between a black man and a white woman in a society which brands such a relationship illegal.

The next novel is even darker. *The Late Bourgeois World* is a steely examination of the entombed white English-speaking world in post-Sharpeville South Africa. Through its protagonist, a young divorced woman, the novel records the futile sabotage attempts of her leftist ex-husband and her own terror in the face of an appeal for help from a member of the black underground. Her bland, white society provides a fog-like emotional foreground through which the fear and impotence of her position loom sharp and menacing.

There is a turning away from this dead end in *A Guest of Honour*. Set in an unidentified African country, the novel examines the problems of newly won independence. The central character is a sympathetic Englishman working as a special consultant. His life is complicated by an unexpected passion for a young white woman, which is described with poignant vitality. His frustrations in the new state are paralleled by growing strife, and he is killed in an arbitrary act of violence.

South Africa is again the setting of *The Conservationist*. Mehring, the successful white industrialist through whose consciousness most of the book unfolds, is perplexed by the unsatisfying nature of his possessions. In particular, his weekend farm is obtruded upon by memories (of his callow, liberal son and his smug ex-lover) and by itinerant blacks. In this world of chimera and unfulfilment only the land remains tangible and stable. Yet it too eludes Mehring. A black corpse buried on his farm has a more legitimate claim to be part of it than any guilt-laden lien Mehring can command. The aridity of *The Conservationist* suggests a new kind of dead end. But its haunting evocation of atrophy is only a further step in the author's remarkable chronicling of decay in her society.

—Rowland Smith

GROSSMAN, Edith (Howitt, née) Searle. New Zealander. Born in Beechworth, Victoria, Australia, in 1863. Educated at Invercargill Grammar School; Christchurch Girls' High School; Canterbury College (junior university scholar), 1881–85, B.A. 1884, M.A. (honours) 1885. Married Joseph Penfound Grossman. Teacher at Wellington Girls' College; writer from 1890. Founding Member, Canterbury Women's Institute. *Died 28 February 1931.*

PUBLICATIONS

Fiction

In Revolt. 1892.
A Knight of the Holy Ghost. 1907.
Hermione. 1908.
The Heart of the Bush. 1910.

Other

In Memoriam Helen Macmillan Brown. 1903.
Life of Helen Macmillan Brown. 1905.

Reading List: "Informing the Void: Initial Cultural Displacement in New Zealand Writing" by Peter Alcock, in *Journal of Commonwealth Literature 6*, 1971.

* * *

Of Edith Searle Grossman's four novels only the last need detain us. As one of the early woman graduates of the University of New Zealand she was naturally involved in the vigorous feminism of the nineties (New Zealand women gained the vote in 1893) as well as the contemporary and allied temperance movement (it was said there were then two causes of death in the colony, drink and drowning – while drunk). It is only in *The Heart of the Bush* that her writing transcends the narrow crusading dogmatism and often crude (though contemporarily relevant) exaggeration of her earlier fiction.

This book has three parts: "Between two hemispheres," "The hidden vale," "The book of Dennis and Adelaide." The first gave its title to the original chapter six of E. H. McCormick's *Letters and Art in New Zealand* (1940), which suggests its value as model treatment of our crisis of "Home" (England) or "home" (New Zealand?!). In this part the heroine, Adelaide Borlase, returned from ten years' European education, must choose between Dennis MacDiarmid, the hired man with whom she had plighted childish troth, and the "faultlessly got up Englishman" Horace Brandon: "somehow, re-entering the scenes of her childhood gave her the sensation of being the same child again, or rather of being two distinct persons who did not agree with each other." MacDiarmid spells out sound colonial sense: "Little girl ..., what have they done to you over there in England?" Adelaide soon comes right – "Dennis, Dennis, I never will be Horace Brandon's wife" – but not without some convincing explanation and inoffensive moralising: the magnificent trees in the bush (sub-tropical vegetation) "mocked old architecture with their own richer loveliness and life," and "you cannot see nearly so far in England," she said, "You are always looking through a kind of film. And there are no heights there and no depths."

"The hidden vale" presents their "bush" honeymoon in strange, presumably Freudian, incidents that climax in a chaste but plainly eucharistic meal ("some hard bread and some of Emmeline's home-made wine") well above the vegetation line when Adelaide is rescued from a glacial crevasse. The highly sentimental part 3 reveals the brisk colonial practicality of Dennis, a virtue in part 1, as a threat to their marriage when he neglects Adelaide for local affairs in the form of a developing dairy factory and frozen meat works. This time it is Dennis who sees the error of his ways and settles for idyllic domesticity. E. H. McCormick points out this is precisely the opposite of the national decision.

Over-written at times, naïve in characterisation, *The Heart of the Bush* is still honest, economic, and concentrates in 300 pages a lively, intelligent, convincing dramatisation of some central problems of this young country then – and now.

—Peter Alcock

GROVE, Frederick Philip. Canadian. Born Felix Paul Berthold Friedrich Greve, in Radomno, Prussia-Poland, 14 February 1879; naturalized citizen, 1921. Educated at St. Pauli school, Hamburg, 1886–95; Gymnasium des Johanneums, Hamburg, 1895–98; University of Bonn, 1898–1900; Maximiliens University, Munich, 1901–02; University of Manitoba, Winnipeg, B.A. 1921. Married Catherine Wiens in 1914; one daughter, one son. Writer and translator in Germany, 1902–09; imprisoned for fraud, 1903–04; emigrated to Canada c. 1909; settled in Manitoba: taught in Haskett, 1913, Winkler, 1913–15, Virdin, 1915–16, Gladstone, 1916–17; Ferguson, 1918, Eden, 1919–22, and Rapid City, 1922–24; Editor, Graphic Press, Ottawa, 1929–31, and Associate Editor, *Canadian Nation*, 1929; manager of a farm in Simcoe, Ontario, 1931–38, and lived on the farm after his retirement. Recipient: Lorne Pierce Gold Medal, 1934; Canadian Writers' Federation Pension, 1944; Governor-General's Award, for non-fiction, 1947. D.Litt.: University of Manitoba, 1945. Fellow, Royal Society of Canada, 1941. *Died 19 August 1948.*

PUBLICATIONS

Collections

Letters, edited by Desmond Pacey. 1975.

Fiction

Fanny Essler (in German). 1905.
Maurermeister Ihles Haus. 1906; translated as *The Master Mason's House,* 1976.
Settlers of the Marsh. 1925.
A Search for America. 1927.
Our Daily Bread. 1928.
The Yoke of Life. 1930.
Fruits of the Earth. 1933.
Two Generations: A Story of Present-Day Ontario. 1939.
The Master of the Mill. 1944.
Consider Her Ways. 1947.
Tales from the Margin: The Selected Short Stories, edited by Desmond Pacey. 1971.

Verse

Wanderungen. 1902.
Helena und Damon (verse drama). 1902.

Other

Oscar Wilde (in German). 1903.
Randarabesken zu Oscar Wilde. 1903.
Over Prairie Trails. 1922.
The Turn of the Year. 1923.
It Needs to Be Said.... 1929.
In Search of Myself. 1946.

Translator of works by Balzac, Robert and Elizabeth Barrett Browning, Cervantes, Ernest Dowson, Dumas, Flaubert, Gide, Le Sage, Meredith, Henri Murger, Pater, Wells, and Wilde into German, 1903–9.

Reading List: *Grove,* 1969, and *FPG: The European Years,* 1973 (includes bibliography), both by Douglas O. Spettigue; *Grove* by Ronald Sutherland, 1969; *Grove* by Desmond Pacey, 1970; *Grove* by Margaret R. Stobie, 1973.

* * *

The Canadian Frederick Philip Grove is now known to have begun his career as the minor German author Felix Paul Greve. Brilliant literary detective work by Douglas Spettigue has established that Greve published at least two novels, a volume of poetry and a verse-drama, two critical works on Oscar Wilde, and numerous translations from English and French. Most of this work in German has passed into obscurity or anonymity, although *Maurermeister Ihles Haus* has been published in English as *The Master Mason's House.* A slightly belated example of European naturalism, the novel foreshadows some of Grove's Canadian fiction in its concern for close description and the conflict between sexes and generations.

The years between 1909, when Grove left Europe in mysterious circumstances and his appearance as a teacher on the Canadian prairies in 1912, are a blank. Events recorded in his autobiography and biographical fiction are entirely untrustworthy before 1912, and frequently after, except as they bear on his novels or as data for psychoanalytic criticism. Of his first two Canadian works, each a series of essays responding to Canadian seasons, *Over Prairie Trails* has been recognised as a significant statement on the implications of man's direct confrontation with the harsh environment of Manitoba in winter. Twenty-five of the 68 short stories he also began writing in the 1920's were collected posthumously as *Tales from the Margin*; as with his novels – his uncollected poetry in English shares only the theme – their strength lies in his description of "the generally tragic reaction of the human soul to the fundamental conditions of man's life on earth." This phrase from *It Needs to Be Said*, essays on literature and nationality, is characteristic of Grove's fiction, particularly the four prairie chronicles which are the source of his contemporary reputation.

That Grove's tragic heroes were usually men and most often pioneers reflects his preoccupation with the eventual futility of human will opposed to a fate dictated by circumstances. Both *Settlers of the Marsh* and *The Yoke of Life* see young men struggling with fate in the form of sexual desire, innocence, and their swampy marginal farmland. The two older men of *Fruits of the Earth* and *Our Daily Bread* are both agrarian patriarchs, tragic in their isolation from their families, their economic success ironic because both are left only with their autocratic wills to sustain them. And each feels betrayed because his wife appears to encourage his children to challenge him by abandoning the farm, a pattern echoed in the slighter *Two Generations*, set in Ontario.

The Master of the Mill carries the idea of will to an extreme through industrial capitalism; a family dynasty and a whole town are enslaved by the mechanical evolution of a flour mill, despite one son's attempt to use it to create a miniature welfare state. *Consider Her Ways*, a science fantasy, postulates the evolution of a species of ants whose intellect is higher than that of man; humans have devolved by choosing the evolutionary path of materialistic "slavemakers." Despite Grove's glacial style, both works are increasingly associated with the beginnings of modernism in Canadian fiction.

—Bruce Nesbitt

GUSTAFSON, Ralph (Barker). Canadian. Born in Lime Ridge, Quebec, 16 August 1909. Educated at Bishop's University, Lennoxville, Quebec, B.A. 1929, M.A. 1930; Oxford University, B.A. 1933. Married Elisabeth Renninger in 1958. Music Master, Bishop's College School, 1930; Master, St. Alban's School, Brockville, Ontario, 1934; worked for the British Information Services, 1942–46. Since 1960, Music Critic, Canadian Broadcasting Corporation; since 1963, Professor of English and Poet-in-Residence, Bishop's University. Recipient: Prix David, 1935; Canada Council Senior Fellowship, 1959, Award, 1968, 1971; Governor-General's Award, 1974; A. J. M. Smith Award, 1975. M.A.: Oxford University, 1963; D.Litt.: Mount Allison University, Sackville, New Brunswick, 1973. Lives in Quebec.

PUBLICATIONS

Verse

The Golden Chalice. 1935.
Alfred the Great (verse play). 1937.
Epithalamium in Time of War. 1941.
Lyrics Unromantic. 1942.
Flight into Darkness: Poems. 1944.
Rivers among Rocks. 1960.
Rocky Mountain Poems. 1960.
Sift in an Hourglass. 1966.
Ixion's Wheel: Poems. 1969.
Theme and Variations for Sounding Brass. 1972.
Selected Poems. 1972.
Fire on Stone. 1974.

Fiction

The Brazen Tower. 1974.

Other

Poetry and Canada. 1945.

Editor, *Anthology of Canadian Poetry (English).* 1942.
Editor, *A Little Anthology of Canadian Poets.* 1943.
Editor, *Canadian Accent: A Collection of Stories and Poems by Contemporary Writers from Canada.* 1944.
Editor, *The Penguin Book of Canadian Verse.* 1958; revised edition, 1967, 1975.

Bibliography: "Ralph Gustafson: A Bibliography in Progress" by L. M. Allison and W. Keitner, in *West Coast Review,* June 1974.

Reading List: "Ralph Gustafson: A Review and Retrospect" by Robin Skelton, in *Mosaic,* 1974.

*   *   *

Ralph Gustafson is one of the most prolific, various and technically accomplished of contemporary Canadian poets. After a somewhat unpromising start with a volume of romantic lyrics and sonnets and a poetic play on the subject of King Alfred in the mid-thirties, Ralph Gustafson found an original style and an individual voice in the sardonic and tender poetry produced during and after World War II. *Flight into Darkness* assimilated, rather than shook off, influences of Hopkins and Donne and demonstrated the relevance of the metaphysical dialectic to the problem of preserving an individual integrity in the kaleidoscopic new world of the post-war breakdown.

The poet's elliptical and intensely allusive style has taken on a new subtlety and his work a wider field of interest since 1960. Travel across Canada, especially to the Rockies and the mountains of the north-west coast, and to Italy, Greece and the Scandinavian countries, has provided the stimulus for a prolific outburst of poetry in which the themes of nature, art, history, love and sex are given a highly individual treatment. As Earle Birney has written: "Ralph Gustafson has a way all his own of fusing music and passion with sophisticated feeling and graceful craft.... A stylist given to paradox and poetic wit, he is nonetheless serious, and his sensitive judgments rise from a warm heart."

—A. J. M. Smith

HALIBURTON, Thomas Chandler. Canadian. Born in Windsor, Nova Scotia, 17 December 1796. Educated at the King's College School, Windsor, Ontario, and King's College, Windsor, B.A. 1815; studied law: admitted to the Nova Scotia bar, 1820. Married 1) Louisa Neville in 1816 (died, 1840), eleven children; 2) Sarah Harriet Williams in 1856. Practised law in Annapolis Royal, Nova Scotia, from 1820; Member for Annapolis Royal, Nova Scotia House of Assembly, 1826–29; Chief Justice of the Inferior Court of Common Pleas, Nova Scotia, 1829–41; Justice of the Nova Scotia Supreme Court, 1841–56; retired to England, 1856, to Isleworth, Middlesex, 1859; Member of Parliament (U.K.) for Launceton, 1859–65. Chairman, Canadian Land and Emigration Company. Member of the Board, British North American Association of London. D.C.L.: Oxford University, 1858. *Died 27 August 1865.*

PUBLICATIONS

Collections

Sam Slick in Pictures: The Best of the Humour of Haliburton, edited by Lorne Pierce. 1956.

Fiction

The Clockmaker; or, The Sayings and Doings of Samuel Slick of Slickville. 3 vols., 1836–40.
The Letter-Bag of the Great Western; or, Life in a Steamer. 1840.
The Attaché; or, Sam Slick in England. 1843.
The Old Judge; or, Life in a Colony. 1849.
Yankee Yarns and Yankee Letters. 1852.
Sam Slick's Wise Saws and Modern Instances; or, What He Said, Did, or Invented. 2 vols., 1853; as Sam Slick in Search of a Wife, 1855.
Nature and Human Nature. 1855.
The Season Ticket. 1860.
The Courtship and Adventures of Jonathan Hombred; or, The Scrapes and Escapes of a Live Yankee. 1860.

Other

A General Description of Nova Scotia. 1823.
An Historical and Statistical Account of Nova Scotia. 2 vols., 1829.
The Bubbles of Canada. 1839.
A Reply to the Report of the Earl of Durham. 1839.
The English in America. 2 vols., 1851; as Rule and Misrule of the English in America. 1851.
An Address on the Present Condition, Resources, and Prospects of British North America. 1857.

Editor, Traits of American Humor by Native Americans. 3 vols., 1852.
Editor, The Americans at Home; or, Byeways, Backwoods, and Prairies. 3 vols., 1854.

Reading List: *Haliburton* by V. L. Chittick, 1924 (includes bibliography); *Language and Vocabulary of Sam Slick* by Elna Bengtsson, 1956; *Canadian History and Haliburton* by Stan Bodvar Liljegren, 1969.

* * *

Thomas Chandler Haliburton, the staunch Canadian Tory and author of numerous nineteenth-century political satires, continues to be read today because of his central character, Sam Slick. In seven volumes of sketches, Haliburton grants the Connecticut Yankee Slick a varied career first as a pedlar in Nova Scotia, then as an American diplomat in England, and finally as a United States Fisheries Commissioner. But Slick is most successful as a literary character in Haliburton's early works. Most notably, in *The Clockmaker, First Series*, Slick effectively voices Haliburton's own criticism of Nova Scotians and of democratic tendencies in colonial government. Slick notes that though provincials or Bluenoses possess vast natural resources, their lives consist of "only one-third work and two-thirds 'blowing time.' " He tells his travelling companion the Squire that "a false pride ... is the ruin of this country. I hope I may be skinned if it ain't." And he mocks the typical Nova Scotian who in chasing his wayward horse "runs fourteen miles to ride two because he is in a tarnation hurry." Furthermore, Slick all but labels the politicians in Halifax as con men. They are, he says, as full of smiles, compliments, and promises as "a dog is full of fleas," and he adds that the Bluenoses who can be fooled by this "deserve to be duped." Through Slick, Haliburton thus shows the Nova Scotians to be victims of their own laziness, false pride, and inefficiency, and he suggests, as he does more forcefully in later volumes, that full-fledged democracy for Nova Scotia is undesirable.

Yet Slick is not merely a spokesman for Haliburton. His Yankee trickery and excessive pride come in for their own share of ridicule. When Slick, using "soft sawder and human natur'," sells a clock worth $6.50 for $40 and a horse worth £10 for £50, the reader's reaction to him is surely ambivalent. And the reader also shares the Squire's observation that "With all his shrewdness to discover, and his humor to ridicule the foibles of others, Mr. Slick was blind to the many defects of his own character, and ... exhibited in all he said and all he did the most overweening conceit himself."

Sam Slick is then clearly of interest to the modern reader as a somewhat complex comic character. He is, however, also interesting for the place he occupies in the history of American humor. Indeed, Slick is, as V. L. Chittick observes in his critical biography of Haliburton, a direct descendent of two very different figures in American humorous writing – Jack Downing and Davy Crockett. Haliburton's use of a Yankee to advise the Nova Scotians and his choice of comic techniques were derived from the Jack Downing stories of Seba Smith. And Haliburton combines these "down-East" traits with the traditions of old Southwestern humor, for Slick's extravagant language and his clock peddling were suggested by the Davy Crockett yarns. Slick is as truly a "ring-tail roarer" as he is a Connecticut Yankee. In fact, this very conbination helped make him a folk hero who, as both Chittick and Richard Chase have commented, influenced Herman Melville's *Moby-Dick*.

Haliburton's distinctive, though largely outdated and reactionary, satiric position and his use of both Downing and Crockett make Sam Slick a rather intriguing creation. Nineteenth-century readers were so interested in this character that the volumes about him went through more than one hundred editions. And modern students of American humor continue to read Thomas Chandler Haliburton's sketches about Sam Slick, for Slick is a character who can command both personal and historical interest.

—Suzanne Marrs

HARPUR, Charles. Australian. Born in Windsor, New South Wales, 23 January 1813. Married Mary Doyle in 1850; five children. Farm worker, Hunter River, New South Wales, 1829; settled in Sydney, and worked as post office clerk and free-lance writer, 1833–39; lived in Singleton and Jerry's Plains, New South Wales, 1839–49; teacher, 1850; sheep farmer, Doyle's Creek, New South Wales, 1851–58; Assistant Gold Commissioner, Araluen, and farmer at Eurobodalla, near Nerrigundah, New South Wales, 1859–66. *Died 10 June 1868.*

Publications

Collections

Selected Poems, edited by Kenneth H. Gifford and Donald F. Hall.   1944.
(Selected Poems), edited by Donovan Clarke.   1963.

Verse

Thoughts: A Series of Sonnets.   1845.
The Bushrangers: A Play, and Other Poems.   1853.
A Poet's Home.   1862.
The Tower of the Dream.   1865.
Poems, edited by H. M. Martin.   1883.
Rose: Love Sonnets to Mary Doyle, edited by C. W. Salier.   1948.

Reading List: *Harpur, An Australian* by James Normington-Rawling, 1962; *Harpur* by Judith Wright, 1963.

* * *

The fact that Charles Harpur's parents were both convicts has occasioned surprise to some of his commentators, who remark on the moralistic emphasis of much that he wrote. But the nineteenth century, even in the colonies, was a moralistic age and, whatever his parentage, Harpur was a conforming member of the colonial intellectual community of his day. Indeed he was conventional and conformist by temperament, in spite of some peccadilloes (undefined) of his own. In his official career he was at times under a cloud for what he called "matters of minor morals and manners" and once confessed to being "somewhat lax in my sexual moralities," but in all probability the point of the criticism was mainly his fondness for the bottle. The history of colonial alcoholism has yet to be written: it will no doubt prove revealing but it will not exhibit Harpur as particularly exceptional.

Harpur first wrote for the Sydney newspapers, especially for the *Empire*, conducted by his friend Henry Parkes, who helped him to publish both prose and verse. A great deal of his writing remains uncollected. Of the poems which have reached the public (in the dubious text of *Poems*, 1883), the outstanding examples are those which, like "The Creek of the Four Graves," "A Storm in the Mountains," or "A Coast View," are most vividly and directly drawn from his experience of bush life and landscape in his early years at Windsor or from his early wanderings among the Blue Mountains. Most of his serious work is in blank verse, though a particularly charming and deservedly popular piece, "Midsummer Noon in the Australian Forest" ("Not a sound disturbs the air,/There is quiet everywhere ...") is patterned in trochaic fours. This piece in particular reflects the thoughts and mood of boyhood and has a notable colonial freshness. In poems of a more ambitiously literary cast he shows an interesting allegiance to romantic models – Milton, Wordsworth, Keats, Shelley, possibly also Tennyson – and qualifies as a true colonial Victorian, but these attempts to be literary and traditional (as in "The Tower of the Dream" or "The Witch of Hebron") do not succeed as do the simple Australian pieces, though they are interesting evidence of an awakening colonial literary sensibility.

—Brian Elliott

HARRIS, (Theodore) Wilson. Guyanese. Born in New Amsterdam, British Guiana, now Guyana, 24 March 1921. Educated at Queen's College, Georgetown, 1934–39; started land surveying, under government auspices, 1939–42: subsequently licensed to practise. Married 1) Cecily Carew in 1945; 2) Margaret Burns Whitaker in 1959. Government Surveyor, 1942–54, and Senior Surveyor, 1955–58, Government of British Guiana; settled in London, 1959; Visiting Lecturer, State University of New York at Buffalo, 1970; Writer-in-Residence, University of the West Indies, and Scarborough College, University of Toronto, 1970; Commonwealth Fellow in Caribbean Literature, University of Leeds, 1971; Visiting Professor, University of Texas, Austin, 1972, and University of Aarhus, 1973; Henfield Writing Fellow, University of East Anglia, Norwich, 1974. Delegate to the National Identity Conference, Brisbane, 1968, and to the Unesco Symposium on Caribbean Literature, Cuba, 1968. Recipient: Arts Council grant, 1968, 1970; Guggenheim Fellowship, 1973.

PUBLICATIONS

Fiction

The Guiana Quartet: Palace of the Peacock, 1960; *The Far Journey of Oudin,* 1961; *The Whole Armour,* 1962; *The Secret Ladder,* 1964.
Heartland. 1964.
The Eye of the Scarecrow. 1965.
The Waiting Room. 1967.
Tumatumari. 1968.
The Sleepers of Roraima (stories). 1970.
Ascent to Omai. 1970.
The Age of the Rainmakers (stories). 1971.
Black Marsden. 1972.
Companions of the Day and Night. 1975.
Genesis of the Clowns. 1975.
Da Silva Da Silva's Cultivated Wilderness, and Genesis of the Clowns. 1977.
The Tree of the Sun. 1978.

Verse

Fetish. 1951.
Eternity to Season. 1954.

Other

Tradition and the West Indian Novel. 1965.
Tradition, The Writer and Society: Critical Essays. 1967.

Reading List: *Harris and the Caribbaean Novel* by Michael Gilkes, 1975; *Enigma of Values* edited by Kirsten Holst Petersen and Anna Rutherford, 1975; *The Naked Design* by Hena Maes-Jelinek, 1976.

*   *   *

Though written some ten to twelve years before his first novel was published, Wilson Harris's poetry is shaped by the vision that was to inspire the form and content of his now considerable fictional "work in progress." This vision has its source in the contrasts, the perpetual motions, and the grandiose nature of his native Guyana which, for him, is informed by the two dimensions of eternity and season and by a spirit born of a history of repetitive conquest. *Eternity to Season* brings together two widely remote civilizations, the Mediterranean presented in "Troy" and the Amerindian evoked in "Behring Straits." Their meeting is indirectly recorded in a third poem called "Amazon," which brings to light the creative potentiality of a people so far divided into oppressor and oppressed, the nameless folk that figures so prominently in much of Harris's fiction. The characters in this modern epic – ordinary Guyanese labourers – are called after Greek mythological heroes, faced with the same fundamental issues as their namesakes and moved by similar aspirations. But the interplay of extremes in nature (which can either merely reflect, or else inspire a deeper vision of, man's own states), the weaving and unravelling of its seasonal manifestations, are incentives to a freedom of spirit and a reconciliation of the heterogeneous elements within themselves and their society that should help them grow out of the fixed postures imposed by history. Thus, using universal myths, Harris adapts them to the West Indian experience (as he was later to elicit new meaning from Amerindian myths in *The Sleepers of Roraima* and *The Age of the Rainmakers*) and shows man's power to change his destiny. Through his poetic sequence a Guyanese consciousness becomes attuned to its own environment (see "Recreation of the Senses") and recognizes in it the native complex of phenomena that must feed the sensibility and the imagination of individual and community. Both strongly philosophical (concerned with concepts of space and time/timelessness) and highly sensuous, this poetry is built on paradoxes; it juxtaposes contradictory images and epithets which create a configuration of material and immaterial perspectives and convey the constant interaction between outer and inner reality. Declaring the imperfection of both heaven and earth, if offers an essentially dynamic and open-ended view of existence seen as a process of reunion and separation, of alternating rebirth and death, with which man must learn to move.

This essential fluidity and its meaning are more clearly realized in Harris's fiction, for they manifest themselves through more individualized and concrete setting and characters. The first cycle of his novels, *The Guiana Quartet* and *Heartland*, offers a composite picture of the country's landscapes and its multi-racial communities. They recreate the major feats and trials of the Guyanese experience in both past and present (conquest, slavery, exploitation, violence, the suppression of racial groups). But as much as historical facts and their consequences, Harris brings to light the basic impulses and motives that generated them and the more insidious and deceptive forms of their contemporary effects. Although Harris's novels differ widely from one another in both form and content, there is a sense in which *Palace of the Peacock*, as "novel of expedition" relating a journey into both outer and inner psychological heartland, prefigures them all. It describes the dislocation of personality, the disintegration of conscious or unconscious attitudes of conquest, that his main characters experience as they progress towards the state of void and namelessness suffered by the victims of history or of individual possessiveness.

This necessary shattering of rigid ways of being leads to partial and unfinished reconstructions in the protagonist's consciousness, unfinished because the dynamic duality achieved between dissolution and recreation is, according to Harris, in the very nature of life. The predicament of Caribbean peoples (or of any individual in a given community), their eclipse and possibility of rebirth through the breakdown of totalitarian assumptions, has inspired Harris's philosophy of existence as illustrated in his fiction. It is also the source of his conception of characters, the structure of his novels and their narrative texture, and his dualistic use of imagery. Harris equates dominant forms in art with static and dominant social structures, and he tries to break out of them. The result is, in his second cycle of novels (from *The Eye of the Scarecrow* to *Ascent to Omai*), a surface fragmentation matched with an underlying sense of unity conveyed through a language that aims at reproducing the interrelatedness of all life, human and natural. In these novels Harris's double preoccupation with the creation of a genuine community and an "art of community" is more evident than ever. The protagonist's consciousness (which is also an artist's) contains the world it explores and envisages a reconciliation of its opposites through a regenerating (and regenerated) imagination and through what is presented in a more recent novel as a "Copernican revolution of sentiment."

This has led to new developments in a third cycle of novels initiated with *Black Marsden*. Here the horizons of the individual consciousness are further widened to contain mankind's "global theatre" within which an attempt is made to bridge the gap between contrasting civilizations and to throw light (as in *Companions of the Day and Night*) on the mutation by which eclipsed peoples are beginning to emerge from their buried condition. This mutation is brought to light by the capacity of individual characters to transform ("revise") given images or "paintings" of the past and harmonize them into a vision of heterogeneous wholeness (as opposed to one-sided totality). In Harris's latest novels this wholeness is perceived through a mosaic of characters and motifs who represent and bring together the two faces of tradition, one assertive and oppressive, the other hardly perceptible and usually ignored because it has grown out of the sufferings of the nameless and the oppressed.

—Hena Maes-Jelinek

HERBERT, (Alfred Francis) Xavier. Australian. Born in Port Hedland, Western Australia, 15 May 1901; moved with his family to Geraldton. Educated in local schools; Christian Brothers College, Fremantle; Technical College, Perth; University of Melbourne, diploma in pharmacy. Served in the Australian Imperial Forces in the Pacific, 1942–44. Began career as a pharmacist; also worked as a deep-sea diver, sailor, miner, and stock rider; free-lance writer from 1925; Superintendent of Aborigines, Darwin, 1935–36. Recipient: Australian Literary Society's Gold Medal, 1939; Miles Franklin Award, 1976. Lives in Redlynch, Queensland.

PUBLICATIONS

Fiction

Capricornia. 1937.
Seven Emus. 1959.
Soldiers' Women. 1961.
Larger Than Life: Twenty Short Stories. 1963.
Poor Fellow My Country. 1975.

Other

Disturbing Element (autobiography). 1963.

Reading List: Introduction by L. T. Hergenham to *Capricornia*, 1972; *Herbert* by Harry P.

Heseltine, 1973; "*Poor Fellow My Country:* Herbert's Masterpiece?" by Laurie Clancy, in *Southerly*, 1977.

* * *

What is principally striking about Xavier Herbert's writing is its energy, often rough but compellingly forceful. The reverse of the medal is an unfortunate tendency to garrulousness (a quantitative, not a qualitative fault), leading to charges of overwriting, first in *Capricornia*, increasingly with *Soldiers' Women*, and finally and most notably – because it is the most sensitive of his books – with *Poor Fellow My Country*. The first and the last are works of major importance. (*Soldiers' Women* is perhaps not major, though it is a record of Australian war-time experience under various social pressures, and does not lack vigour, which is inseparable from Herbert's explosive indignation, on any subject; but its bulk is without the drive which animates the other two.)

Capricornia and *Poor Fellow* are vehicles of a passionate nationalism thwarted by bungling, the point of view being very much Herbert's own, yet unquestionably sincere and unfadingly vehement. There are affinities with the Jindyworobak school of writers in the 1930's, now due for revision and reassessment. Herbert's attachment is to the Australian *land* (a quasi-mystical concept) and, as its animating principle, to the Aborigines seen as a displaced and degraded race. *Capricornia*, with its focus on the Top End, dwells, with political implications, on the ruthless dispossession of the tribes, the relentless devastation of the country for profit and the waste it entails, white and often absentee capitalist exploitation, corruption through miscegenation (epitomized in the story of No-name/Nawnim/Norman Shillingsworth), and the wooden-headed industrialization process exhibited in the building of the railway which goes south but ends nowhere. Herbert's handling of character is often masterly in a satirical manner (there is tremendous comic gusto in the burial service near the beginning of *Capricornia*); the model is obviously Dickens, but the eighteenth-century picaresque is discernible through it too. The impact of *Capricornia* was tremendous in the thirties and remained controversial; after it appeared Herbert was said to be *persona non grata* in certain Top End circles. Nevertheless his heart and interest remained grounded in the north, and the same subject matter provided the motivation for the more seriously and elaborately conceived *Poor Fellow My Country*. This work is also concerned with national issues, the land, the Aborigines (whom he had in the meantime studied much more closely), and the black/white problem, here given a more complex dimension. *Poor Fellow My Country* is Herbert's *apologia*. It is an unwieldy book, of an exuberance hard to do justice to; but certainly it stands out as one of the most remarkable achievements by any Australian writer, whether for its weight or its sometimes superb imaginative insights. Its narrative interest is secondary to its intense, passionate purposiveness: in the end it is a huge, gross poem rather than a story. Its compassion is enormous. So also is its truculence – but that is the man, the style, and inescapable.

Seven Emus is a slight but attractive story not without affinities with Arthur Upfield; it has a texture of odd aboriginal mysteries. *Disturbing Element* is frank, entertaining autobiography, and perhaps the bow is not too coarsely overdrawn. The short stories are lively and readable, with an economy the longer works do not aim at.

—Brian Elliott

HOPE, A(lec) D(erwent). Australian. Born in Cooma, New South Wales, 21 July 1907. Educated at the University of Sydney, B.A. 1928; Oxford University, B.A. 1931. Married Penelope Robinson in 1938; three children. English Teacher, New South Wales Department of Education, 1933–36; Lecturer in English and Education, Sydney Teachers College, 1937–45; Senior Lecturer in English, University of Melbourne, 1945–50. Professor of English, 1951–68, Library Fellow, 1969–72, and since 1968 Professor Emeritus, School of General Studies, Australian National University, Canberra. President, Australian Society of Authors, 1965–66, and Australian Association of Teachers of English, 1966–67. Recipient: Britannica-Australia Award, 1965; Ingram Merrill Foundation Award, 1969. Litt.D.: Australian National University, 1972; University of New England, Armidale, New South Wales. Fellow, Australian Academy of the Humanities. O.B.E. (Officer, Order of the British Empire), 1972. Lives in Canberra.

PUBLICATIONS

Verse

The Wandering Islands. 1955.
Poems. 1960.
(Poems), edited by Douglas Stewart. 1963.
Collected Poems 1930–1965. 1966.
New Poems 1965–1969. 1969.
Dunciad Minor: An Heroick Poem. 1970.
Collected Poems 1930–1970. 1972.
Selected Poems. 1973.
A Late Picking: Poems 1965–1974. 1978.

Other

Australian Literature 1950–1962. 1963.
The Cave and the Spring: Essays on Poetry. 1965.
A Midsummer Eve's Dream: Variations on a Theme by William Dunbar. 1970.
Judith Wright. 1975.

Editor, *Australian Poetry 1960.* 1960.

Bibliography: *Hope: A Bibliography,* 1968.

*   *   *

A. D. Hope is learned, passionate, sceptical – and in his work there is an insistent, almost fierce sense of a Western Latin tradition. Perhaps one is misled by the analogy of the Latin line. It may be that the creative impulse is a sense of discrepancy, an aching consciousness of the dissimilarity between the decorative density of Europe and the emptiness of the arid continent. More probably both impulses work together in the Australian sensibility, sharpening into positive existence the Latin elements – not just the linguistic ones – latent in the English language. Certainly, Hope is concerned, in a way most unusual for those currently writing in English, with order and coherence of feeling and with decorum and regularity in presentation. This preoccupation is a constant presence in the poetry, even if not always successfully realised.

Sexual love is a recurrent theme in Hope's work. Occasionally he celebrates it as the beneficent completion of life and personality. More frequently he is concerned with its turbidity and cruelty. He sees it as incestuous, murderous, carnivorous, or absurd. The sense of unalloyed delight in love, spiritual and physical, in, for example, "The Gateway," is comparatively rare in Hope's poetry. It is true that whenever he writes of love he conveys in a masterly way the pleasure of the senses and the richness and beauty of the body. But there is always something else breaking in, something sinister or ugly or mean. Monstrous and cogent memories from the Old Testament and the classics, which supply many of the fictions used in Hope's verse, intrude on the enclosed world of lovers: reminiscences of Circe surrounded by snouted beasts, of Lot and his daughters "crafty from fear, reckless with joy and greed," of Susannah and the seedy hatred of the Elders, of Pasiphae, filled with the bull's monstrous life, of Odysseus and passion punctured by the ridiculous commonplace.

"The End of a Journey" is an example of Hope's supple virtuosity in modulation, from the stately and measured to the casual and throwaway. It calls up the name of Yeats, and Hope has made no secret of his admiration for Yeats and "that noble, candid speech/In which all things worth saying may be said ...," as well as his strong preference for Yeats over Eliot. But while Yeats is clearly a vital (and absorbed) influence on Hope, his idiom is his own, being at once less gorgeous and Byzantine when full out and more flatly contemporary in the lower register.

There is something on occasion nasty, an occasional gratuitous revelling in the garbage-bin (and perhaps also the puritan self-hatred to which this is often a clue), in a few of Hope's poems, as for example in "Rawhead and Bloody Bones":

> This Belly too commits
> By a strange and self abuse,
> Chin-chopper's titbits,
> Meat of his own mint, chews.

But more often some quality in the tone, a quaver of amusement, a glint of wit, a touch of self-mockery, even a cry of innocent astonishment, shows that the macabre is being put to a more complicated and controlled use. It becomes an instrument instead of a dead end, another gateway through which the poet's imagination can enter an odd, disturbed, but somehow valid world.

The grotesque depends on discrepancy, on a measured friction between manner and material or on discordant experiences crushed together. Both types of contrast contribute to the effect of "The Coasts of Cerigo" and "The Kings," as they do in another startling poem in this genre, "The Dinner." "The Dinner" is of unusual interest; we see in the poem how the imagination of a poet of the grotesque hurls itself from the given situation to one at the extreme point of difference. In this violent dialectical swing the shock of the poem comes from our realising that the second stage, in spite of its immense dissimilarity, is really a development of the first, that it was there all the time grinning under the original elegant surface. We notice, too, how Hope arrives like a poetic zoologist at the second fiercely contrasting situation by a kind of compressed evolutionary method which appears in several poems. The reductive habit of the scientist, his concern with origins and causes, becomes in Hope's hands an instrument of poetic exploration.

One of Hope's favoured metres, the rhymed couplet, is handled with remarkable naturalness, and is used as the instrument of strength rather than delicacy. Indeed the heroic couplet, employed in an easy, open way, is splendidly adapted to communicate the peculiar quality of Hope's poetry which one is aware of even in his earliest, lightest pieces. This is its powerfully – almost physically – energetic character. It is muscular, quick, and solid – with the relaxed poise of the gifted athlete who brings all his force to bear rhythmically and without strain.

Hope is the least neurotic of poets and even when he is scrutinising the stages of his own childhood, as in one of his best poems, "Ascent into Hell," his regard is gravely objective without the least touch of narcissistic droop or any suspicion of anxious self-interest. Right from the start of Hope's poetic career, the reader is aware of the formed personality beneath the finished literary character. It is positive, independent, and radical in the Australian manner – in the manner of the Australian *people*, that is; the accepted Australian literary convention lacked precisely this very virtue. It is free of the fog of middle-class pretension and gentility: sharp where that was bland, and harsh where that was cosy. At the same time Hope's poetry asserts a profound commitment to the great constitutive works of the Western – not just the British – tradition, and, not only in poetry but also in thought and morality, accepts and asserts, namely, the principles of an intellectual aristocracy, and in doing so avoids, or ignores, the clogging dangers of Australian democracy. The result is a powerful and unfashionable maturity which joins a naked freshness of original response to a richly realised conception of an ideal order.

—William Walsh

HYDE, Robin. Pseudonym for Iris Guiver Wilkinson. New Zealander. Born in Cape Town, South Africa, 19 January 1906; emigrated to New Zealand, with her family, as an infant. Educated at Berhampore School, Wellington; Wellington Girls' College; Victoria College, Wellington. Had two children. Staff Member, *Dominion*, Wellington, 1923–26; thereafter worked as a free-lance writer and journalist; Editor, *New Zealand Observer*, 1931–33; lived in China, 1938; settled in England, 1938. *Died* (by suicide) *23 August 1939.*

PUBLICATIONS

Fiction

Passport to Hell: The Story of James Douglas Stark. 1936.
Check to Your King: The Life History of Charles, Baron de Thierry. 1936.
Wednesday's Children. 1937.
Nor the Years Condemn. 1938.
The Godwits Fly. 1938.

Verse

The Desolate Star and Other Poems. 1929.
The Conquerors and Other Poems. 1935.
Persephone in Winter. 1937.
Houses by the Sea and the Later Poems. 1952.

Other

Journalese (reminiscences). 1934.
Dragon Rampant: Reminiscences of the Sino-Japanese War. 1939.

Reading List: *Hyde* by Gloria Rawlinson, 1978.

*   *   *

Robin Hyde was one of the first to explore the New Zealand experience as a poet, novelist and journalist. The mid-1930's marked a transition from the colonial outlook to a growing sense of national identity, and Robin Hyde's place in this context is as vital as it was individualistic. Her prose style, evolved from a diversity of talents and attitudes, is notable for its idiosyncratic blend of poetic imagery, humour, compassionate insight, and journalistic sense of pace. Her present reputation rests largely on two books, *Check to Your King* and *The Godwits Fly*, and a number of anthologised poems.

Check to Your King remains a unique contribution to antipodean history as the first, and to date only, full-length biography of that quixotic character, Charles, Baron de Thierry. De Thierry came to New Zealand in 1837 to claim the 40,000 acre property he had purchased in 1822 through an obliging missionary. Here he intended to found a Utopia for English settlers and Maori people alike, with himself as Sovereign Chief. The collapse of his dreams is told with Robin Hyde's own mixture of humour and sympathy in a narrative that weaves 20th-century hindsight into the 19th-century background. *The Godwits Fly* was acknowledged by Robin Hyde as autobiographical. Eliza Hannay is the central character in this poetic but often acidulous story of suburban life in New Zealand. Eliza's childhood, schooldays, love affairs, and traumatic experience as a single girl escaping to Australia for the birth of a still-born child, are all vividly related. But for most readers Eliza's story is somewhat up-staged by the brilliant portraits of the Hannay parents, the socialistic father and ultra-conservative mother, within whose domestic arena are fought out the social and political arguments that continue to plague our troubled century.

Robin Hyde's other books bear witness to her versatile outlook. *Passport to Hell* recounts the early life of John Douglas Stark, a teenage Bomber in World War I. The often brutal frankness of this book still shocks even post-World War II critics. *Wednesday's Children*, by contrast, mingles shrewd humour and tenderness in its fantasy story of a lonely spinster's dreamed-up children. Robin Hyde's last book, *Dragon Rampant*, relates her travels and experiences in China during the 1938 phase of the Sino-Japanese War, including a horrific account of her life in, and escape from, the Japanese-occupied city of Hsuchowfu.

Robin Hyde's poetry had its own distinctive voice, despite the early influences of Shelley, Yeats, and the Georgian poets. She was hostile to the intellectualism of the 1930's, but even so extended her language and imagery to meet the challenge of modernism, and her own increasing consciousness of the "New Zealand experience." The result was such notable poems as "Thirsty Land," "Journey from New Zealand," and the evocative sequence "Houses by the Sea." Her travels in China also inspired some memorable poems, including a poignant essay on inter-cultural relationships, "What Is It Makes the Stranger?," which has been described by Allen Curnow (in his Introduction to *The Penquin Book of New Zealand Verse*) as "that best of poems by a New Zealander on a pilgrimage of self-discovery."

—Gloria Rawlinson

JHABVALA, Ruth Prawer. British. Born in Cologne, Germany, of Polish parents, 7 May 1927; emigrated to England, as a refugee, 1939; naturalized, 1948. Educated at Hendon County School, London; Queen Mary College, University of London, 1945–51, M.A. in English literature 1951. Married the architect C. S. H. Jhabvala in 1951; three daughters. Lived in India, 1951–77. Recipient: Booker Prize, 1975; Guggenheim grant, 1976.

PUBLICATIONS

Fiction

To Whom She Will. 1955; as *Amrita*, 1956.
The Nature of Passion. 1956.
Esmond in India. 1957.
The Householder. 1960.
Get Ready for Battle. 1962.
Like Birds, Like Fishes and Other Stories. 1963.
A Backward Place. 1965.
A Stronger Climate: 9 Stories. 1968.
An Experience of India (stories). 1971.
A New Dominion. 1973.
Heat and Dust. 1975.
How I Became a Holy Mother and Other Stories. 1976.

Plays

Shakespeare Wallah: A Film, with James Ivory, with *Savages*, by Ivory. 1973.
Autobiography of a Princess, Also Being the Adventures of an American Film Director in the Land of the Maharajas, with James Ivory and John Swope. 1975.

Screenplays: *The Householder*, 1963; *Shakespeare Wallah*, with James Ivory, 1965; *The Guru*, 1968; *Bombay Talkie*, 1970; *Roseland*, 1978; *Hullabaloo over Georgie and Bonnie's Pictures*, 1978.

Television Play: *The Place of Peace*, 1975.

Reading List: *The Fiction of Jhabvala* by Haydu M. Williams, 1973.

* * *

Ruth Prawer Jhabvala was born of Polish parents in Germany in 1927. She moved to England in 1939 and when she was twenty-four she married an Indian architect and went to live in India. All her work up to date, both her novels and short stories, has been concerned with her experience of India. At first Ruth Jhabvala was mesmerised by India; she endeavoured to steep herself completely in Indian life, and her first novels are peopled completely by Indians. This euphoria she said lasted for a decade; then the poverty, hunger, and appalling conditions of which she had at first been oblivious suddenly became visible. This led her to write *Get Ready for Battle*, her one novel that deals with India's social problems.

Ruth Jhabvala is a natural satirist with a sharp eye for hypocrisy and inconsistency. With a delicate irony that reminds one, on occasions, of Jane Austen, she exposes the foibles, weaknesses, and prejudices of her English characters while at the same time acknowledging the problems of those who come to India. Her criticism hardens when she turns to the westernized Indians. "Fashionable chatterers," is how she describes them, "hybrids, neither Western nor Indian, whose days are numbered." She is even more scathing about the latest group of travellers to India, those who belong to the westernized hippy movement. "They're the new sahibs," she says. "They detest India, they speak in the rudest way about the dirt and people cheating them, they're all day hanging outside American Express where their money comes from, then they exchange it on the black market, buy drugs, sell them and move around in filthy, torn clothes, which is a mockery of poverty in India. They're like parasites. Indians detest them and rightly so."

Since 1961 Ruth Jhabvala has collaborated with the film director James Ivory. She has scripted five films for him, including *Shakespeare Wallah* and *Autobiography of a Princess*. There is a close relationship between the latter and *Heat and Dust*, the novel that won Ruth Jhabvala the Booker prize in 1975. In the film and the novel she has turned back to the Raj. In both she has interwoven past and present, counterpointed in such a way as to pick up the slightest nuance and so achieve the maximum effect. Both are minor masterpieces conjuring up a whole world of allusion and illusion.

One has felt in Ruth Jhabvala's writing a continuing and ever-growing sense of alienation and an increasing urgency to leave India. She has now done so. This does not mean she has discarded or rejected her Indian experience. As a critic of her work, Yasmine Gooneratne, has pointed out (in *Kunapipi*, 1978), "She is not the first, nor will she be the last, writer for whom India has provided inspiration, experience, and a starting point; for perhaps her 'Indian' novel will, in the final count, represent merely a milestone along her path to the greatness for which she has the potential."

—Anna Rutherford

KENDALL, Henry (Clarence). Australian. Born near Ulladulla, New South Wales, 18 April 1839. Married Charlotte Rutter in 1868. While a boy, taken by his uncle for two-year cruise in the South Sea Islands, on a whaling ship, 1855–57; shop assistant, Sydney, 1857–61; worked in a solicitor's office, Sydney, 1862–63; worked in the Lands Department of the State Survey Department, 1863, and in the Colonial Secretary's Office, 1864–68; treated for alcoholism, 1871; Clerk in the timber business of Fagan Brothers, Camden Haven, New South Wales, 1873–80; appointed Inspector of State Forests, 1881. *Died 1 August 1882.*

PUBLICATIONS

Collections

Poetical Works, edited by Thomas T. Reed. 1966.

Verse

Poems and Songs. 1862.
The Bronze Trumpet: A Satirical Poem, with others. 1866.
Leaves from Australian Forests. 1869.
Cantata for the Opening Ceremony of the Sydney International Exhibition, music by Paolo Giorza. 1879.
Songs from the Mountains. 1880.
Orara. 1881.
Poems. 1886.

Reading List: *Kendall* by Thomas T. Reed, 1960; *Kendall* by W. H. Wilde, 1976.

*   *   *

Henry Kendall's *Leaves from Australian Forests,* his second book of verse, represents the first successful interweaving in Australian poetry of the two main strands in early colonial literature: the poetry of exile, and the poetry of native, homespun material, springing directly from the poet's own experience. What makes this verse particularly interesting is that Kendall made symbolic use of these two contrasting strands to make a personal statement. He was a complex man, and his verse is far more complex than appears on the surface. It makes no real sense, for instance, to see him as a "nature-poet": his prose contains far more precise, detailed observation of nature than his verse. It is true that he took as his region the fertile, well-watered coastline of North-eastern and South-eastern New South Wales, and that he does convey, impressionistically, the feel of its streams, its "glens," its gorges, and its rainforests. But his verse as a whole makes it plain that these for him were images of innocence, of the fresh promise of early life, and that their resemblance in parts to the green fertile pastures of England represented for him the remote, unsullied past of his own family. His poems about heat, drought and the desert, on the other hand, signified for him the painful present, the decay of his family, the death of youthful promise, the drying up of hope; while the poems about mountains, especially the fine, dedicatory "Ode" in *Songs from the Mountains,* express the longing for that idealised father-figure on whom he would like to have been able to model himself.

Kendall has been over-rated on the one hand as "the sweet singer" by those sympathetic with Victorian romanticism, and on the other for his satirical, political, and heroic verse by those with a special interest in the Augustan tradition. Some of the poems in the Augustan mode are very fine, particularly "King Saul at Gilboa," but they are not his most characteristic. A more fruitful approach to Kendall is to consider him as the first practitioner of a deliberate, sustained symbolism in Australian poetry, and of a personal and confessional verse which is again so much in vogue.

Kendall is above all, as he said himself, a poet of retrospection, of nostalgia for his family's English past. He is preoccupied with his father's fate (father, grandfather, and mother, like himself, were all drunkards) and obsessed with a sense of obscure sin, apart from alcoholic guilt. Over all the verse broods a sense of alienation ("alien" is a recurring adjective), of irremediable solitariness. In many of his best poems, there is a contrast between burning heat and coolness, and between inland Australia and England, always to Australia's disadvantage. The coolness and water are nearly always associated with purity, and the heat and dryness with sin – associations which are developed into a metaphysical opposition in poems like "Orara" and "Mooni," where the "burning outer world" is contrasted with the celestial world which is the hidden source of:

> A radiant brook, unknown to me
> Beyond its upper turn.
>
> The singing silver life I hear,
> Whose home is in the green
> Far-folded woods of fountains clear
> Where I have never been.

The poem affirms the necessity for mystery, for inaccessibility:

> Ah! haply in this sphere of change
> Where shadows spoil the beam,
> It would not do to climb that range
> And test my radiant Dream.
>
> The slightest glimpse of yonder place,
> Untrodden and alone,
> Might wholly kill that nameless grace,
> The charm of the unknown.

Kendall's life, from the beginning almost to the end, was a series of tragic losses, of parents, lover, children, friends, position, and self-respect, though the last few years of it were calm and productive of domestic contentment, in spite of poor health. But the ineradicable sense of the poet's conviction of his own unworthiness fills the reader with unease, especially in poems like "Beyond Kerguelen" (a reminiscence of a voyage as a youth on a sailing ship) and "The Curse of Mother Flood." The curious subterranean resemblances of these two poems suggest that there is much about Kendall still to be explained.

—Dorothy Green

KENEALLY, Thomas (Michael). Australian. Born in Sydney, New South Wales, 7 October 1935. Educated at St. Patrick's College, Strathfield, New South Wales; studied for the priesthood and studied law. Served in the Australian Citizens Military Forces. Married Judith Martin in 1965; two daughters. High school teacher in Sydney, 1960–64; Lecturer in Drama, University of New England, Armidale, New South Wales, 1968–70. Recipient: Commonwealth Literary Fund Fellowship, 1966, 1968, 1972; Miles Franklin Award, 1967, 1968; Captain Cook Bi-Centenary Prize, 1970. Fellow, Royal Society of Literature, 1973.

PUBLICATIONS

Fiction

The Place at Whitton. 1964.
The Fear. 1965.

Bring Larks and Heroes. 1967.
Three Cheers for the Paraclete. 1968.
The Survivor. 1969.
A Dutiful Daughter. 1971.
The Chant of Jimmie Blacksmith. 1972.
Blood Red, Sister Rose. 1974.
Gossip from the Forest. 1975.
Moses the Lawgiver. 1975.
Season in Purgatory. 1976.
Victim of the Aurora. 1977.
Passenger. 1979.

Plays

Halloran's Little Boat (produced 1966).
Childermass (produced 1968).
An Awful Rose (produced 1972).

Television Play: *Essington*, 1974.

Other

Ned Kelly and the City of Bees (juvenile). 1978.

*   *   *

Thomas Keneally, most prolific among contemporary Australian novelists, was first concerned with situations related more or less closely to his own experience – *The Place at Whitton*, a horror-story set in a Catholic seminary, *The Fear*, recalling a wartime childhood, and *Three Cheers for the Paraclete*, a tale of a liberal Catholic priest's conflicts with his superiors.

His third novel, *Bring Larks and Heroes*, made his name. It is set in early Australian convict society, exploring what Keneally has called "the working or absence of conscience" among characters in an intolerable but also inescapable situation. In the same passage he speaks of being "obsessed with the notion of Australia as a country alien to the people who live in it," and something of this informs *The Chant of Jimmie Blacksmith*, the story of a half-aborigine who sought a place in white society, was rebuffed, went berserk, and was pursued to his death by outraged white Australians.

Vitality and vivacity characterise Keneally, the man and the author. He always has a story to tell and is keen to find new ways of telling it, whether in grotesque allegory as in *A Dutiful Daughter*, quasi-historical narrative in *Blood Red, Sister Rose*, the account of Joan of Arc, who fascinates him, or the staccato passages of *Gossip from the Forest* about the Armistice of 1918. Recent novels are *Season in Purgatory*, the story of an English doctor with Yugoslav partisans, and *Victim of the Aurora*, in which Keneally returns to Antarctic exploration, a theme which he had already used in *The Survivor*. *Victim of the Aurora* betrays that tendency to the sensational which characterised some of his earlier work.

He has also written plays. *An Awful Rose* is about a psychologically disorientated religious, and *Halloran's Little Boat* derives from *Bring Larks and Heroes*.

—Arthur Pollard

KINGSLEY, Henry. English. Born in Barnack, Northamptonshire, 2 January 1830; brother of the writer Charles Kingsley. Educated at King's College School, London, 1844–50; Worcester College, Oxford, 1850–53. Married his cousin Sarah Kingsley in 1864. Left university, with other students, to work in the Australian goldmines: worked in Australia, possibly as a drover on a sheep and cattle station in Victoria, as a mounted policeman in Sydney, and as a miner at the Caledonian Goldfields, near Melbourne, 1853–57, then returned to England; settled in Wargrave, near Henley-on-Thames, 1864; Editor, *Edinburgh Daily Review*, 1869–71; settled in London; full-time novelist from 1871. Died 24 May 1876.

PUBLICATIONS

Collections

Novels, edited by C. K. Shorter. 8 vols., 1894–95.

Fiction

The Recollections of Geoffry Hamlyn. 1859.
Ravenshoe. 1862.
Austin Elliot. 1863.
The Hillyars and the Burtons. 1865.
Leighton Court. 1866.
Silcote of Silcotes. 1867.
Mademoiselle Mathilde. 1868.
Stretton. 1869.
Old Margaret. 1871.
Hetty and Other Stories. 1871.
The Harveys. 1872.
Hornby Mills and Other Stories. 1872.
Oakshott Castle. 1873.
Reginald Hetherege. 1874.
Number Seventeen. 1875.
The Grange Garden. 1876.
The Mystery of the Island. 1877.

Other

Tales of Old Travel Re-Narrated. 1869.
The Lost Child (juvenile). 1871.
The Boy in Grey and Other Stories and Sketches (juvenile). 1871.
Valentin: A French Boy's Story of Sedan (juvenile). 1872; revised edition, 1874.
Fireside Studies. 1876.

Editor, *Robinson Crusoe,* by Defoe. 1868.

Reading List: *Kingsley: Towards a Vindication* by S. M. Ellis, 1931 (includes bibliography); *Some Novels of Kingsley* by Leonie Kramer, 1954; *Kingsley and Colonial Fiction* by John

Barnes, 1971; *The Neglected Brother: A Study of Kingsley* by William H. Scheverle, 1971.

* * *

Although he has always been overshadowed by his elder brother, Charles, Henry Kingsley has had a special significance for Australian readers because of his first novel, *Geoffry Hamlyn*. This romance of Australian pioneering was for generations of Australians "the best Australian novel that has been, and probably will be written," as the novelist, Marcus Clarke, wrote. However, to the "offensively Australian" novelist, Joseph Furphy, at the turn of the century, it seemed "an exceedingly trashy and misleading novel," and he dismissed Kingsley's heroes as "slender-witted, virgin-souled, overgrown schoolboys." The very force of Furphy's attack was indicative of the novel's continuing appeal, which lies essentially in its idealised and heroic version of pioneering life. Kingsley transplanted in Australia his ideal of English country life, a group of landed families maintaining the traditional standards of the "big house," and with considerable skill incorporated in his narrative the more picturesque and dramatic elements of Australian station life: a bushfire, a kangaroo hunt, cattle branding, a child lost in the bush, and encounters with aborigines and bushrangers.

Kingsley had gone to the colonies during the gold rushes, and had known only hardship and disappointment during his stay of over four years. In the novel, published on his return to England, he wrote of the years before the gold discoveries in the character of an elderly and successful colonist, looking back in a spirit of affectionate reminiscence on the experiences he shared with his friends. The first volume of *Geoffry Hamlyn* (it was the usual three-volume length) is set in England, and reads like stock romance, written under the strong influence of Walter Scott. It is only when Kingsley moves his characters to Australia at the beginning of the second volume that it becomes more than that. In general, novels about life in the colonies in the mid-nineteenth century tended to be fact – more or less accurate – dressed up as fiction. Of those writing about Australia, Kingsley best realised the possibilities of the subject for romantic fiction.

None of Kingsley's later novels was as good as *Geoffry Hamlyn*, and as a writer he declined rather than matured. In his second novel, *Ravenshoe*, he turned from the land of "sunshine and adventure" to write of what he called, at the end of *Geoffry Hamlyn*, "that charming English country life, the like of which, I take it, no other country can show." This novel has been the most highly praised of all his work, but it is more notable for what it promises than for what it achieves in its handling of the theme of loss of identity which is worked out in a series of complicated family relationships. In *The Hillyars and the Burtons*, which contains a finely evocative account of Chelsea where Kingsley spent his childhood, he again traced the fortunes of a group of colonists, and here he gets closer to the realities of colonial life of his time than he does in *Geoffry Hamlyn*.

Kingsley was not a strong or original writer; increasingly, his fiction was lacking in formal integrity and derivative in its notions of character and motive. Yet, however defective his later work, he never wholly lost his power to create an exciting episode and to evoke the beauty of the landscapes in England and Australia which he had viewed with the eyes of an amateur painter and naturalist. He lacked the intellectual depth and moral stamina of his famous brother, but he had a genuine, if minor, talent for romance. And because of the accident of history he has had an influence on the development of writing in Australia, where he is still read and studied widely.

—John Barnes

KLEIN, A(braham) M(oses). Canadian. Born in Montreal, Quebec, 14 February 1909. Educated at McGill University, Montreal, B.A. 1930; University of Montreal, B.C.L. 1933; called to the Bar of Quebec, 1933. Married Bessie Koslov in 1935; two sons, one daughter. Practised law in Montreal from 1933; subsequently also worked in public relations. Director of Education, Zionist Organization of Canada, 1936–37; Editor, *Canadian Zionist* and *Canadian Jewish Chronicle*. Special Lecturer in Poetry, McGill University, 1946–47; a Founder, *Preview*, *First Statement*, and *Northern Review* magazines, Montreal, in the 1940's. Recipient: Edward Bland Fellowship Prize, 1947; Governor-General's Award, 1949; Province of Quebec Literary Prize, 1952; Kovner Memorial Award, 1952; Lorne Pierce Gold Medal, 1957. *Died 21 August 1972.*

PUBLICATIONS

Collections

Collected Poems, edited by Miriam Waddington. 1974.

Verse

Hath Not a Jew.... 1940.
Poems. 1944.
The Hitleriad. 1944.
Seven Poems. 1947.
Huit Poèmes Canadiens (En Anglais). 1948.
The Rocking Chair and Other Poems. 1948.

Play

Hershel of Ostropol, in *Canadian Jewish Chronicle* 26 and 27, 1939.

Fiction

The Second Scroll. 1951.

Other

Translator, *From Palestine to Israel*, by Moishe Dickstein. 1951.
Translator, *Of Jewish Music, Ancient and Modern*, by Israel Rabinovitch. 1952.

Reading List: *Klein* edited by Tom Marshall, 1970; *Klein* by Miriam Waddington, 1970.

*   *   *

The condition of being Jewish, or more positively the fierce sense of Jewish identity, is the generating feeling and the constitutive, substantial experience of all A. M. Klein's best poetry up to *The Rocking Chair*, where indeed it is still present if in a calmer, more implied manner. And the condition of being Jewish, as Klein felt it, is more perplexing a question than whether or not Klein lost his faith, or regained it, or didn't, as though this were a matter that could be defined in a chart or scheduled on a timetable once for all. The pattern of being Jewish revealed in *Hath Not a Jew* and *Poems* includes, it seems to me, at least three notes: first, the consciousness of the divine as totally other, as the unnameable, unqualified, and absolute ground of being; second, the enjoyment of a rich immediacy of life, and custom, habit, rite, symbol, food, of innumerable significant particulars; and third, stretching between the consciousness of the first and the living of the second, the vital sense of a continuous tradition: a tradition, it may be added, in which doubt and the questioning of reason have their place. To celebrate, to recall, to represent, and in doing so, to defend: these are the aims, not always separate one from another, which inform many of the poems, aims themselves subordinate to the larger purpose of sustaining the tradition and defining the human reality of the Jewish experience.

Klein's evocation of the Jewish sensibility is both broad and fine, joining the accuracy of the intent observer to the warmth of recovered personal experience. It includes history, the poet's own life, festivals, characters, fairy-tales, legends, psalms, the memories of a child, as well as carolling children's songs. It takes in not only sages and saints, children and elves, spidery logicians and gloomy puritans, but also Chaucerian rogues, clowns and dwarfs, unabashed hypocrites, the querulous devotee, the furious preacher, the bawling junk man, the matchmaker – "cupid in a caftan" – and the deprecating self, like the mild Moses who so spared everybody trouble "that in his tomb/He will turn dust to save some room." The rich portraiture and the manifold differences of an old complex society derive from the poet's own life, and especially his childhood, and from a wide erudition fed on Jewish learning and European tradition. The tone is variously reverential and sarcastic, disillusioned and pious, indignant and resigned, witty and sad; the diction is biblical and lavish but also homely and colloquial; and the rhythms, whether solemn or nimble, organic and unforced: the whole is the product of a rarely civilised mind in possession of a marvellously humane tradition.

The world constituted in these Jewish poems has solidity and bloom and an intensely living presence, and just occasionally a taste of molasses. It is also torn and stricken by history, its existence constantly menaced and intermittently ravaged, so that one receives the paradoxical impression of something both ancient and brimming with life standing precariously on the edge of dissolution or – since this phrase may suggest the possibility of inward collapse – expecting some oceanic invasion. Working from deep within this tradition Klein's sensibility manifests the opposed attitudes corresponding to the double character of the Jewish universe: the tenderness and reverence for the humanity embodied in the tradition together with the keenest relish for its unique savour, and the hard reaction to external hostility, a stony pride of resistance.

Klein is one of the few serious Canadian writers untroubled by the problem of identity and free of its attendant, modish hysteria about alienation. His work has in it all the richness, the inclusiveness, of the Jewish character and mind, the product of an ancient, sophisticated, oppressed, and still living tradition. At the same time he is alert to the several nuances of contemporary Canadian life, and the marriage of a suffering but essential serenity with a nervous and accurate response make for a poetry which is altogether independent but also splendidly central.

The Rocking Chair, Klein's final appearance as a poet (apart from the verse in *The Second Scroll*), came out in 1948. A case could be made for its being the best single book of verse ever to be published in Canada and one of the best in English anywhere since the war. Not that it is by any means flawless. There is more than a suspicion of North American molasses in "The Sugaring," as well as rather too much unassimilated Hopkins, a degree too feverish a nostalgia in "The Sisters of the Hôtel Dieu," and more than a hint of linguistic intoxication in "Montreal," repeated readings of which leave one irritated at its contrivance and artificiality. In the achieved poems an imagination charged with history and a consciousness clarified by an ancient coherence are brought to bear on persons, places, things, processes, and conditions – saltily, stingingly, fresh, and Canadian. The past in the poet is locked with the present in the object. The effect is to produce a reality which has both roundness and depth. Each clean surface is backed by a thick supporting texture of allusion and reference from history, literature, traditional assumption, and racial memory and luminous Jewish reverence for the life of the word and the book, an unbroken order or human experience. The interior of the refrigerator deepens into a Laurentian village, "tiered and bright"; the commercial bank opens into a flowering jungle concealing silent beasts pawing the ground; bakers at their ovens appear as Levites at their altars; the dress manufacturer as he fishes becomes "at the end of his filament,/a correspondent of water and of fish"; the Quebec liquor commission store turns magically into Ali Baba's cave, offering the pleasures of "the sycophancy of glass, the palm's cool courtier,/and the feel of straw, all rough and rustical"; the break-up of the ice raises from the tomb "the pyramid fish, the unlockered ships,/and last year's blue and bloated suicides"; the social guilt implied in the pawnshop makes it "Our own gomorrah house,/the sodom that merely to look at makes one salt."

Klein's creative generosity, that is, works first to establish the being of the object, event, place, or experience at the centre of the poem, and then to enlarge its significance. The essential quality and inward shape sustain the meaning. So that, for example, in "The Rocking Chair," "Grain Elevator," "The Spinning Wheel," the thing becomes an image, the image a symbol, the symbol a style of life and feeling. Each of the major poems in *The Rocking Chair* testifies to the ease and authority with which Klein treats his Canadian theme. In this work we see detachment telescoped into identity. In none of the poems is the Jew in Klein ousted by the Canadian. Rather a sensibility fed by one of the most ancient sources of human quality shows itself superbly qualified to cope with a new hospitality to experience, and to see in the Canadian example the universal human thing. So that these poems work by combining distance and intimacy, perspective and grain, and find "the thing that makes them one" in what is common and human.

> Or find it, find it, find it commonplace
> but effective, valid, real, the unity
> In the family feature, the not unsimilar face....

The ironic truth of our strange age, enunciated by Klein in "Portrait of the Poet as Landscape," a poem notable for its wit, strength, and undespairing acceptance of a despairing part, is that the making of these creative connections, the articulation of our human experience, is the business of someone who has been dismissed from real society, the poet. He is missing but not missed, "a Mr. Smith in a hotel register – /incognito, lost...."

—William Walsh

LAMMING, George (Eric). Barbadian. Born in Barbados in 1927. Taught school in Trinidad and Venezuela; host of a book review programme for the West Indian Service of the BBC, London, 1951; member of the faculty of the University of the West Indies, Kingston, Jamaica, 1968. Recipient: Guggenheim Fellowship, 1954; Maugham Award, 1957. Lives in London.

PUBLICATIONS

Fiction

In the Castle of My Skin. 1953.
The Emigrants. 1954.
Of Age and Innocence. 1958.
Season of Adventure. 1960.
Water with Berries. 1971.
Natives of My Person. 1972.

Other

The Pleasures of Exile. 1960.

Editor, *Cannon Shot and Glass Beads.* 1974.

*   *   *

George Lamming's main subject is the development of West Indian society. He seeks to give an imaginative insight into the growth of West Indian sensibility and through that to offer an interpretation of West Indian history. The history of the West Indies consists of a series of journeys, explored by Lamming both as metaphors and as historical facts.

In the Castle of My Skin is a recreation of the world that came into being as a result of the first journey. It recreates the childhood hopes and dreams of a poor West Indian boy with great tenderness, and at the same time it traces the gradual destruction of a village community and the emergence of a new black middle class. *The Emigrants* looks at the meaning of the journey to England which was undertaken by thousands of West Indians during the 1950's. The book explores the clash between the idea of England and the reality as it was experienced by the emigrants. *Of Age and Innocence* is concerned with the voyage back to the West Indies and the journey into independence. It is very concretely a political novel. Lamming says himself that it is "a study in the last stages of colonialism." *Season of Adventure* takes the form of an interior journey, a quest for identity sparked off by the ceremony of souls which is witnessed by the main character. The book is a search for what is to be the cultural base of a true West Indian identity. *Natives of My Person* ends the cycle with the beginning. Set in the sixteenth century, it tells the story of the original journey which was responsible for the society and aspirations of *In the Castle of My Skin.*

In his books Lamming grapples with vital issues, and he has made a major contribution to the understanding of the West Indian psyche. The novels are written with great care and attention to minute details; in this way action, symbol, and metaphor are carefully worked into a coherent pattern. There is, however, a tendency for this carefulness to be overdone which accounts for the occasional heavy and overwritten passages.

—Kirsten Holst Petersen

LAMPMAN, Archibald. Canadian. Born in Morpeth, Ontario, 17 November 1861. Educated at F. W. Barron's School, Gore's Landing, Ontario; Cobourg Collegiate Institute, Ontario (Foundation Scholar); Trinity College School, Port Hope, Ontario, 1876–79; Trinity College, University of Toronto, 1879–82, B.A. in classics 1882. Married Maud Playter in 1887; one son, one daughter. Assistant Master, Orangeville, Ontario High School, 1882; Clerk, Post Office Department, Ottawa, 1883–99. *Died 9 February 1899.*

PUBLICATIONS

Collections

The Poems, edited by Duncan Campbell Scott. 1900.
Selected Poems, edited by Duncan Campbell Scott. 1947.

Verse

Among the Millet and Other Poems. 1888.
Lyrics of Earth. 1895
Alcyone. 1899.
At the Long Sault and Other New Poems, edited by E. K. Brown and Duncan Campbell Scott. 1943.

Other

Letters to Edward William Thomson, 1890–1898, edited by Arthur S. Bourinot. 1956.

Reading List: *The Poetry of Lampman* by Norman Guthrie, 1927; *Lampman, Canadian Poet of Nature* by Carl Connor, 1929; *Ten Canadian Poets* by Desmond Pacey, 1958; *Lampman* edited by Michael Gnarowski, 1970.

* * *

Long regarded by Canadian literary historians as the country's most accomplished nineteenth-century poet writing in English, Archibald Lampman himself recognised that he was "a minor poet of a superior order." His particular excellence lies in his close and accurate description of the extremes of the Canadian environment, and in his ability to express the relationship between those extremes and human moral dilemmas. A talented technician and facile versifier, he also wasted much of his time writing lengthy and undistinguished verse dramas characteristic of what A. J. M. Smith has called "colonial romanticism." Yet by the end of his brief career, his few experiments with free verse and a variety of imagism mark him as the first Canadian poet with a twentieth-century sensibility. That these two aesthetic impulses operated simultaneously defines the quandary of the colonial poet. Nevertheless the more "realistic" of his poems strongly influenced his contemporaries until the late 1920's.

Lampman saw only two volumes of his poetry through the presses: *Among the Millet*, published at his own expense, and *Lyrics of Earth*, issued in an edition of only 550 copies. Both were well received in the small literary community of the time (he was known as well in the United States through his contributions to periodicals in Boston and New York). He died shortly after correcting the proofs of *Alcyone*, and twelve copies were pulled from the standing type. His friend and literary executor Duncan Campbell Scott used Lampman's manuscript books to compile the *Poems*, which went through four editions between 1900 and 1915. Scott was also responsible for a volume of selected poetry in 1925; for a new collection of work from the manuscripts, radically edited in collaboration with E. K. Brown in 1943; and for another selection in 1947. Uniquely for a nineteenth-century Canadian poet, much of Lampman's work remained in print during the half-century between the time of the "Confederation poets" who flourished in the 1890's and the publication explosion of poetry beginning in the late 1950's.

Widely anthologised as a "nature poet" (his derogatory term for critical estimates in his lifetime), Lampman also associated with a miniscule group of pale socialists in Ottawa, and occasionally wrote poetry of social protest. Most of this work remained unpublished until after he died, as nearly one-quarter of his known poetry still does. Collections of some of his prose – he indulged in literary journalism for sixteen months, and lectured infrequently – suggest that he was attracted to large humanistic and literary topics, but that his taste and judgement were at best eccentric. He has not always been well served by his editors, especially of his correspondence. Unabridged and uncensored, it reveals a tortured, confused, and insecure private personality at odds with general critical views of the publicly accessible poet.

—Bruce Nesbitt

LAURENCE, (Jean) Margaret. Canadian. Born in Neepawa, Manitoba, 18 July 1926. Educated at the University of Manitoba, Winnipeg, B.A. 1947. Married John F. Laurence in 1947 (divorced, 1969); one son and one daughter. Lived in Somali and Ghana, 1950–57, and in England; Writer-in-Residence, University of Toronto, 1969–70. Recipient: Beta Sigma Phi award, 1960; President's Medal, University of Western Ontario, 1961, 1962, 1964; Governor-General's Award, 1967, 1975; Canada Council Senior Fellowship, 1967, 1971; Molson Prize, 1974, 1975. Lives in Penn, Buckinghamshire.

PUBLICATIONS

Fiction

This Side Jordan. 1960.
The Tomorrow-Tamer: Stories. 1963.
The Stone Angel. 1964.
A Jest of God. 1966; as *Rachel, Rachel,* n.d.
The Fire-Dwellers. 1969.
A Bird in the House (stories). 1970.
The Diviners. 1974.
Heart of a Stranger (stories). 1977.

Other

The Prophet's Camel Bell (travel). 1963; as *New Wind in a Dry Land*, 1964.
Long Drums and Cannons: Nigerian Dramatists and Novelists, 1952–66. 1968.
Jason's Quest (juvenile). 1970.

Editor, *A Tree for Poverty*. 1954.

Reading List: *Laurence* by Clara Thomas, 1969 (includes bibliography).

* * *

Although nearly half of Margaret Laurence's work has been prompted by her seven years in Africa, her major accomplishment in fiction is an inter-related cycle of short stories and four novels centred in Manawaka, Manitoba, a fictional small town on the Canadian prairies. Her African experience in Somaliland (Somalia) and the Gold Coast (Ghana) eventually resulted in a volume of translations, a travel memoir, a novel, a collection of short stories, and a series of critical essays. Laurence's book for children, *Jason's Quest*, is a moral fable set in London. *Heart of a Stranger* brings together 19 sketches written between 1964 and 1975 as "travels and entertainments ... a record of the long journey back home."

A Tree for Poverty, translations of Somali oral poetry and prose published by the government of the Protectorate, includes examples of formal poetic *gabei*, oral folk-tales, and love-poems, *belwo*. *The Prophet's Camel Bell*, a conventional travel narrative, reflects her recurrent urge to view "the whole of life through different eyes." Laurence's attempts to break out of her preconceptions as an anglophone Canadian in Africa, together with her anti-imperialist sentiments, were strengthened during her five years in Ghana. Her first novel, *This Side Jordan*, dramatises the complexities of the strained racial truce existing in the Gold Coast immediately before independence. The mixed success of her seeing with "different eyes" and experimenting with different voices is also suggested in *The Tomorrow-Tamer*, stories first published between 1956 and 1963. The figure of exile is dominant, whether expatriate or Ghanaian; political statement – particularly deft in the allegory of "Godman's Master" – emerges through both oral tale and tightly constructed Western narrative. The title of Laurence's only book of literary criticism, essays on Nigerian dramatists and novelists writing from 1952 to 1966, is taken from a poem by the late Christopher Okigbo: "long drums and cannons:/the spirit in the ascent." Written before the Biafran War, the longer essays on Soyinka, Clark, Achebe, Tutuola, and Ekwensi (six other authors are considered briefly) explore the ambiguities of language, religion and culture inherent in that difficult "ascent."

Laurence's Canadian fiction may not originally have been conceived as an organic cycle, but the five works taken together comprise an unusually coherent examination of five generations of women. The stories collected as *A Bird in the House* are told by Vanessa MacLeod, a girl growing through the ten terrifying years from childhood to adolescence. Laurence has called the book "fictionalized autobiography"; it is a sensitive tracing of one woman's view of the social history of western Canada during the depression and the Second World War. The small town of Manawaka, with its claustrophobic social structure, immigrant mix, and comfortably visible signs of ancestry, becomes a place which must be escaped in *A Jest of God*. In her late thirties and unmarried, Rachel Cameron is haunted by her mother and religion and sexual frustration. (A film version, *Rachel, Rachel*, inexplicably transposed the location of the novel to the New England area of the United States, thus missing the peculiarly Canadian inhibitions of the 1960's which were vividly evoked by the text.) Rachel's older sister, Stacey MacAindra, is a 39-year-old housewife in Vancouver, smothered by her four children and husband in *The Fire-Dwellers*. Her bitter and humorous memories, fantasies, conversation, and inner thoughts end only in acceptance of her entrapment, despite the ostensible freedom offered by an affair and her life away from Manawaka.

The Diviners, Laurence's most ambitious novel, is recounted by a 47-year-old novelist, Morag Gunn. Her illegitimate teen-age daughter, Pique, was deliberately conceived with a Métis father (mixed French-Canadian and native Indian), and represents the most important of Morag's three quests: for her immediate past, through her own adoptive parents in Manawaka; for her ancestral past, by living in England and taking a Scots lover; and for herself, through her fiction and Pique. The daughter unknowingly brings these three together by melding a series of symbols begun early in Laurence's career. *The Stone Angel*, chronologically her second novel and perhaps her finest, completes the cycle. Hagar Shipley's dying memories are compressed into two or three weeks, when she is 90. Indomitable, sensual, and crusty, she escapes incarceration in an old age home by running away from her elderly children; she finally accepts that her pride has been destructive, and her raging against death comes to be an affirmation of love, both past and present.

—Bruce Nesbitt

LAWLER, Ray(mond Evenor). Australian. Born in Footscray, Melbourne, Victoria, in 1921. Left school at age 13. Married Jacklyn Kelleher; three children. Worked in a factory; then as an actor in variety, Brisbane; as actor and producer, National Theatre Company, Melbourne; and as Director, Melbourne University Repertory Company. Recipient: *Evening Standard* award, 1957.

PUBLICATIONS

Plays

Cradle of Thunder (produced 1949).
Summer of the Seventeenth Doll (produced 1955). 1957.
The Piccadilly Bushman (produced 1959). 1961.
The Unshaven Cheek (produced 1963).
A Breach in the Wall (televised 1967; produced 1970).
The Man Who Shot the Albatross (produced 1972).
Kid Stakes (produced 1975).
Other Times (produced 1976).

Television Plays: *A Breach in the Wall*, 1967; *Cousin Bette* (serialization), from the novel by Balzac, 1971; *The Visitors* (serialization), from the novel by Mary McMinnies, 1972; *Two Women* (serialization), from the novel by Alberto Moravia, 1972; *Mrs. Palfrey at the Claremont*, from the novel by Elizabeth Taylor, 1973; *Seeking the Bubbles*, in *The Love School* series, 1975; *True Patriots All*, 1975; *Husband to Mrs. Fitzherbert*, 1975.

* * *

With his first professionally produced play, *Summer of the Seventeenth Doll*, Ray Lawler established a landmark in Australian drama. The play awakened his country's theatre from a prolonged sleep of adolescence through an incisive attack on national myths, stereotypes, and the clichéd language of earlier plays. Although Lawler's later work has not had the same power or effect, Australian drama unquestionably owes him an enormous debt.

The Doll, as it is known, explores the "mateship" of two sugarcane cutters who work half the year, and their carefree life with their women during the "layoff." This idyllic society, symbolized by the kewpie doll brought home each summer, is torn apart on its seventeenth anniversary, when the characters are forced to see the insubstantiality of their relationships. Blinded by the Australian national myths of male friendship, the submissiveness of women, and the superiority of the country over the city, they are helpless before the inexorable advance of their own lives. Lawler's precise use of the understatement inherent in Australian colloquial speech and his relentless exposure of the myths and illusions surrounding the characters, as well as his strong dramatic construction, give the play the ring of authenticity and an intense power.

After *The Doll*, Lawler left Australia, settling ultimately in Ireland, and his next play, *The Piccadilly Bushman*, examined the ambivalent attachment of Australians to their mother country. Although it reflects Lawler's continuing investigation of national myths, it is weakened first by the already-diminished force of the very myth he was attacking, and second by a failure to weld his theme to his characters, who remain at such a distance from one another that the play's resolution seems contrived and unsatisfying.

Although most of Lawler's work has been realistic, he has worked in other styles. *The Unshaven Cheek*, for example, progresses largely through flashbacks, but his most serious experiment with non-realistic drama has been *The Man Who Shot the Albatross*. This study of Captain Bligh (of the *Bounty*), who served as governor of New South Wales from 1806 to 1808, mixes present experience, memory, and fantasy on a stage divided into several performance areas, and provides a fascinating look at this curious man's mind.

Lawler's most recent work, however, *Kid Stakes* and *Other Times* (known with *The Doll* as *The Doll Trilogy*) marks a return, both theatrically and dramatically to his first success. The new plays mirror the realism and the structure of *The Doll*, and deal with the same characters in years previous to that play's action, but neither has the intensity and life of before. Despite his lack of development, Ray Lawler is nonetheless a talented and able dramatist, whose place in Australian drama is secure.

—Walter Bode

LAWSON, Henry (Hertzberg). Australian. Born in Grenfell, New South Wales, 17 June 1867. Educated at the Eurunderee Public School, 1876; became deaf at age 9. Married Bertha Bredt in 1896 (separated, 1902), one son and one daughter. Held various jobs from age 13 – builder, apprentice to a railway contractor, house painter, and clerk; contributed to his mother's magazines, *Republican* and *Dawn*, Sydney, in the 1880's, and to the *Bulletin*, Sydney, in the 1890's; worked for the labour paper *Brisbane Boomerang* in 1892; laborer in Bourke, 1892–93; telegraph lineman in New Zealand, 1893–94; gold prospector in Western Australia, 1896; teacher, Mangamauna Maori School, 1897–99; returned to Sydney, 1900; lived in London, 1900–03, then settled in Sydney. *Died 2 September 1922.*

Publications

Collections

Prose Works. 2 vols., 1935.
Stories, edited by Cecil Mann. 3 vols., 1964.
Collected Verse, edited by Colin Roderick. 3 vols., 1967–69.
Letters, 1890–1922, edited by Colin Roderick. 1970.
Short Stories and Sketches, 1888–1922, edited by Colin Roderick. 1972.
Autobiographical and Other Writings, 1887–1922, edited by Colin Roderick. 1972.
The Portable Lawson, edited by Brian Kiernan. 1976.

Fiction

Short Stories in Prose and Verse. 1894.
While the Billy Boils (stories). 1896.
On the Track, and Over the Sliprails (stories). 1900.
The Country I Come From (stories). 1901.
Joe Wilson and His Mates (stories). 1901.
Children of the Bush (stories and poems). 1902; as *Send Round the Hat* and *The Romance of the Swag*, 2 vols., 1907.
The Rising of the Court and Other Sketches in Prose and Verse. 1910.
Mateship: A Discursive Yarn. 1911.
The Strangers' Friend. 1911.
Triangles of Life and Other Stories. 1913.

Verse

In the Days When the World Was Wide and Other Verses. 1896.
Verses, Popular and Humorous. 1900.
When I Was King and Other Verses. 1905.
The Elder Son. 1905.
The Skyline Riders and Other Verses. 1910.
A Coronation Ode and Retrospect. 1911.
For Australia and Other Poems. 1913.
My Army, O, My Army! and Other Songs. 1915; as *Songs of the Dardanelles and Other Verses*, 1916.
Selected Poems. 1918.
The Auld Shop and the New. 1923.
Joseph's Dream. 1923.
Winnowed Verse. 1924.
Popular Verses. 1924.
Humorous Verses. 1924.
Poetical Works. 3 vols., 1925.
The Men Who Made Australia. 1950.

Other

A Selection from the Prose Works, edited by George Mackaness. 1928.

Bibliography: *An Annotated Bibliography of Lawson* by George Mackaness, 1951.

Reading List: *Lawson* by Stephen Murray-Smith, 1962; *Lawson: The Grey Dreamer* by Denton Prout, 1963; *Lawson* by Colin Roderick, 1966, and *Lawson: Criticism 1894–1971* edited by Roderick, 1972; *Lawson among Maoris* by Bill Pearson, 1968; *The Receding Wave: Lawson's Prose* by Brian E. Matthews, 1972.

*   *   *

In his verses, sketches, stories, and journalistic pieces, Henry Lawson wrote from his experiences as a worker in both country and city. He was seen as the most representative of Australian writers by his own and later generations: the founder of a native, vernacular literary tradition, and the imaginative historian of the decades between the gold rushes and Federation, the period of transition between a rural and an urban-industrial Australia.

Although he first gained recognition for his ballads, which remain popular, his high critical reputation today rests on the best of his stories. From his early writing, it is apparent that Lawson had two models for fiction. One was the conventional magazine story with a heavily contrived situation and resounding ending – whether melodramatic or humorous. The other was the journalistic sketch, ostensibly not fictional at all. An early example is the genre piece "A Day on a Selection," published in the *Bulletin*, a weekly to which readers contributed paragraph-length sketches and anecdotes typical of Australian life.

Lawson continued to write conventionally plotted stories. Such humorous examples as "The Loaded Dog" and "The Iron Bark Chip" are still entertaining. His artistic development, however, can be seen in terms of his extending, without contrivance, the realistic sketch towards fuller, more rounded stories. His most frequently anthologized story, "The Drover's Wife," is an early example: it is a sketch of a typical bushwoman's experiences shaped around an anecdote.

In 1892, assisted by the *Bulletin*, Lawson visited the real "bush" for the first time. Appalled by the reality that conflicted with its conventional depiction, he determined, like his contemporary Joseph Furphy, to reject "literary" falsification. "The Union Buries Its Dead," a developed sketch of an up-country funeral, explicitly rejects "literary" sentimentality. Still a strikingly modern story, it is an imaginatively realistic appraisal of men on the margin of human existence. Lawson employs an involved narrator speaking colloquially, so avoiding the sense of a patronizing presentation of "low" characters, and the conventional representation of "low" speech found in earlier stories. From this time on, apart from humorous stories, he was to prefer such narration, and to move the sketch towards fuller dramatic and thematic complexity.

The typical Lawson story, which blends reportage with an unobtrusive imaginative structuring, is about adversity in the bush or the city, the consolation of mateship, and the temptation to escape into drink or nostalgia. Two good examples are "Going Blind" and "Telling Mrs. Baker": these illustrate his concern with the need for sympathy in a harsh world, and, particularly, the ambiguous role of the imagination. The imagination can sustain but it can also delude – an underlying personal preoccupation throughout Lawson's work.

The height of his achievement is the sequence of four "Joe Wilson" stories. (Lawson frequently wrote clusters of stories with common characters or themes, but complained that editors disregarded his intentions.) First published in England while he was there in 1901, the sequence brings together all his major themes and presents them with dramatic amplitude. Through Joe Wilson's narration, Lawson resolves his own romantic and realistic tendencies in a recognition of the transient nature of happiness in an adverse world. The sequence contains the greatest single example of his fiction, "Water Them Geraniums." Nothing else in Australian writing, of whatever length, sees further into the disappointments of life yet manages also to find its redeeming significance.

—Brian Kiernan

LAYTON, Irving (Peter). Canadian. Born in Neamtz, Rumania, 12 March 1912; emigrated to Canada in 1913. Educated at Alexandra Public School, Montreal; Byron Bing High School, Montreal; MacDonald College, Sainte Anne de Bellevue, Quebec, B.Sc. in agriculture 1939; McGill University, Montreal, M.A. 1946. Served in the Canadian Army, 1942–43: Lieutenant. Married 1) Betty Frances Sutherland in 1946; one son, one daughter; 2) the writer Aviva Cantor in 1961, one son. Lecturer, Jewish Public Library, Montreal, 1943–58; high school teacher in Montreal, 1954–60; Part-time Lecturer, 1949–65, and Poet-in-Residence, 1965–66, Sir George Williams University, Montreal; Writer-in-Residence, University of Guelph, Ontario, 1968–69. Since 1969, Professor of English Literature, York University, Toronto. Co-Founding Editor, *First Statement,* later *Northern Review,* Montreal, 1941–43; former Associate Editor, *Contact* magazine, Toronto, and *Black Mountain Review,* North Carolina. Recipient: Canada Foundation Fellowship, 1957; Canada Council Award, 1959, 1967, and senior arts grant and travel grant, 1973; Governor-General's Award, 1960; President's Medal, University of Western Ontario, 1961. D.C.L.: Bishop's University, Lennoxville, Quebec, 1970. Lives in Toronto.

PUBLICATIONS

Verse

Here and Now. 1945.
Now Is the Place: Stories and Poems. 1948.
The Black Huntsman. 1951.
Cerberus, with Raymond Souster and Louis Dudek. 1952.
Love the Conqueror Worm. 1953.
In the Midst of My Fever. 1954.
The Cold Green Element. 1955.
The Blue Propeller. 1955.
The Blue Calf and Other Poems. 1956.
Music on a Kazoo. 1956.
Improved Binoculars: Selected Poems. 1956.
A Laughter in the Mind. 1958; augmented edition, 1959.
A Red Carpet for the Sun: Collected Poems. 1959.
The Swinging Flesh (poems and stories). 1961.
Balls for a One-Armed Juggler. 1963.
The Laughing Rooster. 1964.
Collected Poems. 1965.
Periods of the Moon. 1967.

The Shattered Plinths. 1968.
The Whole Bloody Bird (obs, aphs, and pomes). 1969.
Selected Poems, edited by Wynne Francis. 1969.
Five Modern Canadian Poets, with others, edited by Eli Mandel. 1970.
Collected Poems. 1971.
Nail Polish. 1971.
Lovers and Lesser Men. 1973.
Selected Poems. 1974.
The Pole Vaulter. 1974.
Seventy-Five Grub Poems. 1974.
The Unwavering Eye: Selected Poems, 1969–1975. 1975.
Selected Poems. 1977.

Other

Engagements: The Prose of Layton, edited by Seymour Mayne. 1972.
Taking Sides: The Collected Social and Political Writings, edited by Howard Aster. 1977.

Editor, with Louis Dudek, *Canadian Poems 1850–1952.* 1952
Editor, *Pan-ic: A Selection of Contemporary Canadian Poems.* 1958.
Editor, *Poems for 27 Cents.* 1961.
Editor, *Love Where the Nights Are Long: Canadian Love Poems.* 1962.
Editor, *Anvil: A Selection of Workshop Poems.* 1966.
Editor, *Poems to Colour: A Selection of Workshop Poems.* 1970.
Editor, *Anvil Blood: A Selection of Workshop Poems.* 1973.

Bibliography: "Layton: A Bibliography in Progress 1931–1971" by Seymour Mayne, in *West Coast Review,* January 1973.

Reading List: "That Heaven-Sent Lively Ropewalker, Layton" by Hayden Carruth, in *Tamarack Review,* Spring 1966; *Layton* by Eli Mandel, 1969.

* * *

Irving Layton is undoubtedly the most prolific of Canadian poets; since his first book, *Here and Now,* appeared in 1945, hardly a year has passed without another volume or at least a brochure of his verse appearing. He has also written some short stories and a few polemical essays, the best of which were collected by his fellow poet, Seymour Mayne, in a volume entitled *Engagements.* As an editor he has been involved in a number of North American verse magazines, including *First Statement* and *Contact* in Canada, and *Black Mountain Review* in the United States. But is is essentially as a poet that Layton sees himself and makes sure that the world sees him.

Layton is a poet of various styles and equally various levels of quality; he belongs to no school and has borrowed effects from all of them. Readers are often puzzled that so much energy and so much genuine talent should be accompanied by such an evident lack of self-criticism – a lack which means that more than half of any volume Layton publishes is likely to consist of poems that should never have passed beyond the writer's desk. At the same time they are often stirred to admiration by his best poems which, as Northrop Frye has pointed out, reveal Layton as "an erudite elegiac poet, whose technique turns on an aligning of the romantic and the ironic."

Layton's work can really be considered in three phases. He first published, largely at his own expense, a series of thin volumes of verbose and flamboyant verses strong in self-advertisement and in cheap shocks for respectable minds. By the early 1950's, however, Layton was beginning to find himself; in volumes like *The Cold Green Element* his real power as a poet of compassion, in love with the splendour and sad with the transience of life, begins to emerge. It is admirably exemplified in the poem – obliquely celebrating Layton's hero Nietzsche – "The Birth of Tragedy":

> A quiet madman, never far from tears,
>   I lie like a slain thing
>   under the green air the trees
> inhabit, or rest upon a chair
>   towards which the inflammable air
> tumbles on many robins' wings;
>   noting how seasonably
>   leaf and blossom uncurl
> and living things arrange their death,
> while someone from afar off
> blows birthday candles for the world.

The period from about 1953 to 1965 can perhaps be regarded as the climax of Layton's career, when he wrote the series of vivid and moving lyrics and elegies that make his *Collected Poems* of 1965 the true core of his work, its best items rarely equalled by any of the many volumes he has published during the years since then.

It was during the 1960's that Layton moved out of small-press printing into commercial publication, while writing as prolifically as he had always done; in this decade also he became the most popular among the Canadian poets who during this period turned public entertainer, his combination of inspired rhetoric and sexual clowning making him popular with the young audience of the period's counter-culture. What has been really surprising, in view of the volume of work that Layton has continued to produce, is the lack of real change or development in his work since the middle 1960's. His poetry remains essentially didactic and constantly agitated; one encounters repeatedly – and to the degree of boredom – the familiar obsessions with sex, with the poet's ego, with the poet's detractors, with those the poet despises, the glorifications of creativity and life as against order and art, of Dionysus as against Apollo, the hatred of critics, the love for the trival and juvenile epigram, the deliberate Nietzschean waywardness. What has declined is the immediacy of the lyric urge. In recent years Layton has written no poems that really compare with the earlier series of splendidly passionate and compassionate elegies on the human and animal condition which place Layton among the best Canadian poets.

—George Woodcock

LEACOCK, Stephen (Butler). Canadian. Born in Swanmoor, Isle of Wight, Hampshire, England, 30 December 1869; emigrated to Canada with his family, 1876. Educated at Upper Canada College, Toronto, until 1887; University of Toronto, 1887–91, B.A. 1891; University of Chicago, 1899–1903, Ph.D. in political economy 1903. Married Beatrix Hamilton in 1900 (died, 1925), one son. Taught at Uxbridge High School, 1889, Upper Canada College,

1891–99, and the University of Chicago, 1899–1903; Lecturer in Political Science, 1903–06, Associate Professor of Political Science and History, 1906–08, William Dow Professor of Political Economy, and Head of the Department of Political Science and Economics, 1908–36, and Professor Emeritus, 1936–44, McGill University, Montreal. Toured the Empire as a Rhodes Trust Lecturer, 1907–08. Recipient: Lorne Pierce Medal, 1937. Litt.D: Brown University, Providence, Rhode Island, 1917; D.Litt.: University of Toronto, 1919; D.H.L.: Dartmouth College, Hanover, New Hampshire, 1920. Fellow, Royal Society of Canada, 1910. *Died 28 March 1944.*

PUBLICATIONS

Collections

The Best of Leacock, edited by J. B. Priestley.   1957; as *The Bodley Head Leacock,* 1957.

Fiction and Sketches

Literary Lapses: A Book of Sketches.   1910.
Nonsense Novels.   1911.
Sunshine Sketches of a Little Town.   1912.
Behind the Beyond, and Other Contributions to Human Knowledge.   1913.
Arcadian Adventures with the Idle Rich.   1914.
The Methods of Mr. Sellyer: A Book Store Study.   1914.
Moonbeams from the Larger Lunacy.   1915.
Further Foolishness: Sketches and Satires on the Follies of the Day.   1916.
Frenzied Fiction.   1918.
The Hohenzollerns in America, with the Bolsheviks in Berlin and Other Impossibilities.   1918.
Winsome Winnie and Other New Nonsense Novels.   1920.
Over the Footlights.   1923.
College Days.   1923.
The Garden of Folly.   1924.
Winnowed Wisdom.   1926.
Short Circuits.   1928.
The Iron Man and the Tin Woman, with Other Such Futurities.   1929.
Laugh with Leacock: An Anthology.   1930.
The Leacock Book, edited by Ben Travers.   1930.
Wet Wit and Dry Humour.   1931.
Afternoons in Utopia.   1932.
The Dry Pickwick and Other Incongruities.   1932.
The Perfect Salesman, edited by E. V. Knox.   1934.
Funny Pieces.   1936.
Here Are My Lectures and Stories.   1937.
Model Memoirs and Other Sketches from Simple to Serious.   1938.
Too Much College; or, Education Eating Up Life.   1939.
Laugh Parade.   1940.
My Remarkable Uncle and Other Sketches.   1942.
Happy Stories, Just to Laugh At.   1943.
Last Leaves.   1945.

Play

Q, with Basil Macdonald Hastings (produced 1915). 1915.

Verse

Marionettes' Calendar 1916. 1915.
Hellements of Hickonomics in Hiccoughs of Verse Done in Our Social Planning Mill. 1936.

Other

Elements of Political Science. 1906; revised edition, 1921.
Baldwin, LaFontaine, Hincks: Responsible Government. 1907; revised edition, as *Mackenzie, Baldwin, LaFontaine, Hincks,* 1926.
Adventures of the Far North. 1914.
The Dawn of Canadian History. 1914.
The Mariner of St. Malo: A Chronicle of the Voyages of Jacques Cartier. 1914.
Essays and Literary Studies. 1916.
The Unsolved Riddle of Social Justice. 1920.
My Discovery of England. 1922.
Economic Prosperity in the British Empire. 1930.
Mark Twain. 1932.
Back to Prosperity: The Great Opportunity of the Empire Conference. 1932.
Charles Dickens: His Life and Work. 1933.
Lincoln Frees the Slaves. 1934.
Humor, Its Theory and Technique. 1935.
Humor and Humanity. 1937.
My Discovery of the West: A Discussion of East and West in Canada. 1937.
All Right, Mr. Roosevelt. 1939.
Our British Empire: Its Structure, Its History, Its Strength. 1940.
Canada: The Foundations of Its Future. 1941.
Montreal, Seaport and City. 1942.
How to Write. 1943.
My Old College, 1843–1943. 1943.
Canada and the Sea. 1944.
While There Is Time: The Case Against Social Catastrophe. 1945.
The Boy I Left Behind Me (autobiography). 1946.

Editor, *Lahontan's Voyages.* 1932.
Editor, *The Greatest Pages of Dickens.* 1934.
Editor, *The Greatest Pages of American Humor.* 1936.

Bibliography: *Leacock: A Check-List and Index of His Writings* by Gerhard R. Lomer, 1954.

Reading List: *Leacock, Humorist and Humanist* by Ralph L. Curry, 1959; *Leacock: A Biography* by David M. Legate, 1970.

* * *

The first sketch in Stephen Leacock's first humorous work, *Literary Lapses*, describes the narrator's panic-stricken attempt to open a bank account, and money and the antics of those who possess it are the most prominent *leitmotifs* in his subsequent writing. He made his first career as a lecturer in economics, and his second as a quick-witted observer of the quirks and blemishes of the life-style of the brave new world of transatlantic consumerism. When he says, blandly, in *The Garden of Folly*, "Business having become the most important thing in life, it is quite clear that it is destined to swallow up the feeble things that we used to call literature and art," he is recording an uneasy possibility.

Those who admire Leacock have stressed the satirical edge in his writing; others have insisted that he let himself be blunted by success. Certainly his portrait-caricatures of the rogues of big-city as of small-town business are affectionate and even admiring. Perhaps that means that his strength is in irony rather than satire. That could certainly be argued of the best pieces in *Sunshine Sketches of a Little Town*, *Arcadian Adventures with the Idle Rich*, and *The Garden of Folly*. The first of these is set in Mariposa, a "typical" Canadian small-town, the second among the inhabitants of Plutoria Avenue in a "typical" North American city. The stories in each are elaborate anecdotes, spun out by Leacock's ingenuity. He is a raconteur, not, as some have believed, a novelist *manqué*. He is also a parodist, a punster, a compiler of comic lists, and frequently the inventor of spurious documents. *The Garden of Folly* is an example of Leacock's non-fictional style, that of the moral (or mock-moral) essayist. *Nonsense Novels*, *Frenzied Fiction*, and *Winsome Winnie* contain some of his happiest frolics. The ideal reader of Leacock is one who is willing to be silly and ready to indulge an urge to chuckle like the would-be compositors of his first two books, who, he says, found it impossible to print them because they kept falling back "suffocated with laughter and gasping for air."

—Peter Thomson

LEE, John (Alexander). New Zealander. Born in Dunedin, 31 October 1891. Educated in local schools. Served as a sergeant in the New Zealand Expeditionary Forces in World War I, 1915–18: lost an arm in combat; Distinguished Conduct Medal. Married Marie E. Guy in 1919; three children. Farm and factory worker until 1909; joined the New Zealand Public Works Department, 1910; Labour Member of Parliament for Auckland East, 1922–28, and for Grey Lynn, 1931–43: Under-Secretary to the Minister of Finance, 1936–39; Controller of the State Housing Department, 1939–40; expelled from the Labour Party, 1940; Director, Printing Service Ltd., and Democratic Property Ltd., Auckland, 1940–46; Managing Director, Vital Books Ltd., Auckland, from 1950. President, Auckland Rugby League, 1935–40; Member of the Council, New Zealand Booksellers Association, 1959–61; Honorary President, New Zealand Branch, P.E.N., 1969. LL.D.: University of Otago, Dunedin, 1965. Lives in Auckland.

PUBLICATIONS

Fiction

Children of the Poor. 1934.

The Hunted. 1936.
Civilian into Soldier. 1937.
The Yanks Are Coming. 1943.
Shining with the Shiner (stories). 1944.
Shiner Slattery. 1964.

Other

Four Years of Failure: A History of the Smash-and-Grab Government. 1935.
Labour and Prosperity. 1935.
Labour Has a Plan. 1935.
Returned Soldiers – Vote Labour. 1935.
Banking and the New Zealand Labour Government. 1937.
Money Power for the People. 1937.
Socialism in New Zealand. 1938.
A Letter Which Every New Zealander Should Read. 1939.
Debt-Hold, Leasehold, Bankhold, or Prosperityhold. 1940.
The Democratic Labour Party in Business and the Home. 1940.
Expelled from the Labour Party for Telling the Truth. 1940.
Hitler. 1940.
I Fight for New Zealand. 1940.
Mussolini, Apostle of Violence. 1940.
This Debt Slavery (speeches). 1940.
Manufacture or Perish. 1941.
Simple on a Soap-Box (autobiography). 1964.
Rhetoric at the Red Dawn. 1965.
The Lee Way of Speech Training. 1965; as *The Lee Way to Public Speaking*, 1965.
Delinquent Days (autobiography). 1967.
Political Notebooks. 1973.

*   *   *

John Lee wrote both fact and fiction, and it is not easy to draw a sharp line between the two. The reason for this is that all his fictional works have a strong autobiographical element.

He first rose to fame as a writer in 1934 when *Children of the Poor* was published. The narrator-protagonist is the child Albany Porcello, who grows up in the slums of Dunedin in the 1890's. It is a story of a stunted childhood, and of the unremitting poverty which eventually leads to Albany's being made a ward of the state. The book was published anonymously, and created a scandal when it was revealed that it was written by Lee, who was by then a Labour member of parliament. The conservative New Zealand public found it offensive that one of their leading figures and representatives should admit to a delinquent past, a prostitute sister, a drunken grandmother, and a childhood of squalor and poverty. For John Lee made it clear that it was his own past he was revealing through the story of Albany Porcello. No doubt it was the conditions of the 1930's that reminded Lee of his own deprived childhood and led him to write his first novel. He followed it with a sequel, *The Hunted*, which continued the story of Albany and followed his career through reform school, his escape and final recapture. In 1967 Lee published his autobiography, *Delinquent Days*. If one compares the dedication to this work with that of *Children of the Poor* the very close link between fact and fiction is made obvious:

"To daughters of the poor. To errant brats and guttersnipes. To eaters of left-overs, the wearers of cast-offs. To slaves of the wash-tub and scrub-brush, whose children, nevertheless, go to hell. To teachers who adopt, through compulsion or desire, the method of the barrack square. To juvenile culprits fleeing from the inescapable hand of the law, sometimes called justice ... THIS STORY OF THE GUTTER." (*Children of the Poor*)

"To Welfare and Probation Officers, Magistrates and Judges, Jailors and Police, Enlightened or Obscurantist Ministers of Justice and Attorney Generals ... is dedicated this book of one who somehow survived." (*Delinquent Days*)

Lee wrote other works – including a series of very successful sketches, *Shining with the Shiner* and *Shiner Slattery*, which tell of his days when he roamed the New Zealand countryside carrying his swag – but his chief importance lies in his two socially committed novels, *Children of the Poor* and *The Hunted*. In these two works he drew a distinction, not between the good and the bad, but between the "haves" and the "have-nots," and showed that social injustice and poverty could exist as easily in the New World as in the Old.

—Anna Rutherford

LIVESAY, Dorothy. Canadian. Born in Winnipeg, Manitoba, 12 October 1909. Educated at Trinity College, University of Toronto, 1927–31, B.A. 1931; the Sorbonne, Paris, diploma, 1932; London Institute of Education, 1959; University of British Columbia, Vancouver, M.Ed. 1966. Married Duncan Macnair in 1937 (died); one son and one daughter. Social worker, Englewood, New Jersey, 1935–36, and Vancouver, 1936–39, 1953–55; Correspondent, Toronto *Daily Star*, 1946–49; Documentary Scriptwriter, Canadian Broadcasting Corporation, 1950–55; Lecturer in Creative Writing, University of British Columbia, 1955–56, 1965–66; High School Teacher, Vancouver, 1956–58; UNESCO English Specialist, Paris, 1958–60, and Zambia, 1960–63; Writer-in-Residence, University of New Brunswick, Fredericton, 1966–68; Associate Professor of English, University of Alberta, Edmonton, 1968–71; Visiting Lecturer, University of Victoria, British Columbia, 1974–75; Writer-in-Residence, University of Manitoba, Winnipeg, 1975–77, and University of Ottawa, 1977. Editor, *CV/II* magazine. Recipient: Governor-General's Award, 1945, 1948; Lorne Pierce Medal, 1947; President's Medal, University of Western Ontario, 1954; Canada Council grant, 1958, 1964, 1971, 1977. D.Litt.: University of Waterloo, Ontario, 1973.

PUBLICATIONS

Verse

Green Pitcher. 1928.
Signpost. 1932.

Day and Night. 1944.
Poems for People. 1947.
Call My People Home. 1950.
New Poems. 1955.
Selected Poems 1926–1956. 1957.
The Colour of God's Face. 1965.
The Unquiet Bed. 1967.
The Documentaries: Selected Longer Poems. 1968.
Plainsongs. 1969; revised edition, 1971.
Disasters of the Sun. 1971.
Collected Poems: The Two Seasons. 1972.
Nine Poems of Farewell 1972–1973. 1973.
Ice Age. 1975.

Fiction

A Winnipeg Childhood (stories). 1973.

Other

Right Hand, Left Hand (memoirs). 1977.

Editor, *The Collected Poems of Raymond Knister.* 1949.
Editor, with Seymour Mayne, *Forty Women Poets of Canada.* 1971.

Reading List: "Livesay: The Love Poetry" by P. Stevens, in *Canadian Literature,* Winter 1971; "Livesay's Two Seasons" by Robin Skelton, in *Canadian Literature,* Autumn 1973.

* * *

Dorothy Livesay's efflorescence in her later years is remarkable in Canadian poetry. Her two early collections demonstrated a controlled, precise lyric verse, often praised at the time for its "feminine images" and "intense feeling." Reviewers of her overtly political work from the 1930's were reluctant to acknowledge her leftist views, although her reputation as a craftsman was well established by the time her *Selected Poems* appeared; after E. J. Pratt and Earle Birney, and with F. R. Scott, A. M. Klein, and A. J. M. Smith she was considered to be one of the country's half-dozen best poets. With seven new volumes published during the last two decades, together with her *Collected Poems* and a selection, she is now widely regarded as the most mature voice in Canadian feminist poetry. Livesay has long insisted on a "way of looking" that is distinctively from a "womans's eye," and she has edited an anthology of women poets from Canada. *Collected Poems* and *Ice Age* include all her substantial poetry.

Livesay's semi-autobiographical prose reminiscences of her youth, *A Winnipeg Childhood*, suggest the constrained literary environment reflected in her first precocious volume of verse and its sequel. Her personal preoccupations through the 1930's and later can be summed up as "love, politics, the Depression and feminism." A communist for much of that time, she was only occasionally heard in public as a revolutionary; the appearance of *Day and Night* during the Second World War revealed the strength of her commitment to the struggle against fascism and industrial capitalism. Despite the obtrusive rhetoric, her sympathies with the victims of economic and military oppression are strongly realised in the longer poetry of the 1930's and 1940's: the title poems of *Day and Night* and *Call My People Home* (a radio documentary on Japanese-Canadians interned in 1941), and "Prophet of the New World," about the nineteenth-century mystic and revolutionary Riel.

New Poems marked a substantial development. Her usual tight control, frequently emphasized by rhyme, was sharpened by a more objective tone. Later collections continue to demonstrate the dialectic structure of her work, while increasingly they embody "that pull between community and private identity that is characteristic of being a woman." In *The Unquiet Bed* Livesay had found an appropriately intimate voice, one patterned by natural speech rhythms yet preserving the sharp irony which characterizes her most acute work. The "great game" of love can involve both "an itch for the seven-inch/reach" and confidence that "aloneness is the only bliss." In her latest poetry she is secure in her stance as both observer and participant, poet and woman, listening with her "third ear" and knowing that "in the small womb/lies all the lightning."

—Bruce Nesbitt

LOWRY, (Clarence) Malcolm (Boden). English. Born in Liscard, Cheshire, 28 July 1909. Educated at the Braeside School, Cheshire; Caldicote School, Hitchin, Hertfordshire, 1915–23; Leys School, Cambridge, 1927; Weber's School of Modern German, Bonn, 1928; St. Catharine's College, Cambridge, 1929–32, B.A. in English 1932. Married 1) Jan Gabrial in 1934 (divorced, 1940); 2) Margerie Bonner in 1940. Lived in Mexico, 1937–39, Canada, 1940–54, and Sussex, England, 1954–57. Recipient: Governor-General's Award, Canada, 1962. *Died 27 June 1957.*

PUBLICATIONS

Collections

Selected Poems, edited by Earle Birney and Margerie Lowry.   1962.
Selected Letters, edited by Harvey Breit and Margerie Lowry.   1965.

Fiction

Ultramarine.   1933; revised edition, 1962.
Under the Volcano.   1947.
Hear Us, O Lord, from Heaven Thy Dwelling Place (stories).   1961.
Lunar Caustic, edited by Earle Birney and Margerie Lowry.   1968.
Dark as the Grave Wherein My Friend Is Laid, edited by Douglas Day and Margerie Lowry.   1968.
October Ferry to Gabriola, edited by Margerie Lowry.   1970.
China, and Kristbjorg's Story in the Black Hills.   1974.

Play

Notes on a Screenplay for F. Scott Fitzgerald's Tender Is the Night, with Margerie Lowry.   1967.

Verse

Psalms and Songs, edited by Margerie Lowry. 1975.

Bibliography: by Earle Birney, in *Canadian Literature 8,* Spring 1961.

Reading List: *Lowry* by Daniel B. Dodson, 1970; *Lowry: The Man and His Work* edited by George Woodcock, 1971; *Lowry* by W. H. New, 1972; *Lowry: A Biography* by Douglas Day, 1973; *Lowry: His Art and Early Life* by Muriel Bradbrook, 1974; *The Art of Lowry* edited by Anne Smith, 1978.

* * *

Many novelists — Balzac, Zola and Proust among them — have thought of their novels as being parts of some larger life work that would provide an imaginative portrait of their age but would also make some major social or philosophic or psychological statement about the condition of man. Malcolm Lowry, whose reading was vast and whose philosophical wanderings were adventurous and wide, was such an author, but, unlike the other writers I have mentioned, he completed little of the great structure he had foreseen when he conceived the fictional cycle "The Voyage That Never Ends." In fact, during his lifetime Lowry published only two books, *Ultramarine* and, fourteen years later, *Under the Volcano,* the novel on which his reputation now rests. He also published a few stories and poems in periodicals. One novel that appears to have been virtually complete — *In Ballast to the White Sea* — was destroyed when his cabin on Burrard Inlet in British Columbia was burnt down. But the greater part of Lowry's work remained unfinished and unpublished at the time of his death in 1957.

The reasons why Lowry never completed a book after he finished *Under the Volcano* in 1945 are obviously complex, and his alcoholism was probably less a cause than a concurrent symptom of the monumental unsureness that prevented him from being satisfied with almost everything he wrote in his later years. Yet was it unsureness? Could it not have been also a sense that life was continually revising itself? Interpreted in either way, Lowry's failure to complete the ambitious works with which his later years were consumed suggests that he had come to a point when the barriers between art and life were so shredded that they hardly existed.

Certainly this view is borne out by a study of Lowry's books, both those he passed for publication and those which after his death were revised by others and published in his name. *Ultramarine,* written in his very early twenties, is patently autobiographical, based on the voyage which Lowry himself undertook as cabin boy in 1928 on a freighter bound for the China Seas. Only in *Under the Volcano* and in a few of the short stories — notably "The Forest Path to the Spring" — does one have a sense of emerging from the self that was Malcolm Lowry. *Under the Volcano* has often been treated — justly I think — as Lowry's only successful novel. In this story of the almost self-induced murder of Geoffrey Firmin, an alcoholic British consul, the human drama is integrated in a closely knit formal and metaphorical structure, largely cabbalistic in its origins, and the sinister aspects of Mexican life combine with the splendour of the country's topography to symbolize the metaphysical overtones. The strong autobiographical element — for the Consul's disintegrating marriage and his alcoholic adventures in a small Mexican town can easily be correlated to Lowry's own experiences — is exemplarily subsumed in the fictional.

In other words, one can believe in the Consul and his world in the sense of crediting them with an autonomous existence, which is more than one can say for the two novels published after Lowry's death, *Dark as the Grave Wherein My Friend Is Laid* and *October Ferry to Gabriola.* Both of these novels were put together by Lowry's widow Margerie, in one case with the co-operation of Douglas Day, out of a chaos of varying drafts, so that in neither case is one sure that the published version really represents Lowry's final wishes. What is quite clear is that both novels, for all their passages of splendid writing, are amazingly unresolved when one considers how long Lowry was working on them. Wilderness, the leading character of *Dark as the Grave*, and Ethan Llewelyn in *October Ferry*, are all too palpably varying personae who have never completely detached themselves from their creator, and the adventures they undergo, on a trip to Mexico and a trip to Vancouver Island respectively, are elaborations of narratives already contained in Lowry's notebooks, and never sufficiently detached for us to be confident about describing them as fiction. Curiously enough, the very journey symbolism, the escape that in each case does not succeed, is indicative of Lowry's desire to escape from himself, and his difficulty in doing so. It is perhaps significant that the one piece among the works published after his death which stands complete as a work of fictional art is "The Forest Path to the Spring," an extraordinarily evocative novella whose territory never goes beyond the woods and the sea around the little shack in Canada which he loved so deeply. For once, Lowry was not trying frantically – and, because of his eagerness, failing – to escape from himself. More than anything else he wrote in his later years, this brief work is the true Paradiso that balances the Inferno of *Under the Volcano*.

—George Woodcock

MACKENZIE, Kenneth (Ivo). Pseudonym: Seaforth Mackenzie. Australian. Born in Perth, Western Australia, in 1913. Educated at Muresk Agricultural College; studied arts and law at the University of Western Australia, Perth. Married Kate Loveday in 1934; one daughter and one son. Lived in Kurrajong from 1948. Recipient: Commonwealth Literary Fund grant, 1948, 1951, 1955. *Died in January 1955.*

PUBLICATIONS

Collections

The Poems, edited by Evan Jones and Geoffrey Little. 1972.

Verse

Our Earth. 1937.
The Moonlit Doorway. 1944.

Fiction

The Young Desire It. 1937.
Chosen People. 1938.
Dead Men Rising. 1951.
The Refuge: A Confession. 1954.

Other

Editor, *Australian Poetry, 1951–52.* 1952.

Reading List: "A Dead Man Rising: The Poetry of Mackenzie" in *Australian Quarterly 36,* 1964, and *Mackenzie,* 1969, both by Evan Jones; "Mackenzie's Novels" by Peter Cowan, in *Meanjin 24,* 1965; "Mackenzie's Fiction" by R. G. Geering, in *Southerly 26,* 1966.

* * *

Many of Kenneth Mackenzie's poems were not published until 1972, seventeen years after his death. On the basis of his two early books *Our Earth* and *The Moonlit Doorway,* it was possible to regard him mainly as a love-poet, sensual and egoistic. The new volume, almost but not quite complete, revealed that the love-poems were far less dominant than poems about death and nothingness, and that fear of death gave way to a quiet longing for death, or "his brother sleep," submerged beneath the fear in the early verse. Mackenzie's decision to be a writer, and above all, a poet, in a country in which, in his day, it was almost impossible to exist by the pen, kept him all his short life in stark poverty, not mitigated by his alcoholism. One of the editors of his *Poems* has pointed out the remarkable parallels between his life and Dylan Thomas's, though Thomas seems to have died of too much success while Mackenzie succumbed to failure. Yet the disorders of his life were not reflected in the tone of his verse, which became more measured, serene, and controlled as outward circumstances deteriorated. His essential solitariness, with his retreat to the bush, became in the end a source of strength, and the last poems, especially those about the natural world, have a freshness, a joy, and a confidence which have no other source except in this sense of freedom from all earthly ties.

Existential guilt and anxiety are constant notes in the verse from the beginning, as the first poem in *The Moonlit Doorway,* "Heat," indicates. It is the first of many "river" poems, which gains an ironic significance from hindsight: Mackenzie was to drown in a river at the age of forty-two. Of the thirty-five poems on the subject of death, some are associated with love, but many more with fear or anxiety. Mackenzie's adult world is on the whole a painful, candle-lit world, full of dark presences and the need for expiation which is never quite remorse. Many of the poems lament the lost innocence of childhood, and parenthood was not for him a source of joy, as it was for Judith Wright, but an occasion for apology or a plea for forgiveness:

> What shall I say to you in my defence?
> What can I say to mate you with your stars?
> I shall say this: I got you unawares.

The sense of guilt, the anxiety, are conveyed quite often in images of murder, as in "Going Upstairs," for example, a striking if melodramatic poem, which nevertheless displays a gift for the theatrical in the proper sense of the word. It is a remarkable example of Mackenzie's gift for finding a situation to contain emotional mysteries without lapsing into frigid allegory, and the swift transition from the heroic to the sordid and the ridiculous is beautifully accomplished. A similar piece of reductionism occurs in "A Conqueror," one of the best and most neglected of Australian war-poems. The private murders and betrayals of lovers have their counterpart on the world's stage, where the lust for power, which lovers too often mistake for love, becomes destructive on a grand scale.

The poems of the final ten years are much preoccupied with physical pain, his own and other men's, in hospital. Some are pleas for oblivion, but one at least calls in question the genuineness of the death-wish, and prays for time to amend and praise. Mackenzie's poems have the faults associated with these themes. The great deliberation and the unrelenting control give an impression of slowness and monotony. It is best to read them a few at a time. He also has one of the defects of the solitary: frequent outbursts of garrulity. Lacking companionship, he conducts an eternal argument with himself, always "fighting a battle on the brink of time." He also has the narrow range of the solitary, though within that range he saw very deeply, as the references to his wife in "Two Trinities" reveal. His work is self-regarding, ego-centric, but not self-deluding – he does not romanticize his weaknesses, and with all his faults remains on the right side of the thin line between sensitivity and self-indulgence.

He wrote four novels, largely as pot-boilers. But *The Refuge*, about an extraordinary relationship between a journalist, his refugee second wife, and his son by his first wife, is as sensitive, perceptive, and compelling as the best of his verse.

—Dorothy Green

MacLENNAN, (John) Hugh. Canadian. Born in Glace Bay, Nova Scotia, 20 March 1907. Educated at Halifax Academy; Dalhousie University, Halifax, B.A. 1928; Oriel College, Oxford (Rhodes Scholar), B.A., M.A. 1932; Princeton University, New Jersey, Ph.D. 1935. Married 1) Dorothy Duncan in 1936 (died, 1957); 2) Frances Walker in 1959. Classics Master, Lower Canada College, Montreal, 1935–45; full-time writer, 1945–51; Associate Professor, 1951–67, and since 1967 Professor of English, McGill University, Montreal. Recipient: Guggenheim Fellowship, 1943; Governor-General's Award, 1946, 1949, 1960, for nonfiction, 1950, 1955; Lorne Pierce Gold Medal, 1952; Molson Prize, 1966. D.Litt.: University of Western Ontario, London, 1953; University of Manitoba, Winnipeg, 1955; Waterloo Lutheran University, Ontario, 1961; Carleton University, Ottawa, 1967; LL.D.: Dalhousie University, 1956; University of Saskatchewan, Saskatoon, 1959; McMaster University, Hamilton, Ontario, 1965; University of Toronto, 1966; Laurentian University, Sudbury, Ontario, 1966; University of Sherbrooke, Quebec, 1967; University of British Columbia, Vancouver, 1968; St. Mary's University, Halifax, 1968; Mount Alison University, Sackville, New Brunswick, 1969; D.C.L.: Bishop's University, Lennoxville, Quebec, 1965. Fellow, Royal Society of Canada, 1953, and the Royal Society of Literature, England, 1959. C.C. (Companion, Order of Canada), 1967. Lives in Montreal.

PUBLICATIONS

Fiction

Barometer Rising. 1941.
Two Solitudes. 1945.
The Precipice. 1948.
Each Man's Son. 1951.
The Watch That Ends the Night. 1959.
Return of the Sphinx. 1967.

Other

> *Oxyrhynchus: An Economic and Social Study.* 1935.
> *Cross Country.* 1948.
> *Thirty and Three* (essays). 1954.
> *Scotchman's Return and Other Essays.* 1960; as *Scotsman's Return and Other Essays,* 1960.
> *Seven Rivers of Canada.* 1961; as *The Rivers of Canada,* 1961.
> *The Colour of Canada.* 1967.
>
> Editor, *McGill: The Story of a University.* 1960.

Reading List: *MacLennan* by George Woodcock, 1969; *MacLennan* by Peter Buitenhuis, 1969; *MacLennan* by Alec Lucas, 1970; *The Novels of MacLennan* by Robert H. Cockburn, 1970.

* * *

Canadian writers in the English language suffer disadvantages that are unknown to men of letters of other countries. The long and rich history of British literature is part of their heritage but they cannot write as Englishmen lest they become foreigners in their own country. They are North Americans, and the economic, cultural and political influence of the United States is to them immediate and powerful, but as Canadians they cannot themselves participate in the exercise of that influence. They belong to a nation of two languages but to one which, for all that the politicians have decreed, is still far from being bilingual and so they are cut off from the support of their fellow-Canadians who write in French and from a substantial minority of readers in a country which even in its entirety is not plush with enthusiasm for its artists. Faced with all these handicaps and inevitably attracted to one or the other of the two powerful magnets of English-language publishing, London and New York, many Canadian writers have turned their backs on Canadianism while others have been obsessed by it and have become little more than brash heralds of Canadian chauvinism. Among Canadian novelists only Hugh MacLennan has been consistent in his ability to create an essentially Canadian mythology without abdicating the novelist's responsibility to be at once idiosyncratic and universally comprehensible.

It is one of the persistent paradoxes of Canadian literature that so many of its leading exponents are typically Canadian, in that it is a notable trait among Canada's intelligentsia that they have in their heredity and upbringing so many strains that are extra-Canadian. MacLennan, for example, is a fourth generation Nova Scotian, but his father still spoke Gaelic, and the fatalism, the religious fervour, and the mythology of the Highland Scots are as real in the novels of Hugh MacLennan – above all in *Each Man's Son* and *Return of the Sphinx* – as they are in the novels of Scotland-based Scotsmen such as Neil Gunn and Eric Linklater. But if, as has been said, "several of his novels ... can be regarded as transatlantic epilogues to the history of Scottish literature, and the records of a pastoral people battered and bewildered by urban society," nevertheless the most obvious influences on his literary personality are not Scottish, and certainly not Nova Scotian, but Oxford and Princeton, the two great centres of elegant intellectualism in which he was educated.

A dedicated classical scholar, MacLennan has never lacked the courage to attempt in his novels the grandeur of Greek tragedy. The sense of guilt that prevades *The Precipice* is explicitly derived from Canadian Puritanism. *Two Solitudes* is the most complete representation in fictional form of the division between English and French Canada, the schism which, above all others, makes the concept of Canadianism an illusion. *Each Man's Son* mourns the fate of MacLennan's own race, the Highland Scots thrust out of Scotland by poverty and in Nova Scotia damned to abandon their rural tradition and to live by coal-mining. All these are Canadian themes, but they are also parables of man's estate, and in all his work MacLennan holds to his ambition to fuse realism and symbolism.

MacLennan said of his early novels, "I was writing out of a country at that time unknown even to itself," and that consequently he was forced to explore and to explain in detail many aspects of the Canadian character. In the same passage he claims that by the time he came to write his later novels exegesis of this kind was no longer necessary. Yet if there is a blemish in MacLennan's craftsmanship, it springs from his skill as an essayist, and if that blemish exists it is most apparent in the novels written in the 1950's and 1960's, above all in *The Watch That Ends the Night*, in which the narrative is frequently broken by didactic interpolations. And perversely MacLennan's first novel *Barometer Rising* is almost entirely free from expository asides.

Already when he wrote *Barometer Rising* MacLennan was a superior craftsman, capable of handling plot, characterisation, and setting, and already he was concerned to find the parable behind the chronicle. But he would never again find historical events so pliable to his purpose as those which he chronicles in *Barometer Rising*, the Great War and the explosion that wrecked Halifax in 1917. Perhaps no Canadian ever will – for the symbolism of the Halifax disaster is both dramatic and inevitable, and it was the Great War, more even than Confederation, which aroused Canadians to aspirations of nationhood.

—J. E. Morpurgo

MAIR, Charles. Canadian. Born in Lanark, Ontario, 21 September 1838. Educated at Queen's University, Kingston, Ontario. Married Elizabeth Louise MacKenny in 1868 (died, 1906). Entered government service, Ottawa, 1868; involved in the "Canada First" movement, 1868, and was imprisoned at Fort Garry by the rebels in the Riel Rebellion, 1869; escaped to Ontario, and became a fur trader at Portage La Prairie; Quartermaster, Governor-General's Body Guard, 2nd Riel Rebellion, 1885; thereafter served on government expeditions to British Columbia, and worked in the Canadian Immigration Department until 1921. LL.D.: Queen's University, 1926. Fellow, Royal Society of Canada, 1889. *Died 7 July 1927.*

PUBLICATIONS

Verse

Dreamland and Other Poems. 1868.
Tecumseh: A Drama, and Canadian Poems. 1901; revised edition, 1926.

Play

Tecumseh (as *The Red Revolutionary*, produced 1972). 1886.

Other

Through the Mackenzie Basin: A Narrative of the Athabasca and Peace River Treaty Expedition of 1899. 1908.

Reading List: *Mair* by Norman Shrive, 1965.

* * *

Charles Mair holds a place in Canadian literary history for his politics more than for his poetry. In the later 1860's he became a member of that early nationalist movement known as Canada First, and his desire to spread Canadian influence into the yet unsettled prairies led him to take a provocative role at the Red River during the rebellion of 1869. He strongly supported the Canadian party which stood in opposition to Louis Riel and the insurgent Métis. After Riel established his Provisional Government at Fort Garry, Mair became involved in an abortive attempt at armed resistance. He was captured by Riel's militia, and threatened with execution by Riel himself, but escaped to Ontario. In later years he wandered over the west, as a trader, as a land speculator, and in his final years as an immigration agent, a post he continued to hold until the age of 83.

Little of this adventurous life, or of the political fire which it at times projected, is anticipated in Mair's first book of poems, *Dreamland and Other Poems*, which appeared a year before his Red River adventure. It is a volume of somewhat Tennysonian lyrics that are mostly sentimental in tone, and it is mainly redeemed by occasional quite vivid renderings of natural scenes where the Upper Canadian countryside is portrayed with an observation almost pre-Raphaelite in its sharpness and directness.

Mair's nationalism emerges much more emphatically in the verse drama, *Tecumseh*, which deals with the War of 1812 and the role of the Indian leader Tecumseh, whom Mair presents as a symbol of Canadian defiance of American domination. It is a cumbersome work, unviable dramatically, but here and there the experiences of Mair's years in the west shine through in splendid passages describing the prairies before the settlers and the railway came:

> At length we heard a deep and solemn sound –
> Erupted moanings of the troubled earth
> Trembling beneath innumerable feet.
> A growing uproar blending in our ears,
> With noise tumultuous as ocean's surge,
> Of bellowings, fierce breath and battle shock,
> And ardour of unconquerable herds ...
> And, lo! before us lay the tameless stock,
> Slow wending to the northward like a cloud!
> A multitude in motion, dark and dense –
> Far as the eye could reach, and farther still,
> In countless myriads stretched for many a league.

As this passage on the great and vanished bison herds suggests, Mair is principally important in a historical way, not for the quality of his verse, but because he was one of the first poets to see Canada as a man who belonged to the land, a native in feeling as well as by birth, rather than, like most of his contemporaries, as a colonial attempting to recreate the literary culture of the motherland.

—George Woodcock

MAIS, Roger. Jamaican. Born in 1905. Educated at Calabar High School. Worked as civil servant and journalist; also a photographer and painter. Associated with the political activist Norman W. Manley in the 1930's and 1940's: imprisoned for anti-colonial essay for six months in 1944; lived abroad, 1951–54. *Died in 1955.*

PUBLICATIONS

Fiction

And Most of All Man (stories and verse). 1939.
Face and Other Stories. 1942.
The Hills Were Joyful Together. 1953.
Brother Man. 1954.
Black Lightning. 1955.

Play

Atalanta in Calydon, from the play by Swinburne (produced 1950).

Reading List: Introduction by Norman Manley to *Three Novels,* 1966; *Mais* by Jean D'Costa, 1979.

*   *   *

Some understanding of Roger Mais's generation is helpful in the reading of his fiction. He belonged to that group of middle-class intellectuals and political activists who assumed the leadership of mass labour and nationalist movements throughout much of the West Indies during the 1930's and 1940's. This is the group that dominated the slow movement towards nationhood in Jamaica, Trinidad, Barbados, and Guyana, among others. It is therefore no coincidence that Jamaica's late Prime Minister, Norman Manley, wrote the introduction to Mais's *Three Novels* (a reprint of his three major works) for both Manley the political leader and Mais the writer belonged to what Manley describes as "the National Movement." By a similar token it is to be expected that Mais's fiction is marked by a socio-political commitment (to the poor, to the working classes, and to national identity) which he shares with political counterparts like Manley. And this commitment is best exemplified by the three novels on which much of his reputation rests, *The Hills Were Joyful Together, Brother Man,* and *Black Lightning.*

The Hills Were Joyful Together is a novel about victimization, and the victims are the slum dwellers of Jamaica's capital, Kingston. The slum "yard" is a cage, confining its members to a closed cycle of poverty which breeds crime and which in turn removes the slum dweller even further from socio-economic opportunities. And it is also a cage of indiscriminate brutality, the kind that arises from perpetual poverty and involves even the gentle hero, Surjue. In his case poverty leads to a bungled burglary attempt, and to prison where he is shot to death in an attempted escape. Moreover the circumstances of Surjue's imprisonment and death emphasize that the slum yard is not an isolated phenomenon but a symbol of a pervasive social malaise that corrupts all social institutions, including a rather brutish judicial system.

Despite the emphasis on institutional failures in a work like *The Hills* Mais's fiction is not merely one-dimensional social protest. The work also suggests that the human tragedy is compounded by an inscrutable universal fate, but that in the final analysis the individual's salvation, from hostile environment and fate alike, lies in his or her own hands. Thus although he is a failure in one sense, Surjue nevertheless emerges with heroic dimensions because he embodies a certain integrity and nobility which are heightened rather than diminished by his conflict with a brutal world. Similarly, notwithstanding the *public* downfall of the folk preacher, Bra Man, in *Brother Man*, he and his woman Minette enjoy a triumph of sorts, a triumph which flows from their individual strength and from the integrity of their relationship. The practical attempts at brotherhood fail, but Bra Man's dreams of brotherhood are validated by the moral strength of Bra Man the dreamer. And, conversely, Bra Man's *individual* integrity is confirmed by his capacity to seek brotherhood on behalf of his fellow creatures. Finally, this insistence on that inner strength and on those private resources which are necessary for survival in a hostile world is most explicit in the most introspective of the novels, *Black Lightning*. In this work the setting shifts from urban Kingston to rural Jamaica which becomes the background for an intense analysis of private relationships between a selected number of characters. In effect Mais's fiction is simultaneously an act of socio-political commitment and an exploration of that inner life which is essential to the individual who attempts to deal with the world outside.

—Lloyd W. Brown

MANDER, Jane. New Zealander. Born in 1877. *Died in 1949.*

PUBLICATIONS

Fiction

The Story of a New Zealand River. 1920.
The Passionate Puritan. 1921.
The Strange Attraction. 1922.
Allen Adair. 1925; edited by Dorothea Turner, 1971.
The Besieging City. 1926.
Pins and Pinnacles. 1928.

Reading List: *Mander,* 1972, and "*The Story of a New Zealand River:* Perceptions and Prophecies in an Unfixed Society," in *Critical Essays on the New Zealand Novel* edited by Cherry Hankin, 1976, both by Dorothea Turner.

*   *   *

The slender output and belated recognition of Jane Mander have until recently disguised her importance as a seminal figure in New Zealand literature. As her novels were largely ignored on first publication, so did her artistic purposes change, with the result that three of her six novels are of slight critical significance. *The Strange Attraction* now reads like a strident attempt at sensationalism, while in *The Besieging City* and *Pins and Pinnacles* she used New York and London locations in an apparent attempt to extend her readership.

It is on the other three novels with a New Zealand location that Jane Mander's literary stature must rest. *The Story of a New Zealand River* has some of the obvious technical clumsiness of a first novel, in particular a very awkward handling of narrative perspective; yet it remains the definitive fictional study of the puritanism which until recently has dominated New Zealand society, and its naturalistic emphasis on environmental conditioning anticipates the brilliant documentary sections of the undeservedly neglected *The Passionate Puritan*. Mander's fourth novel is, however, her masterpiece. *Allen Adair* deals, like its predecessors, with emergent society in the northern areas of New Zealand, but the texture of human relationships is much more subtle. Here, the former themes of puritanism, self-induced isolation, and frigid marriage are again prominent, but there is also an undercurrent of latent homosexuality between the best-conceived male characters in Jane Mander's essentially feminist fictional world.

It is not surprising that restricted library access and related social attitudes left Jane Mander at her death virtually unknown in her own country, but recent responses indicate that her place is beside Katherine Mansfield and Frank Sargeson as pioneers in the fictional dissection of New Zealand colonial culture.

—Howard McNaughton

MANSFIELD, Katherine. Pseudonym for Kathleen Mansfield Beauchamp. New Zealander. Born in Wellington, 14 October 1888. Educated at a school in Karori; Girls' High School, Wellington, 1898–99; Miss Swainson's School, Wellington, 1900–03; Queen's College, London, 1903–06; Royal Academy of Music, Wellington, 1906–08. Married George Bowden in 1909 (separated, 1909; divorced, 1918); lived with John Middleton Murry from 1912; married him, 1918. Settled in London, 1908; contributed to *The New Age*, 1910–11; contributed to Murry's *Rhythm*, and its successor, *The Blue Review*, and later became his partner, 1911–13; reviewer for the *Westminster Gazette*, 1911–15; Founder, with Murry and D. H. Lawrence, *Signature* magazine, 1916; tubercular: lived for part of each year in the South of France, then Switzerland, from 1916; contributed to the *Athenaeum*, edited by Murry, 1919–20. Recipient: Femina-Vie Heureuse Prize, 1921. *Died 9 January 1923.*

PUBLICATIONS

Collections

Letters, edited by J. Middleton Murry. 2 vols., 1928.
Collected Stories. 1945.
Selected Stories, edited by Dan Davin. 1953.
Letters and Journals: A Selection, edited by C. K. Stead. 1977.

Fiction

In a German Pension (stories). 1911.
Je Ne Parle Pas Français. 1918.

Bliss and Other Stories. 1920.
The Garden Party and Other Stories. 1922.
The Dove's Nest and Other Stories. 1923.
Something Childish and Other Stories. 1924; as *The Little Girl and Other Stories*, 1924.
The Aloe. 1930.
The Mystery of Maata: A Novel, edited by Patrick A. Lawlor. 1946.
Undiscovered Country: The New Zealand Stories, edited by Ian A. Gordon. 1974.

Verse

Poems. 1923.

Other

Journal, edited by J. Middleton Murry. 1927; revised edition, 1934.
Novels and Novelists (reviews), edited by J. Middleton Murry. 1930.
Scrapbook, edited by J. Middleton Murry. 1939.
Letters to John Middleton Murry, 1913–1922, edited by Murry. 1951.
Passionate Pilgrimage: A Love Affair in Letters: Mansfield's Letters to John Middleton Murry from the South of France 1915–1920, edited by Helen McNeish. 1976.
The Urewera Notebook, edited by Ian A. Gordon. 1978.

Translator, with S. S. Koteliansky, *Reminiscences of Leonid Andreyev*, by Gorky. 1928.

Bibliography: *The Critical Bibliography of Mansfield* by Ruth C. Mantz, 1931; *Mansfieldiana: A Brief Mansfield Bibliography* by G. N. Morris, 1948; *Mansfield: Publications in Australia 1907–1909* by Jean E. Stone, 1977.

Reading List: *The Loneliness of Mansfield* by Patrick A. Lawlor, 1950; *Mansfield: A Critical Study* by Sylvia Berkman, 1951; *Mansfield: A Biography* by Antony Alpers, 1953; *Mansfield* by Ian A. Gordon, 1954; *Mansfield* by Saralyn R. Daly, 1965; *Mansfield: An Appraisal* by Nariman Hormasji, 1967; *The Edwardianism of Mansfield* by Frederick J. Foot, 1969; *The Fiction of Mansfield* by Marvin Magalaner, 1971; *Mansfield: A Biography* by Jeffrey Meyers, 1978.

* * *

Katherine Mansfield was the daughter of Harold Beauchamp, a New Zealand merchant and banker. She was educated in various schools in Wellington, and in Queen's College, London, where she had already begun to write. Back in Wellington at the age of 18, she persuaded her family to allow her return to London, and she settled there before she was 20. It took her two years to find an outlet for her short stories. Early in 1910 she was accepted by *The New Age*, for which she produced a series of tartly satirical stories with settings that were familiar from her experiences in England, Belgium, and Bavaria. The Bavarian stories, unsympathetic portrayals of German provincial life, were collected in a volume *In a German Pension*, which was well reviewed.

Katherine Mansfield was by now dissatisfied with the narrow range of story which *The New Age* expected of her (the editor rejected her more romantic writing). A chance meeting with John Middleton Murry, then editing the periodical *Rhythm*, led to an invitation to contribute something different. With the help of one of her old New Zealand diaries, she wrote her first recognisably New Zealand story "The Woman at the Store," and during 1912 and 1913 she provided *Rhythm* and its successor, *The Blue Review*, with a group of stories based on memories of her native country and of her family. She became Murry's lover (they were later married) and his partner. Stories of this period, like "An Indiscreet Journey" and "The Little Governess," show advances both in technique and in sympathy, very different from the brittle satire of her *New Age* contributions.

Early in 1915, her brother arrived from New Zealand on his way to the British army. He was killed in a training accident towards the end of the year and the shock of his death sent Katherine Mansfield into a self-imposed exile in the south of France, where she began writing "recollections of my own country." The first version of this new story was called *The Aloe*. It was later revised and entitled "Prelude," first published in 1918 by Virginia and Leonard Woolf at their Hogarth Press. "The *Prelude* method" – a plotless series of episodes that (in her own words) "just unfolds and opens" – was something quite new in the English short story; and when "Prelude" first appeared in book form in *Bliss and Other Stories* in 1920, Katherine Mansfield was recognised as one of the significant writers in the literary scene of the time. Virginia Woolf, as her recently published letters indicate, was unable to repress feelings of jealousy at this rival talent.

Periodicals were now more hospitable. She returned to *The New Age*, and other journals took her work. Murry's accession in 1919 to the editorship of *The Athenaeum* provided her with the readiest outlet in periodical form for her later work. But by now she had turned ill and had to spend every winter, separated from Murry, in the south of France. Her last year, 1922, was spent in Switzerland, in a vain search for health.

The stories written after the appearance of *Bliss* appeared in the volume that consolidated her reputation, *The Garden Party and Other Stories*. It contained most of her best New Zealand stories ("At the Bay," "The Garden Party," "The Voyage," "The Stranger") but her new stories written with English or continental backgrounds (notably "The Daughters of the Late Colonel" and "Miss Brill") are written with equal sensitivity. After her death, in early 1923, Murry published two more volumes, collected from the periodicals and from her manuscripts.

Technically, Katherine Mansfield made the kind of advance in short-story writing that her contemporaries James Joyce and Virginia Woolf were making in the novel. She was a pioneer in the interior monologue and in the presentation of shifting viewpoints. Most of her best short stories are, without being mere photographic replicas, shaped-up recollections of her family and her New Zealand childhood. Her studies of children (seen through their own eyes and not those of adults) have few equals. Her stories are written in a carefully evolved prose that owes something to the techniques of poetic language: and her best stories measure up to the close analysis that is usually reserved for lyric poetry. Her range of material is not great – children on their own, children reacting to adults, the lonely and isolated woman in a hostile world, these are her main preoccupations. But, granted the narrowness of her range, she is penetrating and superbly effective. Her work has continued to attract.

After her death, Murry collected some of her manuscripts and portions of her notebooks, and published them as the *Journal of Katherine Mansfield*. The quality of the writing ensured it a great success and it became one of the important "confessional" writings of the period. Recent research on her manuscripts has demonstrated that his selection of material was very partial and pietistic. The saintly wraith that emerges from the *Journal* is largely the creation of selective editing. The real Katherine Mansfield was made of much tougher material, a hard-working professional at her trade, and the *Journal* should be regarded with caution by readers seeking biographical enlightenment.

—Ian A. Gordon

MARSH, Dame (Edith) Ngaio. New Zealander. Born in Christchurch, 23 April 1899. Educated at St. Margaret's College, Christchurch, 1910–14; Canterbury University College School of Art, Christchurch, 1915–20. Actress, 1920–23; theatrical producer, 1923–27; interior designer, London, 1928–32; thereafter a full-time writer; served in a Red Cross Unit in World War II; theatrical producer for O'Connor Theatre Management, New Zealand, 1944–52, and Canterbury University; Honorary Lecturer in Drama, Canterbury University, 1948. Recipient: Mystery Writers of America Grand Master Award, 1978. D.Litt.: University of Canterbury, 1963. O.B.E. (Officer, Order of the British Empire), 1948; D.B.E. (Dame Commander, Order of the British Empire), 1966. Fellow, Royal Society of Arts. Lives in Christchurch.

PUBLICATIONS

Fiction

A Man Lay Dead. 1934.
Enter a Murderer. 1935.
Death in Ecstasy. 1936.
The Nursing Home Mystery, with Henry Jellett. 1936.
Vintage Murder. 1937.
Artists in Crime. 1938.
Death in a White Tie. 1938.
Overture to Death. 1939.
Death at the Bar. 1940.
Death of a Peer. 1940; as *Surfeit of Lampreys,* 1941.
Death and the Dancing Footman. 1941.
Colour Scheme. 1943.
Died in the Wool. 1945.
The Final Curtain. 1947.
Swing Brother Swing. 1949; as *A Wreath for Rivera,* 1949.
Opening Night. 1951; as *Night at the Vulcan,* 1951.
Spinsters in Jeopardy. 1953.
Scales of Justice. 1955.
Death of a Fool. 1956; as *Off with His Head,* 1957.
Singing in the Shrouds. 1958.
False Scent. 1959.
Hand in Glove. 1962.
Dead Water. 1963.
Killer Dolphin. 1966; as *Death at the Dolphin,* 1967.
Clutch of Constables. 1968.
When in Rome. 1970.
Tied Up in Tinsel. 1972.
Black As He's Painted. 1974.
Last Ditch. 1977.
Grave Mistake. 1978.

Plays

Surfeit of Lampreys, with Owen B. Howell, from the novel by Marsh (produced 1950).
False Scent, from her own novel (produced 1961).

The Christmas Tree (juvenile). 1962.
A Unicorn for Christmas, music by David Farquhar (produced 1965).
Murder Sails at Midnight (produced 1972).
Television Play: *Evil Liver,* 1975.

Other

New Zealand, with R. M. Burdon. 1942.
A Play Toward: A Note on Play Production. 1946.
Perspectives: The New Zealander and the Visual Arts. 1960.
Play Production. 1960.
New Zealand. 1964.
Black Beech and Honeydew (autobiography). 1965.

* * *

Ngaio Marsh's *Black Beech and Honeydew* is principally about her life as a director-producer in the theatre and includes only passing references to her work as a mystery novelist. One such reference is a modest defence for the work she appears to consider only a means of livelihood rather than a vocation: "Intellectual New Zealand friends tactfully avoid all mention of my published work.... So it was astonishing, that time in England, to find myself broadcasting and being televised and interviewed and it was pleasant to find detective fiction being discussed as a tolerable form of reading by people whose opinion one valued. I suppose the one thing that can always be said in favour of the genre is that inside the convention the author may write with as good a style as he or she can command." Dame Ngaio's command of the genre has enabled her to create a body of work that is in quality, quantity, and popular appeal second only to the achievement of Agatha Christie. She resembles Christie also in the variety and richness of her backgrounds and in the good-humoured tone maintained throughout the novels.

Dame Ngaio has explained in a 1977 edition of *The Writer* that one rainy afternoon in 1933, having read a book by Christie or Sayers, she thought it would be "highly original" to write a mystery novel using the popular parlor game called "Murder" as a plot device. Thus *A Man Lay Dead* is a significant first novel in that it establishes those characteristics that have come to be Marsh's hall-marks: the attitude that fictional murder is primarily a game whose first obligation is to amuse, the interest in the habitations of the gently eccentric British middle and upper classes as locales, and the presentation of her perdurable detective, Roderick Alleyn.

Alleyn, who appears to be a more substantial, less quixotic version of Sayers's Lord Peter Wimsey, dominates virtually all of Dame Ngaio's mystery novels. He is occasionally joined by Nigel Bathgate and Inspector Fox, who play his Watsons. While he shows a remarkable inability to age, he nevertheless manifests a broadening of interests and represents (according to Earl F. Bargainnier in *Armchair Detective,* 1978) the combination of the aristocratic gentleman-detective of the 1930's and the hard-nosed cop of the later police procedurals.

Dame Ngaio has written some travel books about New Zealand and has used her native country as a background for a few of her thrillers, but most often she sets her novels in the British Isles and uses the theatre or a theatrical situation for backgrounds, such as *Opening Night* (*Night at the Vulcan*) and *Overture to Death*. Her experience in the theatre is also reflected in her sharp ear for dialogue and dialect.

—Nancy C. Joyner

MASON, Bruce (Edward George). New Zealander. Born in Wellington, 28 September 1921. Educated at Takapuna Grammar School, Auckland; Wellington Boys' College; Victoria University College, now Victoria University of Wellington, B.A. 1945. Served in the New Zealand Army, 1941–45; Royal New Zealand Naval Volunteer Reserve, 1943–45: Sub-Lieutenant. Married Dr. Diana Manby Shaw in 1945; one son and two daughters. Research Assistant, War History Branch, Wellington, 1946–48; Assistant Curator of Manuscripts, Alexander Turnbull Library, Wellington, 1948–49; travelled in Europe, 1949–51; Public Relations Officer, New Zealand Forest Service, Wellington, 1951–57; Radio Critic, 1955–61, Record Critic, 1961–62, and Music Critic, 1964–69, *New Zealand Listener*, Wellington; Senior Journalist, *Tourist and Publicity*, Wellington, 1957–58; Drama Critic, *Dominion*, Wellington, 1958–60; Editor, *Te Ao Hou* (Maori Affairs), Wellington, 1960–61; Editor, *Act*, Wellington, 1967–70; Senior Copywriter, Wood and Mitchell Advertising, Wellington, 1969–71. President, Secretary, and Committee Member, Unity Theatre, Wellington, 1948–60. New Zealand Delegate, International Drama Conference, Edinburgh, 1963. Full-time actor, producer and director: has directed first productions of most of his own plays, operas for the New Zealand Opera Company, and revues for the Unity Theatre and Downstage, Wellington; has appeared in his own plays for solo actor, in New Zealand, England, and the United States. Recipient: British Drama League Playwriting Competition Prize, five times; Auckland Festival Society National Playwriting Competition Prize, 1958; State Literary Fund Scholarship in Letters, 1973. Lives in Wellington.

PUBLICATIONS

Plays

The Bonds of Love (produced 1953).
The Evening Paper (produced 1953).
The Verdict (produced 1955).
The Licensed Victualler, music by Mason (produced 1955).
A Case in Point (produced 1956).
Wit's End (revue; produced 1956).
The Light Enlarging (produced 1957).
Birds in the Wilderness (produced 1957).
The Pohutukawa Tree (produced 1957). 1960.
The End of the Golden Weather (produced 1960). 1962.
We Don't Want Your Sort Here, music by Mason (cabaret; produced 1961).
Awatea (broadcast 1964; produced 1968). 1969.
Swan Song (broadcast 1964; produced 1965).

The Hand on the Rail (broadcast 1964; produced 1965).
The Counsels of the Wood (produced 1965).
The Waters of Silence, from a work by Vercors (produced 1965).
Hongi (broadcast 1967; produced 1968).   In *Contemporary New Zealand Plays,* edited by Howard McNaughton, 1974.
Zero Inn (produced 1970).   1970.
Not Christmas, But Guy Fawkes (produced 1976).
Courting Blackbird (produced 1976).

Radio Plays: *The Cherry Orchard,* from a play by Chekhov, 1960; *Awatea,* 1964; *Swan Song,* 1964; *The Hand on the Rail,* 1965; *Hongi,* 1967.

Verse

We Don't Want Your Sort Here: A Collection of Light Verse.   1963.

Other

Theatre in Danger, with John Pocock.   1957.
New Zealand Drama: A Parade of Forms and a History.   1972.

Reading List: *Mason* by Howard McNaughton, 1975.

*   *   *

The artistic career of Bruce Mason reflects, in its breadth, the resourcefulness which until recently has been essential to the professional artist in New Zealand. While his earliest short stories were establishing his literary reputation in the late 1940's, he was already gaining the intimate knowledge of all aspects of stage production that was to enable him to write, direct, and act in most of his early plays, in the 1950's. *The Bonds of Love*, *The Evening Paper*, and *The Verdict* brought a new intensity and severity to New Zealand realistic drama, while *The Light Enlarging* and the full-length *Birds in the Wilderness* educated audiences to subtleties of stylised comedy. The constrictions of domestic drama, however, proved increasingly frustrating to a writer with more epic propensities, and an expansion of professional production resources on both radio and stage stimulated Mason into his most ambitious series of plays, the five dramas on Maori themes.

The Pohutukawa Tree quickly became famous through stage, radio, and television productions, and remains the seminal dramatic portrayal of the corrosion between Maori and European culture. Other plays offer a more optimistic resolution to such an issue, all of them written for radio in 1964–5: the controversial *Awatea*, conceived on a scale as grand as that of *The Pohutukawa Tree*, *Swan Song*, a more stylised treatment of the cultural impasse, and *The Hand on the Rail*, an intimate study of the tensions within a bicultural family. Reverting to a more pessimistic tone, *Hongi* is a historical drama with a highly resonant core of ethnic pageantry. All of these later Maori plays have also been radically reshaped and rescripted for the stage, but their production has been limited because they were originally written with lead parts for the great Maori bass singer, the late Inia Te Wiata; only *Awatea* is familiar to theatre audiences, and more subtle plays like *The Hand on the Rail* and *Hongi* have been undeservedly neglected.

Mason's most dramatically innovative work, however, lies in his plays for solo actor. Initially inspired by Emlyn Williams's Dickens performances, he wrote and performed *The End of the Golden Weather*, a study of New Zealand boyhood; between 1959 and 1962 he was engaged in extensive internal tours, and after appearances in London, at the Edinburgh Festival, and in the U.S.A., the popularity of the work is unabated. In 1965, he extended his solo repertoire with *The Counsels of the Wood* and *The Waters of Silence* (adapted from Vercors); though the more exotic content of these works has limited their stage popularity, he has combined them under the title of *Men of Soul* and continues to present the programme during his larger seasons. For his two most recent solo works, both premiered in 1976, Mason has returned to New Zealand material; *Not Christmas, But Guy Fawkes* is based on some of his own short stories and autobiographical pieces, while *Courting Blackbird* is a swift-moving, well-integrated, highly comic anecdotal piece about an expatriate eccentric.

Since the Maori works, Mason's output of plays has been limited, with only *Zero Inn* (1970) making an impact on the stage. His solo theatre, however, has flourished, and his tours continue to be among the most remarkable feats of sustained creativity that the New Zealand stage has seen.

—Howard McNaughton

MASON, R(onald) A(lison) K(ells). New Zealander. Born in Auckland, 10 January 1905. Educated at Panmore School; Auckland Grammar School, 1917–22; Auckland University College, 1926–29, 1938–39, B.A. in classics 1939. Married Dorothea Mary Mould in 1964. Part-time tutor, University Coaching College, Auckland, 1923–29; company secretary, 1933–35; Editor, *Phoenix*, 1933; public works foreman, 1936–39; Editor, *In Print*, 1941–43; Assistant Secretary, Auckland General Labourers Union, and Editor, *Challenge*, 1943–54; landscape gardener from 1956, and part-time school teacher from 1965. Founder Member and Officer, People's Theatre and New Theatre Group, Auckland, 1940–43; first President, New Zealand-China Society. Recipient: New Zealand State Literary Fund award, 1961; Robert Burns Fellowship, University of Otago, 1962. *Died in 1971.*

PUBLICATIONS

Verse

In the Manner of Men. 1923.
The Beggar. 1924.
Penny Broadsheet. 1925.
No New Thing: Poems 1924–1929. 1934.
End of Day. 1936.
This Dark Will Lighten: Selected Poems 1923–1941. 1941.
Recent Poems, with others. 1941.
Collected Poems. 1962.

Plays

To Save Democracy, in *Tomorrow*, 27 April 1938.
Squire Speaks: A Radio Play. 1938.

China (produced 1943). In *China Dances*, 1962.
Refugee (produced 1945).
Daddy, Paddy, and Marty, in *The People's Voice*, April 1950.
Strait Is the Gate (produced 1964).

Other

Frontier Forsaken. 1947.
Rex Fairburn. 1962.
China Dances (miscellany). 1962.

Reading List: *Mason* by Charles Doyle, 1970.

* * *

If any New Zealand poet before James K. Baxter has a claim to continuing international recognition, R. A. K. Mason is the prime candidate. An independent New Zealand poetry begins in 1923 with the publication of Mason's *In the Manner of Men*.

A poet by nature rather than conscious intellectual development, Mason had done most of his best work by the time he was thirty. The poems in his first important small collection *The Beggar* were almost all written before he was eighteen. Although a handful of pieces were added to his last major collection, *This Dark Will Lighten*, the bulk of his slender collected poems were written by 1929 and published, after a series of printing delays, in *No New Thing*.

During the 1930's Mason became more consciously literary and this reduced the tension of his poems. He also turned towards Marxism and developed an interest in a kind of didactic drama. Possibly for these reasons, and because of the thinness of the cultural context in which he had to work, he wrote few poems in the latter half of his life, with the scathing "Sonnet to MacArthur's Eyes" (1950) a notable exception. From 1931 to 1956 he wrote chiefly leftist political journalism, first mainly for the *People's Voice* and then *Challenge*. One small book, *Frontier Forsaken*, deals with the disastrous effects of European colonisation on the Cook Islands. Still of some interest are several of Mason's plays, such as *Squire Speaks* and *China*, the latter a manifestation of his longtime interest in revolutionary China.

Strongly influenced by the Latin classics (especially Horace and Catullus), many of Mason's best poems are rooted also in the New Testament, particularly Christ's Passion. His central theme was grief at the body's death, an unappeasable hunger for personal immortality. From these concerns came his finest poems, such as "Footnote to John, II iv," "On the Swag," "Flow at Full Moon," "Judas Iscariot" (of which Dylan Thomas asked, "Didn't that poem shock people in New Zealand?"), and other compelling pieces, such as "After Death," "The Lesser Stars," and "The Spark's Farewell to its Clay."

Although a major figure in his own country, Mason has had no followers. In style and personality he is idiosyncratic, and the religious element is important to what is best in him; he is thus an odd poet to have sprung from a secular welfare-state society. The meeting-ground is a curious species of puritanism common to the poet and the national psyche.

—Charles Doyle

McAULEY, James (Phillip). Australian. Born in Lakemba, New South Wales, 12 October 1917. Educated at Fort Street High School, Sydney; University of Sydney, M.A., Dip. Ed. Married Norma Abernethy in 1942; four sons, one daughter. Lecturer in Government, Australian School of Pacific Administration, 1946–60; Professor of English, University of Tasmania, Hobart, 1961–76. Founding Editor, *Quadrant*, Sydney, 1956–76. Recipient: Carnegie grant, 1967. Fellow, Australian Academy of the Humanities. *Died 15 October 1976.*

PUBLICATIONS

Verse

The Darkening Ecliptic, with Harold Stewart. 1944; as *Poems,* 1961.
Under Aldebaran. 1946.
A Vision of Ceremony. 1956.
The Six Days of Creation. 1963.
(Poems). 1963.
Caption Quiros: A Poem. 1964.
Surprises of the Sun. 1969.
Collected Poems 1936–1970. 1971.

Other

Poetry and Australian Culture, with *Felons and Folksongs* by Russell B. Ward. 1955.
The End of Modernity: Essays on Literature, Art, and Culture. 1959.
C. J. Brennan. 1963.
Edmund Spenser and George Eliot: A Critical Excursion. 1963.
A Primer of English Versification. 1966; as *Versification: A Short Introduction,* 1966.
The Personal Element in Australian Poetry. 1970.
Christopher Brennan. 1973.
The Grammar of the Real: Selected Prose 1959–1974. 1976.
A Map of Australian Verse. 1976.

Editor, *Generations: Poetry from Chaucer to the Present Day.* 1969.

Reading List: *McAuley: Tradition in Australian Poetry* by Leonie Kramer, 1957; *McAuley* by Vivian Smith, 1965, revised edition, 1970.

*   *   *

James McAuley's work is zestful and, after his conversion to Roman Catholicism in 1952, certain. His was a full life and a firm faith.

Even before 1952, in his first collection *Under Aldebaran* there is much that speaks his dissatisfaction with a materialist society of narrow views and short perspectives. "The True Discovery of Australia," ironic and Gulliverian, has the local reference that the later "Letter to John Dryden" extends in scope. The alignment with Swift and Dryden reminds us not only of McAuley's classicism but also of his focus upon the European inheritance. His editing of *Quadrant* and his work for the Australian Association for Cultural Freedom should be seen as part of the same context as his regard for traditional values, which has received its most closely argued expression in his two prose works, *The End of Modernity* and *The Grammar of the Real*. His most ambitious poem, *Captain Quiros*, records its hero's voyage to establish New Jerusalem in the southern seas. The voyage can easily be applied to McAuley's own spiritual experience in a world from which he felt increasingly isolated but for which he never despaired.

As a poet he applied the strictest standards to sustain the pure dialect of the tribe, working persistently in traditional measures and wanting no other. As early as 1944 with Harold Stewart he perpetrated the Ern Malley hoax, by which several ridiculous pieces were taken seriously by the *avant-garde* as the work of a newly discovered poet. Like Spenser, McAuley "celebrates" secular and divine love, and his second collection was called *A Vision of Ceremony*. For him, in his own phrases, "Beauty is order" ("Envoi") and "Only the simplest forms can hold/A vast complexity" ("An Art of Poetry").

—Arthur Pollard

MITTELHOLZER, Edgar (Austin). Guyanan. Born in New Amsterdam, British Guiana, now Guyana, 16 December 1909. Educated at Berbice High School, New Amsterdam. Served in the Trinidad Navy during World War II. Married 1) Roma Halfhide in 1942 (divorced, 1958), two sons and two daughters; 2) Jacqueline Pointer in 1960, one son. Worked as a customs official, meteorological observer, and journalist, until 1941; settled in London after World War II; member of the Books Department, British Council, London, 1948–52; full-time writer from 1952. Recipient: Guggenheim Fellowship, 1952. *Died 6 May 1965.*

PUBLICATIONS

Fiction

    Corentyne Thunder. 1941.
    A Morning at the Office. 1950; as *A Morning in Trinidad,* 1950.
    Shadows Move among Them. 1951.
    The Children of Kaywana. 1952; as *Kaywana Heritage,* 1976.
    The Weather at Middenshot. 1952.
    The Life and Death of Sylvia. 1953; as *Sylvia,* 1963.
    The Harrowing of Hubertus. 1954; as *Hubertus,* 1955; as *Kaywana Stock,* 1968.
    My Bones and My Flute: A Ghost Story in the Old-Fashioned Manner. 1955.
    Of Trees and the Sea. 1956.
    A Tale of Three Places. 1957.
    Kaywana Blood. 1958; as *The Old Blood,* 1958.
    The Weather Family. 1958.
    The Mad MacMullochs. 1959.
    A Tinkling in the Twilight. 1959.

Latticed Echoes: A Novel in the Leitmotiv Manner. 1960.
Eltonsbrody. 1960.
Thunder Returning: A Novel in the Leitmotiv Manner. 1961.
The Piling of Clouds. 1961.
The Wounded and the Worried. 1962.
Uncle Paul. 1963.
The Jilkington Drama. 1965.
The Aloneness of Mrs. Chatham. 1965.

Other

Creole Chips. 1937.
The Adding Machine: A Fable for Capitalists and Commercialists. 1954.
With a Carib Eye. 1958.
A Swarthy Boy (autobiography). 1963.

Reading List: *Mittelholzer: The Man and His Work* by A. J. Seymour, 1968.

* * *

After World War II when the British Empire began to break up, there was great critical interest in English-language fiction from the Commonwealth countries as a result of what can now be seen as the naive hope that a worldwide English-speaking union might be preserved not through politics, but literature. A particular beneficiary of this short-lived movement was Edgar Mittelholzer, a native of British Guiana, who failed to follow up an exciting start.

His first professional novel, *A Morning at the Office*, was kindly received both in Great Britain and the United States, although reviewers felt that this plotless account of the tensions in a business office where colored clerks outnumber the whites (a kind of microcosm of the dissolving empire) was too thin and unresolved.

Mittelholzer scored an enormous hit, however, with his next novel, *Shadows Move among Them*, a stylish, cryptically ironic tale about a neurotic young man's attempts to gain control of his feelings while visiting a British minister's wise and witty family amidst the ruins of the old Dutch culture in the Guyana jungle. Anthony West compared the work to Norman Douglas's *South Wind* as one which "under cover of light entertainment ... discusses serious ideas sensibly and rationally." The visitor is led, almost unwillingly, out of his manias, West maintained, by the eccentric British family because they were able to deal with the jungle "as something that is there, not as a malicious departure from an ideal setting" (*New Yorker*, 6 October 1951). Other enthusiastic reviewers agreed that this unique fable might provide a model for facing the problems of new cultures evolving from the ruins of old in a world obsessed with guilt and existential despair. Two years after its publication, the novel provided the basis for Moss Hart's popular play, *The Climate of Eden*.

Mittelholzer never returned, however, to the sophisticated vein of this most successful work. His next novel, *The Children of Kaywana*, initiated a long, plodding trilogy that recounts the history of Guyana from its Dutch settlement in the seventeenth century down to 1960 through the lurid and violent doings of the van Groenwegel family. Readers were shocked by its sadism and sensuality, but received more sympathetically its more restrained companion pieces, *The Harrowing of Hubertus* and *Kaywana Blood*, as effective portrayals of three-dimensional characters against the extraordinary background of a jungle society. Reviewers became uneasy, however, as the author neared the present and became involved with "obeah," a local form of voodoo, for the impact of the work dwindled. It remains more important as the picture of an otherwise unchronicled past than for its artistic significance.

Between the first and second volumes of this trilogy, Mittelholzer published two other novels that can now be seen as ominous foreshadowings of those to follow. In the second, *The Life and Death of Sylvia*, he tried again to deal with modern Guyana; but despite the authenticity of the exotic setting, the mixed-blood heroine proved vapid because the author seemed unable to penetrate a woman's mind. He seemed to be running out of materials from his native land. Casting about for a fresh scene to exploit, he had already produced, in *The Weather in Middenshot*, a confused horror story about rural England; but this and others of the same kind to follow proved unsuccessful, although these obscure late novels surely indicate the truth of his report just before his grotesque death (apparently self-inflicted) that his principal interests were oriental occultism and psychical research. His talent was not for constructing histories, but for evoking atmosphere. He won readers as long as he had a tangible new world to offer them; but when his attention shifted from the physical to the metaphysical, the results were disastrous.

—Warren French

MOORE, Brian. Canadian. Born in Belfast, Northern Ireland, 25 August 1921; emigrated to Canada in 1948; moved to the United States in 1959. Educated at St. Malachy's College, Belfast. Served with the British Ministry of War Transport, in North Africa, Italy, and France, 1943–45. Married 1) Jacqueline Scully in 1951; 2) Jean Denney in 1966; one child. Served with the United Nations Relief and Rehabilitation Administration (UNRRA) Mission to Poland, 1946–47; Reporter, *Montreal Gazette*, 1948–52; full-time writer since 1952. Recipient: Authors Club of Great Britain Award, 1956; Beta Sigma Phi Award, 1956; Guggenheim Fellowship, 1959; Governor-General's Award, 1961; National Institute of Arts and Letters grant, 1961; Canada Council Fellowship, 1962; Smith Literary Award, 1973; Black Memorial Award, 1976. Lives in California.

PUBLICATIONS

Fiction

Judith Hearne. 1955; as *The Lonely Passion of Judith Hearne*, 1956.
The Feast of Lupercal. 1957; as *A Moment of Love*, 1965.
The Luck of Ginger Coffey. 1960.
An Answer from Limbo. 1962.
The Emperor of Ice-Cream. 1965.
I Am Mary Dunne. 1968.
Fergus. 1970.
Catholics. 1972.
The Great Victorian Collection. 1975.
The Doctor's Wife. 1976.

Plays

Screenplays: *The Luck of Ginger Coffey*, 1964; *Torn Curtain*, 1966; *The Slave*, 1967; *Catholics*, 1973.

Other

>   *Canada,* with the editors of *Life.* 1963.
>   *The Revolution Script.* 1971.

Reading List: *Moore* by Hallvard Dahlie, 1969 (includes bibliography); *Odysseus Ever Returning* by George Woodcock, 1970.

* * *

    Brian Moore's fiction falls into three groups: the Belfast novels (*Judith Hearne, The Feast of Lupercal,* and *The Emperor of Ice-Cream*); the early North American novels (*The Luck of Ginger Coffey, An Answer from Limbo,* and *I Am Mary Dunne*); and the more recent metaphysical novels (*Fergus, Catholics,* and *The Great Victorian Collection*) written since his move to California some years ago. *The Doctor's Wife* (1976) comes under none of these headings, and must be considered separately since, although touching on areas Moore has already explored in his earlier work, it seems to mark a new departure.
    The Belfast novels revolve around crises in the lives of an alcoholic spinster, a bachelor schoolmaster, and an adolescent boy in revolt against his family. The society Moore depicts – the Belfast of the 1940's – is a bleak and terrible place for the outsider or the transgressor; for the lonely, despairing Judith Hearne, or the incautious Diarmid Devine, who pursues a scandalous if pathetic affair with a Protestant girl, although he is himself a Catholic. But in *The Emperor of Ice-Cream,* which belongs to this early period although written years later, Moore strikes a more optimistic note with his account of a few formative months in the life of a Catholic boy who takes a job as an air-raid warden, thus outraging his old-fashioned, nationalist parents. The job, however, provides him with much picaresque experience of the adult world, and the opportunity to stand on his own feet.
    The protagonists of the Belfast novels know, all too well, who they are. Their relation to the closed society around them is fixed, almost immutable. But in the early North American novels the characters begin to drift away from fixed identity, all but losing themselves in the existential flux of modern life. Ginger Coffey, an Irish immigrant in Montreal, finds his mental categories dissolving as he struggles to land a decent job commensurate with what he assumes to be his social status. In *An Answer from Limbo* an Irish writer living in New York sacrifices his mother for the sake of his work; cuts himself off, as it were, from his own past in order to create himself anew. And in *I Am Mary Dunne* a young woman in the midst of pre-menstrual tension literally forgets her own name and later comes close to suicide.
    A vein of metaphysical speculation, released in Moore by the American experience, is evident in *Fergus, Catholics,* and *The Great Victorian Collection,* in each of which the nature of reality is called into question, and the nature and significance of art or artifice held up for inspection. "The final belief," said Wallace Stevens, evidently one of Moore's favourite poets, "is to believe in a fiction, which you know to be a fiction, there being nothing else"; and this is the theme of the metaphysical novels, where creative activity is itself brought into the centre of the action, literally or symbolically. But in his most recent novel, *The Doctor's Wife,* Moore put aside these considerations in order to revisit earlier scenes. The book is a sort of Irish *Madame Bovary.* The heroine, on holiday in France, breaks with her husband, a Belfast surgeon, and has an ill-fated affair with an American student some years her junior. She is the antithesis of Judith Hearne, with everything that Judith Hearne desired, and she throws it all away, finishing up penniless and alone, but with her integrity undiminished, in a London bedsitter. And if the simple narrative line and the absence of metaphysics seem to represent a regression, we must conclude that Moore is making his world mosaically, not linearly – perhaps a richer and more various way of proceeding.

—Derek Mahon

MORAES, Dom(inic Frank). Indian. Born in Bombay, 19 July 1938; son of Frank Moraes, editor of the *Indian Express*. Educated at Jesus College, Oxford, 1956–59, B.A. in English 1959. Married 1) Judith St. John in 1963 (divorced), one son; 2) Leela Naidu in 1970. Formerly, scriptwriter, Granada Television; Documentary Filmmaker. Since 1971, Editor, *The Asian Magazine*, Hong Kong. Since 1973, Consultant, United Nations Fund for Population Activities. Recipient: Hawthornden Prize, 1958.

PUBLICATIONS

Verse

A Beginning. 1957.
Poems. 1960.
John Nobody. 1965.
Poems 1955–1965. 1966.
Bedlam Etcetera. 1966.

Other

Green Is the Grass (on cricket). 1951.
Gone Away: An Indian Journal. 1960.
My Son's Father: An Autobiography. 1968; as *My Son's Father: A Poet's Autobiography*, 1969.
The Tempest Within: An Account of East Pakistan. 1971.
From East and West: A Collection of Essays. 1971.
A Matter of People. 1974; as *This Burdened Planet*, 1974.

Editor, *Voices for Life: Reflections on the Human Condition.* 1975.

Translator, *The Brass Serpent,* by T. Carmi. 1964.

* * *

Dom Moraes, the son of the distinguished journalist and writer Frank Moraes, is in several ways an interesting literary figure. One of the best known Indian poets writing in English, there is in his poetry, paradoxically, very little of specific "Indianness." In fact, as he himself put it once: "English is the language I think in and write in; I even dream in it ... I don't speak any Indian language – neither Hindi nor my native Konkani." And he spent the most formative years of his life – from 15 to 30 – in England.

Moraes's poetic talent has been an extremely precocious one: at eighteen, he won the Hawthornden Prize for his first collection of poems, *A Beginning*; his second, *Poems*, was a Poetry Book Society choice. The most remarkable quality of his poetry is an unusual combination of romantic naivety with a deep, underlying ironic thrust. This stems from a recurring feeling of loneliness threatening, in the initial stages, to become obsessive self-indulgence: "I have grown up, I think, to live alone,/To keep my old illusions, sometimes dream/Glumly that I am unloved and forlorn ..." ("Autobiography"). This apparently "fluent sentimentality" in fact tempts one, as Harry Fainlight has put it (*Encounter*, November 1961) "to write the whole thing off as a luxury product, the lispings of an elite-poet." The naivety, however, is only apparent, for there is "deceptive strength in this kind of verse; having the courage of one's own naivety is a difficult and promising thing and certainly a much sounder basis for growth than the clever apeing of maturity ...."

This growth registers itself in his gradual awareness of contemporary reality: the loss of identity rendered acute by his dichotomous background as an Indian writing in English, the increasing eruption of violence and disorder. If the Indian landscape is dotted with "hawks," "doe-like girls, the sun, endless delay/Bullocks and Buicks, statesmen like great auks," ("John Nobody") and "the consumptive beggars" with "the thin voice of a shell" ("Gone Away"), he realizes that this is an extension of disorder all over, symbolized by such events as the trial of Milovan Djilas and the atrocities of the Nazis.

From this awareness of a searing landscape arises the insistent longing for love ("Except in you I have no rest/For always with you I am safe"), for the tranquil, almost mystical, vision. This is expressed with great subtlety in, for instance, "Bells for William Wordsworth," in which the Wordsworthian vision does not remain a mere academic exercise ("His work is carefully studied in colleges still") but becomes a significant mode for his own regaining of tranquillity: "I have seen him risen again with the crocus in Spring./I have turned my ear to the wind, I have heard him speaking." The longing for the tranquil vision, for Moraes, is innate to the poet's vocation itself, his preoccupation with words: "I have spent several years fighting with words/And they fight back with words that perplex" ("A Small Whimper"). And eventually it is art that encapsules reality in a deathless way; for, like the stranger catching a "glimpse" of "the miles-off sea" even in the midst of ruins ("kanheri caves"), art ensures resurrection.

Poetry seems to Moraes, however, aesthetically to insulate one from the rough and tumble of life. Probably this accounts for his constant roving and, like V. S. Naipaul, interspersing his creative with non-fictional writing: travelogue, reportage, film-making. *Gone Away* (a record of his travel in India) and *My Son's Father* (autobiography) are written with great subtlety and insight and seem inalienable parts of his creative writing itself.

Moraes's weakness as a poet, however, seems to be the lack of a controlling, focussing centre. In spite of his work's wide-ranging implications, arising out of the incorporation of myth, anthropology, and medieval references, there is an absence of firm roots. Hence the irritating sense of non-belonging perceptible in his poetry.

—M. Sivaramakrishna

MULGAN, John (Alan Edward). New Zealander. Born in Christchurch, 31 December 1911; son of the writer Alan Mulgan. Educated at Maungawhan School, 1917–25; Wellington College, 1925–27; Auckland Grammar School, 1927–30; Auckland University College, 1930–32, B.A. 1932; Oxford University, 1933–35. Served in the British Army in the Middle East and Greece, 1939–45: Lieutenant-Colonel. Married Gabrielle Wanklyn in 1937; one son. Regular contributor to the *Auckland Star*, 1934–37; worked for the Clarendon Press, Oxford, 1935–39. *Died* (by suicide) *25 April 1945*.

PUBLICATIONS

Fiction

Man Alone. 1939.

Other

The Emigrants: Early Travellers to the Antipodes, with Hector Bolitho. 1939.
An Introduction to English Literature, with Dan Davin. 1947.
Report on Experience (autobiography), edited by Jack Bennett. 1947.

Editor, *Poems of Freedom*. 1938.
Editor, *A Concise Oxford Dictionary of English Literature*. 1939.

Reading List: *Mulgan,* 1968, and *Mulgan* (booklet), 1978, both by Paul Day.

*   *   *

A month before his suicide in 1945, John Mulgan described the manuscript of *Report on Experience* as "only the draft and outline of a book I'd like to write." It was nevertheless published two years later, and, although the intended revision and expansion would undoubtedly have made it more substantial, the book reveals a good deal about the author of *Man Alone* and has the direct, transparent style of that remarkable novel. Its mode is autobiographical, but its subject matter goes beyond personal concerns. Social patterns in New Zealand and England between the wars are seen with a shrewd eye and limned with a steady hand, and the rest of the book contains Mulgan's reflections on army life, on the nature of modern warfare, on ideologies and ideals, on the *virtus* ethic, and on wartime Greece. There is a tendency to generalize without supporting evidence or precise definition, and it is in this respect that his report is most obviously incomplete. But it belongs authentically to its period and to the cultural attitudes which shaped Mulgan's imagination.

It is significant that, although the thirties were dominated by widespread economic stress and political struggle, Mulgan's survey of New Zealand life during those years invokes no concepts of class or system. "Doctrinaire allegiances he distrusted absolutely," one of his friends said of him; and the criteria of Mulgan's commentary in *Report on Experience* imply a mellow humanism based on simple communal values. Of the Depression's impact he has this kind of thing to say: "Certain changes came over New Zealand at this time.... It was noticeable that men stopped speaking openly to one another, and the majority favoured a doctrine that every man's duty was to look after himself. This, of course, was the fine old flavour of the pioneers and of rugged, economic liberalism, but I think, from what I have read, that the pioneers turned out to help their neighbours in distress and survived because they lived as a community, and not as men alone."

Accordingly the primary emphasis in *Man Alone* is on the inadequacies of most relationships between people, and between individuals and the land itself, in a country pervaded by mean-spirited materialism. Paul Day has remarked in an essay on *Man Alone* that it shows how, in New Zealand, economic exigencies "provide a grimly constricting rule over human destinies," yet they do so in Mulgan's view not because of political injustices so much as because people force themselves into a narrow, solitary, joyless existence through their own "lust to possess." It is a moral critique rather than a specifically political one that Mulgan offers. This needs emphasizing because the novel's central concerns were sometimes misread when it first appeared. Johnson, the protagonist, is a casual drifter, sceptical of all theories and commitments, and indeed most of the characters are to some degree solitaries. That fact is not changed when, in the brief second part of the novel, Johnson goes off to fight in the Spanish War. A contemporary reviewer misrepresented this ending when he said of Johnson: "It is a mature and conscious socialist who volunteers for the Brigade in Spain," and added that Mulgan's purpose was to reveal "the deepening capitalist crisis." On the contrary, the author continues to underline in this post-script section (written only at the publisher's request to bring the book up to "minimum novel length") Johnson's non-committal view of politics. He goes to Spain merely for the sake of company and excitement.

The original title of the novel was "Talking of War"; but that refers primarily not to any class struggle, nor to international conflict, but to the hostility generated between men and the land by acquisitive individualism.

—Ian Reid

NAIDU, Sarojini (née Chattopadhyaya). Indian. Born in Hyderabad, 13 February 1879. Educated at Madrea University, Hyderabad; King's College, London; Girton College, Cambridge. Married M. G. Naidu in 1898; two sons and two daughters. Involved with the women's movement in India, and the welfare of Indian students: lectured widely in the chief cities of India on questions of social, religious, educational, and national progress; Member of the Bombay Municipality, 1923–29; one of the leaders of the political movement for the freedom of India; travelled throughout East Africa and South Africa on behalf of Indian settlers, 1924; Chairman of the Indian National Congress, 1925; lectured in the United States and Canada, 1928–29; took part in the Round Table Conference, London, 1931; Member, Government of India Deputation to South Africa, 1932; Acting Governor of the United Provinces, 1947. Chancellor, University of Allahabad. Recipient: Kaiser-i-Hind Medal, 1908. Fellow, Royal Society of Literature, 1914. *Died 3 March 1949.*

PUBLICATIONS

Verse

The Golden Threshold. 1905.
The Bird of Time: Songs of Life, and Death, and the Spring. 1912.
The Broken Wing: Songs of Love, Death, and Destiny, 1915–1916. 1917.
The Sceptred Flute: Songs of India. 1928.
Select Poems, edited by H. G. Dalway Turnbull. 1930.
The Feather of the Dawn. 1961.

Other

Speeches and Writings. 1904(?); revised edition, 1925.
The Soul of India. 1917.

Reading List: *Naidu: A Biography* by Padmini Sengupta, 1966.

* * *

Sarojini Naidu was born into a distinguished Bengali family. Her father, Dr. Aghorenath Chattopadhyaya, took his doctorate in Science from the University of Edinburgh in 1877. He was a pioneer in the field of education and founded the Nizam College at Hyderabad. He was also a linguist familiar with French, German, Urdu, and Hindi. Mrs. Naidu reflected in her career a comparable versatility. A sensitive poet, she was also a gifted speaker and an ardent nationalist, playing, as a close associate of Gandhi, a decisive role in the Indian freedom struggle. Above all, she was a rebel: defying all caste inhibitions, she married Dr. Govindarajulu Naidu, a non-Bengali and non-Brahmin.

Mrs. Naidu's poetic career, according to her own account, began early: "One day, when I was eleven, I was sighing over a sum in algebra: it *wouldn't* come right, but instead a whole poem came to me suddenly. I wrote it down." This poetic impulse acquired certitude and definition when she went to England in 1895 for further studies. Here the impact of writers such as Edmund Gosse was decisive. In fact, it was Gosse who advised her to avoid evoking "Anglo-Saxon sentiment in an Anglo-Saxon setting" which would condemn her poetry to derivative mediocrity. Instead, she should give, he felt, "some revelation of the heart of India, some sincere penetrating analysis of native passion."

This was a valuable suggestion and gave direction to Mrs. Naidu's emerging talent; her poetry began evidencing an impressive thematic and descriptive range. Her poetry ranges from exquisite vignettes of Indian life – "The Snake Charmers," "The Bangle-Sellers," "The Weavers" or "The Bazaars of Hyderabad" – to deeply metaphysical contemplation, as in "To a Buddha Seated on a Lotus." Whatever the subject, Mrs. Naidu shows an unusual eye for the descriptive detail and achieves remarkable success in presenting, as James H. Cousins has put it, "the amazing groupings of colour and form, human and natural, that make the surface of life in India a fascinating kaleidoscope." Mrs. Naidu's basic poetic stance, however, is invariably a delicate, almost naïve, sense of romantic wonder and innocence, what Arthur Symons called "a bird-like quality," "a delicately evasive way of writing." This stemmed from, in Mrs. Naidu's own words, "a very fanciful and dreamy nature." This genteel romanticism probably explains her imperviousness to the modernist trends exemplified in the work of her contemporaries Yeats and Eliot. There is in her poetry a profusion of sentiment and images which, lacking an underlying logic of emotion, remain decorative. Even when the poem is ostensibly called "An Indian Love Song," what emerges is not so much specific "Indianness" but a plethora of images: "Like the perfume in the petals of a rose/Hides thy heart within my Bosom, O my love!/Like a garland, like a jewel, like a dove."

What is, however, remarkable in Mrs. Naidu's poetry is its prosodic virtuosity. She handled almost all the English metrical patterns – including difficult ones such as the dactylic – with ease. R. Parthasarathy credits her with "perhaps the finest ear among Indian poets for the sound of English," and cites "Palanguin-bearers" for its "springy and elastic steps":

> Lightly, O lightly we bear her along,
> She sways like a flower in the wind of our song;
> She skims like a bird on the foam of a stream,
> She floats like a laugh from the lips of a dream
> Gaily, O gaily we glide and we sing,
> We bear her along like a pearl on a string.

In effect, while Mrs. Naidu's poetry is fascinating in its evocation of the Indian landscape and prosodically excellent, it seems a bit cloying in its fulsome sentimentality.

—M. Sivaramakrishna

NAIPAUL, V(idiadhar) S(urajprasad). Trinidadian. Born in Trinidad, 17 August 1932. Educated at Queen's Royal College, Port of Spain, Trinidad, 1943–48; University College, Oxford, 1950–54, B.A. (honours) in English 1953. Married Patricia Ann Hale in 1955. Settled in England, 1950; Editor, "Caribbean Voices," BBC, London, 1954–56; Fiction Reviewer, *New Statesman,* London, 1957–61; travelled in the West Indies and South America, 1961, India, 1962–63, Africa, 1966, and the United States and Canada, 1969. Recipient: Rhys Memorial Prize, 1958; Maugham Award, 1961; Phoenix Trust Award, 1962; Hawthornden Prize, 1964; Smith Literary Award, 1968; Arts Council grant, 1969; Booker Prize, 1971.

PUBLICATIONS

Fiction

The Mystic Masseur. 1957.
The Suffrage of Elvira. 1958.
Miguel Street. 1959.
A House for Mr. Biswas. 1961.
Mr. Stone and the Knights Companion. 1963.
The Mimic Men. 1967.
A Flag on the Island (stories). 1967.
In a Free State. 1971.
Guerrillas. 1975.

Other

The Middle Passage: Impressions of Five Societies – British, French and Dutch – in the West Indies and South America. 1962.
An Area of Darkness: An Experience of India. 1964.
The Loss of El Dorado: A History. 1969.
The Overcrowded Barracoon and Other Articles. 1972.
India: A Wounded Civilization. 1977.

Reading List: *The West Indian Novel* by Kenneth Ramchand, 1970; *Naipaul: An Introduction to His Work* by Paul Theroux, 1972; *Naipaul* by Donald Hamner, 1973, and *Naipaul* edited by Hamner, 1978; *Naipaul: A Critical Introduction* by Landeg White, 1975; *Paradoxes of Order: Some Perspectives on the Fiction of Naipaul* by Robert K. Morris, 1975.

* * *

V. S. Naipaul's readers, both private and official, have not been unappreciative, and his publisher has honoured him with a collected edition, a prize usually awarded to the illustrious dead. So much esteem might well have sunk, or at least spoiled, a lesser talent. It has had no such effect on Naipaul, who is undoubtedly a writer of the utmost devotion, as well as a man of rare personal integrity.

It is the life of Trinidad, its workers, peasants, crooks, shopkeepers, local politicians, pundits, which is the body of Naipaul's early novels, *The Mystic Masseur, The Suffrage of Elvira,* and *Miguel Street,* treated with gaiety, malice, the clearest insight, and with an unfailingly lucid and elegant line. It is the world described discursively, and sometimes bitterly, in *The Middle Passage,* a place where neither civilization nor revolution had been created, only plantations and prosperity, neglect and decline. There are two contrasts in this early work: one between the huddled disorder of the place, and the unqualified sharpness and clarity of the writer's definition. The barely controlled chaos, both of place and sensibility, is outlined with a controlled and absolute clarity. It is as though the defining form is not just an instrument of the writer's perception, but a protest of the wholeness of his self against the neurotic muddle of the surroundings. The other contrast is between the flatness and dreariness of village and town, graceless, mean, wretchedly thin, like the village of Fuente Grove, and the brilliance and liveliness of the people, a folk with a genius for vivacity, expressed in an idiom of dancing vitality and wit. The intimate, energetic, sometimes brutal, speech of the people, contrasts with the silken run of the author's own voice, which has a near-Latin order and assurance, and which speaks out of a more inclusive intelligence and for a scheme of values in which judgment is an essential part of registration, and a detached and cultivated irony a key element in the sensibility.

Indian stability, West Indian mobility: not an inaccurate description of the feel of this work.

Naipaul's prose style lacks any awkwardness or arbitrary flush; it is wholly free of the gratuitous and the gesturing. Indeed, it may well seem mild and unemphatic. But it is also lithe, sharp, and definitive. Its grace is no block to a questing analytic capacity. It corresponds in its quiet firmness to some central assurance in the author, and it is this medium which makes it possible for him to fit together a variety of idioms and conversational habits. It corresponds, too, to an unbending honesty, the moral equivalent of clarity of perception; this is a power which enables Naipaul to see his characters in all their contradictory complexity and depth. He is a master of tone, with a capacity to differentiate one from another, and to assemble a variety of tones in consort.

Naipaul's comedy is not one of situation or plot; nor are the characters cartoons or puppets; and if it is satirical that is only so because of the author's sense of the ridiculous and his eye for dishonesty. It has been called malicious but it is hard to see why, since the attitude is neither contemptuous nor patronising, and the author can hardly be condemned for not having as his purpose the wrapping up of reality in cosy illusion. It is a comedy essentially of the individual person in his damaged society, the actual person and the observed setting. But even the gayest, the most deliriously comic persons are frayed with anxieties and hunted by sickness and death.

Naipaul's masterpiece, *A House for Mr. Biswas*, was published early in his career. It is a novel in the grand manner, deliberate, large in scope, constructing a world with authoritative ease, with a central figure, a biographical line, a multitude of grasped minor characters, people seen from within so that they possess an intrinsic, spontaneous vitality, and from without, so that they are located in time and place and in a context of value and feeling. The distaste for certain aspects of humanity, faint in his earlier work, harsher in the discursive books and in his latest novels, is taken up here into a much more inclusive sensibility which is concerned with an essential humanity and which blends unsentimental accuracy in notation with a braced pity and tensed, athletic tolerance. It is a novel which has, too, a more profound value, a deep poetic truth. This is realised in the creative, encompassing metaphor which initiates and sustains the novel. At the root of the metaphor is the idea of slavery. Naipaul had mentioned in an earlier book, *The Middle Passage*, the difficulty of finding in Trinidad physical evidence of slavery. But that palpable absence of external institution does not mean that slavery had not inflicted an incurable wound on the national consciousness. The members of the community in *A House for Mr. Biswas*, even those like the Indians who were exempt from formal, historical slavery, carry about with them in their attitude and posture, in their management of life and feeling, the indelible mark of the slave, who is supremely the unnecessary man. All are impelled by the urgency to demonstrate, to themselves even more than to others, their human necessity. In the earlier novels they did this by bruising themselves absurdly and ineffectively against an indifferent universe. Mr. Biswas constructs the proof of his necessity in both a comic and a most moving way. Saturated as he is with the ethos of the given place, maltreated in peculiar deficiencies and cruelties, he is none the less realised with such complete conviction, so living a reality, that he becomes a model of man, just as the history and situation which formed him are seen to be a metaphor of the process which constitutes any man.

The society (with the history implicit in it) which would produce the wiry, flinching figure of Mr. Biswas (and having done so coldly demonstrate his superfluousness) is evoked with humour for its absurdity, sadness for its cruelty, and precision in everything. This capacity for definition which is also embodiment, for solid and refined denotation, lies at the heart of Naipaul's expressive power. His mind and his language work, not by any poetic murmuration or suggestiveness, but by pointing, by specifying, delimiting, detailing. To arrive at the utmost clarity is Naipaul's artistic purpose; to mark off the detail in its uniqueness, whether it be object or feeling or event, is his method. The details as defined are assembled with such unobtrusive tact, with such a fine sense of what is sufficient, that without display or excess or strain they make a composition lit by a level and equal light, as convincing and as self-endorsing as a natural substance.

The one limitation on the generality, the fullness of grasp, of Naipaul's strong, original work, is something I can only call an over-developed, on occasion even an overwrought, sense of human offensiveness. It corresponds to that flinching distaste for the human skin in *The Mimic Men*. The note is insistent and sometimes shrill. It suggests in the author some radical horror of human flesh. The bias against the ordinary grossness of human beings which is clearly part of Naipaul's sensibility becomes here a rejection of the flesh itself.

If this is weakness, as I think it is, it is also evidence of another, more positive quality of Naipaul's writing. That is his scrupulous honesty in reporting both the facts of the case and his reaction to them. He never fudges a state of affairs or fakes his feelings. He has an eye without prejudice as well as an eye unclouded by fear that he might be prejudiced, a timidity common enough among a number of English writers.

—William Walsh

NARAYAN, R(asipuram) K(rishnaswami). Indian. Born in Madras, 10 October 1906. Educated at Maharaja's College, Mysore, graduated 1930. Full-time writer. Recipient: National Prize of the Indian Literary Academy, 1958; Padma Bhushan, India, 1964; National Association of Independent Schools Award, U.S.A., 1965; English-Speaking Union of the United States award, 1975. Litt.D.: University of Leeds, Yorkshire, 1967. Lives in Mysore, India.

Publications

Fiction

Swami and Friends: A Novel of Malgudi. 1935.
The Bachelor of Arts. 1937.
The Dark Room. 1938.
Cyclone and Other Stories. N.d.
Malgudi Days (stories). 1943.
The English Teacher. 1945; as *Grateful to Life and Death,* 1953.

An Astrologer's Day and Other Stories. 1947.
Mr. Sampath. 1949; as *The Printer of Malgudi,* 1955.
Dodu and Other Stories. 1950(?).
The Financial Expert. 1952.
Waiting for the Mahatma. 1955.
Lawley Road (stories). 1956.
The Guide. 1958.
The Man-Eater of Malgudi. 1961.
Gods, Demons, and Others (stories). 1964.
The Vendor of Sweets. 1967; as *The Sweet Vendor,* 1967.
A Horse and Two Goats (stories). 1970.
The Painter of Signs. 1976.

Other

Mysore. 1944.
My Dateless Diary (travel in America). 1960.
The Ramayana: A Shortened Modern Prose Version of the Indian Epic. 1972.
Reluctant Guru (essays). 1974.
My Days: A Memoir. 1974.
The Mahabharata: A Shortened Modern Prose Version of the Indian Epic. 1978.

Reading List: *Narayan: A Critical Study of His Works* by Haris Raizada, 1969; *The Novels of Narayan* by Lakshmi Holmstrom, 1973; *Narayan* by P. S. Sundaram, 1973.

*　　*　　*

The most immediately striking aspects of the eleven novels of R. K. Narayan are their spatial identity, for all take part in the imagined town of Malgudi, and their temporal continuity, for they take us from the days of the Raj, when the first of them – *Swami and Friends* – was written, down to the independent India whose struggles for self- realization form the background to later books, down through four decades to *The Painter of Signs.*

As Narayan constructs it in the mind's eye from novel to novel, Malgudi is a medium-sized south Indian provincial town, reminiscent of both Mysore and Bangalore, which changes as time goes on; it has an imaginary river where boys can play, saints can bathe ritually, and wives try to drown themselves; behind it lie the equally imaginary Mempi Hills, where townsmen of Malgudi can become anchorites and others, like Vasu in *The Man-Eater of Malgudi,* can work out their rage by hunting.

Yet history has made Malgudi not merely Indian. One of Narayan's main themes is in fact the strange consequences of the continuing influence of a departed alien culture – the British – which offers perhaps the only means by which even an intensely conservative society like that of south India, proud of its traditions, can play a viable role in the modern world. Narayan himself, writing an English more eloquent than that of many English writers, is of course an example of this phenomenon, and it tends to dominate his early novels.

These early novels are all set within the educational system of the Raj, and are Narayan's most autobiographical works: *Swami and Friends* draws heavily on his experience as a mission school boy, *The Bachelor of Arts* on his years as a college student, and *The English Teacher* on his unsuccessful pedagogic career.

Swaminithan and his fellows in *Swami and Friends* are unwitting examples of the contradictions which even in the 1930's Narayan saw entering into the culturally divided lives of modern Indians. They attend a mission school which prepared them for the College in Malgudi where English is the only language of instruction. In this situation they become dedicated to the English game of cricket, and their special form of the quest that dominates all Narayan novels is a comic one, the creation on the waste lots of Malgudi of an M.C.C. which they hope may rival its English namesake.

The alternative to submersion in western models is of course withdrawal into one or other of the interlocking traditional worlds of the village and the life of the wandering holy man, who usually finds his warmest welcome among illiterate peasants. In Narayan's novels such withdrawal often provides a way to self-discovery if not self-transformation.

After winning his degree, Chandran, in *The Bachelor of Arts*, wanders for eight months as a *sanyasin* – a holy beggar – because conflicting horoscopes have prevented him from marrying the girl he fell in love with when he saw her on the riverbank. But he goes through the motions of the holy life without being holy, and his moment of revelation comes when – at a time of drought and starvation – he realizes the fraud he had been foisting on himself as well as on the villagers who have fed him out of their iron rations. He returns to the normal world, becomes a successful small businessman and marries a girl whose stars in their motions dance well with his.

Savitri, the misused wife of *The Dark Room*, runs away from home when her husband carries on a public affair with a young widow, his colleague at the Egladia Insurance Company. She tries to drown herself, but is rescued by a thief and taken to his village, where she becomes servant in the temple until she finds the love of her children calling her back and the middle-class, half-Indian-half-Western world reclaims her.

Raju, in *The Guide*, does not return. Guide to the cave temples of the Malgudi Hills, he becomes involved with a former temple dancer, is led to crime and imprisonment, and then retreats to an old riverside temple. The villages take him for a saint, and he becomes trapped in the role, so that he undertakes a quixotic fast to end a drought and dies when the rains come. Only Jagan, in *The Sweet Vendor*, old, tired of profitable trading, disillusioned and – as he believes – defiled by the behaviour of a westernized son, seems likely to find in his withdrawal the wise detachment he seeks.

On a different, political level, the search for fulfilment outside ordinary currents of middle-class Indian life is portrayed in *Waiting for the Mahatma*. Sriram, rich and immature, falls in love with Bharati, one of the young women devotees who follow the Mahatma on his wanderings, and, when Bharati goes to prison on Gandhi's command, he falls in with a violent revolutionary who leads him into acts of sabotage. Sriram himself is imprisoned, and released in time to join Bharati and witness Gandhi's assassination in 1948.

Gandhi and his death represent an incursion from the outside world that destroys the magic autonomy of Malgudi and makes *Waiting for the Mahatma* at once one of the most interesting and least satisfying of Narayan's novels, largely because of the difference in grain between Gandhi and the people of Malgudi. For if there is one characteristic Narayan's characters share, it is mediocrity. Malgudi is a city of the petty and the unfulfilled and, like Chekhov, Narayan has produced from their very inadequacies, from their weaknesses and shallow pretensions, a combination of sadness and comedy that is irresistibly appealing. And even when the people of Malgudi seek to break out of the circle of their mediocrity, they fail because their ambitions overleap their capacities. The eponymous hero of *Mr. Sampath* sets out to establish in Malgudi a film studio that will rival those of Bombay and Calcutta, but the great epic of Hindu mythology that is to be his first production is ruined by a series of farcical disasters arising out of the jealousies, passions, and sheer inadequacies of Sampath and his associates.

But the ancient Indian myths which Narayan began to read with attention in his middle years are not merely plots for films; his novels recreate them in real life. Weak and inexperienced characters fall under the influence of malign men who are little more than nature forces personified. Such is the evil Dr. Pal in *The Financial Expert*, who sets the money-lender Margyya on his course of prosperity by giving him the copyright on an erotic book, who later corrupts Margyya's son Balu, and who finally encompasses the "financial expert's" ruin by starting the rumours that destroy him. And such too is Vasu the hunter who disrupts the life of the modest little printer Nataraj in *The Man-Eater of Malgudi* and threatens the little town's prosperity by seeking to kill the temple elephant for its ivory. In the end Vasu kills himself with the superhuman power he has not the wisdom to control, and the elephant marches on unharmed while Malgudi settles down again into the peace of mediocrity, a middle-class town in which, creating an ambiance for the sad eccentric characters and their quasi-mythical adventures, the colours and smells of India are so powerfully evoked that anyone who knows India south of Bombay has only to pick up a Narayan novel and read a dozen pages for the whole setting to re-form in his mind's nostril and the chatter of Indian voices to echo again in his ear. In Malgudi's microcosmic Indianness lives the secret of its appeal to readers in so many countries.

—George Woodcock

NEILSON, (John) Shaw. Australian. Born in Peoria, South Australia. 22 February 1872. Educated at State School, Peoria; State School, Minimay, Victoria, 1885–86. Farmer in the bush country, 1902–22; also wrote for the *Bulletin*, Sydney, 1900, *The Book Fellow*, 1907 and from 1911, and *Clarion*, 1908; Messenger, Country Roads Board, Melbourne, 1928–41. Granted Commonwealth Literary Fund pension, 1922. *Died 12 May 1942.*

PUBLICATIONS

Collections

The Poems, edited by A. R. Chisholm. 1965.

Verse

Heart of Spring. 1919.
Ballad and Lyrical Poems. 1923.
New Poems. 1927.
Collected Poems, edited by R. H. Croll. 1934.
Beauty Imposes: Some Recent Verse. 1938.
Unpublished Poems, edited by James Devaney. 1947.
Witnesses of Spring: Unpublished Poems, edited by Judith Wright. 1970.

Bibliography: *Neilson: An Annotated Bibliography and Checklist 1893–1964* by Hugh Anderson, 1964.

Reading List: *Neilson* by James Devaney, 1944; *Neilson* by Judith Wright, 1963 (biography and selected verse); *Neilson* by H. J. Oliver, 1968; *Neilson* by Hugh Anderson and L.J. Blake, 1972.

* * *

Shaw Neilson's work is hard to characterize. He is purely a lyrical poet, and his subjects are those of traditional lyric: the cycle of natural renewal, love, the spring, the beauty and pathos of young girls, children, the way of the animals as superior to the ways of men. Although he knew and loved the Australian back country, his poetry is not particularly tinged with local colour; his tone is not assertively tough nor is he in search of the Australian identity. In a sense, his poems could have emerged from several cultures: delicately mystical, occasionally reminiscent of Blake, or Walter de la Mare, or, in a poem like "The Long Week End" with the colloquially bitter-sweet irony of its refrain, calling to mind John Crowe Ransom:

> Sweet is the white, they say, she will ascend
> To an unstinted country where the days
> Gone without malice there she stays and stays
> Upon the long weekend.

His central poem, "The Orange Tree," is pure poetry, language at its most literary and innocent, the Tree representing the eternal life cycle. The poem is a dialogue between a young girl who hears the deep words of the tree and a sophisticated interlocutor who tries futilely to match his questions with the "mystery" of life, and who is imperatively silenced by the girl at the end of the poem, where questioning is stilled in affirmation:

> Listen! the young girl said. For all
>   Your hapless talk you fail to see
> There is a light, a step, a call
>   This evening in the Orange Tree.
>
> Is it, I said, a waste of love
>   Imperishably old in pain,
> Moving as an affrighted dove
>   Under the sunlight or the rain? ...
>
> Silence! The young girl said. Oh, why
>   Why will you talk to weary me?
> Plague me no longer now for I
>   Am listening like the Orange Tree.

—Ian Fletcher

OKARA, Gabriel (Imomotimi Gbaingbain). Nigerian. Born in Bumodi, Ijaw District, Rivers State, Western Nigeria, 21 April 1921. Educated at the Government College, Umuahia; trained as a bookbinder; studied journalism at Northwestern University, Evanston, Illinois, 1956. Principal Information Officer, Eastern Regional Government, Enugu, until 1967; Biafran Information Officer, Nigerian Civil War, 1967–69; travelled to the United States, with Chinua Achebe and Cyprian Ekwensi, to seek help for Biafra, 1969. Since 1972, Director of the Rivers State Publishing House, Port Harcourt. Recipient: Nigerian Festival of the Arts award, 1953.

PUBLICATIONS

Verse

The Fisherman's Invocation. 1978.

Fiction

The Voice. 1964.

Reading List: *Mother Is Gold* by Adrian A. Roscoe, 1971; *Culture, Tradition, and Society in the West African Novel* by Emmanuel Obiechina, 1975.

* * *

Gabriel Okara has written plays, translated folk material from Ijaw into English, and prepared documentary material for broadcasting. He is known almost exclusively, however, as a poet and as the author of an experimental novel, *The Voice*.

In 1953 Okara's poem "The Call of the River Nun" won the best all-round award in the Nigerian Festival of Arts. Like much of his poetry it has undercurrents of melancholy. The poet writes, with a slightly adolescent plangency, of how the River Nun beckons him into the mainstream of life. Later poems have been more symbolic including "The Snow Flakes Sail Gently Down," invoking impressions of exile while wintering in America:

> Then I dreamed a dream
> in my dead sleep. But I dreamed
> not of earth dying and elms a vigil
> keeping. I dreamed of birds, black
> birds flying in my inside, nesting
> and hatching on oil palms, bearing suns
> for fruits and with roots denting the
> uprooters' spades.

Okara's poems are deeply felt and usually introspective, though he is as concerned for the loss of traditional life in Nigeria as he is for his own state of mind brought about by the transition.

The Voice enjoys a reputation as a *succès d'estime*, for Okara attempted a semi-poetic novel which would render into an English equivalent some of the rhythms and sense of imagery found in his own vernacular, Ijaw. The novel is referred to whenever the possibilities of an African English are discussed. It is a short, partly allegorical novel presenting a struggle between the individual and his community; it is so lucid and distilled that it is likely to survive as a classic of African writing. In many ways *The Voice* is the archetypal rural novel in West Africa, confronting old and new values in a modern setting and demonstrating the rooted idealism which many African writers in the early 1960's believed to be the salvation of Africa. Okolo, whose name means "voice," embodies the author's faith in the liberty of personal conscience.

—Alastair Niven

OKIGBO, Christopher (Ifenayichukwu). Nigerian. Born in Ojoto, Onitsha Province, East Central State, 16 August 1932. Educated at the Government College, Umuahia; University College, Ibadan, 1951–56, B.A. in classics 1956. Served as a Major in the Biafran Army: killed in action, 1967. Married Sefi, daughter of the Attah of Igberra, in 1963; one daughter. Worked for the Nigerian Tobacco Company and the United African Company; Private Secretary to the Federal Minister of Research and Information, 1956–58; Latin Teacher, Fiditi Grammar School, near Ibadan, 1959–60; Librarian, University of Nigeria, Nsukka, then Enugu, 1960–62; West Africa Representative, Cambridge University Press, 1962–66. West African Editor, *Transition* magazine, Kampala, Uganda; Editor, Mbari Press, Ibadan. Founder, with Chinua Achebe, of Citadel Books Ltd., Enugu, 1967. Recipient: Dakar Festival of Negro Arts Poetry Prize, 1966. *Died in August 1967.*

PUBLICATIONS

Verse

Heavensgate. 1962.
Limits. 1964.
Labyrinths, with Path of Thunder. 1971.

Reading List: *The Trial of Okigbo* by Ali A. Mazrui, 1971; *Okigbo: Creative Rhetoric* by Sunday O Anozie, 1972.

*   *   *

In the Introduction to *Labyrinths*, Christopher Okigbo wrote:

> Although these poems were written and published separately, they are, in fact, organically related.
> *Heavensgate* was originally conceived as an Easter sequence. It later grew into ... an offering to Idoto, the village stream of which I drank, in which I washed, as a child....
> *Limits* and *Distances* are man's outer and inner worlds projected.... Both parts of *Silences* were inspired by the Western Nigeria crisis of 1962, and the death of Patrice Lamumba....
> *Labyrinths* is thus a fable of man's perennial quest for fulfilment ... a poet-protagonist is assumed throughout ... larger than Orpheus: one with a load of destiny on his head, rather like Gilgamesh, like Aeneas ... like the Fisher King of Eliot's *Waste Land*....

The comment makes very clear the kind of poet Okigbo was. He had an urgent sense of the poetic future of a country only recently released from pre-literacy. His education in Classical and British literature combined with his life's knowledge of Ibo ethic, myth, and verbal folk poetry allowed him to see man's past as much more interwoven than has been supposed and African culture no less rich than that of the West. Okigbo's poetry does not try to merge Ibo, Nigerian, African backgrounds or poetry with British or Classical, but to show them as if from one, perhaps the same, antecedent. In *Silences* he writes, "One dips one's tongue in ocean, and begins / To cry to the mushroom of the sky."

Okigbo made no effort to solve problems which such attitudes as that of the Negritude of the 1950's posed. English was for him his own tongue, and he did not think of using any other for his poetry. In fact, there are strong echoes from other English writers — in *Limits*, for instance, of Eliot, John Wain, even de la Mare — mingled with references to Ibo myth and ritual:

>Hurry on down—
>>Thro' the cinder market —
>
>Hurry on down
>>in the wake of the dream;
>
>Hurry on down —
>>To rockpoint of Cable,
>
>To pull by the rope
>>the big white elephant ...
>
>& *the mortar is not yet dry*
>& *the mortar is not yet dry*....

Okigbo's double background makes for richness of substance and metaphor. Intensity of feeling carries this intellectual poet still further. He acknowledges his debt to Gerard Manley Hopkins in his " Lament of the Silent Sisters," a poem prophetic of his own death:

>Chorus: We carry in our worlds that flourish
>Our worlds that have failed ...
>
>Crier: This is our swan song
>This is the sigh of our spirits.

Okibo was a religious, philosophic poet of great promise.

—Anne Tibble

PAGE, P(atricia) K(athleen). Canadian. Born in Swanage, Dorset, England, 23 November 1916; emigrated to Canada, 1919. Educated at St. Hilda's School for Girls, Calgary, Alberta; Art Students' League, and Pratt Institute, New York; studied art privately in Brazil and New York. Married William Arthur Irwin in 1950; three step-children. Formerly, sales clerk and radio actress, St. John, New Brunswick; filing clerk and historical researcher, Montreal, and a Founding Editor, *Preview*, Montreal; Script Writer, National Film Board, Ottawa, 1946–50. Painter, as P. K. Irwin: one-man shows at Picture Loan Society, Toronto, 1960; Galeria de Arte Moderna, Mexico City, 1962, and Art Gallery of Greater Victoria, 1965; works included in the collections of the National Gallery of Canada, Ottawa; Art Gallery of Toronto; Vancouver Art Gallery. Recipient: Governor-General's Award, 1955. Member, Academia Brazileira de Letras, Rio de Janeiro. Lives in Victoria, British Columbia.

PUBLICATIONS

Verse

Unit of Five, with others. 1944.
As Ten as Twenty. 1946.
The Metal and the Flower. 1954.
Cry Ararat! Poems New and Selected. 1967.
Leviathan in a Pool. 1973.

Fiction

The Sun and the Moon. 1944.
The Sun and the Moon and Other Fictions. 1973.

Reading List: *The Bush Garden: Essays on the Canadian Imagination* by Northrop Frye, 1971; "The Poetry of Page" by A. J. M. Smith, in *Canadian Literature*, Autumn 1971.

* * *

P. K. Page is a poet with two careers. She played a considerable role among the Montreal poets of the early 1940's, being one of the founding editors of the historic Canadian poetry magazine *Preview*, and she continued writing verse until the early 1950's. There followed a period of travel in Latin America, Australia, and the United States, during which she wrote comparatively little, and developed a parallel talent as a painter under the name of P. K. Irwin. Returning to Canada in 1964, she began to write poetry again, and in recent years has reoccupied her leading position among active Canadian writers.

P. K. Page's early poetry tended to take on some of the flavour of English 1930's verse, concerning itself with themes of social protest and showing the formal influence of Auden and Spender. By the end of the 1940's she was moving into a more individual kind of expression, terse and ironic, and was concerning herself less with socio-political situations than with individual predicaments – the plights of solitary people or of those whom circumstances subjected to contempt; satire and compassion are unusually mingled in these middle poems.

In her later work, P. K. Page has moved towards a stark, purified poetry of great tonal attractiveness, and at the same time towards metaphysical intents, and an almost mystical concern for the view out from the mind towards images that promise integration. Her poem, "Cry Ararat!," in the volume with the same name, is typical of this trend, as the final lines eloquently demonstrate:

> The leaves that make the tree by day,
> the green twig the dove saw fit
> to lift across a world of water
> break in a wave about our feet.
> The bird in the thicket with his whistle
> the crystal lizard in the grass
> the star and shell
> tassel and bell
> of wild flowers blowing where we pass,
> this flora-fauna flotsam, pick and touch,
> requires the focus of the total I.

A single leaf can block a mountainside;
all Ararat be conjured by a leaf.

As well as her poetry and painting, P. K. Page has produced a small amount of fiction. The novel she published in 1944 under the pseudonym of Judith Cape, *The Sun and the Moon*, was a work of romantic symbolism, and the same is true of her haunting and highly ambivalent short stories.

—George Woodcock

PALMER, (Edward) Vance. Australian. Born in Bundaberg, Queensland, 28 August 1885. Educated at Ipswich Boys' Grammar School, Queensland, 1899–1901. Served in the Australian Imperial Forces in World War I. Married Janet Higgins in 1914. Journalist in Brisbane, 1901–05; free-lance writer in London, 1905–08; worked as a tutor, bookkeeper, and bush worker, in Australia, 1909; returned to London, 1910, and wrote for *New Age*, *Guardian Fortnightly*, and *British Review*; lived in Melbourne, 1915–25; associated with *Fellowship* literary magazine from 1917; Founder, with Louis Esson, Pioneer Players, in the 1920's; settled temporarily in Caloundra, Queensland, 1925, but returned to Melbourne. Chairman of the Advisory Board, Commonwealth Literary Fund, 1947–53. Recipient: Australian Literature Society Medal, 1930. *Died 15 July 1959.*

PUBLICATIONS

Fiction

The World of Men (stories). 1915.
The Shantykeeper's Daughter. 1920.
The Boss of Killara. 1922.
The Enchanted Island. 1923.
The Outpost. 1924; revised edition, as *Hurricane*, 1935.
Cronulla: A Story of Station Life. 1924.
The Man Hamilton. 1928.
Men Are Human. 1930.
The Passage. 1930.
Separate Lives (stories). 1931.
Daybreak. 1932.
The Swayne Family. 1934.
Sea and Spinifex (stories). 1934.
Legend for Sanderson. 1937.
Cyclone. 1947.

Golconda. 1948.
Let the Birds Fly (stories). 1955.
Seedtime. 1957.
The Rainbow Bird and Other Stories, edited by A. Edwards. 1957.
The Big Fellow. 1959.

Plays

The Prisoner (produced 1919). In *The Black Horse and Other Plays,* 1924.
A Happy Family (produced 1921).
Telling Mrs. Baker, from the story by Henry Lawson (produced 1922). In *The Black Horse and Other Plays,* 1924.
The Black Horse (produced 1923). In *The Black Horse and Other Plays,* 1924.
Travellers (produced 1923). In *The Black Horse and Other Plays,* 1924.
The Black Horse and Other Plays. 1924.
Ancestors, in *Best Australian One-Act Plays.* 1937.
Hail Tomorrow. 1947.

Verse

The Forerunners. 1915.
The Camp. 1920.

Other

National Portraits. 1940; revised edition, 1954.
A. G. Stephens: His Life and Work. 1941.
Frank Wilmot (Furnley Maurice). 1942.
Louis Esson and the Australian Theatre. 1948.
The Legend of the Nineties. 1954.
Intimate Portraits and Other Pieces: Essays and Articles, edited by H. P. Heseltine. 1969.

Editor, *Such Is Life,* by Joseph Furphy. 1937.
Editor, *Coast to Coast: Australian Stories 1944.* 1945.
Editor, *Old Australian Bush Ballads,* music by Margaret Sutherland. 1951.

Reading List: in *Meanjin 18,* 1959; *Palmer* by H. P. Heseltine, 1970; *Palmer,* 1971, and *Vance and Nettie Palmer,* 1975, both by Vivian Smith; *Dream and Disillusion* by David Walker, 1976.

* * *

"There'll be little care for beauty in the world they build tomorrow,/But these are my people, and I'm with them to the end." These lines from an early poem of Vance Palmer's express the conscious commitment that governed the whole of his work as a writer. But though Palmer saw himself as contributing to the creation of a national culture by portraying what he regarded as "an Australia of the spirit," his writing was not distinctively Australian in its style or idiom. Unlike the nationalist writers of an earlier generation whom he so admired – Lawson and Furphy – he had limited command of the vernacular, and his identification with ordinary Australians was more a matter of intellectual choice than instinctive feeling. In the history of Australian writing, Palmer occupies a special place, because of his dedication to the cause of a national literature. As a man of letters, he saw himself as having a role to play in the shaping of national values.

Palmer's creative output included poems, plays, novels, short stories, essays, and broadcast talks. His poems and plays are minor work, though the plays have a continuing interest because of Palmer's association with the Pioneer Players group, which attempted to create a national theatre on the model of the Abbey Theatre in Dublin. His novels and short stories represent him at his strongest. Beginning with conventional station romances, he matured steadily, and with *The Passage* he established himself as a significant Australian novelist. This novel, centering on the figure of the fisherman Lew Callaway, exemplifies Palmer's concern with the inward life of ordinary people. "My task is to set down Australian rhythms," he once said, and this simple yet challenging ambition underlies all his fiction.

With the exception of *The Big Fellow*, none of Palmer's novels is wholly satisfying. They are well-made; they focus on interesting themes; they examine the texture of human experience with intelligence and delicacy; but, with all their craftsmanship, they do not get enough of the very feel of life. *The Big Fellow*, however, is a moving novel, in which Palmer expressed more fully than elsewhere his personal vision of things. It is the third volume of a trilogy, begun with *Golconda* and continued with *Seedtime*, dealing with the public themes that preoccupied him throughout his life – his conviction that the essential values of Australian society had been defined in the 1890's and his profound belief in the responsibility of the individual to the community. But what gives *The Big Fellow* its distinctive strength is its quiet revelation of the inner life of the central character, a politician facing a crisis in which all the values of his life are questioned. Through the character of Macy Donovan, Palmer presents more fully than anywhere else his personal vision of life's meanings.

The subtle understanding which Palmer shows in his portrayal of Donovan's sense of inescapable loneliness is more often to be found in his short stories, especially in *Let the Birds Fly*. It was in the restricted scope of the short story that Palmer could best express his own sensitive, romantic yearning for beauty and his wry awareness of the inevitable defeats the romantic must face. His stories of childhood – notably "The Rainbow Bird," "The Foal," "Josie," and "Mathieson's Wife" – are especially attractive in their restrained and sympathetic evocation of immature states of feeling.

Alongside the best of Palmer's creative writing must be set the best of his non-fiction prose. He contributed to many journals on a variety of topics and was a very successful radio book-reviewer. The magazine article, the radio talk, and the public lecture were forms he handled with ease. He had a remarkable ability to present ideas in an easily understood form without distorting or over-simplifying them, and the best of his journalism, along with his book of literary history, *The Legend of the Nineties*, will continue to be read with pleasure by all conditions of men.

—John Barnes

PATERSON, Andrew Barton. Australian. Born in Narrambla, near Orange, New South Wales, 17 February 1864. Educated at school in Binalong; preparatory school in Sydney; Sydney Grammar School; University of Sydney; entered in the Roll of Solicitors. Ambulance Driver, Australian Hospital, Boulogne, 1914–15, and served in the British Red Cross Centre in Egypt and Palestine, 1916–18: Major. Married Alice Walker in 1903; one son and one daughter. Practised law in Sydney: Managing Clerk, later Partner, W. William Street, until 1900; Contributor to the *Sydney Bulletin* after 1886; War Correspondent for *Sydney Morning Herald* and *Melbourne Argus* during the Boer War, 1899–1901; *Sydney Morning Herald* Correspondent in China, 1901, and England, 1902; Editor, *Evening News*, Sydney, 1903–06, and *Town and Country Journal*, Sydney, 1906–08; Editor, *Sydney Sportsman*, 1921–30; freelance journalist for *Smith's Weekly* in the early 1930's. C.B.E. (Commander, Order of the British Empire), 1939. *Died 5 February 1941.*

PUBLICATIONS

Collections

The World of "Banjo" Paterson: His Stories, Travels, War Reports, and Advice to Racegoers, edited by Clement Semmler. 1967.

Verse

The Man from Snowy River and Other Verses. 1895.
Rio Grande's Last Race and Other Verses. 1902.
Saltbush Bill, J.P., and Other Verses. 1917.
Collected Verse. 1921.
The Animals Noah Forgot (juvenile). 1933.

Plays

Radio Series: *The Land of Adventure,* 1930's.

Fiction

An Outback Marriage. 1906.
Three Elephant Power and Other Stories. 1917.
The Shearer's Colt. 1936.

Other

Australia for the Australians Showing the Necessity for Land Reform. 1889.
Happy Dispatches. 1934.

Editor, *The Old Bush Songs.* 1905.

Reading List: *Paterson,* 1965, *The Banjo of the Bush,* 1966, and *Paterson,* 1967, all by Clement Semmler; *Paterson* by Lorna Ollif, 1971.

* * *

The status of the popular ballad in Australia (with a run from about the mid-1880's to about 1930) was unique in its day. Andrew Barton Paterson was one of its most distinguished creators. Unlike his contemporary Henry Lawson, he accented the cheerful aspects of colonial life. Whereas Lawson saw life from ground-level (he identifies with underdogs, swagmen, and job-seekers), Paterson is reputed to have looked on the world as a rider, with the advantageous elevation of horseback to lift up his mood. His verses, incidentally, are full of a variety of riding rhythms, vigorous in style and full of joy in their motion.

Paterson has a strong predilection for energy and movement, but as a rule the action becomes suffused with reflection: "In my wild erratic fancy visions come to me of Clancy/ Gone a-droving 'down the Cooper' where the Western drovers go...." It is not merely what Clancy does, but what he enjoys that is exciting: "And he sees the vision splendid of the sunlit plains extended,/And at night the wondrous glory of the everlasting stars." In "The Man from Snowy River" action and reflection form a common conclusion as Paterson's imagination pursues the spirit of heroism into myth:

> And where around the Overflow the reed-beds sweep and sway
> To the breezes, and the rolling plains are wide,
> The Man from Snowy River is a household word today,
> And the stockmen tell the story of his ride.

Clancy and the Man and sundry other heroes of Paterson's fancy have become Australian myth-figures today. His poetical compass is not wide – there are repetitions – but for all that he epitomizes, as does also Lawson in his different way, one of the major aspects of Colonial life – in Paterson's case, a cheerful if also distinctly conservative one. Much of what he writes is from the heart of an imaginative boy; he preserves a boy's delight in nature. He also preserves a very lively, perhaps essentially a boy's sense of humour, as witness that infectious Australian comic classic "The Man from Ironbark." Not the least of his achievements was in being the author of another work of comic (and equally grotesque) genius, the ballad of "Waltzing Matilda," now an Australian national song.

Paterson's prose was less distinguished than his verse, but includes some good colonial fiction, a few excellent short stories, and much lively journalism ranging from war correspondence to "advice to racegoers."

—Brian Elliott

PATON, Alan (Stewart). South African. Born in Pietermaritzburg, Natal, 11 January 1903. Educated at Maritzburg College, University of Natal, B.Sc. 1923, B.Ed. 1966. Married 1) Doris Francis in 1928 (died, 1967), two sons; 2) Anne Hopkins in 1969. Schoolteacher in Natal, in a native school and at Pietermaritzburg College, 1925–35; Principal, Diepkloof Reformatory, Johannesburg, 1935–48; full-time writer since 1948. Honorary Commissioner, Toc H Southern Africa, Botha's Hill, Natal, 1949–58; President of the Convocation, University of Natal, 1951–55, 1957–59; Founder and President, Liberal Party of South Africa, 1958–68; Chubb Fellow, Yale University, New Haven, Connecticut, 1973. Since 1969, Honorary President, South African National Union of Students. Recipient: Anisfield-Wolf Award, 1948; Newspaper Guild of New York Award, 1949; Freedom House Award,

1960; Free Academy of Arts Medal, Hamburg, 1960; National Conference of Christians and Jews Brotherhood Award, 1962; International League for Human Rights prize, 1977. L.H.D.: Yale University, 1954; D.Litt.: Kenyon College, Gambier, Ohio, 1962; University of Natal, 1968; Harvard University, Cambridge, Massachusetts, 1971; Trent University, Peterborough, Ontario, 1971; Rhodes University, Grahamstown, South Africa, 1972; Willamette University, Salem, Oregon, 1974; D.D.: University of Edinburgh, 1971. Fellow, Royal Society of Literature, 1961; Honorary Member, Free Academy of Arts, Hamburg, 1961. Lives in Hillcrest, Natal.

PUBLICATIONS

Fiction

Meditation for a Young Boy Confirmed (story). 1944.
Cry, The Beloved Country. 1948.
Too Late the Phalarope. 1953.
Debbie Go Home: Stories. 1961; as *Tales from a Troubled Land*, 1965.

Play

Sponono, with Krishna Shah, from a story by Paton (produced 1964). 1965.

Other

South Africa Today. 1951.
The Land and the People of South Africa. 1955; as *South Africa and Her People*, 1955; revised edition, 1965, 1971.
South Africa in Transition. 1956.
Hope for South Africa. 1958.
Hofmeyr. 1964; abridged, as *South African Tragedy: The Life and Times of Jan Hofmeyr*, 1965.
The Long View. 1968.
Instrument of Thy Peace: The Prayer of St. Francis. 1968.
Kontakion for You Departed. 1969; as *For You Departed*, 1969.
Case History of a Pinky. 1972.
Apartheid and the Archbishop: The Life and Times of Geoffrey Clayton, Archbishop of Cape Town. 1973.
Knocking at the Door: Shorter Writings, edited by Colin Gardner. 1975.

Reading List: *Paton* by Edward Callan, 1968.

*   *   *

Alan Paton is a liberal white South African. He was national president of the Liberal Party in South Africa until its disbandment in 1968. The unenviable position not only colours his writing, it also provides the subject matter: apartheid and its moral, psychological, and economic consequences. In what is probably the most famous novel to come out of South Africa, *Cry, The Beloved Country*, Paton explores this theme from two points of view. The old, simple, and humble black priest Steven Kumalo goes to Johannesburg in search of his son who has become a juvenile delinquent. His descent into the underworld of Johannesburg is registered through his horrified and honest eyes in a biblical language of great simplicity and beauty. When he finds his son it is too late; the boy is on trial for the murder of a white man. The bitter irony of the situation becomes clear when it is revealed that the murdered man was a "good" white man who worked hard to change the apartheid system. The next part of the book is devoted to the father of the murdered man Jarvis, Sr., who tries to comprehend his son's ideas as he reads through his papers. In the final section Kumalo and Jarvis reach an understanding, and through this Paton advocates a solution to the South African situation based on a combination of black humility and honesty and white American-inspired democratic liberalism.

Paton's position as principal of a reformatory for delinquent African boys has given him an insight into the criminal world of Johannesburg which he uses in *Cry, The Beloved Country*. In his collection of short stories *Debbie Go Home*, he explores this world and its inhabitants in a realistic fashion which does not leave room for the humility of Steven Kumalo.

Paton is, however, at his very best when he explores the Calvinist Boer mind as he does in *Too Late the Phalarope*, an excellent but much ignored book. It tells the story of the policeman Pieter van Vlaanderen, a pillar of the Boer community, and his silent agonizing fight against his desire to sleep with the black girl Stephanie. He finally loses the battle, is inevitably discovered and destroyed. The reasons for his desires and actions are explained very convincingly as the short comings of Calvinist morality – lack of love, fear of sexuality, and perverse colour prejudice. The book deserves all the attention which has been showered upon the more popular *Cry, The Beloved Country*.

—Kirsten Holst Petersen

p'BITEK, Okot. Ugandan. Born in Gulu, Acoli District, Northern Uganda, in 1931. Educated at Gulu High School; King's College, Budo, Uganda; University of Bristol, Certificate in Education; University of Wales, Aberystwyth, LL.B.; Oxford University, B.Litt. in social anthropology 1963. Lecturer in Sociology at Makerere University College, and Director of the Uganda National Theatre and Uganda National Cultural Center, all Kampala, 1964–68; Founder, Kisumu Arts Festival, Kenya, 1968; Fellow, International Writing Program, University of Iowa, Iowa City, 1969–70; Senior Research Fellow, Institute of African Studies, Nairobi, 1971. Lives in Kisumu, Kenya.

PUBLICATIONS

Verse

Lak tar miyo kinyero wi lobo? (in Acoli: Are your teeth white, then laugh!). 1953.
The Song of Lawino (translated from Acoli by the author). 1966.
Song of Ocol. 1970.
The Song of a Prisoner. 1970.
Two Songs: The Song of a Prisoner, The Song of Malaya. 1971.
The Horn of My Love (Acoli traditional songs, translated by the author). 1974.
The Hare and the Hornbill. 1978.

* * *

PUBLICATIONS

Verse

Lak tar miyo kinyero wi lobo? (in Acoli: Are your teeth white, then laugh!).   1953.
The Song of Lawino (translated from Acoli by the author).   1966.
Song of Ocol.   1970.
The Song of a Prisoner.   1970.
Two Songs: The Song of a Prisoner, The Song of Malaya.   1971.
The Horn of My Love (Acoli traditional songs, translated by the author).   1974.
The Hare and the Hornbill.   1978.

*   *   *

Okot p'Bitek is a scholar as well as a poet and a novelist. *Song of Lawino* is a traditional story in verse of an Acoli wife, as if told by herself, of her husband's turning, in his desire to be "modern," to Clementine who "aspires/To look like a white woman" ("And she believes/ That this is beautiful"):

> I do not deny
> I am a little jealous.
> It is no good lying,
> We all suffer from a little jealousy....
>
> How many kids
> Has this woman sucked?
> The empty bags on her chest
> Are completely flattened, dried.
> Perhaps she has aborted many!
> Perhaps she has thrown her twins
> In the pit latrine!

The story contains a revealing character-sketch of the husband, Okol, floundering among the problems of *Uhuru* (freedom). It is a useful stroke to have made a woman the mouthpiece while there are still too few women writing in Africa. *Two Songs: Song of a Prisoner, Song of Malaya* are in similar, short-lined, graphic verse, the first song from the mouth of a man, the second from an unmarried woman. They are biting yet compassionate satires on an emergent African society torn between its own rich traditions and a seductive, materialist modernity passed on by British and American "imperialist progress"; *Song of a Prisoner* reveals, behind this "false dawn" of assassinations, corruption great and small, tyrants and blustering power, an enduring reality of life outside the "brash new towns" – the burning optimism of the people of Africa in the face of hardship and humiliation as in the known face of hunger: "Brother/How could I/So poor/Cold/Limping/Weak/Hungry like an empty tomb/A young tree/Burnt out/By the fierce wild fire/Of Uhuru/How could I/Inspire you/To such heights of brutality?".

What p'Bitek is writing is essentially a new kind of verse. Not only is he combining modern verse-form with oral form and content: he is showing how that form *is* the oral form. Yet, beside his stark concern with human essentials, the content of some modern Western verse can sound trivial, precious, oblique, too personal, materialist. Almost the only other poetry like p'Bitek's, since the 1960's, has come from South Africa, Russia, Chile, East Europe. In his own preface to *The Horn of My Love*, he explains: "Missionaries, anthropologists, musicologists and folklorists have plucked songs, stories, proverbs, riddles etc. from their social backgrounds and, after killing them by analysis, have buried them in inaccessible and learned journals, and in expensive technical books. I believe that literature, like all the other creative arts, is there, first and foremost, to be enjoyed." Writing by Africans alone, p'Bitek thinks, can secure the development of African literature.

—Anne Tibble

PORTER, Hal. Australian. Born in Albert Park, Melbourne, Victoria, 16 February 1911. Educated at Kensington State School, 1917; Bairnsdale State School, Victoria, 1918–21; Bairnsdale High School, 1922–26. Married Olivia Parnham in 1939 (divorced, 1943). Cadet Reporter, *Bairnsdale Advertiser*, 1927; Schoolmaster, Victorian Education Department, 1927–37, 1940; Queen's College, Adelaide, 1941–42; Prince Alfred College, Kent Town, South Australia, 1943–46; Hutchins School, Hobart, Tasmania, 1946–47; Knox Grammar School, Sydney, 1947; Ballarat College, Victoria, 1948–49; Nijimura School, Kure, Japan (Australian Army Education), 1949–50; Director, National Theatre, Hobart, 1951–53; Chief Librarian of Bairnsdale and Shepparton, Victoria, 1953–61; full-time writer from 1961. Australian Writers Representative, Edinburgh Festival, 1962; Lecturer for the Australian Department of External Affairs, in Japan, 1967. Recipient: Sydney Sesquicentenary Prize, 1938; Commonwealth Literary Fund Fellowship, 1956, 1960, 1964, 1968, and Subsidy, 1957, 1962, 1967; Sydney Journalists' Club Prize, 1959, for drama, 1961; *Encyclopaedia Britannica* Award, 1967; Captain Cook Bi-Centenary Prize, 1970. Lives in Garvoc, Victoria.

PUBLICATIONS

Fiction

Short Stories. 1942.
A Handful of Pennies. 1958.
The Tilted Cross. 1961.
A Bachelor's Children. 1962.
The Cats of Venice (stories). 1965.
Mr. Butterfry and Other Tales of New Japan. 1970.
Selected Stories, edited by Leonie Kramer. 1971.
The Right Thing. 1971.
Fredo Fuss Love Life (stories). 1974.

Plays

The Tower (produced 1964). 1963.
The Professor (as *Toda-San,* produced 1965; as *The Professor,* produced 1965). 1966.
Eden House (produced 1969; as *Home on a Pig's Back,* produced 1972). 1969.
Parker (produced 1972).

Verse

The Hexagon. 1956.
Elijah's Ravens. 1968.
In an Australian Country Graveyard and Other Poems. 1973.

Other

The Watcher on the Cast-Iron Balcony (autobiography). 1963.
Australian Stars of Stage and Screen. 1965.
The Paper Chase (autobiography). 1966.
The Actors: An Image of the New Japan. 1968.
Criss-Cross (autobiography). 1973.
The Extra (autobiography). 1976.

Editor, *Australian Poetry 1957.* 1957.
Editor, *Coast to Coast 1961–1962.* 1963.
Editor, *It Could Be You.* 1972.

Bibliography: *A Bibliography of Porter* by Janette Finch, 1966.

Reading List: *Porter* by Mary Lord, 1974.

*   *   *

Hal Porter is not only one of Australia's finest short-story writers but he has also written one of the very best of all Australian autobiographies. The title of the first volume of this work is *The Watcher on the Cast-Iron Balcony*; the watcher is Porter, and it is in this role that we find him in both his autobiography and his fiction. The role itself creates a duality between Hal Porter the writer and Hal Porter the man. As the watcher, the artist, he is alone, isolated, detached, endeavouring always to be objective, to sift the real from the non-real. "This watching, this down-gazing, this faraway staring, is an exercise in solitude and non-involvement." But the community is there "to rob him of aloneness and content." For Porter is not only a spectator, he is also a participant; his fiction as well as his autobiography is written out of his own personal experience. He comments on his method of writing (in *Southerly*, 1969):

> pure fiction, and flights of fancy are utterly beyond me. As a result another preoccupation is necessary. This is with the mechanics of transmuting actual personal experience, or the witnessed experiences of others, into what reads (I pray!) like true to life fiction.... Many characters, settings, and situations, already tied up in a "plot," are filched, holus-bolus, with the insolence of a shop-lifter, straight out of "life."

Of course, as an artist he will shape his material; he may be, as he writes in *The Paper Chase*, a "restless picker-up" but he is also a "ruthless pruner," and it is in the pruning that his imagination is at work – in the artist's sensitivity to the essentials, and in the ability to arrange "the million bits of the answer into One Answer." The One Answer is what Porter is seeking; the question he asks is: what is real? Rarely do his characters know the truth; many of them live, and some of them even die, with their illusions.

In the second volume of his autobiography, *The Paper Chase*, Porter tells of his methods when he is looking back on past experience. "As always, when writing of a past self, I try to put down what is felt 'then' even if 'now' has changed the feeling." "Francis Silver," one of the best known of Porter's stories, is an excellent example of Porter at work. The narration passes through several Hal Porters, the naïve boy, the romantic adolescent, the idealistic youth, the bitter and cynical young adult and the writer aware of "one disconcerting, even disenchanting thing: what one oneself remembers is not what others remember." The concern of the story is with the question of true identity; it deals with a moment of initiation when a youthful illusion is shattered by a harsh reality. Such moments occur quite frequently in Porter's work, and the often savage and grotesque nature of the reversal suggests the bitterness of one who feels that perhaps life is a fraud.

Any reader must be immediately aware that Porter has an eye that is gluttonous for details. He has said in the article already mentioned:

> In more intense forms of writing – the short story, for instance – effects must be made quickly, and often on many planes in immediately sequent sentences. Even if one splurge or over-express, one dares not falter on minutiae: dress, vehicles, customs, moral quirks, peculiar snobberies, atmospheric tone, and – above all – conversation.... To write down what is literally heard, to tape-record as it were in writing is to miss the point: the eye does not hear. The reader has to be tricked with a selection of words which "look" like what is supposed to be "heard." Acquiring the necessary illusionist's skill, ... has been another of my preoccupations.

Through his assembling of all the details Porter not only recaptures another age but also the people who lived in it. In *The Paper Chase* he said, "The quality of one's connection with people through their relation with things, tunes, scents, sounds, and so on is a subject of great allure, its existence a great blessing." This is the special significance of things for Porter; they are "evidences of humanity ... threads resistant to time and space." As such they are man's protection against mutability, against the destructive element in time, which so often creates an illusion out of what was once a reality. The details, the picture, the song, remain to defy time.

In "Francis Silver" the destruction of the lock of hair signifies the destruction of yet another illusion for the young man. The stench reminds us of the ugliness, perhaps the evil of reality; the agony is that of a youth stripped of one more romantic ideal. He goes out cynically to perform his first adult chore, which ironically enough is to perpetuate an illusion. Only the watcher will remain aware of the reality.

—Anna Rutherford

PRATT, E(dwin) J(ohn). Canadian. Born in Western Bay, Newfoundland, 4 February 1883. Draper's apprentice, St. John's, Newfoundland, 1898–1901; educated at Methodist College, St. John's, 1901–03; school teacher and student preacher, Newfoundland, 1903–07; Victoria College, University of Toronto, 1907–17, B.A. 1911, B.D. 1913, M.A. 1915, Ph.D. 1917; ordained in the Methodist Church. Demonstrator and Lecturer in Psychology, University College, 1911–17, and Associate Professor of English, 1919–33, Professor of English, 1933–53, and Emeritus Professor, 1953–64, Victoria College, University of Toronto. Editor, *Canadian Poetry* magazine, Toronto, 1936–42; Member, Editorial Board, *Saturday Night*, Toronto, 1952. Recipient: Governor-General's Award, 1937, 1949, 1952; Lorne Pierce Gold Medal, 1940; University of Alberta Gold Medal for Literature, 1951; Canada Council grant, 1958, and medal, 1961. D.Litt.: University of Manitoba, Winnipeg, 1945; McGill University, Montreal, 1949; University of Toronto, 1953; Assumption

University, Windsor, Ontario, 1955; University of New Brunswick, Fredericton, 1957; University of Western Ontario, London, 1957; Memorial University of Newfoundland, St. John's, 1961; LL.D.: Queen's University, Kingston, Ontario, 1949; D.C.L.: Bishop's University, Lennoxville, Quebec, 1949. Fellow, Royal Society of Canada, 1930. C.M.G. (Companion, Order of St. Michael and St. George), 1946. *Died 26 April 1964.*

PUBLICATIONS

Collections

Selected Poems, edited by Peter Buitenhuis.   1968.

Verse

Rachel: A Story of the Sea.   1917.
Newfoundland Verse.   1923.
The Witches' Brew.   1925.
Titans.   1926.
The Iron Door: An Ode.   1927.
The Roosevelt and the Antinoe.   1930.
Verses of the Sea.   1930.
Many Moods.   1932.
The Titanic.   1935.
The Fable of the Goats and Other Poems.   1937.
Brébeuf and His Brethren.   1940.
Dunkirk.   1941.
Still Life and Other Verse.   1943.
Collected Poems.   1944; revised edition, edited by Northrop Frye, 1958.
They Are Returning.   1945.
Behind the Log.   1947.
Ten Selected Poems.   1947.
Towards the Last Spike: A Verse Panorama of the Struggle to Build the First Canadian Transcontinental.   1952.
Here the Tides Flow.   1962.

Other

Studies in Pauline Eschatology and Its Background.   1917.

Editor, *Under the Greenwood Tree,* by Thomas Hardy.   1937.
Editor, *Heroic Tales in Verse.*   1941.

Reading List: *Pratt: The Man and His Poetry* by H. W. Wells and C. F. Klinck, 1947; *The Poetry of Pratt* by John Sutherland, 1956; *Pratt* by Milton T. Wilson, 1969; *Pratt* by David G. Pitt, 1969; *Pratt: The Evolutionary Vision* by Sandra Djwa, 1974.

*   *   *

Widely regarded as Canada's pre-eminent narrative poet, E. J. Pratt embodied in his work a nineteenth-century concern for social Darwinism and an evolving "instinct for what is imaginatively central in Canadian sensibility" (Northrop Frye). An ordained Methodist minister who wrote his M.A. and Ph.D. theses on demonology and Pauline eschatology, he experienced a crisis of faith which has caused him to be viewed variously an an atheist, Christian humanist, and agnostic. Similar ambiguity has hedged judgements about his shorter lyric poems and longer comic extravaganzas. His narrative fables and epics, particularly *Brébeuf and His Brethren*, best demonstrate his pre-occupation with themes of primaeval conflict, his fascination with technical language, and his dexterity in establishing the dramatic coherency of his stories in verse.

Four collections of Pratt's shorter poems were published between 1923 and 1943 (*Newfoundland Verse*, *Many Moods*, *The Fable of the Goats*, and *Still Life*); with some of his later poems, most are included in the second edition of the *Collected Poems*. Their tone is remarkably consistent: calm and flat, covering a moment of violence and usually concluding with a rhetorical comment. Pratt was not attracted by post-Edwardian experiments in form, and very few of these poems are in free verse. He almost never wrote about love. His most frequently anthologized short works, such as "The Shark" and "Sea-Gulls," centre on Newfoundland and the sea, or on the simultaneity of the evolutionary process, as in "The Prize Cat" and "From Stone to Steel."

Pratt's early personal and stylistic difficulties in reconciling orthodox Christianity with the aftermath of the First World War, a natural world indifferent to man, are evident in his first narratives: "Clay" (1917, published in part in *Newfoundland Verse*) and *Rachel*. *The Witches' Brew*, a farce about the effects of alcohol on fish, pointed more clearly to the elastic line, hyperbolic language, and juxtaposition of sober detail with vaulting commentary, all of which would mark his mature long poems. The formulation of *The Iron Door* as a dream-vision did not bear out his attempt to rationalize belief in the face of his mother's death. Thereafter he would continue to construct epic battles as metaphors for the persistence and frailty of human will, the kind of battles he dramatized in "The Cachalot" and "The Great Feud." Published together as *Titans*, his first major work, both poems set out the struggle between evolutionary Titans and Olympians: in the first, a giant squid against a sperm whale, and in the second (sub-titled "A Dream of a Pleiocene Armageddon") the animals of the land led by an ape against those of the sea, with admixtures of grotesque comedy. Man kills one victor and is himself drowned in "The Cachalot"; man's solitary ancestor remains alive in "The Great Feud."

Pratt's poetic response to the political and economic dialectic of the 1930's was curiously muted. "The Fable of the Goats," omitted from the *Collected Poems*, offers peace in our time as a solution to the Spanish Civil War. His choice of the metaphor of a gigantic dinner for "The Depression Ends" appears perversely blinkered as a political statement. More characteristic of his larger attitudes are two of the three epics set at sea: *The Roosevelt and the Antinoe* and *The Titanic*, with their themes of human rescue partially thwarted and of the limits of technology in saving man. The American ship *Roosevelt* aids the sinking British *Antinoe*, but the sea can master both. The iceberg of *The Titanic* assumes a related role, a morally neutral force which seems – but only seems – to strike man down for his pride and arrogance. The Second World War provided Pratt with a properly grand stage for his complicated concept of heroism: rhetorically in the propagandistic *Dunkirk*; intimately in the North Atlantic convoy duty described in *Behind the Log*; and mythically in "The Truant," a debate between representative man and the Panjandrum who personifies the mechanistic principle of the universe, the perfect dictator. That Pratt should later describe Canada's far western mountain ranges as "seas" is appropriate, as is his concern with individual rather than collective human effort in his last narrative, *Towards the Last Spike*. Here the construction of the transcontinental railway in the 1870's and 1880's is transmuted into an ironic commentary on the triumph of will over environment, the need to establish an empire of communication over what man sees to be moral chaos, and the belief that technological progress is a metaphor for human evolution.

Brébeuf and His Brethren, Pratt's finest (and longest) narrative, is patterned on the way of the cross in its exploration of faith in seventeenth-century New France. (It is partly based on events chronicled in the Jesuit *Relations*.) The conflict of Indian and priest moves to the inevitable martyrdom of Brébeuf and Lalement. Pratt's objectivity, careful pacing, and smooth manipulation of a quarter-century's dialogue and description conclude with a contemporary Mass at the shrine of the martyrs. The final ironies of the poem characterize Pratt's own views on man's fate in a world always new to him. The value of human life lies in the persistence of individual struggle against our collective self-willed suicide.

—Bruce Nesbitt

PRICHARD, Katharine Susannah. Australian. Born in Levuka, Fiji, 4 December 1883; emigrated with her family to Australia, 1886. Educated at home, and at South Melbourne College. Married Hugo Throssell in 1919 (died, 1933); one son. Worked as a governess in South Gippsland, and as a teacher at Christ Church Grammar School, Melbourne; journalist for the Melbourne *Herald* and *New Idea*, Sydney; free-lance journalist in London and Europe, 1908; Editor, Melbourne *Herald*'s "Women's Work" column 1908–12; returned to London, and worked as a free-lance journalist, 1912–16: Correspondent in France, 1916; full-time writer from 1916; settled in Greenmount, Western Australia; member of the Australian Communist Party from 1920. *Died 20 October 1969.*

PUBLICATIONS

Fiction

The Pioneers. 1915; revised edition, 1963.
Windlestraws. 1916.
The Black Opal. 1921.
Working Bullocks. 1926.
The Wild Oats of Han (juvenile). 1928; revised edition, 1968.
Coonardoo, The Well in the Shadow. 1929.
Haxby's Circus, The Lightest, Brightest Little Show on Earth. 1930; as *Fay's Circus,* 1931.
Kiss on the Lips and Other Stories. 1932.
Intimate Strangers. 1937.
Moon of Desire. 1941.
Potch and Colour (stories). 1944.
The Roaring Nineties: A Story of the Goldfields of Western Australia. 1946.
Golden Miles. 1948.
Winged Seeds. 1950.
N'Goola and Other Stories. 1959.
Subtle Flame. 1967.
Moggie and Her Circus Pony (juvenile). 1967.
Happiness: Selected Short Stories. 1967.

Plays

The Burglar (produced 1910).
The Pioneers (produced 1923).   In *Best Australian One-Act Plays,* 1937.
Brumby Innes (produced 1972).   1927.

Verse

Clovelly Verses.   1913.
Earth Lover.   1930.
The Earth Lover and Other Verses.   1932.

Other

The New Order.   1921.
Marx: The Man and His Work.   1922.
The Materialist Conception.   1922.
The Real Russia.   1935.
Why I Am a Communist.   1950(?).
Child of the Hurricane: An Autobiography.   1963.
On Strenuous Wings: A Half-Century of Selected Writings, edited by Joan Williams.   1965.

Editor, with others, *Australian New Writing 1–3.* 3 vols., 1943–45.

Reading List: "Prichard Issue" of *Overland 12,* 1959; *Prichard* by H. Drake-Brockman, 1967.

*   *   *

In 1915 Katharine Susannah Prichard's first novel, *The Pioneers*, won the Hodder and Stoughton prize in the Australian section of their prize for Dominion novels. She had done what she had set out to do, namely, "proved ability to 'succeed' abroad." Having done so she returned to Australia: "I wanted to live and write in Australia about the country and its people." While in England she had been shocked by the appalling slum conditions. The Russian revolution and the doctrines of Marx and Engels were to give direction to her indignation, and when the Australian Communist Party was formed in 1920 she joined it. So, added to her aim of "knowing the Australian people and interpreting them to themselves" was the additional one of propagating the socialist doctrine both in her life and in her work. As Jack Lindsay wrote, "[Her work] is a creative development of the Marxist concepts of what humanises and what alienates, born out of an artist's deep sympathy for, and understanding of, her fellow men."

She had inherited the democratic, humanist tradition of the 1890's. However, while she shared with the nationalist, realist writers of that period a firm belief in mateship, in the virtues of the working people, the ordinary Australians, she did not share Lawson's picture of "a grey and distressing country. I wanted," she said, "to bring a realisation of the beauty and vigour of our life to Australian literature." What impresses one is her evocative portrayal of the land in which her characters live and which she so obviously loved. Her settings were wide, varying from the opal fields in *The Black Opal*, the timber country in *Working Bullocks*, the small town circuit in *Haxby's Circus*, the outback station in *Coonardoo*, the gold fields in her trilogy *The Roaring Nineties*, *Golden Miles*, and *Winged Seeds*. But no matter how varied the setting the same theme emerged. Always her concern was for the little man in his struggle against exploitive capitalism: her aim was to show how under that system man became alienated not only from his fellow men but also from himself and nature. It is not surprising that Prichard should turn her attention to the most exploited group in Australia, the aborigines. *Coonardoo*, which was to have a powerful effect on the white conscience, is not simply the tragedy of a single person but of a whole people, a tragedy for which the white population was directly responsible.

It has been argued by some that her political commitment has been detrimental to her artistic achievement. In reply to such critics one could quote Lunuchansky: "Of what do you accuse me? Of the fact that the great flames of my fervour to transform the world are burning in my art too?" What inspires one in Prichard's works is the vitalism that informs them. There is in her writing an affirmation of a life force that will continue to struggle in spite of the most appalling conditions and against what seem to be insurmountable odds. As Sam told Han in the first work Katharine Susannah Prichard wrote (*The Wild Oats of Han*), "You've just got to shake your fist at Life and say: 'You can't break me. You can't!' "

While her reputation rests essentially on her novels and short stories, mention should also be made of the seventeen plays she wrote, three of which have been produced. One of them, *Brumby Innes* (1927), won the Triad competition and then waited forty-five years for production. When it was eventually produced in 1972 it was greeted with acclaim by the critics, one of whom wrote, "Anyone thinking of putting indigenous ingredients together and writing The Great Australian Play can screw the cap back on his pen and take himself off quietly to the pub. It has been belatedly discovered that Katharine Susannah Prichard wrote it in 1927." There is no doubt at all that she is assured of a permanent place in Australian literature.

—Anna Rutherford

PURDY, Al(fred Wellington). Canadian. Born in Wooller, Ontario, 30 December 1918. Educated at Dufferin Public School, Trenton, Ontario; Albert College, Belleville, Ontario; Trenton Collegiate Institute, Ontario. Served with the Royal Canadian Air Force during World War II. Married Eurithe Parkhurst in 1941; one son. Has held numerous jobs; taught at Simon Fraser University, Burnaby, British Columbia, Spring 1970; Poet-in-Residence, Loyola College, Montreal, 1973; Artist-in-Residence, University of Manitoba, Winnipeg, 1975–76. Recipient: Canada Council Fellowship, 1960, 1965, Senior Literary Fellowship, 1968, 1971, award, 1973, and grant, 1974; President's Medal, University of Western Ontario, 1964; Governor-General's Award, 1966. Lives in Ontario.

PUBLICATIONS

Verse

The Enchanted Echo. 1944.
Pressed on Sand. 1955.

Emu, Remember! 1956.
The Crafte So Longe to Lerne. 1959.
Poems for All the Annettes. 1962.
The Blur in Between: Poems 1960–61. 1962.
The Cariboo Horses. 1965.
North of Summer: Poems from Baffin Island. 1967.
Poems for All the Annettes (selected poems). 1968.
Wild Grape Wine. 1968.
Spring Song. 1968.
Love in a Burning Building. 1970.
The Quest for Ouzo. 1970.
Selected Poems. 1972.
Hiroshima Poems. 1972.
On the Bearpaw Sea. 1973.
Sex and Death. 1973.
In Search of Owen Roblin. 1974.
Sundance at Dusk. 1976.

Other

Editor, *The New Romans: Candid Canadian Opinions of the United States.* 1968.
Editor, *Fifteen Winds: A Selection of Modern Canadian Poems.* 1969.
Editor, *I've Tasted My Blood: Poems 1956–1968,* by Milton Acorn. 1969.
Editor, *Storm Warning: The New Canadian Poets.* 1971.

Reading List: *Purdy* by George Bowering, 1970.

* * *

From an unpromising beginning in the early 1940's, Al Purdy has made himself one of the liveliest, most prolific, and most respected Canadian poets. He is also one of the four or five most accomplished. From a purveyor of banalities, both in theme and technique, he has developed into a subtle and wide-ranging craftsman, ear and eye sensitively attuned to the human scene. A self-taught poet, he took a long time to work through certain habits and attitudes gathered in from the British tradition, but by the late 1950's his distinctive gifts had begun to show through. Eclectic in means, Protean in personality, his work seems to have cohered through the discovered sense of *locus* first apparent in such poems as "At Roblin Lake" (*The Crafte So Longe to Lerne*).

His work advanced greatly in the early 1960's, as is evident in *Poems for All the Annettes*, a collection full of a new energy, in which an earlier introversion has given way, importantly, to a telling exploration of individual relationships, as in "House Guest" and "Archaeology of Snow." Beyond this, Purdy shows in poems such as "The Old Woman and the Mayflowers" how a landscape may discover its myths in the character of its people.

The Cariboo Horses is in many ways Purdy's best book. In a book in which time and space, spartan time and empty – or snow-filled – space, predominate, he makes effective technical use of the continuous-present verb form. If *Poems for All the Annettes* marks the moment when Purdy's creative energies gathered decisively, *The Cariboo Horses* follows up by confirming that he is a *Canadian* poet. The book includes "The Madwoman in the Train," remarkable both as a subtle handling of the traditional sestina and as a deployment of psychological perspective.

It was Purdy who started the trend in Canada towards books of poems with a single, usually historical, thematic focus – in *North of Summer*. But his real métier is a kind of discursive lyric which he has, with mastery, made peculiarly his own. From *Wild Grape Wine* to *Sundance at Dusk* his repeated tactic has been to infuse information (geographical, historical, cultural, scientific) with emotion, as in "The Runners," "The Horses of the Agawa," and "Sundance." He handles the contemporary device of minimal punctuation well, and his best work evinces an easy and energetic handling of line and a peculiarly personal tone which is compounded of nostalgia and irony. The strong personality which gives his work its particular quality is held in balance by a high degree of professionalism.

—Charles Doyle

RAO, Raja. Indian. Born in Hassan, Mysore, 21 November 1909. Educated at Nizam College, Hyderabad, University of Madras, B.A. in English 1929; University of Montpellier, France, 1929–30; the Sorbonne, Paris, 1930–33. Married 1) Camille Mouly in 1931; 2) Katherine Jones in 1965; one son. Has spent half of his life in France; now lives half the year in India and half in Europe and the United States. Since 1965, Professor of Philosophy, teaching one semester a year, University of Texas, Austin. Recipient: Academy of Indian Literature Prize, 1964; Padma Bhushan, Government of India, 1969.

PUBLICATIONS

Fiction

Kanthapura. 1938.
The Cow of the Barricades and Other Stories. 1947.
The Serpent and the Rope. 1960.
The Cat and Shakespeare: A Tale of India. 1965.
Comrade Kirillov. 1976.
The Policeman and the Rose. 1977.

Other

Whither India, with Iqbal Singh. 1948.

Editor, with Iqbal Singh, *Changing India.* 1939.

Reading List: *Rao* by M. K. Naik, 1972; *Rao: A Critical Study of His Work* by C. D. Narasimhaiah, 1973.

* * *

As the author of only half a dozen published works, one of which is a collection of short-stories and two of which are of novella length, Raja Rao runs the risk of not having written enough to be regarded as a major Indian novelist. Yet the publication of his first novel, *Kanthapura*, established him as an important writer, while *The Serpent and the Rope*, on which he had been working for many years, has increasingly become the focal point of critical work on Indian fiction in English.

Rao has written short stories from his teens onwards. Some of them (including a few in French) are obscurely hidden away in esoteric magazines, but the best of his early work appeared in *The Cow of the Barricades and Other Stories*. Stories like "Javni," set in Rao's home city of Mysore, or "Akkayya" (the name means "elder sister") show his early preoccupation both with social conditions in India and with the values to be accorded womanhood. A third concern of Rao's later and maturer work, the encounter of Indian and European cultural history, is indicated by the story "Nimka."

Kanthapura is set in a village of that name in the valleys of Himavathi, some distance from Mysore in South India. In the Foreword to the novel Rao says, "The telling has not been easy. One has to convey in a language that is not one's own the spirit that is one's own." The novel deals with the impact of Gandhian principles upon a traditional community. Rao brings the village to life with remarkable feeling, though at times the English he uses seems to strain against the problems of unsophisticated people which he is trying to render. The result may seem a little cloudy or sometimes self-consciously poetic.

C. D. Narasimhaiah, an eminent Indian critic, writes at the start of his book on Rao, "That Raja Rao is India's most significant novelist writing in the English language today is now indisputable." The claim is based on the centrality in Indian fiction of *The Serpent and the Rope*. This novel is written on a more ambitious scale than any other English-language work from India. Drawing on traditional legends from *The Ramayana* and attempting at moments a linguistic synthesis of English meaning and Sanskrit rhythms, the novel explores the relationship of India and Europe through the marriage of its protagonists Rama and Madeleine. The novelist shows a deep awareness of the spiritual and historic links between European and Asian culture, between Catholicism, Hinduism, and Buddhism, between the heresies of east and west. Though the novel is primarily philosophical it does not read like an abstract treatise. Most criticism centres on whether Rao has created proper characters, or merely ideological symbols, on whether or not his interpretation of the Feminine Principle is sentimental, and on the degree to which a deliberately open-ended novel (for Rama does not fulfil his quest) can be considered an achieved work of art.

The Serpent and the Rope has been followed by two short novels, *The Cat and Shakespeare* and *Comrade Kirillov*, in which Rao writes philosophical explorations of the Indian-ness of India.

—Alastair Niven

REANEY, James (Crerar). Canadian. Born near Stratford, Ontario, 1 September 1926. Educated at Elmhurst Public School, Easthope Township, Perth County; Stratford High School; University College, University of Toronto (Epstein Award, 1948), B.A. in English 1948, M.A. 1949, Ph.D. 1956. Married Colleen Thibaudeau in 1951; one son and one daughter. Member of the English faculty, 1949–57, and Assistant Professor of English, 1957–60, University of Manitoba, Winnipeg. Associate Professor, 1960–63, and since 1964 Professor of English, Middlesex College, University of Western Ontario, London. Founding Editor, *Alphabet* magazine, London, Ontario, 1960–71. Active in little theatre groups in

Winnipeg and London. Recipient: Governor-General's Award, 1950, 1959, 1963; President's Medal, University of Western Ontario, 1955, 1958; Chalmers Award, 1975, 1976. Lives in Ontario.

PUBLICATIONS

Plays

Night-Blooming Cereus (broadcast 1959; produced 1960). In *The Killdeer and Other Plays*, 1962.
The Killdeer (produced 1960). In *The Killdeer and Other Plays*, 1962; revised version (produced 1970), in *Masks of Childhood*, 1972.
One-Man Masque (produced 1960). In *The Killdeer and Other Plays*, 1962.
The Easter Egg (produced 1962). In *Masks of Childhood*, 1972.
The Killdeer and Other Plays. 1962.
Sun and Moon (produced 1972). In *The Killdeer and Other Plays*, 1962.
Names and Nicknames (produced 1963). In *Apple Butter and Other Plays*, 1973.
Apple Butter (puppet play; produced 1965). In *Apple Butter and Other Plays*, 1973.
Let's Make a Carol: A Play with Music for Children, music by John Beckwith. 1965.
Listen to the Wind (produced 1965). 1972.
Colours in the Dark (produced 1967). 1970.
Three Desks (produced 1967). In *Masks of Childhood*, 1972.
Masks of Childhood (includes *The Killdeer, Three Desks, The Easter Egg*), edited by Brian Parker. 1972.
Apple Butter and Other Plays for Children (includes *Names and Nicknames, Ignoramus, Geography Match*). 1973.
The Donnellys: A Trilogy:
  1. *Sticks and Stones* (produced 1973). 1975.
  2. *The Saint Nicholas Hotel* (produced 1974). 1976.
  3. *Handcuffs* (produced 1975). 1977.
All the Bees and All the Keys (for children), music by John Beckwith. 1976.
The Dismissal. 1978.

Radio Play: *Night-Blooming Cereus*, 1959.

Verse

The Red Heart. 1949.
A Suit of Nettles. 1958.
Twelve Letters to a Small Town. 1962.
The Dance of Death at London, Ontario. 1963.
Poems, edited by Germaine Warkentin. 1972.
Selected Longer Poems, edited by Germaine Warkentin. 1976.
Selected Shorter Poems, edited by Germaine Warkentin. 1976.

Other

The Boy with an "R" in His Hand (juvenile). 1965.
Twenty Barrels. 1976.

Reading List: *Reaney* by Alvin A. Lee, 1968; *Reaney* by Ross G. Woodman, 1971; *Reaney* by James Stewart Reaney, 1976.

*　*　*

James Reaney is probably the best Canadian playwright writing today, yet, paradoxically, his plays are less performed than those of many other dramatists. This is so largely because the conception that Reaney has of the theatre does not accord well with the taste for either naturalism – the theatre of social comment – or surrealism – the theatre of the absurd. Not only do his plays have many and rapidly shifting scenes, but his characters inhabit a world of fragile Proustian nostalgic fantasy that is almost operatic.

It is easy to see Reaney as outside the mainstream not only of Canadian playwriting and literature, but of modern English literature generally. (This may in part account for his former neglect among the fashionable theatrical circles of Toronto – a city he long ago came to think of as Blake's City of Destruction.) But his debt is to a tradition of fantasy that is pre-eminently late nineteenth century. This influence comes strongly from the early Yeats, but it is also indebted to the Brontës (Reaney takes the name Branwell in his long poem *A Suit of Nettles*), and, one can't help feeling, to the Henry James of *The Turn of the Screw* and *Owen Wingrave*. Indeed, in *Listen to the Wind*, the protagonist is called Owen and proceeds to stage within the play another play called *The Saga of Caresfoot Court*. Reaney based this on his own childhood experience of reading Rider Haggard's *Dawn*, but it owes a good deal also to the tradition of the Gothic tale out of *Wuthering Heights*.

Indeed, it is in Reaney's taste for melodrama – the sudden reversals in the last acts, for instance – that he is weakest. His attempt to justify melodrama by claiming for it another and truer world – "the patterns in it are not only sensational but deadly accurate" – is only partly succesful. The "strong pattern" of melodrama can easily obscure the significant moral exploration of the play, as the exterior story of *Listen to the Wind* very nearly does.

But if the theatre of fantasy works against naturalism, it also, allied with strong lexical whimsy, works against the excesses of melodrama. The playbox of *Colours in the Dark* is not only a way of explaining the longing to get back home to childhood's Eden; it is also an outward and visible sign of those wordlists that Reaney loves – the inventory of the world. The naming of things is as important to him as it is for Eliot in *Old Possum's Book of Practical Cats*, and shares something of that whimsical attitude to the serious matter of language. "What did the Indians call you?/For you do not flow/With English accents," asks Reaney addressing the Avon River in his set of poems *Twelve Letters to a Small Town*. And this concern with names is uppermost in *Names and Nicknames* especially. But it is a characteristic concern of all his plays and poetry. We never forget Reaney the classicist by training. "Most of those words you've no idea of their meaning, but we're sowing them in your mind anyhow," says Polly in *Easter Egg*; and elsewhere, in *Masks of Childhood*, we have a fantasia on the street names of Winnipeg, ending in a whoop – "I Winnipeg ... She Winnipeggied ... They Winnipugged."

Reaney's language spars with his imagery and by its whimsy prevents the apocalyptic metaphors from becoming bombastic. The verse many be Blakean but it is spoken in the dialect of John Clare. Reaney's debt to Blake, via Frye's *Fearful Symmetry*, is a stated one, but Walt Disney and Mother Goose are there as well. This is most obvious in his poem sequence, *A Suit of Nettles* in which barnyard animals become part of a complex allegory that owes something to Spenser and mediaeval flyting. Reaney has a sense of the landscape that reminds us more of Palmer than of Blake, though it is the voice of the *Prophetic Books* that speaks in *Colours in the Dark*:

> We sit by the fire and hear the rushing sound
> Of the wind that comes from Temiskaming
> Algoma, Patricia
> Down from the north over the wilderness.

But for Reaney there is none of Blake's sense of contraries or great loss and fall. Innocence is accessible if we can but find the way, or rather listen to the children who, like the children in *Burnt Norton*, know it. Their music has the apocalyptic quality of the poetry of Leonard Cohen: "I saw the sundogs barking/On either side of the sun." This surrealist strain in him combines with his other theme, death, in a sequence of poems, *The Dance of Death at London, Ontario*, illustrated by the well-known Canadian painter Jack Chambers. In the same year that *Nettles* was published, a critic said of Chambers that he too had captured in his paintings "The Life of Death in London Ontario." Chambers insisted that he was not a surrealist or even a hyper-realist but a "perceptual realist," and doubtless this is a more accurate term for Reaney's work as well.

In that world objects have a life that is almost Dickensian (again the connection to Victorian fantasy). "I'll be the orange devil waiting in the stove/I'll be the chimney trumpeting the night," says Madam Fay in *The Killdeer*. And it is the cry of the killdeer – plaintive (like Reaney's search for the ancestors and the past that will make sense of the present) and deceiving (as Eli in that play recognizes, "It's another clock in another time") – that is a paradigm of Reaney's work. In that sense he speaks for the English Canada that he knows and loves – one of great farmhouses surrounded by large trees on summer afternoons among musty books where "long, long ago" is as real as here and now, the world of Blake and Spenser, Yeats and Rider Haggard, as immediate as the killdeer and the barnyard geese.

Reaney's major achievement has been his recently completed Donnellys trilogy. In those plays he has managed to capture a myth that is both poetic and destructive, universal and local – and for the first time in English Canadian culture. For Reaney James Donnelly is still there in Biddulph Township, not a ghost but a myth. The shifts through time and game and song achieve this in the plays.

The drift from real to fantasy in most of his plays (*The Dismissal* is an exception) is encouraged by the elements – the wind to which the children listen or the detailed catalogues of flowers and animals. It shares something with O'Neill and Miller, but its closest analogy is the late Shakespearean romances where Illyria is a pattern of England as Caresfoot Court becomes a way of understanding Ontario, and Pericles goes searching for the lost child, Marina, that is himself.

—D.D.C. Chambers

REEVES, William Pember. New Zealander. Born in Lyttleton, 10 February 1857. Educated at Christ's College Grammar School, Christchurch, 1867–74; admitted as barrister and solicitor. Married Magdalen Stuart Robison in 1885; two daughters. Worked as a Reporter for the Canterbury Law School; Editor of the Canterbury *Times* in the 1880's; Staff Member, subsequently Editor, Lyttleton *Times*, from 1889; Liberal Member of the New Zealand House of Representatives for St. Albans, 1887–90, and for Christchurch, 1890–96; Minister of Education, Labour and Justice, 1891–96; New Zealand Agent-General in London, 1896–1909, and High Commissioner, 1905–09; Director, London School of Economics, 1908–19; Chairman, National Bank of New Zealand, London, 1917–32. Member of the Senate, University of London, 1902–19; Chairman, Anglo-Hellenic League. Ph.D.: University of Athens, 1919. Knight of the Redeemer, Greece, 1914. *Died 15 May 1932.*

PUBLICATIONS

Verse

> *Colonial Couplets*, with G. P. Williams. 1889.
> *In Double Harness*, with G. P. Williams. 1891.
> *New Zealand and Other Poems.* 1898.
> (*Poems*). N.d.
> *The Passing of the Forest and Other Verse.* 1925.

Other

> *Some Historical Articles on Communism and Socialism.* 1890.
> *Reform and Experiment in New Zealand.* 1896.
> *The Fortunate Isles.* 1897.
> *The Working of Women's Suffrage in New Zealand and South Australia*, with Sir John Cockburn. 1897.
> *New Zealand.* 1898.
> *The Long White Cloud: Ao Tea Roa* (history of New Zealand). 1898.
> *State Experiments in Australia and New Zealand.* 2 vols., 1902.
> *A Council of the Empire.* 1907.
> *The New Zealand's Shipping Company's Pocket Book: An Interesting Guide for Passengers.* 1908.
> *New Zealand* ("described"). 1908.
> *A Plea for a More Civilized Epirus.* 1913.
> *Albania and Epirus.* 1914.
> *An Appeal for the Liberation and Union of the Hellenic Race.* 1918.
> *The Great Powers and the Eastern Christians: Christiani ad Leones! A Protest.* 1922.
>
> Editor, with Ernest Speight, *The Imperial Reader: An Account of the Territories Forming the British Empire.* 1906.

Reading List: *Reeves: New Zealand Fabian*, 1965, and *Reeves*, 1969, both by Keith Sinclair.

* * *

William Pember Reeves was the most interesting and accomplished poet in nineteenth-century New Zealand. Yet, like most of the New Zealanders who produced readable verse in the colonial period (and they were few in number and modest in achievement), Reeves was a man for whom poetry was a minor activity in a life devoted largely to other things, pre-eminently politics, though sport, journalism, and historical writing were among his other accomplishments. His poetry was merely a civilised diversion, a private recreation taken up in the interstices of a busy public life. Nonetheless, despite the limitations of the Victorian verse tradition within which he worked, something of his emotional and intellectual engagement with the land and people of New Zealand spilled over into his poetry. A handful of his poems retain an interest for later generations of New Zealanders partly because they anticipate the concerns of the more authentically indigenous writers who emerged in the 1920's and 1930's, and partly because they document (sometimes unconsciously) a significant phase in the history of the nation's consciousness.

Reeves's one significant collection was *New Zealand and Other Poems*, published in London shortly after he had left New Zealand to settle permanently in England. It included the best of his verses in his first two books, *Colonial Couplets* and *In Double Harness*, both written in collaboration with G. P. Williams. *The Passing of the Forest and Other Verse*, privately published late in life, largely reprinted the contents of the earlier book, and added only one new poem of significance, "The Colonist in His Garden." This poem begins with a letter to a colonist from a friend in England attempting to persuade him to return to civilization. He cites the familiar complaints about life in the colonies: "lonely," "empty," "without a past," "commonplace," "Where men but talk of gold and sheep/And think of sheep and gold." The colonist replies with a spirited defense of colonial life:

> "No art?" Who serve an art more great
> Than we, rough architects of State
> With the old Earth at strife?

But what makes the poem interesting today is the revelation of attitudes beneath the surface of the conscious argument; the bold colonial assertiveness wears thin and reveals the cringing defensiveness beneath. The New World is defended on the grounds that it is a home away from Home, just like the old country only better:

> And with my flowers about her spread
> (None brighter than her shining head),
> The lady of my close,
> My daughter, walks in girlhood fair.
> Friend, could I rear in England's air
> A sweeter English rose?

A further unconscious irony is that this poem was written after Reeves himself had made the decision to leave New Zealand and settle in England. In its analysis of the colonial condition this poem anticipates the work of later New Zealand poets such as Ursula Bethell, A. R. D. Fairburn, and Allen Curnow.

Other poems by Reeves which prefigure the work of later generations are "The Passing of the Forest" (a once famous but incurably portentous and sentimental account of the destruction by the settlers of the native forests), "Fragments from *Tasman, a Poem*" (anticipating the interest in the history of the country of the poets of the thirties), "New Zealand" (an early instance of nationalism), and "Nox Benigna" (a descriptive poem in which truth to landscape and region asserts itself over the conventions of English Romantic poetry which vitiated most descriptive poetry in the colonial period). Reeves pointed the way to the eventual emergence of an authentic native tradition in New Zealand poetry.

—Peter Simpson

REID, Vic(tor Stafford). Jamaican. Born in Jamaica, 1 May 1913. Educated in Jamaica. Married; four children. Reporter, editor, and foreign correspondent for various newspapers; worked in advertising; currently, managing director and chairman of a printing and publishing company in Kingston, Jamaica; has travelled extensively in the Americas, Africa, Europe, and the Middle East. Recipient: Guggenheim Fellowship, 1959; Canada Council Fellowship; Mexican Writers Fellowship. Lives in Kingston, Jamaica.

PUBLICATIONS

Fiction

New Day. 1949.
The Leopard. 1958.
Mount Ephraim. 1972.
The Sun and Juan de Bolas. 1974.

Other

Sixty-Five (juvenile). 1960.
The Young Warriors (juvenile). 1967.
Buildings in Jamaica. 1970.

* * *

Vic Reid's novel *New Day* is a landmark in Caribbean literature. As Gerald Moore remarked in *The Chosen Tongue*, "discovery in the cultural sense comes with a realization that one is neither a rootless being devoid of identity, nor a lost son of Africa or Asia, but a man made by this island now." For the people of Jamaica this discovery was made when Vic Reid's novel *New Day* was published in 1949.

The novel spans a period of eighty years, from the time of the Morant Bay Rebellion in 1865 when the constitution was abolished till 1944 when constitution rule was once more returned to the people, and there was a promise at least of a "new day." The narrator is the eighty-seven-year-old Johnny Campbell. On the eve of independence he looks back to the past, and it is through his reminiscences that we trace the history of Jamaica and its people. Through Johnny Campbell, Reid has given us an artist's interpretation of eighty years of Jamaican history and of the people and forces that have shaped this history.

The final section of the novel has come in for some criticism. Sylvia Wynter (in *Savacou 5*, 1971) writes:

> Garth is made to bear the weight of an expectation that can never be realized. Whilst the first part of the book parallels and patterns the structure of its society, and reflects its failure to satisfy human needs, the third part fails by ignoring the fact that a change in the superstructure of the plantation, a new Constitution, even Independence, were changes which left the basic system untouched; and which only prolonged the inevitable and inbuilt confrontation.

Reid ignores this situation. Unlike George Beckford in *Persistent Poverty* or George Lamming in his novel *Natives of My Person*, he fails to point out that what in fact has happened in Caribbean society is that the old masters and colonizers have been replaced by new ones. But as Mervyn Morris said, "That there was more to see ... does not invalidate the book."

The whole work is in dialect. By making the language of the people an acceptable literary medium, Reid paved the way for other writers such as Samuel Selvon.

Mention should also be made of Reid's novel *The Leopard*. The setting this time is Kenya; the book was written to counterbalance the flood of anti-Kikuyu literature that followed the Mau-Mau uprising. The narrator is Nebu, the African; the conflict between him and Gibson, the white settler, the leopard, the destroyer of harmony in the natural world, is symbolic of the black-white conflict in Africa. Interest centres eventually on Toto, the half-caste child of

Nebu and Mrs. Gibson, who is alienated from both his European and Kikuyu ancestry. It is Toto's alienation that in Kenneth Ramchand's opinion makes "*The Leopard* in its finest aspect a parable on the relationship between alienated West Indian and embarrassing African ancestry" (*The West Indian Novel and Its Background*, 1970).

While *The Leopard* has been acclaimed by a number of critics it is almost certain that Vic Reid's reputation will rest on his novel *New Day*.

—Anna Rutherford

RICHARDSON, Henry Handel. Pseudonym for Ethel Florence Lindesay Richardson Robertson. Australian. Born in Melbourne, Victoria, 3 January 1870. Educated at the Presbyterian Ladies' College, Melbourne; studied music at the Leipzig Conservatorium, 1887–90. Married John G. Robertson in 1895 (died, 1933). Lived in Strasbourg, 1895–1903, in London, 1903, and in Sussex from 1933; writer from 1908. Recipient: Australian Literature Society Gold Medal, 1929. *Died 20 March 1946.*

PUBLICATIONS

Fiction

Maurice Guest. 1908.
The Getting of Wisdom. 1910.
Australia Felix. 1917; *The Way Home*, 1925; *Ultima Thule*, 1929; complete version, as *The Fortunes of Richard Mahony*, 1930.
The End of a Childhood and Other Stories. 1934.
The Young Cosima. 1939.

Other

Two Studies. 1931.
Myself When Young. 1948.
Letters to Nettie Palmer, edited by Karl-Johan Rossing. 1953.

Translator, *Siren Voices*, by J. P. Jacobsen. 1896.
Translator, *The Fisher Lass*, by B. Bjørnson. 1896.

Bibliography: "Richardson: An Annotated Bibliography of Writings about Her" by Verna D. Wittock, in *English Literature in Transition 6*, 1964.

Reading List: *Richardson: A Study* by Nettie Palmer, 1950; *Richardson and Some of Her Sources*, 1954, *A Companion to Australia Felix*, 1962, and *Richardson*, 1966, all by Leonie Kramer; *Richardson* by Vincent Buckley, 1961; *Ulysses Bound: Richardson and Her Fiction* by Dorothy Green, 1973 (includes bibliography).

* * *

Henry Handel Richardson's novels and short stories are at once intensely personal and part of a powerful literary tradition. As an expatriate in late 19th-century Germany, she found herself for the first time psychologically and intellectually at home in a milieu in which the polarities of existence, permanence and change, and the attempt to reconcile or transcend them were the dominant concerns of thinkers and artists. Her heroes (and heroines) are always "in flight"; even an old woman on her death-bed in the story "Mary Christina" wants to get up and go away, "far away." Richardson's true place, therefore, is within the German Romantic tradition that took its rise in Goethe, and no estimate of her achievement can afford to ignore the influence on her work of her husband, John George Robertson, for whom Goethe was the supreme artist. Robertson, one of the most distinguished German and Scandinavian scholars of his day, was for thirty years Professor of Germanic and Scandinavian Languages at London University, inaugurating the first systematic study of these subjects in Britain. It is not surprising that these are the influences felt most in Richardson's work, not those of the Russians or the French as is sometimes claimed.

Richardson's early childhood was tragic and her girlhood unhappy; her novels are the result of bringing to bear on these painful memories her later experience as a music-student in Leipzig and what she absorbed at the side of her husband. It was Robertson who first documented, as a philologist, the transition from the concept of art as mimesis to the assertion of the primacy of the imagination in artistic creation. Traces of Robertson's account of the relationship between truth and fiction and of the function of the imagination can be clearly discerned in Richardson's work, from *Maurice Guest* and *The Getting of Wisdom* to the late short stories. These new ideas shed light on her past and on her country's past, and enabled her to make symbolic use of both. Australia, and especially the Australia of the gold-rush period, was the perfect image of flux and instability, while the search for gold was itself an ancient symbol of the longing for wholeness, for permanence, which her divided nature craved. *The Fortunes of Richard Mahony* is only marginally a realistic period novel about an emigrant doctor; it is much more a novel about a state of mind and a metaphysic; its deceptively commonplace domestic mould, the skilled psychological presentation of the conflict of wills and purposes between husband and wife, have blinded many critics to its complexity.

Richardson had been writing for thirty years before the publication of the final volume of the trilogy, *Ultima Thule*, brought her sudden fame. The two previous volumes, *Australia Felix* and *The Way Home*, about Mahony's early struggles, his rise to unexpected riches, and his sudden loss of fortune, appeared too far apart in time to make the impact they deserved, and it is true their significance is not wholly clear without the third volume, which is much more self-contained.

Selected details from her father's life provided the scaffolding for the novel, but the temperament with which she endowed Mahony is much more her own than her father's. The fusing of fact and fiction results in a work of art which is a great parable of the deepest longings of the human spirit, embodied in Mahony and his wife Mary, by means of a narrative method which can be justly called dialectic. Richardson is a master of telling and climactic scenes, and the one in which Mahony finally goes out of his mind, as he burns his deeds, his scrip, his insurance policies – everything to do with money – is one of the most memorable images of the contradictions of rising capitalism in modern literature. At the same time, the relentless unfolding of the novel, its sombre tones, place it, if not on the same level, at least in the same category, as Sophoclean tragedy. The great Oedipean theme is inescapable Destiny; that of *Richard Mahony* is the limitless unpredictability of the genotype, the stubborn core of irrationality at the heart of things that all flesh must accept.

The same theme sounds in the first novel, *Maurice Guest*, though it is not yet a major one. Richardson was more concerned, when she began to write, about her two painful and impossible love-experiences, and the book is an exploration of the nature of love. On a surface level, it draws on her life as a music-student, and on her considerable professional competence as pianist and composer, for its realistic and figurative content. The book was as innovative as *Richard Mahony* was to be, though Richardson has never been given due credit for originality. *Maurice Guest* is one of the earliest full-length portraits of the "outsider" figure in English, and the first to treat homosexuality openly, though the term is not used; the first to treat Freudian ideas critically, the first to present Nietzchean ideas ironically – so subtly indeed that she was accused later of being a Nietzchean. The novel anatomizes a number of human relationships that normally come under the heading "love" and exposes them for what they are: different forms of narcissism. Real love, in which the one seeks the happiness of the other, is defined by its absence, though Richardson has something positive to say on behalf of the obsessive personality in her summing-up. The heroine of the book is modelled externally on Eleonora Duse, and her violinist lover, Schilsky, is an ironic portrait of the young Richard Strauss; the central character, Maurice, and the heroine are a composite, psychologically, of Richardson herself, but so detached and objective is her style that there is no way of knowing this without biographical assistance. The novel was deeply influenced by Jacobsen's *Niels Lyhne*, and, more superficially, by D'Annunzio's *Il Fuoco*, but, when all debts are acknowledged, *Maurice Guest* is unmistakably Richardson's own creation, felt upon her pulses. The book was one of the best pillaged works of its day, admired and imitated by fellow-novelists, and then ignored, its pioneering of the "outsider" theme unrecognised. *The Getting of Wisdom*, written concurrently with *Maurice Guest*, but published two years later, handles the same theme more lightly in the setting of a Melbourne girls' school. Its relationship with *Richard Mahony* is direct: the wisdom Laura learns so painfully is that which Mahony attempts to convey to his wife in *The Way Home*: "*Panta rei* is the eternal truth; *semper idem* the lie we long to see confirmed."

The short stories, *The End of a Childhood*, are conceived with great insight and beautifully shaped. With one or two exceptions, they are sombre in tone, especially when dealing with sexual deviance or themes of alienation. The best of them is perhaps "Mary Christina," an early story originally entitled "Death." It is a powerful evocation of the physical sensations of dying and the nearest Richardson came to nihilism. (Her usual attitude to the "great mystery" she shared with Spiritualists like Sir Oliver Lodge; she was a member of the Society for Psychical Research for many years, but her temper was sceptical rather than dogmatic.)

Her prose is remarkable for its rhythms and its elegiac tone rather than for its diction and she is not to be judged according to the canons of lyric poetry but by the strengths proper to a novelist: characterisation and organisation. Through all the changes of literary fashion since the 1920's, Richardson has remained the most permanently satisfying of Australian novelists.

—Dorothy Green

RICHLER, Mordecai. Canadian. Born in Montreal, Quebec, 27 January 1931. Educated at the Montreal Hebrew Academy; Baron Byng High School, Montreal; Sir George Williams University, Montreal, 1948–50. Married Florence Wood in 1959; three sons and two daughters. Lived in Europe, 1959–72; Writer-in-Residence, Sir George Williams University, 1968–69; Visiting Professor, Carleton University, Ottawa, 1972–74. Member for Canada, Editorial Board, Book-of-the-Month Club, since 1976. Recipient: President's Medal, University of Western Ontario, for non-fiction, 1959; Canada Council Junior Arts Fellowship, 1959, 1960, and Senior Arts Fellowship, 1966; Guggenheim Fellowship, 1961; Governor-General's Award, 1969, 1971; Writers Guild of America award, 1974; British Film Festival Golden Bear, 1974; Canadian Library Association English Medal Award, for children's book, 1976. Lives in Montreal.

PUBLICATIONS

Fiction

The Acrobats. 1954; as *Wicked We Love,* n.d.
Son of a Smaller Hero. 1955.
A Choice of Enemies. 1957.
The Apprenticeship of Duddy Kravitz. 1959.
The Incomparable Atuk. 1963; as *Stick Your Neck Out,* 1963.
Cocksure. 1968.
The Street: Stories. 1969.
St. Urbain's Horseman. 1971.
Notes on an Endangered Species and Others (stories). 1974.

Plays

Screenplays: *Dearth of a Salesman,* 1957; *No Love for Johnnie,* with Nicholas Phipps, 1961; *Tiara Tahiti,* with Geoffrey Cotterell and Ivan Foxwell, 1962; *The Wild and the Willing (Young and Willing),* with Nicholas Phipps, 1962; *Life at the Top,* 1965; *The Apprenticeship of Duddy Kravitz,* 1974; *Fun with Dick and Jane,* with David Giler and Jerry Belson, 1977.

Radio Play: *It's Harder to Be Anybody,* 1961.

Television Plays: *Trouble with Benny,* 1959; *The Apprenticeship of Duddy Kravitz,* from his own novel, 1961; *The Fall of Mendel Crick,* from a story by Isaac Babel, 1963.

Other

Hunting Tigers under Glass: Essays and Reports. 1969.
Shovelling Trouble. 1972.
Jacob Two-Two Meets the Hooded Fang (juvenile). 1975.
Creativity and the University, with André Fortier and Rollo May. 1975.
Images of Spain. 1977.

Editor, *Canadian Writing Today.* 1970.

Reading List: *Richler* by George Woodcock, 1970; *Richler* edited by G. David Sheps, 1970; *Richler* by Robert Fulford, 1971.

* * *

Mordecai Richler, the Canadian novelist and essayist, was born in Montreal of a Jewish family which originated in Russia and Poland. Of his novels, *The Apprenticeship of Duddy Kravitz* and *St. Urbain's Horseman* are not only the most ambitious in scale but the ones that have earned most critical praise. Many of his novels have enjoyed remarkable sales, especially the temptingly titled *Cocksure,* a bawdy and satirical fantasy about modish London. His collection of essays, *Hunting Tigers under Glass,* includes witty but perceptive pieces on Expo 67 and Norman Mailer, as well as the sharply ironic "Jews in Sport."

Jewishness is the subject and Jewish is the tone of all Richler's work. Though he knows the slicker business world of Jewish enterprise, mocking it with brio in several of his books, he writes more feelingly of the Jewish minority in French-speaking Montreal. Duddy Kravitz, who has also become the subject of a successful Canadian film based on Richler's novel, has been described as "a two-timing, trouble-making, self-pitying, anti-goy young Jew from a Montreal back-street." Richler portrays him with an almost total lack of sentimentality. Similar lives are presented in *St. Urbain's Horseman* and in a collection of short stories entitled *The Street*. In *St. Urbain's Horseman* Richler links Canadian experience with the Nazi treatment of the Jews, providing his novel with a deeper compassion than has been obvious in earlier work.

Richler's combination of abrasive humour and racy style can lead him into cynicism, even meretriciousness. *Cocksure*, like *The Incomparable Atuk* whose central character is an Eskimo poet taken up by a public relations officer, makes splendid fun of media techniques and of trendy attitudes. Both novels, however, partly fall victim to the superficiality they seek to satirise.

Richler enjoys great popular success but is regarded with some suspicion by critics for his apparent lack of seriousness. In his best work, however, he writes with such shrewd observation of minority groups that he is likely to be assured a lasting place among the leaders of Canadian fiction. He has also worked on several film scripts, including John Braine's *Life at the Top*, as a result of which the film world plays an important part in many of his writings. He lived mainly in Europe from 1959 to 1972, which may account for a sense of rootlessness running through some of his work.

—Alastair Niven

ROBERTS, Sir Charles G(eorge) D(ouglas). Canadian. Born in Douglas, New Brunswick, 10 January 1860. Eduated at the Collegiate School, Fredericton, New Brunswick, 1874–76; University of New Brunswick, Fredericton (Douglas Medal in Latin and Greek; Alumni Gold Medal for Latin Essay), 1876–81, B.A. (honours) in mental and moral science and political economy 1879, M.A. 1881. Served in the British Army, 1914–15: Captain; transferred to the Canadian Army, 1916: Major; subsequently worked with Lord Beaverbrook on the Canadian War Records. Married 1) Mary Isabel Fenety in 1880 (died, 1930), three sons and one daughter; 2) Joan Montgomery in 1943. Headmaster, Chatham Grammar School, New Brunswick, 1879–81, and York Street School, Fredericton, 1881–83; Editor, *This Week*, Toronto, 1883–84; Professor of English and French, 1885–88, and Professor of English and Economics, 1888–95, King's College, Windsor, Nova Scotia; Associate Editor, *The Illustrated American*, New York, 1897–98; Co-Editor, The Nineteenth Century series, 1900–05; lived in England, 1911–25. Recipient: Lorne Pierce Medal, 1926. LL.D.: University of New Brunswick, 1906. Fellow, 1890, and President of Section II, 1933, Royal Society of Canada; Fellow, Royal Society of Literature, 1892; Member, National Institute of Arts and Letters, 1898. Knighted, 1935. *Died 26 November 1943.*

PUBLICATIONS

Collections

Selected Poems, edited by Desmond Pacey. 1956.

Verse

Orion and Other Poems. 1880.
Later Poems. 1881.
Later Poems. 1882.
In Divers Tones. 1886.
Autotochthon. 1889.
Songs of the Common Day, and Ave: An Ode for the Shelley Centenary. 1893.
The Book of the Native. 1896.
New York Nocturnes and Other Poems. 1898.
Poems. 1901.
The Book of the Rose. 1903.
Poems. 1907.
New Poems. 1919.
The Sweet o' the Year and Other Poems. 1925.
The Vagrant of Time. 1927; revised edition, 1927.
Be Quiet Wind: Unsaid. 1929.
The Iceberg and Other Poems. 1934.
Selected Poems. 1936.
Twilight over Shaugamauk and Three Other Poems. 1937.
Canada Speaks of Britain and Other Poems of the War. 1941.

Fiction

The Raid from Beauséjour, and How the Carter Boys Lifted the Mortgage: Two Stories of Acadie. 1894; *The Raid from Beauséjour* published as *The Young Acadian,* 1907.
Reube Dare's Shad Boat: A Tale of the Tide Country. 1895; as *The Cruise of the Yacht "Dido,"* 1906.
Around the Campfire. 1896.
The Forge in the Forest, Being the Narrative of the Acadian Ranger, Jean de Mer. 1896.
Earth's Enigmas: A Book of Animal and Nature Life. 1896; revised edition, 1903.
A Sister to Evangeline, Being the Story of Yvonne de Lamourie. 1898; as *Lovers in Acadie,* 1924.
The Heart of the Ancient Wood. 1900.
By the Marshes of Minas (stories). 1900.
Barbara Ladd. 1902.
The Kindred of the Wild: A Book of Animal Life. 1902.
The Prisoner of Mademoiselle: A Love Story. 1904.
The Watchers of the Trails: A Book of Animal Life. 1904.
Red Fox: The Story of His Adventurous Career. 1905.
The Heart That Knows. 1906.
The Haunters of the Silences: A Book of Animal Life. 1907.
In the Deep of the Snow. 1907.
The Red Oxen of Bonval (stories). 1908.
The House in the Water: A Book of Animal Life. 1908.
The Backwoodsmen. 1909.
Kings in Exile. 1909.
Neighbours Unknown. 1910.
More Kindred of the Wild. 1911.
Babes of the Wild. 1912; as *Children of the Wild,* 1913.
The Feet of the Furtive. 1912.
A Balkan Prince. 1913.
Cock Crow (stories). 1913.

Hoof and Claw. 1913.
The Secret Trails. 1916.
The Ledge on Bald Face. 1918; as *Jim: The Story of a Backwoods Police Dog,* 1919.
In the Morning of Time (stories). 1919.
Wisdom of the Wilderness. 1922.
They Who Walk in the Wild. 1924.
Eyes of the Wilderness. 1933.
Further Animal Stories. 1935.
Thirteen Bears, edited by Ethel Hume Bennett. 1947.
Forest Folk, edited by Ethel Hume Bennett. 1949.
The Last Barrier and Other Stories. 1958.
Kings of Beasts and Other Stories, edited by Joseph Gold. 1967.

Other

The Canadian Guide-Book: A Tourist's and Sportsman's Guide to Eastern Canada and Newfoundland. 1892.
The Land of Evangeline and the Gateways Thither. 1894.
A History of Canada for High Schools and Academies. 1897.
Discoveries and Explorations in the Century (nineteenth-century series). 1904.
Canada in Flanders, vol. 3. 1918.

Editor, *Poems of Wild Life.* 1888.
Editor, *Northland Lyrics,* by William Carmon Roberts, Theodore Roberts, and Elizabeth Roberts McDonald. 1899.
Editor, *Alastor and Adonais,* by Shelley. 1902.
Editor, with Arthur L. Tunnell, *A Standard Dictionary of Canadian Biography: The Canadian Who Was Who.* 2 vols., 1934–38.
Editor, with Arthur L. Tunnell, *The Canadian Who's Who,* vols. II and III. 1936–39.
Editor, *Flying Colours: An Anthology.* 1942.

Translator, *The Canadians of Old,* by Philippe Aubert de Gaspé. 1890; as *Cameron of Lochiel,* 1905.

Reading List; *Roberts* by Elsie M. Pomeroy, 1943, and *Tributes Through the Years: The Centenary of the Birth of Roberts,* edited by Pomeroy, 1959; *Roberts* by William J. Keith, 1969.

*   *   *

Charles G. D. Roberts is now most remembered as a poet, but he wrote far more prose than verse in a long life, much of which had to be supported by the proceeds of free-lance writing. He wrote a *History of Canada* and a number of historical novels about Canada's early centuries. He also wrote what today we might term environmental romances like *The Heart of the Ancient Wood* and *In the Morning of Time,* in which he somewhat implausibly portrayed men and women trying to reconcile themselves with the world of nature. Most of his energy, however, went into the writing of stories about animals, of which, in all, he published no less than twenty volumes.

As several critics have pointed out, Roberts pioneered a peculiarly Canadian type of animal story which does not attempt to anthropomorphize the characters, as English stories of the same kind do, or to turn them into symbols of destiny, as American writers from Melville onwards have been tempted to do. Roberts sees the animals with great empathy for the non-human beings they are, with whom we may identify only because they too are victims of destiny. Consequently the best of his fiction in this genre, in collections like *The Kindred of the Wild*, *The Watchers of the Trails* and *Neighbours Unknown*, has a kind of inward authenticity that is still appealing.

In his first volume of verse, *Orion and Other Poems*, Roberts seemed to be setting out, in poems many of which retell the myths of classical antiquity, to prove that a Canadian poet could be as capable as any English versifier of handling traditional themes and forms. His manifest success in this aim made Roberts the leader among the group of young men – including Archibald Lampman, Bliss Carman, and Duncan Campbell Scott – who later became known as the Confederation Poets, the first real school of Canadian poetry.

It was in later volumes, like *In Divers Tones*, which included the famous nostalgic landscape poem "Tantramer Revisited," and *Songs of the Common Day*, that Roberts really found his style, applying the techniques he had learnt from the English poets to a vision of the Canadian terrain and Canadian country life as they really were and not as sham English settings. Later in life, he moved forward technically, and "The Iceberg," written in the 1930's, was one of the earliest Canadian poems to use free verse with effect.

Roberts never sprang completely free of the tone and even the diction of Victorian neo-romanticism, but by his passionate exploration of the Canadian scene as a theme for poetry he did more than any other Canadian poet writing in the nineteenth century to establish a native poetic tradition.

—George Woodcock

ROSS, Sinclair. Canadian. Born in Shellbrook, Saskatchewan, 22 January 1908. Served in the Canadian Army, 1942–45. Worked for the Royal Bank of Canada for 43 years: in Winnipeg, 1931–42, and in Montreal, 1946–68; now retired. Lives in Malaga, Spain.

PUBLICATIONS

Fiction

> *As for Me and My House.* 1941.
> *The Well.* 1958.
> *The Lamp at Noon and Other Stories.* 1968.
> *Whir of Gold.* 1970.
> *Sawbones Memorial.* 1974.

Reading List: "Ross's Ambivalent World" by W. H. New, in *Canadian Literature*, Spring 1969; "No Other Way: Ross's Stories and Novels" by Sandra Djwa, in *Canadian Literature*, Winter 1971.

* * *

Sinclair Ross has written chiefly about the harshness of life on the Canadian prairie. His early stories and first novel, *As for Me and My House*, set against the drought and depression of the 1930's are established classics of Canadian literature. Ross describes the wind, the dust storms, and the fierce extremes of climate with powerful accuracy, but what is remarkable is the way he uses the details of setting as symbolic counters for human emotions. For example, the drought and vast distances between prairie farms reflect the spiritual dryness and the loneliness felt by the characters. Ross describes the efforts of the farmers and the people of the small prairie towns to wrest a living from their bleak environment, and in his style there is a taut, spare quality which is the perfect measure of man's struggle to endure. Ross's stories focus on three main figures: the farmer, physically strong but inarticulate, who pits himself against the adversities of the land; the young wife and mother who longs for a closer relationship with her husband and dreams of their moving away from the lonely farm; and the child who escapes into an imaginative world of his own making suggested by a fragment of music or by the spirit and freedom of a horse.

"The Lamp at Noon," "Cornet at Night," and "One's a Heifer" are fine stories, yet Ross's masterpiece is the novel *As for Me and My House*, which documents the repressed lives of a preacher and his wife in a small town during the depression. The story is told in diary form by the wife, Mrs. Bentley, who craves for intimacy with her silent, aloof husband, and who plots their escape from the town. Her husband, however, effects his own escape by closing himself in his study where he tries to paint. The form of the novel is striking, for the repressed, claustrophobic existence of the characters is perfectly rendered by the secretive and repetitious entries Mrs. Bentley makes in her daybook. The artist's struggle to find himself gives the novel a universal theme, but the artist's story is told unconventionally by means of the wife's observations rather than through the artist's consciousness. What is more impressive, however, is the author's creation of his female narrator; seldom has a male writer portrayed a woman so credibly or sympathetically.

Ross's output has been small. *The Well* and *Whir of Gold*, conventionally plotted narratives, have added little to his reputation, but in writing *Sawbones Memorial*, the story of a small town doctor, Ross found another fictional structure which vividly renders the life of the prairies. There is no narration in *Sawbones Memorial*, only the drama-like presentation of conversations and memories on the night of the doctor's retirement party, but this unique form serves once again to chronicle man's struggle to survive in a harsh land and his instinct to dream of a better life.

—David Stouck

RUDD, Steele. Pseudonym for Arthur Hoey Davis. Australian. Born in Drayton, Queensland, 14 November 1868. Educated in the Emu Creek State School. Married twice; three sons and one daughter from the first marriage. Worked on sheep and cattle stations in Queensland, 1880–86; settled in Brisbane, 1886, and entered the Queensland Civil Service: Junior Clerk in the office of the Curator of Intestate Estates, 1886–88; Clerk in the Sheriff's Office, 1889–1902, and Under-Sheriff, 1902–03; full-time writer from 1903; columnist for newspapers in Brisbane, and for the Sydney *Bulletin*; Founding Editor, *Steele Rudd's Magazine*, Brisbane and Sydney, 1904–08, 1923–30. Died 11 October 1935.

PUBLICATIONS

Fiction

On Our Selection! 1899.
Our New Selection. 1903.
Sandy's Selection. 1904.
Back at Our Selection. 1906.
The Poor Parson. 1907.
In Australia. 1908.
Dad in Politics and Other Stories. 1908; as *For Life and Other Stories*, 1908.
Stocking Our Selection. 1909.
Duncan McClure. 1909.
From Selection to City. 1909.
On an Australian Farm. 1910.
The Dashwoods. 1911.
The Book of Dan. 1911.
The Old Homestead. 1917.
Memoirs of Corporal Keeley. 1918.
Grandpa's Selection. 1919.
We Kaytons. 1921; as *Kayton's Selection*, 1926.
On Emu Creek. 1923.
Me an' th' Son. 1924.
The Rudd Family. 1926.
The Miserable Clerk. 1926.
The Romance of Runnibede. 1927 (?).
Green Grey Homestead. 1934.

* * *

Arthur Hoey Davis's singular achievement was his creation, as "Steele Rudd," of an enduring Australian mythology. It epitomizes the struggle of the common man-on-the-land to accept and adapt to the basic rural environment; the "selector" (unlike the earlier and wealthier "squatter") was the nearest equivalent to a European peasant settler, dogged, independent, and hard-working, and he was endowed with a similar tenacity and energy. In modern times the character of Dad Rudd, with the rest of the Rudd family – Dan, Dave, Kate, Mabel, Joe, a colonially extensive tribe – is perhaps not so convincingly representative of the Australian farmer, who with time has become relatively more prosperous and relatively more conservative. But Davis's vision was of the selector's world in its primary phase, and the picture had great vigour. His characters were from the first grotesques; the humour was a horse-laugh. All this became easy to caricature, a fact which accounts for the (artistic) corruption which in its later days descended on the legend when it became the material for comic strip presentation in newspapers; but this was something outside Davis's invention, imposed by popular success itself. In order to preserve proportion a discriminating reader will always go to Davis's early books; those first stories have a colonial freshness that is as true as the characters are good. And it is a tribute to their integrity that, even in the corruption of the Rudds in later days, only the literary proprieties suffered – nothing could destroy their essential innocence or the warmth of their humanity. When Davis took his rural characters to town and Dad entered politics they still kept their rural identity and colour. Their truth, not their subtlety, preserves them; they are comic ghosts and phantoms and as such do not sustain for long – but phantoms also have great perdurability, and these will always remain ready to imaginative recall as long as Australians are disposed to turn back romantically to those phases of early history which represent their struggle to possess their own landscape, those bad old days of frustration and despair which, in their innermost hearts, they really treasure as the golden age of their national pride. To this mythological phenomenon, even now in these very different times, "Steele Rudd" still holds one of the essential keys.

—Brian Elliott

SARGESON, Frank. New Zealander. Born in Hamilton, 23 March 1903. Educated at Hamilton High School; University of New Zealand; admitted as a Solicitor of the Supreme Court of New Zealand, 1926. Estates Clerk, New Zealand Public Trust, Wellington, 1928–29; has also worked as a journalist. Recipient: Centennial Literary Competition prize, 1940; New Zealand Government literary pension, 1947–68; Hubert Church Prize, 1952, 1968; Katherine Mansfield Award, 1965. D.H.L.: University of Auckland, 1974. Lives in Auckland.

PUBLICATIONS

Fiction

Conversation with My Uncle and Other Sketches. 1936.
A Man and His Wife (stories). 1940.
When the Wind Blows. 1945.
That Summer and Other Stories. 1946.
I Saw in My Dream. 1949.
I for One.... 1954.
Collected Stories 1935–1963, edited by Bill Pearson. 1964; revised edition, as *The Stories 1935–1973,* 1973.
Memoirs of a Peon. 1965.
The Hangover. 1967.
Joy of the Worm. 1969.
Man of England Now (includes *Game of Hide and Seek* and *I for One* ...). 1972.
Sunset Village. 1976.

Plays

A Time for Sowing (produced 1961). In *Wrestling with the Angel,* 1964.
The Cradle and the Egg (produced 1962). In *Wrestling with the Angel,* 1964.
Wrestling with the Angel: Two Plays. 1964.

Other

Once Is Enough: A Memoir. 1972.
More Than Enough. 1975.
Never Enough! (memoirs). 1977.

Editor, *Speaking for Ourselves: A Collection of New Zealand Stories.* 1945.

Bibliography: in *The Stories,* 1973.

Reading List: *The Puritan and the Wolf: A Symposium of Critical Essays on the Work of Sargeson* edited by Helen Shaw, 1955; *Sargeson* by H. Winston Rhodes, 1969; *Sargeson in His Time* by Dennis McEldowney, 1977.

* * *

Thirty years ago Frank Sargeson already occupied a pre-eminent position among New Zealand prose-writers on the strength of the unspectacular but carefully crafted short stories which he had been producing since the mid-1930's. Yet this body of work, though respected and influential, was very small, and he added only two book-length publications in the period up to 1964. As Sargeson had reached his sixties, it would have been pardonable then to suppose that his career was virtually over. But the publication of his *Collected Stories* in 1964 not only confirmed the excellence and exemplary quality of his achievement in the short-story form; it also initiated a remarkable late flowering: four novels, a brace of plays, two volumes of autobiography, novellas, and various contributions to periodicals. While extending his achievement, however, these writings of recent years have in general confirmed its nature and direction. Sargeson's chief virtues derive from a preoccupation with the distinctive contours of New Zealand speech, with language not as a mere tool for the writer but as his material, a medium which carries the imprint of a particular place and time.

Reading through his *Collected Stories,* arranged in chronological sequence, one notices an increasing sophistication of technique; yet throughout the steady development – from the direct and even moralistic sketches of early years, through the subtler artistry of stories like "A Man and His Wife," to the more inventive disposition of materials in stories of the 1950's and 1960's – certain essential elements stay constant. Most obviously, these are all very brief tales; they have a confined span of action; they deal with small groups of characters; they are almost always narrated from within the consciousness of one of these characters; and they keep strictly to an idiom appropriate to that consciousness, an idiom which is therefore often flat and muted. In short, the formal aspects of his stories are characterized by stringent limitation. Take for example "I've Lost My Pal" (*Conversation with My Uncle*). It contains only three characters, one of them the narrator, who simply relates how his friend came to be murdered by a fellow-worker. What gives it potency is the fact that we observe through eyes that do not see the whole truth. The very inadequacy of the narrator's concluding comments forces us to sift everything that has been said and make our own independent judgement about the attitudes of George the murderer, Tom the victim, and the narrator himself. This kind of experiment in attenuation is repeated in story after story, most impressively in the novella *That Summer,* in which a soft-hearted and almost simple-minded rolling stone called Bill recounts some of his experiences during a few weeks of the depression. He feels deeply, but cannot get beyond a formulaic slang in expressing his feelings. As he moves in random fashion from place to place we meet his few casual acquaintances; but although the setting is urban no sense of social relationships emerges, and although his dealings with other people are full of nuance he is not conscious of it. Sargeson's achievement in *That Summer* is to have utilized these self-imposed limitations in such a way that they give moving emphasis to the central thematic issues.

For his first novel, *I Saw in My Dream*, Sargeson abandoned the first-person narrative stance, but the point of view is still strictly limited. We remain within the narrow orbit of the central character's circumstances, and whatever occurs is refracted through his consciousness. The structure is essentially linear, having length without substantial breadth, and once again there is no attempt to depict directly an extensive social milieu. Society takes the shape of claustrophobic, puritanical family pressures.

Even more confined is the scale of *I for One* ..., a novella in diary form in which a very sheltered spinster reflects on her experiences over a brief period. The technique of narration is a little less reductive than in the earlier stories, since Katherine is sufficiently self-aware and articulate to be able to record happenings and feelings with some precision. But the action is as tightly circumscribed as ever; the little that does actually take place does so offstage.

Sargeson's most impressive single work is *Memoirs of a Peon*. Instead of the flat, laconic language of the short stories, he now couches his first-person narration in an elaborate style of comic circumlocution and bookish artifice. The wordy protagonist is Michael Newhouse, a latter-day suburban Casanova, and much of the story consists of his mock-heroic accounts of his amorous exploits and embarrassments. In an odd way, the verbosity becomes as limiting as the deadpan plainness had formerly been: since Newhouse processes his personal history periphrastically, there is a tendency for moral distinctions to be blurred while minutiae get focal attention.

In *The Hangover*, as in so much of his work, Sargeson directs his unblinking but not uncompassionate gaze towards an adolescent who is struggling to reconcile the disturbing facts of his widening world with the severe assumptions derived from a narrowly religious upbringing. Alan, with his hungover puritanism, is cast in the same mould as the central figures of "A Good Boy" (*Conversation with My Uncle*) and of *I Saw in My Dream*. Indeed, the anatomy of puritanism is Sargeson's obsessive subject. In *The Hangover* this familiarity of material is modified with some formal novelty: the narrative perspective shifts from time to time so that we are freed for a while from Alan's onion-peel mind to follow the thoughts or doings of some other person. Nevertheless, secondary characters are not numerous and are so treated that we regard them as subordinate parts of a simple design, economically drawn, whose main component is the frustrated Alan.

Joy of the Worm is an exercise in garrulity, and doesn't quite succeed. Material that might have made a fine sketch has been inflated to furnish 150 pages without acquiring real amplitude in the process. Sargeson has attempted something difficult: to sustain our interest in two bores, the Reverend James Bohun and his son Jeremy. Bohun senior is a bookworm whose chief joy is savouring Gibbon and Hooker – and reproducing their cadences in flatulent discourse of his own. (The "worm" of the title also signifies sexuality – both Bohuns are supposed to be splendidly potent – and mortality.) Bohun junior is a nonentity. There is something inert about this narrative; the inner action is as uneventful as the external. The relationship between father and son and the marital relationships of each are examined at some length, but nothing much is elicited. In an interview, Sargeson said he intended the book to be "a celebration of the Bohun vitality," but this quality fails to come through dramatically enough to be convincing. The novel is by no means merely tedious; Sargeson's mimic gift is amusingly displayed in the numerous letters, from various hands, which carry much of the story, and the reader who knows his Virgil and Catullus will relish some incidental allusions. But such things only thicken the texture without giving it a full-bodied flavour.

There is no room here for discussion of Sargeson's two plays, published together as *Wrestling with the Angel*, or of his three-part memoir. A fine capstone to his oeuvre appeared in 1976: *Sunset Village* is set in a cluster of pensioner flats which are suddenly exposed to public scrutiny when it seems that one of the inmates has been murdered. The old

Sargesonian motif of sexual concealment reappears, and the satirical irony that pervades so much of his later work is again incisively present. In all, *Sunset Village* provides a pleasant blend of the formal economy which governed Sargeson's earliest writings and the mellow comedy which released such an unexpectedly prolific flow of new fiction in his autumnal years.

—Ian Reid

SAVERY, Henry. Australian. Born in Butcombe, Somerset, England, 4 August 1791; transported to Australia, 1825. Married Eliza Elliott in 1815 (separated, 1829); one son. Apprentice in Bristol; thereafter worked as a sugar refiner and newspaper editor; convicted of forgery, 1825: death sentence changed to transport to Hobart Town: worked as a clerk in the Colonial Secretary's and Colonial Treasurer's offices, 1825–27; worked for the Superintendent of Van Diemen's Land Establishment, 1827–29; imprisoned for debt, 1829–30; given ticket of leave, 1832; farmer, 1832–38; granted conditional pardon, 1838; convicted of forgery, 1840, and imprisoned in Port Arthur. *Died 6 February 1842.*

PUBLICATIONS

Fiction

    The Hermit in Van Diemen's Land. 1829.
    Quintus Servinton: A Tale Founded upon Incidents of Real Occurrence. 3 vols., 1830–31; edited by Cecil H. Hadgraft, 1962.

*   *   *

Henry Savery was a well-educated, rich Bristol merchant who, because of financial difficulties, committed forgery and was subsequently condemned to death. The day before he was to be executed the sentence was commuted to deportation for life to Australia. Seventeen years later he died in the notorious convict prison in Port Arthur. Doubt surrounds the manner of his death, namely whether he cut his throat or whether he suffered a stroke. What is certain is that he died in the most miserable of circumstances. His claim to fame lies in his authorship of the first Australian novel, *Quintus Servinton.*

Prior to writing the novel Savery had written another book, *The Hermit of Van Diemen's Land.* This consisted of a series of sketches written while serving a prison sentence and published separately at first in the *Colonial Times* under the pseudonym of Simon Stokeley. The pseudonym was necessary, as convicts were forbidden to write for the press and were punished with transportation to the dreaded Macquarie Harbour if they did so. It was modelled on a contemporary English work, *The Hermit in London.* The series were in letter form and bore some resemblance to Goldsmith's Chinese Letters (published in volume form as *The Citizen of the World*). There are also some undertones of *The Spectator.* The book is particularly interesting for the light it throws on the social life of Hobart under Governor Arthur's rule. The "hermit," under the guise of an Englishman visiting Tasmania, satirizes Hobart society and its leading citizens. The satire was a little too close to the bone, for it involved the publisher in a libel suit and cost him £80.

Two years later *Quintus Servinton* was published. The novel is obviously autobiographical. Picaresque in structure, it follows the events of Savery's own life. Up until his crime and deportation it is realistic, but when the facts become unpalatable Savery romanticizes, and the novel displays some of the worst excesses of the early 19th-century English novel of this kind. Fiction was much kinder than fate to Savery. Having done penance for his sins, Quintus is permitted to return to England where he lives happily ever after. "The stains that had marked him were removed by the discipline he had been made to endure." The moral preached is the typical Victorian moral, "crime does not pay," and the novel follows the pattern of several other books dealing with the convict theme. Sin is synonymous with crime; Australia is the purgatory where expiation must take place before one can return to "that other Paradise."

Its literary merit, though slight, lies in the power to tell a story. It is, however, an important social document because of the picture it gives of convict life and society in the early days of Australia's history.

—Anna Rutherford

SCHREINER, Olive (Emilie Albertina). South African. Born in Wittebergen mission station, Cape of Good Hope, 24 March 1855. Largely self-educated. Married Samuel Cronwright in 1894; one daughter. Governess to the Orpen family children, in South Africa, 1874–81; lived in England, 1881–89; writer from 1882; lived in South Africa, 1890–1913; returned to England, 1913. *Died 10 December 1920.*

PUBLICATIONS

Collections

The Letters, edited by S. C. Cronwright-Schreiner. 1924.
A Selection, edited by Uys Krige. 1968.

Fiction

The Story of an African Farm. 1883.
Dreams. 1891.
Dream Life and Real Life. 1893.
Trooper Peter Halket of Mashonaland. 1897.
Stories, Dreams, and Allegories, edited by S. C. Cronwright-Schreiner. 1923.
From Man to Man; or, Perhaps Only –. 1926.
Undine. 1928.

Other

> *The Political Situation in Cape Colony,* with S. C. Cronwright-Schreiner. 1896.
> *The English-South African's View of the Situation: Words in Season.* 1899.
> *Closer Union: A Letter on the South African Union and the Principles of Government.* 1909.
> *Woman and Labour.* 1911.
> *Thoughts on South Africa.* 1923.

Reading List: *The Life of Schreiner* by S. C. Cronwright-Schreiner, 1924; *Schreiner: A Study in Latent Meanings* by Marion V. Friedmann, 1954; *Schreiner* by Michael Harmel, 1955; *Schreiner, Her Friends and Times* by Daisy Adler, 1955; *Schreiner: Portrait of a South African Woman* by Johannes Meintjes, 1965; *Until the Heart Changes: A Garland for Schreiner* by Zelda Friedlander, 1967; *Schreiner: A Short Guide to Her Writings* by Ridley Beeton, 1974.

* * *

Olive Schreiner had her first novel, *The Story of an African Farm,* published when she was in her twenties. For the remaining years of her life, apart from occasional journalism and a few allegories, she produced one short propagandist novel about the Boer War, *Trooper Peter Halket of Mashonaland,* and a major non-fictional study, *Woman and Labour.* After her death her husband published a fairly disastrous forerunner to *The Story of an African Farm, Undine,* which she had written in early youth, and *From Man to Man* on which she had been working at the time of her death. All these works, apart from *The Story of an African Farm,* are almost entirely unread today, and even her most famous novel which won her instant celebrity is now neglected. Olive Schreiner's South African background has perhaps not helped her reputation. Pro-Boer in the Boer War and a pacifist in the World War she hardly curried favour with the English-speaking world, while her sympathy for all sections of the African population has not endeared her to the ruling party in South Africa. It would, however, be hard to deny her skill in evoking the harsh beauty of her native land. Her attacks on orthodox religion won her fame in 1883, but when *From Man to Man* was published they already seemed out of date. The loose allegorical structure of her novels full of long sermons in favour of feminism or against religious orthodoxy makes them difficult reading, and as novels they cannot be ranked very highly in spite of moments of inspired lyricism. As a feminist, however, Olive Schreiner deserves more recognition than she has been given: the predicament of Undine, of Lyndall in *The Story of an African Farm,* and of Rebekah in *From Man to Man,* all prevented from fulfilling their aspirations, is fairly and poignantly presented, and Olive Schreiner's shriller successors could learn much from her.

—T. J. Winnifrith

SCOTT, Duncan Campbell. Canadian. Born in Ottawa, Ontario, 2 August 1862. Educated at Smiths Falls High School, Ontario, 1874–75; Wesleyan College, Stanstead, Quebec, 1877–79. Married 1) Belle Warner Botsford in 1894 (died, 1929), one daughter; 2) Desiree Elise Aylen in 1931. Joined Department of Indian Affairs, Ottawa, 1879: Clerk Third Class, 1879–93; Chief Clerk, 1893–96; Secretary of the Department, 1896–1909;

Superintendent of Indian Education, 1909–23; Deputy Superintendent General, 1923 until his retirement, 1932. Columnist, *Toronto Globe*, 1892–93; President, Ottawa Drama League; President, Canadian Authors Association, 1931–33. Recipient: Lorne Pierce Medal, 1927. D.Litt.: University of Toronto, 1922; LL.D.: Queen's University, Kingston, Ontario, 1939. Fellow, 1899, Honorary Secretary, 1911–21, and President, 1921–22, Royal Society of Canada; Fellow, Royal Society of Literature (England). C.M.G. (Companion, Order of St. Michael and St. George), 1934. *Died 19 December 1947.*

PUBLICATIONS

Collections

Selected Poems. 1951.
Selected Stories, edited by Glenn Clever. 1972.

Verse

The Magic House and Other Poems. 1893.
Labor and the Angel. 1898.
New World Lyrics and Ballads. 1905.
Via Borealis. 1906.
Lines in Memory of Edmund Morris. 1915.
Lundy's Lane and Other Poems. 1916.
To the Canadian Mothers, and Three Other Poems. 1917.
Beauty and Life. 1921.
Byron on Wordsworth, Being Undiscovered Stanzas of Don Juan. 1924 (?).
The Poems. 1926.
The Green Cloister: Later Poems. 1935.

Plays

Pierre (produced 1921). In *Canadian Plays from Hart House Theatre 1*, edited by Vincent Massey, 1926.
Prologue (produced 1923). In *The Poems*, 1926.
Joy! Joy! Joy! (produced 1927).

Fiction (stories)

In the Village of Viger. 1896.
The Witching of Elspie. 1923.

Other

John Graves Simcoe (biography). 1905.
Notes on the Meeting Place of the First Parliament of Upper Canada and the Early Buildings at Niagara. 1913.
The Administration of Indian Affairs in Canada. 1931.

Walter J. Phillips, R.C.A. (biography). 1947.
The Circle of Affection and Other Pieces in Prose and Verse. 1947.
Some Letters, edited by Arthur S. Bourinot. 1959; *More Letters,* 1960.

Editor, *The Poems of Archibald Lampman.* 1900; selection, 1947.
Editor, with Pelham Edgar, *The Makers of Canada.* 20 vols., 1903–08.
Editor, *The People of the Plains,* by Amelia Anne Paget. 1909.
Editor, *Lyrics of Earth: Sonnets and Ballads,* by Archibald Lampman. 1925.

Reading List: *Ten Canadian Poets* by Desmond Pacey, 1958; essay by A. J. M. Smith, in *Our Living Tradition* edited by R. McDougall, 1959.

* * *

Duncan Campbell Scott had a long poetic career; his first book, *The Magic House*, appeared in 1893, and his last, *The Circle of Affection*, appeared in the year of his death, 1947. He also had experiences unusual among poets in his day, for in 1879 he became a clerk in the Indian Branch in Ottawa, and continued in the service until 1932. In his work Scott had to undertake long, arduous journeys into the northern wilderness where he came into close contact with Indians, Métis, loggers, and trappers; he treasured these experiences, and the tales he heard on his travels, for use in his poetry.

Scott was not only a poet. He published two volumes of short stories, *In the Village of Viger* and *The Witching of Elspie*, both of them set in the pietist and superstition-ridden rural Quebec of the late nineteenth century. Some of these stories are humorous, others are eerie, and others have a grim starkness that reminds one of some of Scott's own poems about Indian life. His play *Pierre* was also set among French Canadians.

It is as a poet, however, that Scott is most interesting. His first volume, *The Magic House*, consisted mainly of descriptive lyrics, conventional in form and sentiment. But in his second book, *Labor and the Angel*, he displayed a real distinctiveness, not only in the romantic narrative poem "The Piper of Arll," but also in the first of his poems about the northland wilderness and the harsh life of the nomad Indian hunters. His experiences in the north continued to haunt him, and almost every later volume down to *The Green Cloister* in 1935 contained Indian poems, of which "The Onondaga Madonna," "At Gull Lake, 1810," and "The Forsaken," a poignant narrative of an old woman left to die by her tribe, are among the best-known of Canadian poems.

Scott in fact wrote two very different kinds of poem. There were the conventional and rather Tennysonian lyrics, concerned often with wild nature, sonorous and mood-provoked but essentially unexperimental, and there were the poems of the northern wilderness and of Indian life in which he strived for a stark and vivid authenticity and achieved it by breaking away from Victorian conventions to use irregular verse forms, hard images, and often harsh words. In these northern poems Scott, more than any of his contemporaries, anticipated the poets of the 1930's who took Canadian poetry out of its colonial past and into modern times.

—George Woodcock

SCOTT, F(rancis) R(eginald). Canadian. Born in Quebec City, 1 August 1899. Educated at Quebec High School; Bishop's College, Lennoxville, Quebec, B.A. 1919; Magdalen College, Oxford (Rhodes Scholar), 1920–23, B.A. 1922, B.Litt. 1923; McGill University, Montreal, B.C.L. 1927; called to the Quebec Bar, 1927; Queen's Counsel, Quebec, 1961.

Married Marian Mildred Dale in 1928; one son. Teacher, Quebec High School, 1919, Bishop's College School, Lennoxville, 1920, and Lower Canada College, Montreal, 1923; Assistant Professor of Federal and Constitutional Law, 1928–34, Professor of Civil Law, 1934–54, Macdonald Professor of Law, 1955–67, Dean of the Faculty of Law, 1961–64, and Visiting Professor in the French Canada Studies Programme, 1967–69, McGill University. Visiting Professor, University of Toronto Law School, 1953–54, Michigan State University, East Lansing, 1957, and Dalhousie University, Halifax, Nova Scotia, 1969–71. Co-Founding Editor, with A. J. M. Smith, *McGill Fortnightly Review*, Montreal, 1925–27; Editor, *Canada Mercury*, 1928, *Canada Forum*, 1936–39, *Preview*, Montreal, 1942–45, and *Northern Review*, Montreal, 1945–47. President, League for Social Reconstruction, 1935–36; Member, National Council, Penal Association of Canada, 1935–46; Member, National Executive, Canadian Institute of International Affairs, 1935–50; National Chairman, Canadian Cooperative Commonwealth Federation Party, 1942–50; U.N. Technical Assistant, Burma, 1952; Chairman, Legal Research Committee, Canadian Bar Association, 1954–56; Chairman, Canadian Writers Conference, 1955; Civil Liberties Counsel before the Supreme Court of Canada, 1956–64; Member, Royal Commission on Bilingualism and Biculturalism, 1963–71. Recipient: Guggenheim Fellowship, 1940; Royal Society of Canada Lorne Pierce Medal, 1962; Banff Springs Festival Gold Medal, 1958; Quebec Government Prize, 1964; Canada Council Molson Award, 1965, and grant, 1974. LL.D.: Dalhousie University, 1958; University of Manitoba, Winnipeg, 1961; Queen's University, Kingston, Ontario, 1964; University of British Columbia, Vancouver, 1965; University of Montreal, 1966; Osgoode Hall Law School, Downsview, Ontario, 1966; McGill University, 1967; LL.B.: University of Saskatchewan, Saskatoon, 1965. Fellow, Royal Society of Canada, 1947. Honorary Member, American Academy of Arts and Sciences, 1967. C.C. (Companion, Order of Canada), 1967. Lives in Montreal.

PUBLICATIONS

Verse

Overture. 1945.
Events and Signals. 1954.
The Eye of the Needle: Satires, Sorties, Sundries. 1957.
Signature. 1964.
Selected Poems. 1966.
Trouvailles: Poems from Prose. 1967.
The Dance Is One. 1973.

Other

Canada Today: A Study of Her National Interests and National Policy. 1938.
Make This Your Canada: A Review of C. C. F. History and Policy, with David Lewis. 1943.
Canada after the War: Attitudes of Political, Social, and Economic Policies in Post-War Canada, with Alexander Brady. 1944.
Cooperation for What? United States and Britain's Commonwealth. 1944.
The World's Civil Service. 1954.
Evolving Canadian Federalism. 1958.
The Canadian Constitution and Human Rights (radio talks). 1959.
Civil Liberties and Canadian Federalism. 1959.

Dialogue sur la Traduction, with Anne Hébert. 1970.
Essays on the Constitution. 1977.

Editor, with A. J. M. Smith, *New Provinces: Poems of Several Authors.* 1936.
Editor, with A. J. M. Smith, *The Blasted Pine: An Anthology of Satire, Invective and Disrespectful Verse, Chiefly by Canadian Writers.* 1957; revised edition, 1967.
Editor, with Michael Oliver, *Quebec States Her Case: Speeches and Articles from Quebec in the Years of Unrest.* 1964.

Translator, *St. Denys Garneau and Anne Hébert.* 1961.
Translator, *Poems of French Canada.* 1976.

Reading List: *Ten Canadian Poets* by Desmond Pacey, 1958; *The McGill Movement: A. J. M. Smith, Scott, and Leo Kennedy* edited by Peter Stevens, 1969; "The Road Back to Eden: The Poetry of Scott," in *Queen's Quarterly,* Autumn 1972.

* * *

The humanistic irony which informs F. R. Scott's finest work has characterized his multiple career since the 1930's: political theorist, academic lawyer, satirist, translator, editor, and, above all, socially sensitive poet. His most mature poetry is best seen in his *Selected Poems* and its sequel, *The Dance Is One.* Scott's early verse was influenced by imagism and marked by a strong formal sense, both of which served him well in tracing the harsh environment of northern Quebec and Canada. His precise, occasionally brittle diction matched the dominant imagery of stone, water, snow, and ice. Many of his descriptions of man's place in this "inarticulate, arctic" landscape have come to be regarded as major statements in the transformation of colonial romanticism into modernism in Canadian poetry. Later his rhythms became looser and his verse more free, but his fascination with the relation of language and meaning is still reflected in the concreteness and careful rhetoric of even his most delicate lyrics.

Language as playful dance is central to Scott's aesthetic, just as satire is an essential part of his humanism. Here his political and social vision finds its best expression in verse, and his popular reputation is largely founded on his acerbic humour. His targets are usually institutional and structural dangers, follies, and quirks, rather than individual foibles, for he has been a socialist nearly as long as he has written poetry. *The Eye of the Needle* and *Trouvailles* (a collection of found poems) gather his most familiar observations on Canadian politics, history, literature, class structure, bi-culturalism, and social stupidities – the subjects of his co-edited anthology of "satire, invective and disrespectful verse."

That Scott should have received a Governor-General's Award, not for his poetry but for the retrospective collection *Essays on the Constitution,* is itself ironic, notwithstanding his substantial contributions to Canadian law, legal education, and constitutional theory. The essays incorporate forty years' writing on civil liberties, federalism (both topics of a separate book), human rights, labour relations, public policy, and sovereignty – issues with which he had been actively involved since the beginning of his career as a professor of law. Scott is well-known for his participation in two major civil rights cases in Quebec during the 1950's, and for his role in the founding of the Co-operative Commonwealth Federation (C.C.F., now N.D.P.), the first successful democratic socialist party in Canada. Less known are his pamphlets and books on law and politics, both polemical and academic. As national chairman of the C.C.F., he co-authored a lengthy statement on the history and principles of the party, *Make This Your Canada.*

Scott's strong beliefs about the bilingual nature of Canadian federation are mirrored in his translations of Québécois poetry into English. His *Dialogue sur la Traduction* records progressively his various translations of Anne Hébert's "Tombeau des Rois," and his correspondence with her. His translated *Poems of French Canada* is evidence of his conviction that "translation is not only an art in itself, it is also an essential ingredient in Canada's political entity."

—Bruce Nesbitt

SELVON, Samuel (Dickson). Trinidadian. Born in Trinidad, 20 May 1923. Educated at Naparima College, Trinidad, 1935–39. Served as a wireless operator with the Trinidad Royal Naval Volunteer Reserve, 1940–45. Married 1) Draupadi Persaud in 1947, one son; 2) Althea Nesta Daroux in 1963, two sons and one daughter. Journalist, *Trinidad Guardian*, 1946–50; civil servant, in the High Commission, London, 1950–53; full-time writer from 1954. Recipient: Guggenheim Fellowship, 1954, 1968; Society of Authors Travelling Scholarship, 1958; Trinidad Government Scholarship, 1962; Arts Council of Great Britain grant, 1967, 1968; Humming Bird Medal, Trinidad, 1969. Lives in London.

PUBLICATIONS

Fiction

A Brighter Sun. 1952.
An Island Is a World. 1955.
The Lonely Londoners. 1956.
Turn Again, Tiger. 1958.
Ways of Sunlight (stories). 1958.
I Hear Thunder. 1963.
The Housing Lark. 1965.
The Plains of Caroni. 1969.
Those Who Eat the Cascadura. 1972.
Moses Ascending. 1975.

Plays

Radio Plays: *Lost Property*, 1965; *A House for Teona*, 1965; *A Highway in the Sun*, 1967; *Rain Stop Play*, 1967; *You Right in the Smoke*, 1968; *Worse Than Their Bite*, 1968; *Bringing in the Sheaves*, 1969; *Perchance to Dream*, 1969; *Eldorado West One*, 1969; *Home Sweet India*, 1970; *Mary Shut Your Gate*, 1971; *The Magic Stick*, from work by I. Khan, 1971; *Voyage to Trinidad*, 1971; *Those Who Eat the Crocodile*, 1971; *Water for Veronica*, 1972; *Cry Baby Brackley*, 1972; *Harvest in Wilderness*, 1972; *Zeppi's Machine*, 1977.

Reading List: *The West Indian Novel* by Kenneth Ramchand, 1970.

* * *

In the 1950's there was a major exodus of writers from the Caribbean to London. These included V. S. Naipaul, Wilson Harris, George Lamming, Edgar Mittelholzer, Andrew Salkey, and Samuel Selvon. They left the Caribbean, like thousands of other West Indians, with the hope of a bright new future in the mother country. On arrival their hopes were soon dashed. Instead of a welcome they were met with open hostility, rejection, exploitation, and racial prejudice. Several of the above mentioned writers have written about the lives of these unwanted immigrants in England but none as successfully as Samuel Selvon. In books like *The Lonely Londoners*, *Ways of Sunlight*, and *The Housing Lark*, he describes in tragi-comic fashion the ordinary everyday lives of the simple West Indian immigrants in London and the loneliness that lies behind their lives. "It have people living in London," remarks one of Selvon's characters, "who don't know what happening in the room next to them, far more the street, or how other people living. London is a place like that" (*The Lonely Londoners*).

While Selvon is probably best known for his stories set amongst the West Indian community in London it could be argued that his finest work is his first novel, *A Brighter Sun*. The novel is set in Trinidad and describes the attempt of a young East Indian peasant, Tiger, to establish an identity. But the novel is not only a description of Tiger's growing awareness of self; it is also an attempt on Selvon's part to show the various ethnic groups in the Caribbean struggling to establish a single Caribbean identity. For, unlike V. S. Naipaul, Selvon believes this to be a possibility if all the races co-operate. This single identity is symbolized by Tiger's house which the various races help him to build.

A Brighter Sun has another claim to fame, and that is because of Selvon's use of dialect. "It is in this novel," remarked the West Indian critic, Kenneth Ramchand, "that dialect first becomes the language of consciousness in West Indian fiction." Selvon was not only the first to use and explore dialect successfully in this way; he still remains without equal in this field.

—Anna Rutherford

SERVICE, Robert (William). Canadian. Born in Preston, Lancashire, England, 16 January 1874; emigrated to Canada, 1894. Educated at Hill Head High School, Glasgow; University of Glasgow. Served as an ambulance driver, 1914–16, and in Canadian Army Intelligence, 1916–18. Married Germaine Bourgoin in 1913; one daughter. Worked in the Commercial Bank of Scotland; in the Canadian Bank of Commerce, Kamloops, 1904, Whitehorse, 1904–07, Dawson, 1908–10, and Victoria, 1910–12; War Correspondent, *Toronto Star*, 1912.Travelled in Russia, Africa and the South Seas; lived in France from 1912. Died 11 September 1958.

PUBLICATIONS

Collections

Collected Poems. 1961.
Later Collected Verse. 1965.

Verse

    Songs of a Sourdough. 1907.
    The Spell of the Yukon and Other Verses. 1907.
    Ballads of a Cheechako. 1909.
    Rhymes of a Rolling Stone. 1912.
    The Rhymes of a Red-Cross Man. 1916.
    Selected Poems. 1917.
    The Shooting of Dan McGrew and Other Verses. 1920.
    Ballads of a Bohemian. 1921.
    Complete Poetical Works. 1921; as *Collected Verse,* 1930.
    Complete Poems. 1933.
    Twenty Bath-Tub Ballads. 1939.
    Bar-Room Ballads. 1940.
    Complete Poems. 1940.
    Songs of a Sun-Lover. 1949.
    Rhymes of a Roughneck. 1950.
    Lyrics of a Lowbrow. 1951.
    Rhymes of a Rebel. 1952.
    Songs for My Supper. 1953.
    Carols of an Old Codger. 1954.
    More Collected Verse. 1955.
    Rhymes for My Rags. 1956.
    Songs of the High North. 1958.

Fiction

    The Trail of '98. 1910.
    The Pretender. 1914.
    The Poisoned Paradise. 1922.
    The Roughneck. 1923.
    The Master of the Microbe. 1926.
    The House of Fear. 1927.

Other

    Why Not Grow Young? or, Living for Longevity. 1928.
    Ploughman of the Moon: An Adventure in Memory. 1945.
    Harper of Heaven: A Further Adventure in Memory. 1948.

Reading List: *Service* by Carl F. Klinck, 1976.

* * *

    Robert Service arrived in Alaska too late for the Gold Rush of 1898, but his successful career rested almost exclusively on two narrative poems about it: "The Shooting of Dan McGrew" and "The Cremation of Sam McGee." He wrote these and other, similar *Songs of a Sourdough* (as he titled his first collection) largely to amuse companions in the Yukon where he worked in a bank. The popularity of this early work – 1,700 copies were sold from galley sheets alone, by word of mouth among the typesetters and proof-readers, apparently – insured Service's financial security. He further chronicled that final American horizon in *The*

Trail of '98, a novel purporting to be "an authentic record ... tragic and moral in its implications" but which sacrificed characterization for melodrama and substituted lyrical flights about the terrain for psychological probing of motives and actions. Service seems to have read little, declaring late in life, "The Classics! Well, most of them bore me/The Moderns I don't understand." He aspired to be "The Bret Harte of the Northland," however, and obviously he knew the work of such oddly matched influences as Rudyard Kipling and Eugene Field.

Service abandoned the Yukon for France shortly after his early success and never returned. His popular verse narratives about Claw-Fingered Kitty, Pious Pete, One-Eyed Mike, The Dago Kid, Gum-Boot Ben, and Muckluck Meg afforded him the leisure to please readers content with romanticized tragedies and comic turns decked out in neat rhymes. (Service later guessed he had written about 30,000 couplets during his career.) Other novels followed as well, all either mysterious, violent, coarse, or lurid: *The Pretender* is about the literary life in the Latin Quarter before the First World War; *The Poisoned Paradise* complicates the same subject with gambling during the 1920's; *The House of Fear*, an overwrought gothic horror story, concluded his half-dozen ventures in this genre.

Some of Service's war poems, in *The Rhymes of a Red-Cross Man*, are of interest because they capture conflicting attitudes toward patriotism and fear through the colloquial speech of enlisted men. Two volumes of autobiography, although of little historical value, offer a readable account of a comfortable man well aware of his modest talents. "For God-sake, don't call me a poet,/For I've never been guilty of that," he wrote in one of the rhymed homilies that filled some 2,000 pages of published work. Well into his eighties, he wrote to his publisher: "Alas, my belly is concave,/My locks no longer wavy;/But though I've one foot in the grave,/The other's in the gravy."

Robert Service was probably too aware of his limitations to be an entirely successful novelist: his own sense of irony too often takes over, alienating his readers from his characters. This is particularly true in *The Trail of '98*, his most valuable work of fiction. His verse narratives, however, are always likely to draw readers who enjoy romance and adventure laced with inexhaustible rhyme and wit.

—Bruce Kellner

SHADBOLT, Maurice (Francis Richard). New Zealander. Born in Auckland, 4 June 1932. Educated at Te Kuiti High School; Avondale College; University of Auckland. Married twice; three sons and one daughter. Journalist for various New Zealand publications, 1952–54; documentary scriptwriter and director for the New Zealand National Film Unit, 1954–57; full-time writer from 1957; lived in London and Spain, 1957–60, then returned to New Zealand. Recipient: Hubert Church Memorial Award, 1959; New Zealand State Literary Fellowship, 1960, 1970; Katherine Mansfield Award, 1963, 1967; Robert Burns Fellowship, Otago University, 1963; National Association of Independent Schools Award, U.S.A., 1966; Freda Buckland Award, 1969; Pacific Area Travel Association Award, for non-fiction, 1971; James Wattie Award, 1973. Lives in Auckland.

PUBLICATIONS

Fiction

The New Zealanders: A Sequence of Stories. 1959.

Summer Fires and Winter Country (stories). 1963.
Among the Cinders. 1965.
The Presence of Music: 3 Novellas. 1967.
This Summer's Dolphin. 1969.
An Ear of the Dragon. 1971.
Strangers and Journeys. 1972.
A Touch of Clay. 1974.
Danger Zone. 1976.

Other

New Zealand: Gift of the Sea, with Brian Blake. 1963.
The Shell Guide to New Zealand. 1968.
Isles of the South Pacific, with Olaf Ruhen. 1968.

Reading List: *Shadbolt* by Conrad Bollinger, 1975; "Ambition and Accomplishment in Shadbolt's *Strangers and Journeys*" by Lawrence Jones, in *Critical Essays on the New Zealand Novel* edited by Cherry Hankin, 1976.

*   *   *

Maurice Shadbolt has said of his work that "as a man of my time and place ... I have simply tried to make sense of it." Certainly his fiction, taken collectively, does attempt to make sense of contemporary New Zealand, forming a picture with three dimensions – social, historical, and personal.

Read as social documents, Shadbolt's works show the major currents of the time and place. The change from a rural to an urban society, with the resultant growth of urban and suburban discontents, is evident, especially in the stories of *Summer Fires and Winter Country.* The decline of political activism in the 1950's, discouraged both by the rigidities of the Cold War and the complacency engendered by the Welfare State, is seen in the stories of *The New Zealanders* and in the middle sections of *Strangers and Journeys,* while the last sections of that book and the more recent novels show the rebirth of political activism in the 1960's and 1970's in relation to Vietnam, ecological issues (*A Touch of Clay*), and French nuclear testing (*Danger Zone*). Another recurring theme, prominent in *The Presence of Music* and *Strangers and Journeys,* has been the place of the artist in helping to mould the national sensibility of a society that is still "shapeless, half-formed, indistinct."

Shadbolt's picture of the "bruised Eden" of contemporary New Zealand is given depth by the historical dimension, for, with his own family roots reaching back to the early European settlement, he sees the present as the result of past attempts to impose European dreams on Pacific islands. These dreams, the pioneer dream of a pastoral paradise and the political dream of the just city, are touched upon in *Among the Cinders* and *A Touch of Clay,* but they are developed most fully in *Strangers and Journeys,* where the failure of the dreams of the fathers is visited upon the sons.

Social and historical concerns, however, have merely formed a background to Shadbolt's primary theme of personal relationships – sexual, familial, and between male friends. In a society lacking the direction of a religious faith or a political ideology, and deprived of the challenge of the physical struggle for survival, personal relationships become the only source of meaning and the real "danger zone" in which one is tested. Repeatedly Shadbolt shows the weight that personal relations must carry, how fragile they are, how difficult it is to maintain relationships that are honest, mutual, responsible, non-exploiting.

Shadbolt's portrait of New Zealand is presented artfully, especially in the handling of multiple plots and time-levels and of recurring images and motifs. However, facility can pass into slickness, especially in the mannered style and in the tendency to melodramatic plotting and stereotyped characters. Only in such stories as "The Strangers," "The Room," and "Figures of Light" and in the first section of *Strangers and Journeys* is Shadbolt entirely successful, but all the books have impressive sequences and all contribute to his account of his time and place.

—Lawrence Jones

SINGH, Khushwant. Indian. Born in Hadali, India, now Pakistan, 2 February 1915. Educated at the Modern School, Delhi; St. Stephen's College, Delhi; Government College, Lahore, B.A. 1934; King's College, London, LL.B. 1938; called to the Bar, Inner Temple, London, 1938. Married Kaval Malik in 1939; two children. Practising lawyer, High Court, Lahore, 1939–47; Press Attaché, Indian Foreign Service, in London and Ottawa, 1947–51; member of the staff of the Department of Mass Communications, UNESCO, Paris, 1954–56; Editor, *Yejna*, an Indian government publication, New Delhi, 1956–58; Visiting Lecturer, Oxford University, 1964, University of Rochester, New York, 1965, Princetown University, New Jersey, 1967, University of Hawaii, Honolulu, 1967, and Swarthmore College, Pennsylvania, 1969; Editor of *The Illustrated Weekly of India*, Bombay, from 1969. Head of the Indian Delegation, Writers Conference, Manila, 1965. Recipient: Padma Bhushan, Government of India, 1974. Lives in Bombay.

PUBLICATIONS

Fiction

The Mark of Vishnu and Other Stories. 1950.
Train to Pakistan. 1955; as *Mano Majra*, 1956.
I Shall Not Hear the Nightingale. 1959.
The Voice of God and Other Stories. N.d.
A Bride for the Sahib and Other Stories. N.d.
Black Jasmine. 1971.

Other

The Sikhs. 1952.
Jupji: The Sikh Morning Prayer. 1959.
The Sikhs Today: Their Religion, History, Culture Customs, and Way of Life. 1959; revised edition, 1964.
Fall of the Kingdom of the Punjab. 1962.
A History of the Sikhs, 1469–1964. 2 vols., 1963–66.
Ranjit Singh: Maharajah of the Punjab, 1780–1839. 1963.
Shri Ram: A Biography, with Arun Joshi. 1963.
Ghadar, 1919: India's First Armed Revolution, with Satindra Singh. 1966.
Homage to Guru Gobind Singh, with Suneet Veer Singh. 1966.

Hymns of Nanak the Guru. 1969.
Singh's India (essays), edited by Rahul Singh. N.d.

Editor, *A Note on G. V. Desani's "All about H. Hatterr" and "Hali,"* with Peter Russell. 1952.
Editor, with Jays Thadani, *Land of the Five Rivers: Stories of the Punjab.* 1965.
Editor, *Sunset of the Sikh Empire,* by Sita Ram Kohli. 1967.
Editor, *I Believe.* 1971.
Editor, *Love and Friendship.* 1974.
Editor, *Sacred Writings of the Sikhs.* N.d.

Translator, with M. A. Husain, *Umrao Jan Ada: Courtesan of Lucknow,* by Mohammed Ruswa. 1961.
Translator, *The Skeleton,* by Amrita Pritam. 1964.
Translator, *I Take This Woman,* by Rajinder Singh Bedi. N.d.

Reading List: *Singh* by V. A. Shahane, 1972.

* * *

Although he is a prolific and distinguished Sikh historian and editor, Khushwant Singh's reputation as a fiction writer rests solely upon *Mano Majra* (also published in the United States under the title *Train to Pakistan*), a harrowing tale of events along the borders of the newly divided nations of India and Pakistan in the summer of 1947.

The atrocities that accompanied the division of these nations had an enormously depressing effect on a world that had just fought a long, bitter war to defeat practitioners of genocide. The somewhat artificial division of the subcontinent (the boundaries remain in dispute) had been strictly along religious lines: Pakistan was to be a nation of Moslems; India, of Hindus, Sikhs, and what Singh calls "pseudo Christians." There were, however, colonies of non-coreligionists left within each nation. Rather than settle down to peaceful coexistence or permit a passive exchange of populations, partisans on both sides set out on a violent campaign of annihilating the communities that were trapped on their ancestral lands beyond friendly borders.

Mano Majra is laid against a background of this ruthless and senseless mass destruction. This powerful novel derives its title from a squalid border town, where a rail line crosses from India into Pakistan. At first this mixed community of Sikhs and Moslems is undisturbed by the violence that is breaking out elsewhere on the frontier, but inevitably it, too, is caught up in the mass hysteria as ominous "ghost trains" of slain Sikhs begin to arrive in town from across the border. Agitation for reprisals follows when the Moslems of the town are at last rounded up and fanatics urge the Sikhs of the community to kill their former neighbors as the train carrying them to Pakistan passes through town.

Singh's story contrasts the ineffectualness of the educated and ruling classes with the power of the violent and irrational peasants. Singh's terse fable suggests a profound disillusionment with the power of law, reason, and intellect in the face of elemental human passions. The philosophy that sparked his tale seems to be expressed through the thoughts of Iqbal, the young radical, as he realizes his helplessness and drifts off into a drugged sleep the night of the climatic incident of the train's passing: "If you look at things as they are ... there does not seem to be a code either of man or of God on which one can pattern one's conduct. ... In such circumstances what can you do but cultivate an utter indifference to all values? Nothing matters."

The same disillusioned tone characterizes Singh's second novel, *I Shall Not Hear the Nightingale,* but the rather wooden tale is almost overwhelmed by heavy-handed ironies. The action occurs about five years before that of the earlier novel, at a time when the British are expressing a willingness to get out of India once the Axis nations have been defeated in World War II. The novel takes a much dimmer view of the human capacity for compassion and self-sacrifice than *Mano Majra* (at one point Sher Singh reflects that "for him loyalties were not as important as the ability to get away with the impression of having them").

His ironic stories resemble Angus Wilson's and express a similar disillusionment about man's rationality. Singh is a brilliant, sardonic observer of a world undergoing convulsive changes; and his novels provide a unique insight into one of the major political catastrophes of this century. His difficulties in fusing his editorial comments with the action in his stories, however, cause his novels to remain principally dramatized essays.

—Warren French

SLESSOR, Kenneth. Australian. Born in Orange, New South Wales, 27 March 1901. Educated at Mowbray House School, Chatswood; North Shore School, Sydney, 1910–19; Sydney Grammar School. Married 1) Noela Senior in 1922 (died 1945); 2) Pauline Wallace in 1951 (marriage dissolved, 1961), one son. Reporter for *The Sun*, Sydney, 1920–24, 1926; a Founding Editor, *Vision*, 1923–24; staff member of *Punch*, Melbourne, and the *Melbourne Herald*, 1925; staff member, 1927, Associate Editor, 1936, and Editor, *Smith's Weekly*, Sydney, and Editor-in-Chief of Smith's Newspapers, 1939; Official War Correspondent for the Australian Forces in the U.K., the Middle East, Greece, and New Guinea, 1940–44; Leader Writer and Literary Editor of *The Sun*, Sydney, 1944–57; Editor of *Southerly*, Sydney, 1956–61; Leader Writer for the *Daily Telegraph*, Sydney, 1957–69. Member of the Advisory Board, Commonwealth Literary Fund, from 1953, and the National Literature Board of Review, from 1968. O.B.E. (Officer, Order of the British Empire), 1959. Died in 1971.

PUBLICATIONS

Verse

Thief of the Moon. 1924.
Earth-Visitors. 1926.
Trio, with Harley Matthews and Colin Simpson. 1931.
Darlinghurst Nights. 1931.
Cuckooz Contrey. 1932.
Five Bells: XX Poems. 1939.
One Hundred Poems, 1919–1939. 1944; revised edition, as *Poems,* 1957.

Other

Portrait of Sydney. 1951.
The Grapes Are Growing: The Story of Australian Wine. 1963.
Life at the Cross (on King's Cross, Sydney). 1965.
Canberra. 1966.
Bread and Wine: Selected Prose. 1970.

Editor, with Jack Lindsay, *Poetry in Australia.* 1923.
Editor, *Australian Poetry.* 1945.
Editor, with John Thompson and R. G. Howarth, *The Penguin Book of Australian Verse.* 1958.

Reading List: *Slessor* by Max Harris, 1963; *Slessor* by Graham Burns, 1963; *Slessor* by Clement Semmler, 1966; *Critical Essays on Slessor* edited by A. K. Thomson, 1968; *Slessor* by Herbert C. Jaffa, 1971.

*   *   *

Kenneth Slessor's considerable reputation in Australia as a poet rests on a collection of 104 poems containing what he wished to preserve. After 1947 he ceased to write verse, because, he said, he had nothing more to say. Slessor is given most of the credit for having introduced modernism into Australian poetry, and, along with his contemporary FitzGerald, he certainly announced many of the themes to be developed by younger writers: time, history, voyages, symbolic landscape. Slessor is also pre-eminently the poet of the city of Sydney and its harbour near which he lived most of his adult life. His excursions into the countryside produce little but images of horror and sterility.

Much of his work in the early 1920's was influenced by his association with the artist Norman Lindsay and his son Jack in literary enterprises intended to bring about a cultural renascence in Australia, free from "decadent" European modernism as well as from nationalism. The basis of these ideas was a woolly kind of Nietzscheanism, a rather frenzied vitalism which found curiously static expression in Norman Lindsay's drawings of satyrs and centaurs. Slessor's poems "Thieves' Kitchen," with its romantic abstractions, and "Marco Polo," with its decorative gestures and its undergraduate finale, for all their rhythmic energy are hardly less factitious than the drawings, though pieces like "Heine in Paris" and "Nuremburg" show a genuine individuality and a luxuriant imagination. Slessor's preoccupation with historical subjects was mainly a form of escape from an unsatisfactory present; history was not a process of which he was a living part and which required understanding. All Slessor's dissatisfactions with the modern world, his distress at the eternal flux of life, his sense of the frustration of man's aspirations, issue simply in rage or lamentation. There is no attempt to reason out an explanation why the world has come to be the way it is, no suggestion that poetry might contribute its mite towards the mitigation of human misery. A late poem like "Gulliver," for example, a horrifying indictment of man trapped in the trivialities of modern life, differs from the youthful "Marco Polo" only in its surface realism, its conversational tone, its physical immediacy. The yearning to be "anywhere but here" is the same.

The difference between Slessor and the poet he most resembles, Thomas Hardy, is instructive. Among the poets known to have influenced Slessor, Tennyson, de la Mare, Housman, and T. S. Eliot, Hardy's name is never mentioned. But his debt to Hardy is acknowledged in a short story Slessor wrote for the magazine *Vision* in 1923; it is clear that he took the image of the face trapped behind a pane of glass, which haunts his verse from first to last, from Hardy's "The Face at the Casement" on which he based his story. Hardy took a dim view of man's estate: man seemed to be nothing but the puppet of blind forces, a spectacle to make the gods yawn (as in Slessor's "The Old Play"). One may not like the metaphysic Hardy constructed to deal with the universe he saw, but at least it made possible a way of life not in danger of collapsing into dandyism. Slessor concurs with Hardy's pessimism, his nostalgia, but he has no countervailing argument: it is a concurrence only in mourning. Slessor remained a romantic throughout his career, but what appealed to him in romanticism was its grotesque, flamboyant aspects and a certain mindless sensuality, not its confrontation with a vision of what man might be.

Nevertheless, in spite of reservations about the intellectual content of Slessor's poems, his contribution towards liberating the language of Australian poetry can hardly be overestimated, and, in spite of the contradictions of the *Vision* program (a national re-birth without nationalism), Slessor developed new lyrical energies in proliferating images and exploring rhythmical possibilities with a zest that denies the elegiac mood characteristic of so much of his verse. He and FitzGerald set new standards in poetry, Slessor in his dedication to technical perfection, FitzGerald in his insistence on solid content and precise thinking.

It is not surprising that an elegy is the peak of Slessor's achievement: the long poem *Five Bells* which re-lives the drowning of an artist friend in Sydney Harbour. All Slessor's preoccupations are gathered up in this poem: his favourite image, the pane of glass, which becomes the port-holes of space through which the dead man is desperately trying to communicate with the living: his other favourite image, the sea, whose eternal movement represents the flux, the destructive aspect of time; the harbour, which represents some sort of permanence within this flux; the sense of human alienation, of fruitful contacts, frustrated by separation or death; of self-alienation, the figure at the window watching a life in which he can never take part. The poem opens with the sound of ship's bells in the harbour marking the watches against a memorable vision of the water at night:

> Deep and dissolving verticals of light
> Ferry the falls of moonshine down. Five bells
> Coldly rung out in a machine's voice. Night and water
> Pour to one rip of darkness, the Harbour floats
> In air, the Cross hangs upside down in water.

The bell recalls the image of the dead Joe and starts off a series of agonised attempts to reconstruct his life and find a meaning in it. All Slessor can remember in the end are little disconnected episodes and the poem comes slowly to an end, not with the conclusion that there is nothing to know but that the poet himself is inadequate to the effort of knowing it. Like all good elegies, *Five Bells* is at once a cry of grief for a particular being and a lament for the general human condition. Protest against death is Slessor's most constant theme, but his anguish does not lead him into nihilism: he does not prefer non-being to the pain of knowing he must die. Slessor's defence against the charge of nihilism can be seen in the last two lines of "South Country," which indicates that death, the norm, is threatened by life, not the other way round: "Something below pushed up a knob of skull,/Feeling its way to air."

The poem "Sleep" reveals Slessor's facility in image-making. Here we find a single idea under the control of one dominating image, and the result is a perfect unity of form and concept. One of the last poems, "Beach Burial," is even more memorable, a triumph of vowel and consonantal music and rhythmical fitness, as well as a most moving and humble tribute to the drowned merchant seamen of the Second World War. *Bread and Wine*, a collection of his best journalistic pieces, includes some fine examples of his work as a war correspondent, as well as his rare literary criticism. The excellence of his prose makes one regret that so much of his talent was expended on ephemeral journalism.

—Dorothy Green

SMITH, A(rthur) J(ames) M(arshall). American. Born in Montreal, Quebec, Canada, 8 November 1902; emigrated to the United States, 1930; naturalized, 1941. Educated at McGill University, Montreal (Editor, *McGill Literary Supplement*), B.Sc. in arts 1925, M.A. 1926; University of Edinburgh, 1926–28, Ph.D. 1931. Married Jeannie Dougal Robins in 1927; one son. Assistant Professor, Ball State Teachers College, Muncie, Indiana, 1930–31; Instructor, Doane College, Crete, Nebraska, 1934–35; Assistant Professor, University of South Dakota, Vermillion, 1935–36. Instructor, 1931–33, since 1936 Member of the English

Department, and since 1960 Professor of English and Poet-in-Residence, Michigan State University, East Lansing; now retired. Visiting Professor, University of Toronto, 1944–45, University of Washington, Seattle, 1949, Queen's University, Kingston, Ontario, 1952, 1960, University of British Columbia, Vancouver, 1956, Dalhousie University, Halifax, Nova Scota, 1966–67, Sir George Williams University, Montreal, Summers 1967, 1969, State University of New York at Stony Brook, 1969, and McGill University, 1969–70. Recipient: Guggenheim Fellowship, 1941, 1942; Governor-General's Award, 1944; Rockefeller Fellowship, 1944; Lorne Pierce Medal, 1966; Canada Centennial Medal, 1967; Canada Council Medal, 1968. D.Litt.: McGill University, 1958; LL.D.: Queen's University, 1966; Dalhousie University, 1969; D.C.L.: Bishop's University, Lennoxville, Quebec, 1967. Lives in East Lansing, Michigan.

PUBLICATIONS

Verse

News of the Phoenix and Other Poems. 1943.
A Sort of Ecstasy: Poems New and Selected. 1954.
Collected Poems. 1962.
Poems: New and Collected. 1967.

Other

Some Poems of E. J. Pratt: Aspects of Imagery and Theme. 1969.
Towards a View of Canadian Letters: Selected Critical Essays 1928–1972. 1973.

Editor, with F. R. Scott, *New Provinces: Poems of Several Authors.* 1936.
Editor, *The Book of Canadian Poetry.* 1943.
Editor, *Seven Centuries of Verse: English and American, from the Early English Lyrics to the Present Day.* 1947.
Editor, *The Worldly Muse: An Anthology of Serious Light Verse.* 1951.
Editor, with M. L. Rosenthal, *Exploring Poetry.* 1955; revised edition, 1973.
Editor, with F. R. Scott, *The Blasted Pine: An Anthology of Satire, Invective and Disrespectful Verse, Chiefly by Canadian Writers.* 1957; revised edition, 1967.
Editor, *The Oxford Book of Canadian Verse: In English and French.* 1960; revised edition, 1965.
Editor, *Masks of Fiction: Canadian Critics on Canadian Prose.* 1961.
Editor, *Masks of Poetry: Canadian Critics on Canadian Verse.* 1962.
Editor, *Essays for College Writing.* 1965.
Editor, *The Book of Canadian Prose.* 2 vols, 1965–73.
Editor, *100 Poems: Chaucer to Dylan Thomas.* 1965.
Editor, *Modern Canadian Verse: In English and French.* 1967.
Editor, *The Collected Poems of Anne Wilkinson and a Prose Memoir.* 1968.
Editor, *The Canadian Century* (anthology). 1975.

Reading List: *Ten Canadian Poets* by Desmond Pacey, 1958; *The McGill Movement: Smith, F. R. Scott, and Leo Kennedy* edited by Peter Stevens, 1969; *Odysseus Ever Returning* by George Woodcock, 1970.

* * *

Though almost his whole academic life was lived in the United States, A. J. M. Smith has been one of the most influential figures in the Canadian modernist movement, as an editor and anthologist, as a critic, and as a poet. In the *McGill Literary Supplement* and the *McGill Fortnightly Review* he and F. R. Scott, while still students between 1924 and 1927, virtually launched the evolution that took Canadian poetry out of the colonial into the cosmopolitan stage; and as early as 1928, in a historic article in the *Canadian Forum* entitled "Wanted – Canadian Criticism," Smith put forward the argument that to be mature in a creative sense, a culture needed also a tradition of criticism. Over the years he has done a great deal to create that tradition in the essays on Canadian poets and on their cultural ambiance which in 1973 he collected in *Towards a View of Canadian Letters*.

But Smith's essays are hardly more than an iceberg's tip in considering his importance as a critic, which is much more substantially expressed in the series of notable anthologies in which he revealed the nature of Canadian poetry as an identifiable tradition. These begin with *New Provinces*, in which he and F. R. Scott gathered in 1936 the work of the few modernist poets then working in Canada. A few years later, Smith published *The Book of Canadian Poetry*, which he specifically entitled "a critical and historical anthology"; this was the first work that went through the whole of Canadian poetry from its colonial beginnings and performed an act of critical evaluation which established the important Canadian poets and their dominant manners and themes. Selection itself was, in this pioneer collection, a critical act; few people have disputed the canon of significant Canadian poetry which Smith established in *The Book of Canadian Poetry* and reinforced in successive editions. In 1960 he published *The Oxford Book of Canadian Verse*, the first definitive anthology of poems in Canada's two major languages, and in 1967 *Modern Canadian Verse: In English and French*. In all these volumes the selection was reinforced by perceptive commentary, and, if Smith's anthologies are not unquestioningly accepted as the definitive statements on the development of poetry in Canada, they have greatly influenced trends in literary history and critical evaluation alike.

As a poet Smith (who began to attract international attention during the 1930's when his work was published in journals like *New Verse*) is an artist whose self-criticism has been almost fanatical. His four volumes of highly metaphysical poetry, beginning with *News of the Phoenix* and ending with *Poems: New and Selected*, are rigorously chosen, and in every case except the first book contain old poems carefully revised, as well as new ones; the *Collected Poems* honed down the canon to a hundred pieces, all that Smith wished to keep from more than thirty years writing poetry.

Comparing these poems which appear again and again in different versions, one has the impression that Smith is a poet little bound by time. He began to attract attention in the 1930's, but Yeats and the Sitwells seem his natural siblings rather than the Auden-Spender circle. And if the world Smith creates in his poems is autonomous in time – a kind of poetic Laputa that might dip down as easily in the seventeenth century as in the twentieth – it seems equally free in place.

Admittedly, there are a very few poems which seem to declare a parochial preference. Smith proclaims his intention

> To hold in a verse as austere
> As the spirit of prairie and river,
> Lonely, unbuyable, dear,
> The North, as a need and for ever.

But even in his rather imagistic poems on Canadian landscapes the result has little of guidebook topography; rather, the glimpse one receives is of a detached and personal world, so that the familiar cedar and firs and wild duck calls in a poem like "The Lonely Land" lead us into a country in feeling as mythological as any painted by Poussin for the encounter of Gods and mortals:

> This is a beauty
> of dissonance
> this resonance
> of stony strand
> this smoky cry
> curled over a black pine
> like a broken
> and wind-battered branch
> when the wind
> bends the tops of the pines
> and curdles the sky
> from the north.

Smith's aims are spareness, clarity, balance, the austerity of a latter-day classicism enriched by the discoveries of the Symbolists and the Imagists. Unlike the wildly intuitive versifier he celebrated in "One Sort of Poet," Smith never sings, "*Let it come! Let it come!*" His poems are carefully worked to the last safe moment of polishing. One is aware of the unending search for words that are "crisp and sharp and small," for a form as "skintight" as the stallions of his "Far West." Occasionally the visions clarified through Smith's bright glass are too sharp for comfort, the detachment too remote for feeling to survive. More often, they are saved by the dense impact of the darker shapes that lie within the crystal, the "shadows I have seen, of me deemed deeper/That backed on nothing in the horrid air."

It is this enduring sense of the shapeless beyond shape that gives Smith's best poems their peculiar rightness of tension, and make his austerities so rich in implication.

—George Woodcock

SOUSTER, (Holmes) Raymond. Canadian. Born in Toronto, Ontario, 15 January 1921. Educated at University of Toronto schools; Humberside Collegiate Institute, Toronto, 1938–39. Served in the Royal Canadian Air Force, 1941–45. Married Rosalie Lena Geralde in 1947. Since 1939, Staff Member, and currently Securities Custodian, Canadian Imperial Bank of Commerce, Toronto. Editor, *Direction*, Sydney, Nova Scotia, 1943–46; Co-Editor, *Contact*, Toronto, 1952–54; Editor, *Combustion*, Toronto, 1957–60. Chairman, League of Canadian Poets, 1968–72. Recipient: Governor-General's Award, 1965; President's Medal, University of Western Ontario, 1967; Centennial Medal, 1967. Lives in Toronto.

PUBLICATIONS

Verse

Unit of Five, with others, edited by Ronald Hambleton. 1944.
When We Are Young. 1946.
Go to Sleep, World. 1947.

City Hall Street. 1951.
Cerberus, with Louis Dudek and Irving Layton. 1952.
Shake Hands with the Hangman. 1953.
A Dream That Is Dying. 1954.
For What Time Slays. 1955.
Walking Death. 1955.
Selected Poems, edited by Louis Dudek. 1956.
Crèpe-Hanger's Carnival: Selected Poems 1955–58. 1958.
Place of Meeting: Poems 1958–60. 1962.
A Local Pride. 1962.
12 New Poems. 1964.
The Colour of the Times: The Collected Poems. 1964.
Ten Elephants on Yonge Street. 1965.
As Is. 1967.
Lost and Found: Uncollected Poems. 1968.
So Far So Good: Poems 1938–1968. 1969.
The Years. 1971.
Selected Poems. 1972.
Change-Up: New Poems. 1974.
Rain Check. 1975.
Extra Innings. 1977.

Fiction

The Winter of the Time. 1949.
On Target. 1973.

Other

Editor, *Poets 56: Ten Younger English-Canadians.* 1956.
Editor, *Experiment: Poems 1923–1929,* by W. W. E. Ross. 1958.
Editor, *New Wave Canada: The New Explosion in Canadian Poetry.* 1966.
Editor, with John Robert Colombo, *Shapes and Sounds: Poems of W. W. E. Ross.* 1968.
Editor, with Douglas Lochhead, *Made in Canada: New Poems of the Seventies.* 1970.
Editor, with Richard Woollatt, *Generation Now* (textbook). 1970.
Editor, with Douglas Lochhead, *100 Poems of Nineteenth Century Canada* (textbook). 1973.
Editor, with Richard Woollatt, *Sights and Sounds* (textbook). 1973.
Editor, with Richard Woollatt, *These Loved, These Hated Lands* (textbook). 1974.

Reading List: "Groundhog among the Stars" by Louis Dudek, in *Canadian Literature,* Autumn 1964; "To Souster with Vermont" by Hayden Carruth, in *Tamarack Review,* Winter 1965.

* * *

Raymond Souster represents the second generation of modern Canadian poets, the poets who rejected the influence of the English poets of the 1930's who had dominated their predecessors, and looked to American poets like Ezra Pound and William Carlos Williams, less as models than as guides to the acquisition of a way of speaking proper to their experience as North Americans. What distinguishes Souster from the poets with whom he shared that direction in the 1940's, such as Irving Layton and Louis Dudek, is the modesty of presence and the quietness of voice he has adopted. His work is entirely lacking in the histrionics of being a poet.

There are other items of traditional poetic baggage Souster has abandoned in his efforts to write a poetry of direct experience. He avoids not only metrical forms but also recondite allusions, archaisms, even symbolism – everything, in other words, that can impede his search for the pure image, or even the pure imageless voice that can convey truly an experience or an emotion.

Souster's poems tend to be short, colloquial in diction, frequently epigrammatic, aiming at the sharp and often ironic insight into a specific situation that expands in the mind to an insight into existence itself. He has been writing with such consistent regularity over the past thirty years that his books offer many examples of the kind of self-contained yet resonantly allusive poem which, at his best, he creates. A good example, for its combination of brevity and intensity, is the six-line poem "The Six-Quart Basket":

> The six-quart basket
> one side gone
> half the handle torn off
>
> sits in the centre of the lawn
> and slowly fills up
> with the white fruits of the snow.

Other poems are less lucid because their feeling is darker, and, for all Souster's evident enjoyment of the bright surface of the earth and the occasional haunting nostalgia of his poems, the dominant mood that underlies them is perhaps best summed up in his own lines:

> life isn't a matter of luck
> of good fortune, it's whether
> the heart can keep singing
> when there's really no reason
> why it should

—George Woodcock

SOYINKA, Wole (Akinwande Oluwole Soyinka). Nigerian. Born in Abeokuta, Western Nigeria, 13 July 1934. Educated at the Government College, Ibadan; University of Leeds, Yorkshire, 1954–57, B.A. (honours) in English. Married; one son and three daughters. Play Reader, Royal Court Theatre, London, 1958–59; Research Fellow in Drama, University of Ibadan, 1960–61; Lecturer in English, University of Ife, 1962–63; Senior Lecturer in English, University of Lagos, 1964–67; Political Prisoner, for alleged pro-Biafra activities,

Kaduna Prison, 1967–69; Director of the School of Drama, University of Ibadan, 1969–72. Research Professor in Drama, 1972–75, and since 1975 Professor of Comparative Literature, University of Ife. Founding Director of the Orisun Theatre and The 1960 Masks Theatre, Lagos and Ibadan. Recipient: Dakar Negro Arts Festival award, 1966; John Whiting Award, 1966. D.Litt.: University of Leeds, 1973. Lives in Nigeria.

PUBLICATIONS

Plays

The Swamp Dwellers (produced 1958). In *Three Plays*, 1963.
The Lion and the Jewel (produced 1959). 1963.
The Invention (produced 1959).
A Dance of the Forests (produced 1960). 1963.
The Trial of Brother Jero (produced 1960). In *Three Plays*, 1963.
Camwood on the Leaves (broadcast 1960). 1973.
Three Plays. 1963.
The Strong Breed (produced 1964). In *Three Plays*, 1963.
Kongi's Harvest (produced 1964). 1967.
Before the Blackout (produced 1964). N.d. (1965?).
The Road (produced 1965). 1965.
Madmen and Specialists (produced 1970; revised version, produced 1971). 1971.
The Jero Plays: The Trials of Brother Jero and Jero's Metamorphosis. 1973.
The Bacchae: A Communion Rite, from the play by Euripides (produced 1973). 1973.
Collected Plays:
  I. *A Dance of the Forests, The Swamp Dwellers, The Strong Breed, The Road, The Bacchae.* 1973.
  II. *The Lion and the Jewel, Kongi's Harvest, The Trials of Brother Jero, Jero's Metamorphosis, Madmen and Specialists.* 1974.
Death and the King's Horseman. 1975.

Screenplay: *Kongi's Harvest,* 1970.

Radio Play: *Camwood on the Leaves,* 1960.

Television Documentaries: *Joshua: A Nigerian Portrait,* 1962; *Culture in Transition,* 1963.

Fiction

The Interpreters. 1965.
Season of Anomy. 1973.

Verse

Idanre and Other Poems. 1967.
Poems from Prison. 1969.
A Shuttle in the Crypt. 1972.
Ogun Abibiman. 1977.

Other

The Man Died: Prison Notes. 1972.
In Person: Achebe, Awooner, and Soyinka at the University of Washington. 1975.
Myth, Literature, and the African World. 1976.

Editor, *Poems of Black Africa.* 1975.

Translator, *The Forest of a Thousand Daemons: A Hunter's Saga,* by D. A. Fagunwa. 1968.

Reading List: *Mother Is Gold: A Study in West African Literature* by A. Roscoe, 1971; *Soyinka* by Gerald H. Moore, 1971, revised edition, 1978; *The Writing of Soyinka* by Eldred D. Jones, 1973; *The Movement of Transition: A Study of the Plays of Soyinka* by Oyin Ogunba, 1975.

* * *

Wole Soyinka is not only Nigeria's leading playwright but possibly the most versatile writer at work in Africa today, having also excelled as a poet, novelist, essayist, critic, editor, and translator. Born in 1934, Soyinka was educated in Ibadan and Leeds. On his return to Nigeria in 1960, after nearly six years in Europe (one result of which was the much-anthologised poem "Telephone Conversation," in which he wittily sums up on the racial prejudice of English landladies), Soyinka was appointed to a number of university posts. These afforded him, particularly at Ibadan and Ife, the chance to produce his own plays, sometimes acting in them himself. He also worked for Nigerian radio and television, and formed an acting company in Lagos called The 1960 Masks. Soyinka was arrested by the Federal Government in 1967 for alleged pro-Biafran activity. The result of his experiences in solitary confinement at Kaduna Prison are recorded with great bitterness in *The Man Died*, a set of prison notes which make little attempt to enter the fashionable spirit of magnanimity which followed the Federal victory.

Soyinka's early work as a dramatist showed his skill as a comic writer. In both *The Swamp Dwellers* and *The Lion and the Jewel* he deals with traditional village life, but in the second he is already experimenting with mime and dance elements as an integral part of the comedy.

Soyinka's plays have subsequently become more technically daring. In *A Dance of the Forests*, his highly ambiguous celebration of Nigerian independence, the mortal world and the divine are brought into conjunction in a half-satirical, half-fantastic blend of traditional Yoruba imagery, dance motifs, and masque. Soyinka has written ironic comedies like his Jero plays, where the main character is a charlatan preacher all too easily exploiting the gullibility of his fellow countrymen, but his most significant dramatic work in recent years is probably *Madmen and Specialists*. This play arises from the mood of war, and the aftermath of war, but the form it takes shows the influence of experimental drama in America (where an early version was first staged) and Europe. Recent work, such as *Death and the King's Horseman* and his new version of *The Bacchae* of Euripides, commissioned for performance by the National Theatre in London, show a growing concern to relate African experience with European.

Soyinka has always tried to express a broad humanity in his work which will not be narrowly nationalistic. Many of his cultural principals are set out in an illuminating critical book, *Myth, Literature, and the African World*. Here he admits a recognizable distinction between African and European aesthetics but believes that they should not operate in isolation from each other.

As a novelist Soyinka has been the subject of some controversy. *The Interpreters* has probably gained in reputation in recent years as African fiction in English has faced up to more contemporaneous themes and more complex relationships. The book concerns a group of young Nigerian intellectuals, capturing, largely through dialogue, their idealism and anticipation about the development of the new Africa. *Season of Anomy* may seem to possess a Joycean difficulty of presentation, but it corresponds to *Madmen and Specialists* in its attempts to make sense of the recent devastations of war. The publisher's description is apt – "an expression of the affirmative, humane response to chaos and blind social forces." Soyinka has also translated *The Forest of a Thousand Daemons*, a Yoruba novel by D. O. Fagunwa. The folk and fantasy material with which it deals has often been reflected in Soyinka's plays.

Idanre and *A Shuttle in the Crypt* are two collections of verse, written over several years. The tone of the second collection is even bleaker than the first, distilling not just the horror and pity of war but the sterility of modern politics:

> They do not bleed
> On whom the dunghill falls, nor they
> Whose bones are sucked of marrow
> In noon perversions of inhuman tongues.
> They do not bleed whose breaths are stilled
> In sludges or sewers, who slither down
> To death on the burst tumour of hate's
> Inventive mind, through chasms of the flight
> Of earth from rites of defilement,
> Dark of abomination. They do not bleed
> Whose wombs are bared to leprous lust

This extract from the long poem "Conversation at Night with a Cockroach" captures the morbid pessimism out of which Soyinka is only just beginning to emerge through the affirmative quality of works like *Season of Anomy*.

—Alastair Niven

STEAD, C(hristian) K(arlson). New Zealander. Born in Auckland, 17 October 1932. Educated at Mount Albert Grammar School; University of Auckland, B.A. 1954, M.A. (honours) 1955; University of Bristol (Michael Hiatt Baker Scholar), Ph.D. 1961. Married Kathleen Elizabeth Roberts in 1955; two daughters and one son. Lecturer in English, University of New England, Armidale, New South Wales, 1956–57. Lecturer in English, 1959–61, Senior Lecturer, 1962–63, Associate Professor, 1964–67, and since 1967 Professor of English, University of Auckland. Chairman, New Zealand Literary Fund Advisory Committee. Recipient: Poetry Awards Incorporated prize, 1955; Winn-Manson Katherine Mansfield Award, for fiction and for essay, 1960, and Fellowship, 1972; Nuffield Travelling Fellowship, 1965; Jessie McKay Award, 1972; New Zealand Book Award, 1975. Lives in Auckland.

PUBLICATIONS

Verse

Whether the Will Is Free: Poems 1954–62. 1964.

Crossing the Bar. 1972.
Quesada: Poems 1972–1974. 1975.

Fiction

Smith's Dream. 1971.

Other

The New Poetic: Yeats to Eliot. 1964.

Editor, *New Zealand Short Stories: Second Series.* 1966.
Editor, *Measure for Measure: A Casebook.* 1971.
Editor, *The Letters and Journals of Katherine Mansfield: A Selection.* 1977.

Reading List: essay by Roy Fuller, in *London Magazine,* July 1964; by James Bertram in *Islands 2,* 1972.

* * *

C. K. Stead's *The New Poetic* illustrates his robust, clear-eyed criticism and special skill in the analysis of a text. Many consider Stead's chief distinction as a writer is as a critic. The most substantial of his prose writings is *Smith's Dream*, a kind of political novel set in a New Zealand that has become dominated by a Fascist dictator who is supported by a strong American military presence. The author's interest is in events rather than the springs of action, personal or political, and he shows considerable narrative skill. The tale has been made into the film *Sleeping Dogs*.

As a poet Stead is not prolific but through his three volumes of verse he has established a solid reputation in his country. *Whether the Will Is Free* is apprentice work strongly influenced by the poets he has chosen for models. The best-known of these early poems is "Pictures from a Gallery Underseas." Stead's poetry has the qualities of good expository prose, clarity, firmness of exposition, and a strong sense of organisation. Its inspiration is often literary but the language has the vitality of common speech and a natural rhythm. The poems in *Crossing the Bar* are poems of statement rather than exploration. He comments on American politics, the nature and importance of poetry, literary events like Auden's sixtieth birthday. There are, too, personal poems like the moving "A Small Registry of Births and Deaths" on his experience of fatherhood. Caesar is a dominant figure in the book. From him the poet has learnt his style, his Rome anticipates modern America: "What Wolf began, Eagle accomplishes." A good deal of Stead's political thinking is summed up in a striking statement of the consequences of political miscalculation: "Minerva had a mouse in mind./It was a weasel, tore her beak." Caesar the victorious soldier is Stead himself fighting that campaign with his "Enemy, brother, Lucifer/My own self" whose outcome is poetry.

The title sequence of *Quesada* is an extended allusion to the questing Don Quixote. The style of the volume is more relaxed than that of the other books, and more open to experience. Confessedly secular in outlook and without a mythopoeic imagination Stead writes verse that frequently lacks any sense of the mystery of life, something essential to the truest poetry. The deficiency is to some extent compensated for when he writes in the Romantic mode of the earlier part of this last volume. Besides the image of Quesada, romantic and compassionate, the book contains an admirable evocation of the South of France.

—F. M. McKay

STEAD, Christina (Ellen). Australian. Born in Rockdale, Sydney, New South Wales, 17 July 1902. Educated at Sydney University Teachers' College, graduated 1922. Married William James Blake in 1952 (died, 1968). Demonstrator, Sydney University Teachers' College, in Sydney schools, 1922–24; secretary in Sydney, 1925–28; moved to Europe, 1928, and worked as a clerk in offices in London, 1928–29, and in Paris, 1930–35; moved to the United States, 1935: Senior Writer, Metro-Goldwyn-Mayer, Hollywood, 1943; Instructor, New York University, 1943–44; returned to Australia. Since 1969, Fellow in Creative Arts, Australian National University, Canberra. Recipient: Arts Council of Great Britain grant, 1967; Patrick White Award, 1974. Lives in Hurstville, New South Wales.

PUBLICATIONS

Fiction

The Salzburg Tales. 1934.
Seven Poor Men of Sydney. 1934.
The Beauties and Furies. 1936.
House of All Nations. 1938.
The Man Who Loved Children. 1940.
For Love Alone. 1944.
Letty Fox: Her Luck. 1946.
A Little Tea, A Little Chat. 1948.
The People with the Dogs. 1952.
Dark Places of the Heart. 1966; as *Cotters' England,* 1967.
The Puzzleheaded Girl: 4 Novellas. 1967.
The Little Hotel. 1974.
Miss Herbert (The Suburban Wife). 1976.

Other

Editor, with William J. Blake, *Modern Women in Love.* 1945.
Editor, *Great Stories of the South Sea Islands.* 1956.

Translator, *Colour of Asia,* by Fernand Gigon. 1955.
Translator, *The Candid Killer,* by Jean Giltène. 1956.
Translator, *In Balloon and Bathyscaphe,* by August Piccard. 1956.

Reading List: "Stead Issue" of *Southerly,* 1962; *Stead,* 1969, and *Stead,* 1969, both by R. G. Geering.

* * *

The author of the most powerful, brilliant and individual Australian novel during the last fifty years has been, like several of Australia's best novelists, an expatriate. Her *House of All Nations,* the most cosmopolitan of her books, has been generously acclaimed in America, but has attracted little serious criticism in her own country. Its complexity, its exuberant detail, its large cast of 159 characters, may have been too much for reviewers to handle, and its form (a series of 104 scenes) presents a kaleidoscopic surface bewildering to readers accustomed to the conventional linear development of a story. Equally baffling, perhaps, is the author's political and moral stance; the book is obviously the work of a radical with a knowledge of Marxism, but there is much in it which would not please the orthodox Marxist, however unflattering its picture of finance capitalism. One suspects that reviewers find Stead's X-ray eye unnerving.

Of all Australian novelists, Christina Stead is most unmistakably a novelist born. Others may surpass her in philosophic coherence or tighter organisation, but not in native genius which finds expression in prose of surpassing richness, ease, and variety, not in range and clarity of observation and in vivid, firm characterisation. With these gifts, which she exercises as easily as a virtuoso violinist playing cadenzas, are allied a penetrating intelligence, an intense curiosity with a sensual quality reminiscent of Tolstoy's, a vision entirely individual, rich with quirks and prejudices, and a compassionate tolerance that stops well short of facile indifference. She may observe rather than judge, but her mind is not an empty room for winds to blow through. There is a strong biological base to Christina Stead's approach to fiction, inherited from her naturalist father. It is discernible in all her books, but is openly present in *The Man Who Loved Children*, a novel based on Australian experience but set in America, in which she analyses dramatically the influences of heredity, association, environment, and circumstances, which combine to produce a genius. This book, and the earlier *The Salzburg Tales* and *Seven Poor Men of Sydney*, show that her interests, unlike those of her social realist contemporaries inside and outside Australia, were not in the common man but in the uncommon man. There is a strong ingredient of the fantastic, even of the grotesque or the supernatural, in her work, though she would probably argue, like Carlos Fuentes, that the "normal" is nowhere to be found. Be that as it may, it is impossible to agree with the American critic and poet Randall Jarrell that the Pollitt family in *The Man Who Loved Children* is in any sense typical or representative. If the "seven poor men" have any reality at all, they are certainly far from being ordinary, and the gallery of story-tellers who tell the tales in *The Salzburg Tales* are as rich and bizarre as the stories they tell.

Christina Stead is above all an observer of the human scene, whose eye is alive to every detail and nuance and who is a full, precise recorder of what she sees. The more unusual and intrinsically interesting the objects under her observation, the greater the heights to which she rises; she has no talent for glorifying domestic trivia. The magnificent *House of All Nations*, furthest removed from the terrain thought proper for female novelists, shows her genius uninhibited. The novel plunges us into the mythomaniac world of finance of the Banque Mercure and its fascinating director Jules Bertillon, charming, unmoral, imaginative, and a compelling talker, whose luck is fabulous and whose dominant instinct is play. Every facet of his world glitters on the pages: speculation, commercial deals, stock manipulations, tax frauds, gambling for control of others – in short a kind of financial totalitarianism analogous to the political totalitarianism spreading over Europe in the late 1930's. Yet all this is refracted through a transforming imagination which understands poetically the intoxication of financial power; the result is prose of a richness rare in modern times.

Most of her other books are in some way concerned with the fortunes of women, though it is a mistake to see her as a feminist: for her, love between men and women is the natural expression of the human libido. The point of view of Teresa in *For Love Alone* is still the basis of her philosophy of life: Teresa's search for the right to love and the right to personal freedom are aspects of the same quest. Love and life are indistinguishable and life without love is not life at all. But it should be noted that this quest is an affair of "exchange": the capacity to love does not imply a demand to be loved. Jonathan Crow's real sin in *For Love Alone* is not so much that he does not return Teresa's love, but that he is incapable of being touched by it, of accepting it; hence the identification of him with the diabolical, a state which is seen as pitiful, as much as malevolent. In *The Puzzleheaded Girl*, one of four novellas published under that title, Stead returned to the theme of incapacity for love, this time in a woman.

As a novelist, Christina Stead's truest begetter is perhaps Dickens. She has the same talent for creating freestanding characters who owe their reality to the element of caricature in their construction, and who, like Mr. Micawber, pass into the language and become independent of their origins. Sam Pollitt, "the man who loved children," is of this kind and so is his wife Henny. The novel in which they appear was probably the first to be designed as deliberately "ecological"; it is one of several examples of the innovatory qualities in Australian women novelists which have been given little recognition, either at home or abroad.

—Dorothy Green

STEWART, Douglas (Alexander). Australian. Born in Eltham, New Zealand, 6 May 1913. Educated at New Plymouth Boys High School; Victoria University College, Wellington. Married Margaret Coen in 1946; one daughter. Literary Editor, *The Bulletin*, Sydney, 1940–61; Literary Adviser, Angus and Robertson, publishers, Sydney, 1961–73. Recipient: *Encyclopaedia Britannica* Award, 1968; Wilke Award, for non-fiction, 1975. O.B.E. (Officer, Order of the British Empire). Lives in Sydney.

PUBLICATIONS

Verse

Green Lions. 1937.
The White Cry. 1939.
Elegy for an Airman. 1940.
Sonnets to the Unknown Soldier. 1941.
The Dosser in Springtime. 1946.
Glencoe. 1947.
Sun Orchids. 1952.
The Birdsville Track and Other Poems. 1955.
Rutherford and Other Poems. 1962.
The Garden of Ships: A Poem. 1962.
(Poems). 1963; as *Selected Poems*, 1969, 1973.
Collected Poems, 1936–1967. 1967.

Plays

Ned Kelly (produced 1944). 1943.
The Fire on the Snow and The Golden Lover: Two Plays for Radio. 1944.
Shipwreck (produced 1948). 1947.
Four Plays (includes *The Fire on the Snow, The Golden Lover, Ned Kelly, Shipwreck*). 1958.
Fisher's Ghost: The Historical Comedy (produced 1961). 1960.

Radio Plays: *The Fire on the Snow*, 1941; *The Golden Lover*, 1943; *The Earthquake Shakes the Land*, 1944.

Fiction

A Girl with Red Hair and Other Stories. 1944.

Other

The Flesh and the Spirit: An Outlook on Literature. 1948.
The Seven Rivers (on angling). 1966.
The Broad Stream (criticism). 1975.
Norman Lindsay: A Personal Memoir. 1975.

Editor, *Coast to Coast: Australian Stories.* 1945.
Editor, with Nancy Keesing, *Australian Bush Ballads.* 1955.
Editor, with Nancy Keesing, *Old Bush Songs and Rhymes of Colonial Times, Enlarged and Revised from the Collection of A. B. Paterson.* 1957.
Editor, *Voyager Poems.* 1960.
Editor, *The Book of Bellerive,* by Joseph Tischler. 1961.
Editor, *(Poems),* by A. D. Hope. 1963.
Editor, *Modern Australian Verse: Poetry in Australia II.* 1964.
Editor, *Selected Poems,* by Hugh McCrae. 1966.
Editor, *Short Stories of Australia: The Lawson Tradition.* 1967.
Editor, with Nancy Keesing, *The Pacific Book of Bush Ballads.* 1967.
Editor, with Nancy Keesing. *Bush Songs, Ballads, and Other Verse.* 1968.
Editor, with Beatrice Davis, *Best Australian Short Stories.* 1971.
Editor, *The Wide Brown Land: A New Selection of Australian Verse.* 1971.
Editor, *Australia Fair.* 1976.

Reading List: *Stewart* by Nancy Keesing, 1965; *Stewart* by Clement Semmler, 1975.

* * *

Douglas Stewart is one of the most prolific and versatile of Australian writers. Well-known as a poet and radio playwright, he has also written short stories, essays, and biography. His account of the Sydney *Bulletin,* whose Red Page he edited from 1940 to 1960, is lively, informative, and graceful, and an important contribution to local literary history.

Stewart's *Collected Poems* assembled the best of his verse from 1936 onwards. Though he is a New Zealander by birth, few native Australians have developes Stewart's feeling for Australian landscape and animal life. His relationship with the natural world has been in turns egocentric, anthropomorphic, even animistic, but in the later poems it has become fraternal and non-attached. Where once he would have wished an insect to look at the world as a man would, he now tries to see the world, not merely as an insect would see it, which would be affectation, but through the eyes of an insect without surrendering the vision of a man. Courtesy is what distinguishes Stewart's attitude to the non-human world, and the reserve which is part of his own nature is scrupulously respected in other creatures, as the volume *Sun Orchids* makes clear. The mood of his verse is primarily one of good humour and well-being, and, in a darkening world living on the edge of a balance of terror, such a mood strikes many readers as superficial and evasive. The long narrative poem *Rutherford,* for instance, in spite of some fine passages, never really comes to grip with the central moral problem of post-Baconian science, while the weight of the verse suggests that the author shares the fuzzy optimism of his hero. Against this, however, should be set the magnificent ballad-sequence, *Glencoe,* with its fine structural coherence, its dramatic appropriateness and the timeless urgency of its theme: the wanton spirit of senseless faction in mankind which guarantees the suffering of the innocent. The main part of the sequence ends with one of Stewart's finest lyrics, the lament "Sigh, wind in the pine", with its grim warning:

> Oh life is fierce and wild
> And the heart of the earth is stone,
> And the hand of a murdered child
> Will not bear thinking on.
>
> Sigh, wind in the pine,
> Cover it over with snow;
> But terrible things were done
> Long, long ago.

The poem was written not long after another massacre: Hiroshima.

Those who deny Stewart the capacity for reflection must take *Glencoe* into account. They must also consider that his reflective exercises are as a rule conducted far below the surface of his poems, as the early poem "The River" makes plain: what he sees he has no objection to sharing, what he really thinks or feels, he seems to regard as largely his own business. His principal gift as a poet is the ability to transfigure the commonplace, to catch a moment of heightened experience and endow it with a history. The facility with which he seizes the poetic moment has sometimes led him into verbosity through over-exercise, and in some of his occasional verse there is a sense of strain. At times indeed he can degenerate into producing a kind of poetic "chirruping." Stewart's preoccupation with an immediate moment of intense awareness has tended to obscure the metaphysical base from which he works, expressed in paradoxical images of fire and snow, heat and cold, which perhaps hint at a struggle between the rational and the irrational in his own nature. Flame and snow come together in "Day and Night with Snow" (an early poem) and in "Flowering Place" (one of his most recent), while variants of the same image crop up in "Spider Gums," "The River," and "Flower of Winter." There is nothing static about this symbolism: fire is as much an image of destruction as it is of the continuity of life; snow, as much an image of potentiality, of steadfastness, as of death. His grasp of this archetypal imagery seems to be intuitional rather than intellectual, but for a lyrist, this is hardly a disadvantage.

The lack of intellectual rigour, however, becomes something of an obstacle in his prose work, especially in the literary criticism, in spite of its general good sense. His criticism, in *The Flesh and the Spirit* and *The Broad Stream*, belongs to the same impressionist genre, without being as captious or exhibitionist, as that of his more famous predecessor on the *Bulletin*, A. G. Stephens. It is intuitional, idiosyncratic, intensely subjective, capable of crystallising the essentials of a work under scrutiny, but liable to the temptations of large, arresting generalisations which will not stand up to close analysis because they take little account of what is extra-literary. It is never dull, always stimulating, often prejudiced, on occasions brilliant, and like much of the verse, often humorous.

Stewart's plays, written mainly for radio and all in verse, are strangely static: there is a much more genuinely dramatic element in the *Glencoe* ballads, or the poem "Terra Australis" than in *Fire on the Snow* or *Ned Kelly*. It is odd, for instance, that a dramatist should always choose situations which involve the characters in so much merely waiting around and talking. *Fire on the Snow*, about Scott's last expedition, unlike *Ned Kelly* and *Shipwreck*, is in addition devoid of human conflict; the enemy is nature, and endurance the only possible response. Written for radio, it is not a play for the theatre at all; and even *Ned Kelly*, which lends itself more easily to the stage, almost founders from excessive verbalisation. *Shipwreck* is a more shapely drama, in which the tendency to lyric expansion is kept under control. Even so, there is too much reliance at certain points on clumsy reporting of off-stage events. This play, however, is securely founded on a real moral conflict: whether a captain is justified in making a dangerous journey to bring help to his shipwrecked crew and passengers, when he must leave them on the verge of mutiny under precarious control.

Shipwreck is perhaps the strongest and most interesting of Stewart's plays. But *The Golden Lover*, on a New Zealand theme, is the most endearing. It dramatises the difficulty of choosing between dream and reality, between unearthly, intense love and domestic security; and in the Maori girl Tawhai, her lumpish husband Ruarangi, and Whana, the "golden lover" from the people of the Mist, Stewart has succeeded in creating three of his most convincing characters. As with *Ned Kelly*, however, the ending is left ambiguous; or rather it seems to be ambiguous until we reflect that the voices of commonsense have been given all the best tunes. It is difficult to avoid the conclusion, when one considers all the plays together, that the one value Stewart unequivocally endorses is sheer survival.

It is in the prose, finally, especially the biographical writing on Kenneth Slessor and Norman Lindsay, that doubts make themselves felt about Stewart's ultimate seriousness. The weight given to the superficial picturesqueness of some of the figures he admires, the flavour of old boy nostalgia for Bohemia, seem to sort ill with the realities of the life the world has known since Hiroshima. Nevertheless, it is possible that the generally light-hearted and circumspect temper of Stewart's writing may conceal a deep ineradicable pessimism, even disgust, about human nature, and that he has turned away to the natural world, content only with the surface pleasures of human society. Two passages in *Shipwreck* may crystallise his view of humanity; when Heynorick, the "observing" butler says suddenly, echoing Hamlet – "The appalling things that happen between sky and earth/Where the beast called man walks upright!" – and when Pelsart tells the condemned sailor: "I cannot pity you, prisoner; but, sometimes, my friends,/I am sorry for the race of men, trapped on this planet."

—Dorothy Green

STOW, (Julian) Randolph. Australian. Born in Geraldton, Western Australia, 28 November 1935. Educated at Guildford Grammar School, Western Australia; University of Western Australia, Nedlands, B.A. 1956. Formerly an anthropological assistant, working in Northwest Australia and Papua New Guinea; taught at the University of Adelaide, 1957; Lecturer in English Literature, University of Leeds, Yorkshire, 1962, and University of Western Australia, 1963–64; Lecturer in English and Commonwealth Literature, University of Leeds, 1968–69. Recipient: Australian Literary Society Gold Medal, 1957, 1958; Miles Franklin Award, 1958; Commonwealth Fund's Harkness Travelling Fellowship, 1964–66; Britannica Australia Award, 1966.

PUBLICATIONS

Fiction

A Haunted Land. 1956.
The Bystander. 1957.
To the Islands. 1958.
Tourmaline. 1963.
The Merry-Go-Round in the Sea. 1965.

Plays

Eight Songs for a Mad King, music by Peter Maxwell Davies. 1969.
Miss Donnithorne's Maggot, music by Peter Maxwell Davies. 1974.

Verse

Act One. 1957.
Outrider: Poems 1956–1962. 1962.
A Counterfeit Silence: Selected Poems. 1969.

Other

Midnite: The Story of a Wild Colonial Boy (juvenile). 1967.

Editor, *Australian Poetry 1964*   1964.

Bibliography: *Stow: A Bibliography* by P. A. O'Brien, 1968.

Reading List: "Outsider Looking Out" by W. H. New, in *Critique 9*, 1967; "Waste Places, Dry Souls" by Jennifer Wightman, in *Meanjin*, June 1969; *The Merry-Go-Round in the Sea* by Edriss Noall, 1971.

* * *

Randolph Stow's reputation as a novelist is based upon five novels which were published by the time he was thirty. These youthful works are rooted in his fascination with family, with the inescapable inheritance of the blood, and his intense feeling for the landscapes of childhood. "I say we have a bitter heritage, but that is not to run it down," says the narrator in *Tourmaline*, and that might serve as an epigraph for all of Stow's fiction. The theme of a "bitter heritage" is central to the first two novels, which are set in the West Australian countryside where Stow grew up. *A Haunted Land* is a vividly imagined but melodramatic story of the Maguire family last century. *The Bystander* concerns Maguire descendants, whose emotional lives are still clouded by the effects of the turbulent family past. This second novel, though it still has a Gothic flavour in places, is more firmly anchored in social observation and realistic psychology than the first, and indicates how rapidly Stow's talent developed.

With his third novel, *To the Islands*, Stow sought to extend his range and to escape the criticism of improbability that had been made of his first two attempts to write fiction. "This is not, by intention, a realistic novel" he announced in an Author's Note; and though the details are realistic, the action is boldly symbolic. The central figure is the aging missionary, Heriot, who leaves the Christian mission in north-western Australia, to which he has devoted his life, and wanders in search of the "islands of the dead" of aboriginal myth. His journey is a journey into the "strange country" of the self, but Stow does not succeed in giving his symbolism the dramatic substance and logic that Patrick White achieves in *Voss*, a novel with which it is inevitably compared.

In strikingly different ways the next two novels focus on the moral discoveries to be made in that "strange country" of a man's own being: their concern is with the meaning of selfhood. *Tourmaline* is Stow's most ambitious experiment in non-naturalistic fiction. Behind it lies his belief, expressed in an article in *Westerly*, 1961, that Australia is an "enormous symbol," and "because of its bareness, its absolute simplicity, a truer and broader symbol of the human environment than any European writer could create from the complex material of Europe." Tourmaline, a desolate country town to which the false hope of reviving life comes in the form of a supposed water diviner, is a kind of Australian waste land, which Stow pictures in images recalling some of Sidney Nolan's paintings. The novel is carefully composed in a mannered, almost ritualistic prose, aiming to direct the reader to the mythic dimensions of the setting and narrative.

More successful is *The Merry-Go-Round in the Sea*, Stow's most sustained piece of realism. With a strong autobiographical base, it is wonderfully evocative of the world as a child knows it. Stow traces the growth of Rob Coram from his earliest memories to adolescence with a warmth and sureness of insight. The boy is at the end made painfully aware that he must depend upon himself, when his loved older cousin, Rick Maplestead, decides to reject Australia and the family to which the boy feels himself proud to belong. With the recognition of his responsibility to himself the boy is ready for coming manhood: "The world and the clan and Australia had been a myth of his mind, and he had been, all the time, an individual." Whereas *Tourmaline* is a skeletal, allegorical work, shaped to express Stow's acceptance of the Taoist vision of existence, *Merry-Go-Round* has all the solidity of remembrance of things past, recreating places and atmospheres and personalities with a loving care for sensuous detail, while yet suggesting the symbolic values this experience holds. In this novel Stow seemed to have begun a new phase as a novelist, but so far no further novels have appeared.

Though he has – perhaps temporarily – ceased to write fiction, Stow has continued to write poetry. The themes of his poetry have been those of his fiction, the most striking correspondence being the series of variations on the themes of the Tao, which Stow entitled "The Testament of Tourmaline." Stow's poetry, always technically accomplished and free of modishness, has not received the recognition it deserves. It is a poetry of passionate utterance, controlled by a traditional sense of form and often distinguished by a memorable command of phrase and rhythm. Stow has written several fine sequences, such as "Stations" (a "suite for three voices and three generations") and "Thailand Railway"; and more recently *Eight Songs for a Mad King* (with music by Peter Maxwell Davies) and a libretto, *Miss Donnithorne's Maggot*. Stow is most often thought of as a poet of lyrical feeling, but he has a gift for parody and satire which finds expression in occasional poems and in his delightful children's story, *Midnite*. This tale of a bushranger with a gang of animals gives him opportunities to mock Australian literary preoccupations. The two sides of Stow can be seen by comparing a serious poem such as "The Singing Bones" with the hilarious treatment of the same theme in *Midnite*.

Now in his forties, Stow is a gifted writer whose achievements in fiction and poetry are already considerable. His recent interest in the relationship of poetry and music would seem to point to the possibility of a new development in his career.

—John Barnes

TAGORE, Sir Rabindranath. Indian. Born in Calcutta, 6 May 1861; son of Maharshi Tagore, grandson of Prince Tagore. Educated privately; University College, University of London, 1878–80. Married Mrinalinidebi in 1884; one son and one daughter. Managed family estates at Shileida from 1885; founded the Santiniketan, a school to blend Eastern and Western philosophical/educational systems, Bolpur, Bengal, 1901, which later developed into an international institution called Visva-Bharti; visited England, 1912; contributed regularly to the *Visvabharati Quarterly*; delivered the Hibbert Lectures, Oxford University, 1930. Began painting, 1929: exhibitions in Moscow, Berlin, Munich, Paris, and New York. Recipient: Nobel Prize for Literature, 1913. D.Lit.: University of Calcutta; Hindu University, Benares; University of Dacca; Osmania University, Hyderabad; D.Litt.: Oxford University. Knighted, 1915; resigned knighthood in 1919 as protest against British policies in the Punjab. Wrote in Bengali and translated his own works into English. *Died 7 August 1941.*

PUBLICATIONS (in English)

Collections

A Tagore Reader, edited by Amiya Chakravarty. 1961.

Verse

Gitanjali. 1912.
The Gardener. 1913.
The Crescent Moon: Child-Poems. 1913.
Fruit-Gathering. 1916.
Lover's Gift, and Crossing. 1918.
Poems. 1922.
The Curse at Farewell, translated by Edward Thompson. 1924.
Fireflies. 1928.
Fifteen Poems. 1928.
Sheaves: Poems and Songs, edited and translated by Nagendranath Gupta. 1929.
The Child. 1931.
The Golden Boat, translated by Chabani Bhattacharya. 1932.
Poems, edited by Krishna Kripalani. 1942.
A Flight of Swans, translated by Aurobindo Bose. 1955.
Syamali, translated by Sheila Chatterjee. 1955.
The Herald of Spring, translated by Aurobindo Bose. 1957.
Wings of Death: The Last Poems, translated by Aurobindo Bose. 1960.
Devouring Love, translated by Shakuntala Sastri. 1961.
A Bunch of Poems, translated by Monika Varma. 1966.
One Hundred and One. 1967.
Last Poems, translated by Pritish Nandy. 1973.
Later Poems, translated by Aurobindo Bose. 1974.

Plays

The Post Office, translated by Devabrata Mukerjee (produced 1913). 1914.
Citra. 1914.
The King of the Dark Chamber. 1914.
Malini, translated by Kshitish Chandra Sen (produced 1915). In *Sacrifice and Other Plays*, 1917.
The Cycle of Spring. 1917.
Sacrifice and Other Plays (includes *Malini; Sanyas, or, The Ascetic; The King and the Queen*). 1917.
Sacrifice (produced 1918). In *Sacrifice and Other Plays*, 1917.

The King and the Queen (produced 1919). In *Sacrifice and Other Plays*, 1917.
The Fugitive. 1918.
The Mother's Prayer (produced 1920). 1919.
Autumn Festival (produced 1920).
The Farewell Curse, The Deserted Mother, The Sinner, Suttee (produced 1920).
The Farewell (produced 1924).
Three Plays (includes *Muktadhara, Natir Puja, Candalika*), translated by Marjorie Sykes. 1950.

Fiction

Glimpses of Bengal Life (stories). 1913.
The Stone and Other Stories, translated by C. F. Andrews and others. 1916.
Mashi and Other Stories. 1918.
The Parrot's Training. 1918.
The Home and the World, translated by Surendranath Tagore. 1919.
The Wreck. 1921.
Gora. 1924.
Broken Ties and Other Stories. 1925.
Two Sisters, translated by Krishna Kripalani. 1943.
Farewell My Friend, with The Garden, translated by Krishna Kripalani. 1946.
Four Chapters, translated by Surendranath Tagore. 1950.
More Stories from Tagore. 1951.
Binodini, translated by Krishna Kripalani. 1959.
The Runaway and Other Stories, edited by Somnath Maitra. 1959.
Caturanga, translated by Asok Mitra. 1963.
Lipika, translated by Indu Dutt. 1969.
The Broken Nest, translated by Mary M. Lagos and Supriya Sen. 1971.

Other

Sadhana: The Realisation of Life. 1913.
Stray Birds (aphorisms). 1916.
My Reminiscences, translated by Surendranath Tagore. 1917.
Letters. 1917.
Nationalism. 1917.
Personality: Lectures Delivered in America. 1917.
Greater India (lectures). 1921.
Thought Relics. 1921.
Creative Unity. 1922.
The Visvabharati, with C. F. Andrews. 1923.
Letters from Abroad, edited by C. F. Andrews. 1924; revised edition, as *Letters to a Friend*, 1928.
Talks in China. 1925.
Lectures and Addresses, edited by Anthony X. Soares. 1928.
City and Village. 1928.
The Religion of Man. 1932.
Collected Poems and Plays. 1936.
Man (lectures). 1937.
My Boyhood Days. 1940.
Eighty Years, and Selections. 1941.
A Tagore Testament. 1953.

Our Universe, translated by Indu Dutt. 1958.
Letters from Russia, translated by Sasadhar Sinha. 1960.
Tagore, Pioneer in Education: Essays and Exchanges Between Tagore and L. K. Elmhirst. 1961.
A Visit to Japan, translated by Shakuntala Shastri. 1961.
Towards Universal Man. 1961.
On Art and Aesthetics. 1961.
The Diary of Westward Voyage, translated by Indu Dutt. 1962.
On Rural Reconstruction. 1962.
The Cooperative Principle. 1963.
Boundless Sky (miscellany). 1964.
The Housewarming and Other Selected Writings, edited by Amiya Chakravarty. 1965.

Reading List: *Tagore, Poet and Thinker* by Mohinimohana Bhattarcharya, 1961; *The Lute and the Plough: A Life of Tagore* by G. D. Khanolkar, 1963; *Ravindranath's Poetry* by Dattatuaya Muley, 1964; *Rabindranath* by Sati Ghosh, 1966; *Tagore: His Mind and Art* by Birenda C. Chakravorty, 1971.

* * *

The complexity of Rabindranath Tagore's genius and the extraordinary range of his intellectual and artistic interests have been noted by scholars in India and the West alike. While hailed primarily as a poet, Tagore excelled as a dramatist, essayist, novelist, short story writer, and, in non-literary endeavors, as painter, philosopher, educator, musician, social reformer, and ambassador of good will to cultures as diverse as China, the United States, and Latin America. Tagore's creative versatility serves to confirm his own belief that most great artists function at higher levels of awareness, often experiencing a natural, spontaneous urge for total Self-realization, which in Vedanta (the highest aspect of Hindu philosophy) is called Unity Consciousness.

This principle of unity (*Sahitya*) is the focal point of Tagore's aesthetic philosophy; derived from the root *Sahit,* meaning "to be with," the word *Sahitya* is the Sanskrit term for both "unity" and "literature." In his book *Sahitya* (1908) Tagore emphasizes that man's sense of oneness with the rest of creation is the root of all aesthetic delight; the poet is essentially restating the Vedantic view of art, which holds that artistic expression has its basis in states of consciousness and that the highest creative expression can only follow from the artist's own direct experience of pure consciousness (*Turiya*). In *Sahityer Pathe* (1926) the poet states, "Aesthetic delight is such a sense of harmony beyond the object that it does not delay in merging with our consciousness. In this case the revelation of the truth of the object is the same as the revelation of my consciousness" (p. 45). The distinguishing characteristic of all great artists, according to Tagore, is their ability to enlarge their own consciousness to the point that it becomes one with the Universal Self, thereby intuiting or reflecting all other selves.

In this regard Tagore considers the writing of poetry to be a spiritual discipline, a kind of *via purgativa.* Thus he shares the Hindu view of art as *Sadhana* – the process of spiritual training which transforms consciousness in such a way that the artist (individual self) can no longer be separated from his art (Universal Self). In *The Cycle of Spring* (1917) Tagore states: "The secret of all art lies in self-[as opposed to Self] forgetfulness. The poet or artist sets free the poet or artist in us" (p. 77). Tagore emphasizes the ability of art to raise the consciousness of not only the artist, but the perceiver as well: "True art withdraws our thoughts from the mere machinery of life, and lifts our souls above the meanness of it. It releases the self from the restless activities of the world and takes us out of the noisy sickroom of ourselves" (ibid).

Critics generally recognize three major stages in the poetic development of Tagore: 1) "romantic" poetry expressing a vague longing for essence transcending the mutability of matter (pre-*Gitanjali*, 1878–1908); 2) "mystic" poetry describing the synthesis of matter and spirit (*Gitanjali*, 1909–1915); 3) "realist" poetry defining the role of duality in the human experience (post-*Gitanjali*, 1916–1941). Tagore's early poetry, of which *Chitra* is a good example, consists largely of verse narrative, miscellaneous poems, songs, and poetic drama. *Gitanjali*, for which Tagore was awarded the Nobel Prize in 1913, consists primarily of his prose translations of selected lyrics from the 1910 Bengali version of *Gitanjali* and *Gitalipi*. *Gitanjali*, which literally means "Song Offerings," is a long, free-verse poem which depicts the author's growth of consciousness from "drunk delight" (*Ananda*) in creation as a child, at the start of the poem, to the acceptance of and thus transcendence of the cycle of birth-and-death (*Samsara*) when he is an old man at the end. Tagore's later poetry, from *Fruit-Gathering* (1916) on, far exceeds his earlier poetry both in volume and quality. Tagore left much of his later work untranslated, but what we do have in English reveals a poet keenly aware of the fragmentation experienced by modern man, yet confident in man's ability to achieve unity through the creative processes and the evolution of his awareness.

—Gail and H.A. Mirza

TENNANT, Kylie. Australian. Born in Manly, New South Wales, 12 March 1912. Educated at Brighton College, Manly; University of Sydney, 1931. Married Lewis C. Rodd in 1932; two children. Full-time writer, 1935–59; worked as journalist, publisher's reader, literary adviser, and editor, 1959–69; resumed full-time writing career, 1969. Life Patron, Fellowship of Australian Writers; Member, Commonwealth Literary Fund Advisory Board, 1961–73. Recipient: S.H. Prior Memorial Prize, 1935, 1941; Australian Literary Society Gold Medal, 1941; Commonwealth Jubilee Stage Prize, 1951. Lives in Hunter's Hill, New South Wales.

PUBLICATIONS

Fiction

Tiburon. 1935.
Foveaux. 1939.
The Battlers. 1941.
Ride On Stranger. 1943.
Time Enough Later. 1943.
Lost Haven. 1945.
The Joyful Condemned. 1953; complete version, as *Tell Morning This,* 1967.
The Honey Flow. 1956.
Ma Jones and the Little White Cannibals (stories). 1967.

Plays

Tether a Dragon. 1952.

John o' the Forest and Other Plays (juvenile). 1952.
The Bells of the City and Other Plays (juvenile). 1955.
The Bushranger's Christmas Eve and Other Plays (juvenile). 1959.

Other

Australia: Her Story: Notes on a Nation. 1953; revised edition, 1964, 1971.
Long John Silver: The Story of the Film. 1953.
The Development of the Australian Novel. 1958.
All the Proud Tribesmen (juvenile). 1959.
Speak You So Gently (travel). 1959.
Trail Blazers of the Air. 1965.
The Australian Essay, with L. C. Rodd. 1968.
Evatt: Politics and Justice (biography). 1970.
The Man on the Headland (biography). 1971.

Editor, *Great Stories of Australia 1–7.* 7 vols., 1963–66.
Editor, *Summer's Tales 1* and *2.* 1964, 1965.

Reading List: *The Novels of Tennant* by Margaret Dick, 1966 (includes bibliography).

* * *

Kylie Tennant once remarked that the Australian novel "eats its peas with its knife," and her own fiction has been something of an embarrassment to those who want literature to be a well-mannered business. She shows on the one hand a capacity for inventive zest and intellectual alertness that few Australian novelists of her generation can match, yet on the other a disconcerting penchant for throwing aesthetic decorum to the winds. She would no doubt admit cheerfully that there are rough patches in her writing, that her techniques are often unsubtle, and that the usual structure of her narratives is casual to the point of untidiness.

Similarly she declines to be solemn about her convictions, or even to admit that she holds any creed. Told once that all serious writers should develop some philosophy, she quipped that it "sounded like growing a moustache to hide my weak mouth." A target for ridicule throughout her work is any pretentious or zealous brand of system-mongering; repeatedly the author mocks those intent on "gnawing and nagging and converting and proselytizing," as she puts it in *Ride On Stranger,* whose heroine Shannon is one of several Tennant characters engaged in steering an honest course between the Scylla of dogmatic idealism and the Charybdis of sterile cynicism. Like many Australian writers before her, she tends to extend her sympathy more readily to the underdog, the battler, than to the well-off and cultivated areas of society, and on that basis some critics have placed her within the so-called "democratic tradition" said to derive from Lawson, Furphy, and others. But as Xavier Pons demonstrates in an article on *The Battlers,* her best-known novel (*Australian Literary Studies,* October 1974), Tennant rejects the spirit of that tradition; it was essentially optimistic, anticipating a fine future for Australian society, whereas she implicitly suggests in her fiction that the facts of experience belie any meliorist faith. Like her character Shannon, Tennant apparently can "not believe that half a dozen changes in the social system would cleanse the sewers of human ignorance and stupidity." We are our own victims.

Compassionate humour is Tennant's response to this dismal spectacle. She admires resilience, unpretentious integrity, and vitality; but she can take a wry pleasure in depicting all sorts of vice and folly without becoming uncharitable towards her own creatures. Her novels swarm with a wide variety of people and activities, and, formally considered, they are more remarkable for profusion than for proportion. But they testify consistently, in the very inclusiveness of their structure, to the breadth of Kylie Tennant's concerns.

—Ian Reid

TUTUOLA, Amos. Nigerian. Born in Abeokuta, Western Nigeria, in June 1920. Educated at the Anglican Central School, Abeokuta. Served as a blacksmith in the Royal Air Force, in Lagos, 1943–46. Married Victoria Tutuola in 1947; four sons and four daughters. Since 1956, Stores Officer, Nigerian Broadcasting Corporation, Ibadan. Founder, Mbari Club of Nigerian Writers. Lives in Ibadan.

PUBLICATIONS

Fiction

The Palm-Wine Drinkard and His Dead Palm-Wine Tapster in the Dead's Town. 1952.
My Life in the Bush of Ghosts. 1954.
Simbi and the Satyr of the Dark Jungle. 1955.
The Brave African Huntress. 1958.
The Feather Woman of the Jungle. 1962.
Abaiyi and His Inherited Poverty. 1967.

Reading List: *Tutuola* by Harold R. Collins, 1969; *Tutuola* edited by Bernth Lindfors, 1978.

* * *

Amos Tutuola's writing is, in a sense, a historical accident. A Yoruba who was taught English for six years at primary school level in colonial Nigeria, he chose to write his stories in English and was published in England largely as a curiosity – not so much for his tales, which are wholly African, but for the entertainment value of his highly idiosyncratic English. Praised by Dylan Thomas for the originality of his language, he was nonetheless read in Europe chiefly as a primitive. He was praised for what was called his "mixture of sophistication, superstition and primitivism, and above all for the incantatory juggling with the English language" (*Times Literary Supplement*, 1962). Consequently he was at first condemned in Africa, on the grounds that he misrepresented his country and his culture. He is a historical accident because the combination of his peculiar talent and the patronising colonial attitude which found entertainment in his English and so brought him into print was a chance conjunction of unique circumstances.

At a distance from the tensions of colonial Nigeria and the early days of independence it is possible to locate qualities in Tutuola which derive less from his use of English than from his free-flowing way of telling a story. His English does have a refreshing vigour and originality, involving for instance an occasional redeployment of stock phrases with precision as well as force (Ajaiyi's inherited poverty is one example). Omolara Leslie (*Journal of Commonwealth Literature 9*, 1970) calls it speaking Yoruba in English words. It has a freedom and confidence, a flow, which further years of learning English in a pedagogic situation would certainly have impeded. The same unselfconsciousness gives the episodic stories and their background a powerful coherence. No less a voice than Chinua Achebe (*Morning Yet on Creation Day*, 1975) has warmly defended Tutuola's integrity as an African writing of his time and for his culture.

—Andrew Gurr

van der POST, Laurens (Jan). South African. Born in Philippolis, 13 December 1906. Educated at Grey College, Bloemfontein. Served in the British Army, in the Western Desert and the Far East, in World War II; Prisoner of War, in Java, 1943–45; Military Attaché to the British Minister, Batavia, 1945–47: C.B.E. (Commander, Order of the British Empire), 1947. Married 1) Marjorie Wendt in 1929 (divorced, 1947), one son and one daughter; 2) the writer Ingaret Giffard in 1949. Farmer in the Orange Free State, South Africa, 1948–65. Explorer: has made several missions to Africa for the Colonial Development Corporation and the British Government, including a mission to Kalahari, 1952. Recipient: Anisfield-Wolf Award, 1951; National Association of Independent Schools Award, U.S.A., 1959; South African Central News Agency Prize, 1963, 1967. D.Litt.: University of Natal, Pietermaritzburg, 1965. Fellow, Royal Society of Literature, 1955. Lives in London and in Aldeburgh, Suffolk.

PUBLICATIONS

Fiction

In a Province. 1934.
The Face Beside the Fire. 1953.
Flamingo Feather. 1955.
A Bar of Shadow. 1956.
The Seed and the Sower (includes *A Bar of Shadow* and *The Sword and the Doll*). 1963.
The Hunter and the Whale: A Tale of Africa. 1967.
A Story like the Wind. 1972.
A Far-Off Place. 1974.
A Mantis Carol. 1975.

Plays

Screenplays: *The Lost World of the Kalahari*, 1956; *A Region of Shadow*, 1971; *The Story of Carl Gustav Jung*, 1971.

Other

> *Venture to the Interior.* 1951.
> *The Dark Eye in Africa.* 1955.
> *The Lost World of the Kalahari.* 1958.
> *The Heart of the Hunter.* 1961.
> *Journey into Russia.* 1964; as *A View of All the Russias,* 1964.
> *A Portrait of All the Russias.* 1967.
> *A Portrait of Japan.* 1968.
> *The Night of the New Moon: August 6, 1945 ... Hiroshima.* 1970.
> *African Cooking,* with the editors of *Time-Life.* 1970.
> *Man and the Shadow.* 1971.
> *Jung and the Story of Our Time: A Personal Experience.* 1975.
> *First Catch Your Eland: A Taste of Africa.* 1977.

Reading List: *van der Post* by Frederic I. Carpenter, 1969.

* * *

Laurens van der Post's fictional world is, like his real one, an intensely masculine world concerned with war, exploration, and adventure. It is for the most part set in his native South Africa and his main attraction as a writer lies in his capacity to recreate the South African landscape and fauna with a vividness and enthusiasm which are obviously born out of a great love for, and knowledge of, the country. However, van der Post also deals with social tensions. In *In a Province* a young white South African and his black friend who gets into trouble with the law become involved with communists and are finally killed. Though van der Post deplores racial discrimination, he has fought a life-long battle against what he sees as "communist subversion." This theme reappears in *Flamingo Feather* which, with its fast, exciting action and romantic/mystic tone, should appeal to the adventurer in each of us. *The Face Beside the Fire* is an altogether different novel, dealing with the problems of a South African writer in London and attempting an understanding of the psychological problems of alienation. *The Seed and the Sower* consists of three long short stories dealing with war and focussing on the life of a prisoner-of-war. They all draw their material from the author's experience as a prisoner-of-war in Japan during the Second World War. Van der Post's most widely read books, however, remain his accounts of expeditions into remote parts of Africa (*Venture to the Interior* and *The Lost World of the Kalahari*) in which he does not attempt any fictionalization of his material but describes his adventures as they happened.

—Kirsten Holst Petersen

WALCOTT, Derek (Alton). Jamaican. Born in Castries, St. Lucia, West Indies, 23 January 1930. Educated at St. Mary's College, St. Lucia; University of the West Indies, Kingston, Jamaica, B.A. 1953. Married; three children. Taught at St. Mary's College and Jamaica College. Formerly, Feature Writer, *Public Opinion,* Kingston, and *Trinidad Guardian,* Port-of-Spain. Since 1959, Founding Director, Trinidad Theatre Workshop. Recipient: Rockefeller Fellowship, for drama, 1957; Guinness Award, 1961; Heinemann Award, 1966; Cholmondeley Award, 1969; Order of the Humming Bird, Trinidad and Tobago, 1969; Obie Award, for drama, 1971. Lives in Trinidad.

PUBLICATIONS

Verse

Twenty-Five Poems. 1948.
Epitaph for the Young. 1949.
Poems. 1953.
In a Green Night: Poems 1948–1960. 1962.
Selected Poems. 1964.
The Castaway and Other Poems. 1965.
The Gulf and Other Poems. 1969.
Another Life. 1973.
Sea Grapes. 1976.
Selected Poems, edited by O. R. Dathorne. 1977.

Plays

Henri Christophe: A Chronicle (produced 1950). 1950
Henri Dernier: A Play for Radio Production. 1951.
Sea at Dauphin (produced 1954). 1954.
Ione: A Play with Music (produced 1957). 1954.
Drums and Colours (produced 1958). In *Caribbean Quarterly 1* and *2*, 1961.
Ti-Jean and His Brothers, music by André Tanker (produced 1958). In *The Dream on Monkey Mountain and Others Plays*, 1971.
Malcochon; or, Six in the Rain (produced 1959). In *The Dream on Monkey Mountain and Other Plays*, 1971.
The Dream on Monkey Mountain (produced 1967). In *The Dream on Monkey Mountain and Other Plays*, 1971.
In a Fine Castle (produced 1970).
The Dream on Monkey Mountain and Other Plays (includes *Ti-Jean and His Brothers, Malcochon, Sea at Dauphin,* and the essay "What the Twilight Says"). 1971.
The Charlatan, music by Galt MacDermot (produced 1974).
The Joker of Seville, and O Babylon! 1978.

Reading List: *Walcott: "Another Life"* by Edward Baugh, 1978.

* * *

The first and simplest pleasure offered by Derek Walcott's poetry is the sense of being alive and out-of-doors in the West Indies: sand and salt on the skin, sunlight and space and the open beach, sea-grapes and sea-almonds, liners and islands, where always "The starved eye devours the seascape for the morsel of a sail,/The horizon threads it infinitely."

Walcott was a painter before he was a poet, and as a youth set off with a friend around his native island of Santa Lucia to put it on canvas and thus create it in the imagination. Later he found he could do the work of creation better with words and metaphor, and that this too was needed:

> For no-one had yet written of this landscape
> that it was possible, though there were sounds
> given to its varieties of wood.

Walcott has kept his painter's eye, and is especially aware of effects of light. He often compares life with art ("Tables in the trees, like entering Renoir"), as indeed he often quotes or echoes lines from the English Metaphysicals, Tennyson, Eliot, Dylan Thomas, and others. These things, taken together with the high polish of his verse, have sometimes led to accusations of virtuoso artificiality and preciosity. But, though there may be some lapses which deserve such strictures, it is precisely the successful transmuting of life into art which makes Walcott's achievement so important.

At his best he fuses the outward scene with inward experience and with a form of English words, resonant within the tradition of literature in English but also appropriate to the particular occasion, all in one single act of perception. In so doing he enhances and illustrates (in the Renaissance sense of that word) the landscape and the human lives that are found on the islands. It is not surprising, perhaps, that he should be such a good love poet, for the experience of love has this same quality of enhancing places: "But islands can only exist/If we have loved in them."

Love, the creation of a centre of consciousness, and a relationship of security with the place one lives are particularly important in societies where a history of slavery, cultural deprivation, colonial dependency, and, latterly, tourism have combined to reinforce the more generalized modern feelings of alienation and contingency. Walcott's work may therefore be quite as socially important as that of more obsessively socially-orientated West Indian writers.

Walcott by no means ignores the well-known dilemmas of the West Indian situation. In "Ruins of a Great House" he works out in a complex fashion his relationship with men like Ralegh, "ancestral murderers and poets," with England and the English language, and with the earlier history of a ruined plantation house. Here and elsewhere he is aware that he has one white grandfather, who like many others "drunkenly seeded their archipelago." When the Mau Mau insurrection in Kenya occurs, he cannot give murderers on either side his blessing though "poisoned with the blood of both," and when he sees television film of the Biafran war he notes "The soldiers' helmeted shadows could have been white." In general his aim seems to be not to make rhetoric out of the past, but to transcend it: "All in compassion ends/So differently from what the heart arranged."

Walcott is also a successful and prolific playwright, the founder-director of the Trinidad Theatre Workshop, a travelling group of players who move around the Caribbean. Whereas the poetry is almost entirely in standard English, the plays are largely in the creole idiom of the West Indies. A further linguistic complication is that the popular language of Walcott's home island is a Creole French (as on Jean Rhys's home island of Dominica) and the French phrases and songs of the islands also find their way in quotation, and, with their special intonations, into his work.

In his best-known play, *Dream on Monkey Mountain*, Makak the charcoal-burner lives in utter degradation, dreams he is king of a united Africa, yet has to go on living in the everyday world. "The problem," Walcott said in an interview (*New Yorker*, 26 June 1971), "is to recognize our African origins but not to romanticize them." Generally, one feels that Walcott has little sympathy for exploitation of the past by modern ideologists, even if they are negro ideologists, and some of his bitterest lines are reserved for post-independence politicians. Against their power and rhetoric he sets out on a subtler and more revolutionary course:

> I sought more power than you, more fame than yours,
> I was more hermetic, I knew the commonweal,
> I pretended subtly to lose myself in crowds
> knowing my passage would alter their reflection

and at the same time to redeem the past

> Its racial quarrels blown like smoke to sea.
> From all that sorrow, beauty is our gain
> Though it may not seem so
> To an old fisherman rowing home in the rain.

—Ned Thomas

WARUNG, Price. Pseudonym for William Astley. Australian. Born in Liverpool, Lancashire, England, 13 August 1855; emigrated with his family to Australia in 1859, and settled in Richmond, Victoria. Educated at St. Stephen's School, Richmond, and at the Model School, Carlton, Victoria. Married Louisa Frances Cape in 1884. Founding Editor, *Richmond Guardian*, 1875; member of staff of the *Riverine Herald*, Echuca, 1876–77; suffered a nervous breakdown, 1878–80; correspondent in Casterton and Melbourne, 1881–82; Editor, *Australian Graphic*, Sydney, 1883; reporter for the Warnambool *Standard*, Sydney *Globe*, Bathurst *Times*, Tumut *Independent*, and the Bathurst *Free Press*, 1884–90; settled in Sydney, 1891; columnist for the Sydney *Bulletin*, 1890–93; Managing Editor, *Australian Workman*, 1893. Granted Commonwealth Literary Fund pension, 1908. Died 5 October 1911.

PUBLICATIONS

Fiction

Tales of the Convict System. 1892.
Tales of the Early Days. 1894.
Tales of the Old Regime, and The Bullet of the Fated Ten. 1897.
Tales of the Isle of Death (Norfolk Island). 1898.
Half-Crown Bob and Tales of the Riverine. 1898.

Other

Labor in Politics: A Criticism and Appeal. 1893.
The Federal Capital: An Argument for the Western Site. 1903.

* * *

Price Warung was the pseudonym used by William Astley whose main claim to fame lies in his tales of the Australian convict system. Astley wrote ninety-four stories of convict life which, with few exceptions, were published between the years 1890 and 1892 in *The Bulletin*, the journal which played a major role in the creation of an indigenous literature in Australia. *The Bulletin*'s motto was "Temper, democratic; bias, offensively Australian," and it was one that Astley could agree with wholeheartedly. Astley was a radical and a nationalist. He saw himself as a missionary who was going to help bring about a new Australia in which capitalism would be replaced by socialism and the wealth taken from the few and shared out among the many.

Not all of Astley's stories are set in a penal colony — they move from free settlements to places of secondary punishment — but they are all concerned in some way or other with convict life and present a similar thesis. Astley's aim was to show that the convicts were more sinned against than sinning, and that the real villains were the British capitalists and imperialists. In a period of increasing nationalistic fervour it is easy to see the reason for the popularity of his stories. His stories all reveal the horror of a cruel and corrupt system and on a larger scale the inhumanity of man to man. Such a theme easily lends itself to the macabre and the melodramatic, and, striving for powerful effects, Astley made full use of both, unfortunately too much so. He was so involved with his thesis, of bringing home the message, that he lacked the detachment so necessary for artistic achievement. The artist is swamped by the polemicist. His plots are contrived, his characters stereotyped. Even his stories which have not got a convict theme (for example, *Tales of the Riverine*) reveal the same flaws.

There has been a recent revival of interest in Astley's work, not because of its literary merit but because of the renewed interest by Australians in their past and of any interpretation of it that might reveal the truth behind the fiction.

—Anna Rutherford

WEBB, Francis (Charles). Australian. Born in Adelaide, South Australia, 8 February 1925. Educated at Christian Brothers schools, Chatswood and Lewisham; University of Sydney. Served in the Royal Australian Air Force in Canada, during World War II. Worked for various Canadian publishers. Recipient: Commonwealth Literary Fund Fellowship, 1960. *Died in 1973.*

PUBLICATIONS

Verse

A Drum for Ben Boyd. 1948.
Leichhardt in Theatre. 1952.
Birthday. 1953.
Socrates and Other Poems. 1961.
The Ghost of the Cock. 1964.
Collected Poems. 1969.

Reading List: "The World of Webb" by Sylvia Lawson, in *Australian Letters,* 1961; "The Poetry of Webb" by Vincent Buckley, in *Meanjin,* 1963.

* * *

Of the younger modern Australian poets of this century, Francis Webb, on the publication of his *A Drum for Ben Boyd* became one of the two leading figures, with David Campbell. Webb's early death cut his achievement short. Webb spent much of his adult life in mental hospitals and a good deal of his poetry undoubtedly attempts to convey experiences peculiar to what are called psychotic states of mind. It is inevitable, therefore, that he should have enjoyed a kind of *succès de scandale* on that account. But much of his poetry is genuinely visionary poetry, the result of a more than ordinarily lucid and energetic way of seeing, of an imagination and a sensibility of greater scope and intensity than usual.

It would be a mistake to see in Webb's early poems, written before his illness, the preoccupations with night, death, dream, eccentricity, solitude, silence, obscure terrors, and rejections that merely bespeak the alienated mind. What most characterises his verse is its immense vitality, its positiveness. Even its privacies are not egocentric. These are not poems of withdrawal, but of reaching out; in contrast to many more "normal" poets, Webb did not "live the life of monologue." Poetry for him was a means of keeping in touch with reality; his early poem, "Compliments of the Audience," is an affirmation of faith in images, which, he argues, are all that emerge to testify to reality from the blackness of memory, the blurred barrenness of thought. *A Drum for Ben Boyd*, a sequence of poems by various speakers giving their different impressions of the merchant-adventurer Boyd, was a remarkable performance for a young man of 22, especially since, in an era of historic poems, it questioned the validity of historiography. His second long poem, *Leichhardt in Theatre*, was no less challenging, and contains perhaps the central symbol of Webb's belief system: the "nomad horseman energy." Other preoccupations which bind the work as a whole together are his interest in music, in painting, and in everything to do with the sea. He gives special importance to laughter, as his last long poem, *Ghost of the Cock*, demonstrates, and the clown image is a recurrent one. Leichhardt, for instance, is presented as part-clown, part-hero.

Webb's greatest technical strength lies in his appeal to the ear. He handles the language as a musician handles tones and produces a rich concourse of sound which carries its own meaning, even if the mind is slow to interpret it. This gift is most in evidence perhaps in the volume *Socrates*, which also shows him in full possession of his visionary world. All his key experiences come together in this book: his Catholic faith, war-time flying, music, the sea, his own illness, his need for monastic solitude. There is much of the "desert father" in Webb's verse: his passionate nature made it necessary for him to turn all women into the Virgin, all children into the infant Christ. The poem "For Ethel" is the nearest we get to any sense of an earthly, particular woman. It is in a poem about a new-born child that Webb comes closest to intimate human contact, with all his senses sharpened, particularly the sense of touch: it is one of the most beautiful of all contemporary Nativity poems, as the opening stanza suggests:

> Christmas is in the air.
> You are given into my hands
> Out of quiet, loneliest lands.
> My trembling is all my prayer.
> To blown straw was given
> All the fullness of heaven.

Webb was too rich and complex a poet to yield himself to short analysis. Perhaps some glimpse of the man and the poet is revealed in his lines about Socrates, musing on the relationship between his soul and his body, as the "chains" of earthly ties are about to be loosed:

> Chains grapple with me gently, as old friends,
> The subtle iron lends its tinklings to my move.
> And it is all of love; for I see Andromeda musing,
> Given back to entire music, swathed in frail silver links:
> They chime, climb or sink with gain or fail of pulse,
> And all about, incurious hulls and the long, long flutes of the sea.

—Dorothy Green

WHITE, Patrick (Victor Martindale). Australian. Born in London, England, 28 May 1912. Educated at schools in Australia, 1919–25; Cheltenham College, 1925–29; King's College, Cambridge, 1932–35, B.A. in modern languages 1935. Served in the Royal Air Force as an Intelligence Officer, in the Middle East, 1940–45. Travelled in Europe and the United States, and lived in London, before World War II; writer from 1938; returned to Australia after the war. Recipient: Australian Literary Society Gold Medal, 1956; Miles Franklin Award, 1958, 1962; Smith Literary Award, 1959; National Conference of Christians and Jews' Brotherhood Award, 1962; Nobel Prize for Literature, 1973. A.C. (Companion, Order of Australia), 1975. Lives in Sydney.

PUBLICATIONS

Fiction

Happy Valley. 1939.
The Living and the Dead. 1941.
The Aunt's Story. 1948.
The Tree of Man. 1955.
Voss. 1957.
Riders in the Chariot. 1961.
The Burnt Ones (stories). 1964.
The Solid Mandala. 1966.
The Vivisector. 1970.
The Eye of the Storm. 1973.
The Cockatoos: Shorter Novels and Stories. 1974.
A Fringe of Leaves. 1976.

Plays

Return to Abyssinia (produced 1947).
The Ham Funeral (produced 1961). In *Four Plays,* 1965.
The Season at Sarsaparilla (produced 1962). In *Four Plays,* 1965.
A Cheery Soul (produced 1963). In *Four Plays,* 1965.
Night on Bald Mountain (produced 1964). In *Four Plays,* 1965.
Four Plays. 1965.
Big Toys (produced 1977).

Verse

The Ploughman and Other Poems. 1935.

Bibliography: *A Bibliography of White* by Janette Finch, 1966.

Reading List: *White* by Geoffrey Dutton, 1961; *White* by Robert F. Brissenden, 1966; *White* by Barry Argyle, 1967; *The Mystery of Unity: Theme and Technique in the Novels of White* by Patricia A. Morley, 1972; *The Eye in the Mandala: White, A Vision of Man and God* by Peter Beatson, 1976; *White's Fiction* by William Walsh, 1978.

* * *

Patrick White comes from a pioneering Australian family, although he was born in London. He travelled widely in Europe and the U.S.A. before World War II, and also lived in London where he was much involved with the theatre, a life-long passion. Part of the depth and intensity of his view of the world comes from his experience of its newer and older civilizations.

His first novel, *Happy Valley* (which he will not allow to be reprinted), was highly praised by some of the most eminent contemporary English critics and writers. It is an uneven but powerful work, set in the high, cold country of southern New South Wales, where he had worked as a jackeroo (an Australian term for a young man learning the skills of managing sheep or cattle). Its immaturity shows in the strong stylistic influence of Joyce, its maturity in its characteristic searching assessment of the causes of human failure.

The Living and the Dead is set in the England of the second and third decades of the twentieth century, and is a harsh judgement of a society more dead than living, softened by the refusal of some of the characters, especially female, to "behave in the convention of a clever age that encouraged corrosiveness, destruction." It is also the first of White's many onslaughts on "the disgusting, the nauseating aspect of the human ego." White's deepest and most consistent purpose in all his work is the offering of signposts on the road to humility. He is a profoundly religious writer, not bound to any creed.

White's original genius appears unmistakably in his next novel, *The Aunt's Story*. The aunt is a spinster, Theodora Goodman, who although lonely and "leathery" has an extraordinarily rich understanding of life and people. Her story moves from reality to illusion, in Australia, Europe and the U.S.A.; she is broken by her longing, but inability, to reconcile the two.

White's next novel, *The Tree of Man*, is the result of his decision to return to Australia after the war, where he settled on a farm near Castle Hill, on the edge of Sydney, with a Greek friend and partner, Manoly Lascaris. All his subsequent books are, in a sense, his attempts to populate what he once called "The Great Australian Emptiness." His love-hate relationship with his own country (for some years now he has lived in Sydney) has in recent years extended to an active involvement in public issues, especially over the constitutional crisis of 1975, surprising perhaps in someone who guards his privacy so fiercely.

The Tree of Man is White's tribute to the ability of ordinary men and women to survive against the elemental and inhuman forces of nature in Australia; ironically, the action takes place on the outskirts of Sydney, and not in the immensities of the outback. Into these surroundings White plunged his next hero. *Voss* is a novel about a German explorer in New South Wales, Queensland, and the Northern Territory, some of the inspiration for which came from White's reading of the journals of the explorers E. J. Eyre and Ludwig Leichhardt. With *The Tree of Man* and *Voss* White secured his international reputation. In *The Tree of Man* he attempted to explain the ordinary. In *Voss* he took an extraordinary hero into an extraordinary country, with the Aborigines leading Voss on to further mysteries of magic and death. But the explorer's real journey is in the purification of his soul through torments of both agony and joy, understood only by the partner of his spiritual life, Laura Trevelyan, who remains in Sydney.

However, no discussion of White's work should be involved exclusively with the spiritual. White is also a master of social comedy, with a classical eye and ear for pretension and vulgarity, and an equally classical, if perhaps surprising, love of knockabout farce and bawdry.

White's next novel, *Riders in the Chariot*, brings a European experience of war and racial persecution into the stifling bourgeois normality of White's mythical Sydney suburb, Sarsaparilla. But, as the title indicates, understanding is only achieved by those who see that life is "streaming with implications," those with the vision of the Chariot. The range of the book may be hinted at by the individuality of the "Riders": Himmelfarb, the Jewish migrant; Miss Hare, a slightly dotty old lady; Mrs. Godbold, a working-class woman (and one of White's great gallery of women without whom the world would collapse); and Alf Dubbo, an Aboriginal artist who is also familiar with booze and the brothel.

In the early 1960's White's energies shifted temporarily to the theatre and the short story.

An early (1947) play, *The Ham Funeral*, was produced in Adelaide for the first time in 1961, followed in rapid succession by *The Season at Sarsaparilla*, *A Cheery Soul* (adapted from a short story), and *Night on Bald Mountain*. These plays came from a deep and long-felt passion for the theatre, but White, disillusioned with the intrigues of theatrical life, turned his back on the stage until 1976, when spurred on by contemporary Australian social and political corruption, he wrote *Big Toys*, which had a long run in various Australian capital cities in 1977.

The Solid Mandala, set in Sydney, is perhaps the most tightly knit, difficult, yet rewarding of White's novels. The twin brothers, Waldo and Arthur Brown, are in many ways the two halves of human nature, knowledge and intuition, fancy and imagination.

The Vivisector, a novel about an artist and the nature of art itself, is the most unsparing and uncompromising of White's works. As the title suggests, no compromise is possible for a true artist, doomed to loneliness, uncomforted by love or sex because both are in competition with art. It is a bleak philosophy, but, as so often with White, it must be emphasized that there is always comedy, from wit to bawdry, from irony to hilarity, which is present not for light relief but because White is always conscious of the human comedy beyond the individual tragedy.

White's recent novel *A Fringe of Leaves* is immediately accessible, with an unexpected tenderness considering the violence of the action: 19th-century shipwreck and murder, and the ordeal of a white woman, naked except for a fringe of leaves, among wild Aborigines, who may be "wild" but in fact have plenty to teach her.

White's genius shows no sign of slackening in its attack or invention. He has more novels on the way, and a film (based on a short story), *The Night the Prowler*, was made in 1977. His intense individuality comes in life from his depth and clarity of vision, and in literature from his unmistakable style, which is based on the widest expansion of metaphor; to adapt De Quincey's words, his style "cannot be regarded as a *dress* or alien covering, but it becomes the *incarnation* of his thoughts."

—Geoffrey Dutton

WILKINSON, Anne (Cochran Boyd). Canadian. Born in Toronto, Ontario, 21 September 1910. Educated privately. Married Frederik R. Wilkinson in 1932 (divorced, 1953); two sons and one daughter. Co-Founding Editor, *Tamarack Review*, Toronto, 1956. Died 10 May 1961.

PUBLICATIONS

Collections

Collected Poems, and a Prose Memoir, edited by A. J. M. Smith. 1968.

Verse

Counterpoint to Sleep. 1951.
The Hangman Ties the Holly. 1955.

Other

Lions in the Way: A Discursive History of the Oslers. 1956.
Swann and Daphne (juvenile). 1960.

* * *

Anne Wilkinson's work is beautifully of a piece, and part of the impressive effect her poetry makes on the reader is the result of the precision and firmness of her literary identity. All the poems, however varied, strike one as issuing from a single source. She brings to mind the name of Hopkins, not in any passive or imitative way but in the intensity and singularity of her sensibility. Her disinterestedness is quite pure, her eye bent without distraction upon the object, and yet the savour of inimitable individuality, of the presence of the author in every syllable, is unmistakable. She is capable of taking a single image, as in her exquisite poem "Lens," and of deriving from it a substantial poem. But all the generation is from within, so that there is no sense of the softness or accretion of pointless apposition – as there is in her weaker production. The pose in "Lens," as in all her best work, is perfect because of the clarity and force, almost the ferocity, of the vision.

She is fascinated by the variety and the continuity of sense-experience, by its blending and blurring of the physical and the psychological, by its organic relationship with the vegetable world at one end of the scale ("Still Life," "A Poet's-Eye View," "Summer Acres") and at the other by its extension into the psychic world ("The Puritan," "After Reading Kafka," "To a Psycho-Neurotic"). Such activity of the senses in the poet produces, as we see, for example, in Wordsworth's *The Prelude*, a world of exceptional presence and brilliance, the mind of the poet being in its creativity almost the opposite to the mere registering instrument advanced by Locke as a mental model. The more vital the subject in fact, the more powerful the object. Thus for Anne Wilkinson even the formless flow of time is something ferocious, "Time is tiger." The external world appears as "The striped, discerning tiger"; the poet's relations with it as dangerous and terrifying, as in "Poem of Anxiety":

> When night's at large in the jungle
> I go fearful
> Lest I kiss or claw his eye.
> Too whoo, too whit, who's who
> When all the jungle reeks?

To say that Anne Wilkinson's poetry is saturated with sense-experience is to say that she is infatuated with existence, the senses being for her the immediate and subtlest entrance into life. This is why her best work gives the reader the sense of sharing an entranced experience of pure existence. It is this model or shape of perfection she struggles to make the rest of living, and even the act of dying, conform to, just as it is the inwardness and sincerity with which the effort is made that confers on her poetry an extraordinary distinction and integrity.

There are two initiating and sustaining conceptions in Anne Wilkinson's poetry: a deep conviction about the unity of existence, which does not exclude a fine sense of its manifold distinctions; and a vibrant joy in the face of existence, which can go with the most intimate experience of grimness and pain. The first never puffs into grandiosity, the second does not slump into complacency because the poetry is marked by qualities tending constantly to work for poise and actuality, wit, continuity, palpability. It is this recovering, connecting, particularizing, palpable tradition of poetry, a line joining Robert Graves to Gerard Manley Hopkins and Keats to Donne, which Anne Wilkinson represents so strongly in Canadian literature.

If poetry as illumination of the present is the burden of the first part of the poem "Lens," poetry as the recovery of the past is that of the second. The augmentation of being becomes the rescuing of it. The imagery of eye, lens, and light turns into one of film and dark room where "the years/Lie in solution." It is because of man's unbroken connection with his own beginnings, human, animal, natural, that the poet's imagination can sharpen into needlepoint precision what lies vaguely latent in the consciousness:

>A stripe of tiger, curled
>And sleeping on the ribs of reason
>Prints as clear
>As Eve and Adam, pearled
>With sweat, staring at an applecore....

—William Walsh

WILSON, Ethel. English/Canadian. Born in South Africa, 20 January 1888. Educated at Trinity Hall, Southport, Lancashire. Married Dr. Wallace Wilson (died). Taught in the public schools of Vancouver, British Columbia. Recipient: Canada Council Medal, 1962; Lorne Pierce Medal, 1964. D.Litt.: University of British Columbia, Vancouver, 1955. Medal of Service, Order of Canada, 1970. Lives in Vancouver.

PUBLICATIONS

Fiction

Hetty Dorval. 1947.
The Innocent Traveller. 1949.
The Equations of Love, with Tuesday and Wednesday, and Lilly's Story. 1952.
Swamp Angel. 1954.
Love and Salt Water. 1956.
Mrs. Golightly and Other Stories. 1961.

Reading List: *Wilson* by Desmond Pacey, 1967.

* * *

The Canadian writer Ethel Wilson sets her novels and stories largely in her home province of British Columbia. The ocean, the mountains, and the rain forests form a backdrop to her fiction and frequently carry symbolic associations in the development of a story. But while Mrs. Wilson is a realist, faithful to her region, her fiction is informed throughout by the universal problem of human relationships – their complexity, their difficulty. Mrs. Wilson's fictional world is peopled with eccentrics and lonely individuals who do not easily relate to others, but who experience nonetheless a profound need for some form of human community. The concern with communication is imbedded in Mrs. Wilson's style. She has said she likes best the formal and simple sentence, clear and unloaded; but while the simple style forms the matrix of her prose, her writing is nonetheless marked by stylistic quirks – curious repetitions, illogical statements, ellipses. The failure of men to communicate with each other is the thematic corollary to this style and the gaps in Mrs. Wilson's writing represent forms of arrest and discontinuity in the flow of human relationships.

The recurrent drama in Mrs. Wilson's fiction is the lonely quest of a young woman, orphaned and cut off from familiar surroundings, to discover her identity and to forge a link with the human community at large. The link is hard to establish, and Mrs. Wilson reveals the many ways by which human contacts are broken. In *Hetty Dorval* jealousy and guilt bring the girl narrator to a state of bitter isolation at the end of the novel, while in the story "Mrs. Golightly and the First Convention" shyness keeps the heroine from enjoying her holiday and the company of other women. In *Swamp Angel* the heroine's desire for mastery in every situation prevents her from forming lasting human ties until near the end of the novel when she begins to test an old woman's observation that we are all part of "the everlasting web" of creation. Mrs. Wilson is fascinated with lonely, anonymous individuals who retreat from human contacts and she gives us on a philosophical level a complementary vision of the universe as an ungoverned void subject to accident and chance. But at the same time she refers us frequently in her writing to Donne's admonition that "No man is an Island," and insists on the humanist's values of love, faith, and responsibility. Mrs. Wilson's fiction is of a consistently high level artistically and to single out her masterwork would be simply to indicate a personal preference.

—David Stouck

WRIGHT, Judith. Australian. Born in Armidale, New South Wales, 31 May 1915. Educated at New England Girls School, Armidale; University of Sydney, B.A. Married J. P. McKinney; one daughter. Secretary, J. Walter Thompson, advertising agency, Sydney, 1938–39; Secretary, University of Sydney, 1940–42; Clerk, Australian Universities Commission, Brisbane, 1944–46; Statistical Research Officer, University of Queensland, Brisbane, 1946–49. Since 1967, Honours Tutor in English, University of Queensland. Commonwealth Literary Fund Lecturer, Australia, 1949, 1962; Guest Delegate, World Poetry Conference, Canada, 1967; Creative Arts Fellow, Australian National University, Canberra, 1974. Co-Founder and President, Wildlife Preservation Society of Queensland, 1962–65. Recipient: Grace Leven Prize, 1949, 1972; Commonwealth Literary Fund Fellowship, 1964; *Encyclopaedia Britannica* Award, 1964; Fellowship of Australian Writers Robert Frost Medal, 1975. D.Litt.: University of Queensland, 1962; University of New England, Armidale, 1963. Fellow of the Australian Academy of the Humanities, 1970. Lives in North Tamborine, Queensland.

PUBLICATIONS

Verse

The Moving Image. 1946.
Woman to Man. 1949.
The Gateway. 1953.
The Two Fires. 1955.
Birds. 1962.
(Poems). 1963.
Five Senses: Selected Poems. 1963.
City Sunrise. 1964.
The Other Half. 1966.
Collected Poems 1942–1970. 1971.
Alive. 1973.
Fourth Quarter. 1978.
The Double Tree: Selected Poems 1942–1976. 1978.

Fiction

The Nature of Love. 1966.

Other

The Generations of Men. 1959.
King of the Dingoes (juvenile). 1959.
Range the Mountains High (juvenile). 1962.
Shaw Neilson (biography and selected verse). 1963.
Charles Harpur. 1963.
The Day the Mountains Played (juvenile). 1963.
Country Towns (juvenile). 1964.
Preoccupations in Australian Poetry. 1965.
The River and the Road (juvenile). 1966; revised edition, 1971.
Henry Lawson. 1967.
Conservation as an Emerging Concept. 1971.
Because I Was Invited (essays). 1976.

Editor, *Australian Poetry 1948.* 1948.
Editor, *A Book of Australian Verse.* 1956; revised edition, 1968.
Editor, *New Land, New Language: An Anthology of Australian Verse.* 1957.
Editor, with A. K. Thomson, *The Poet's Pen.* 1966.
Editor, *Witnesses of Spring: Unpublished Poems,* by Shaw Neilson. 1970.

Reading List: *Critical Essays on Wright* edited by A. K. Thomson, 1968; *Wright* by A. D. Hope, 1975.

*   *   *

Judith Wright has such an awareness of time and place that she seems to look beyond these categories. "The Cycads" (*The Moving Image*), whose "smooth dark flames flicker at time's own root," is a fair representative of this attitude. She sees Australia as an age-old country, but it is also her "blood's country." These poems have a firmly realised local habitation in New England, its landscape, history, and early life, particularly in her recognition of the inescapable association of man and the land where he finds himself. In her most famous poem, "Bullocky," she celebrates an early worker, compelled and driven mad by his environment, but his bones are now everlastingly part of it.

This ability for genuinely fundamental perceptions appears again in *Woman to Man* which records the primitive and elemental awareness of woman in several of its poems dealing with such experiences as conception, pregnancy, and parturition, what A. D. Hope has called "the continuous epic of generation." Relying much on Blake's idea of the double-vision, she grapples in *The Gateway* and in *The Two Fires* with the problem of time, the life that grows from the birth, and, beyond that, with Blakean influences, the doors of eternity, the first steps towards a later recognition of the ability of the five senses to "gather into a meaning/all acts, all presences/ ... a rhythm that dances/and is not mine."

Another influence at work in this period, and later, is T. S. Eliot, whose *Four Quartets* no doubt seemed relevant both to Wright's struggles with the problems of time and also with those which she was conscious of having – "My speech inexact, my note not right" – with language. She was wrestling with philosophical difficulties.

Birds is a return to what she calls the "reverence of the heart." She had became co-founder and president of the Wild Life Preservation Society of Queensland, and *Birds*, a book of light-weight poems, probably represents a necessary breathing-space before the next phase.

Five Senses suggests reassurance and reconciliation. The troubles of the 1950's give way to a sense of fulfilment, aptly represented by the poem "For My Daughter," growing up, growing away, the mother ready to accept the new relationship. Likewise, "Turning Fifty" (*The Other Half*) reflects a mood of acceptance; and "Shadow," the new section in *Collected Poems 1942–1970*, speaks of completeness as she elegises her husband: "Growing beyond your life into your vision,/at last you proved the circle and stepped clear." *Alive* concerns itself with her own process of ageing, but, just as in the 1950's the atomic bomb had troubled her, so in this collection and in "Shadow" she was disturbed by Vietnam and the spoliation of the Australian natural environment. Her later work, competent though it generally is, is rarely so richly satisfying as her first two collections. It does not have that intuitive metaphysical depth that characterises the earlier work.

She has written extensively in the field of literary criticism; *Preoccupations in Australian Poetry* and *Because I Was Invited* collect her best work. The latter also contains many of her articles on conservation. She also wrote short stories and novels for children. As a critic, she is no systematiser but rather a defender of what she likes; she has made a case particularly for such early Australian poets as Harpur, Baylebridge, and Shaw Neilson, who are all too easily underrated.

—Arthur Pollard

NOTES ON CONTRIBUTORS

ALCOCK, Peter. Senior Lecturer in English, Massey University, Palmerston North, New Zealand; Associate Editor of *World Literature Written in English* and bibliographer for *Journal of Commonwealth Literature*. Member of the Executive Committee, Association for Commonwealth Literature and Literature and Language, 1968–77. **Essays:** Blanche Baughan; Denis Glover; Edith Searle Grossman.

BARNES, John. Chairman of the Department of English, La Trobe University, Bundoora, Australia. Author of articles on Peter Cowan, Hal Porter, and Patrick White. **Essays:** Henry Kingsley; Vance Palmer; Randolph Stow.

BODE, Walter. Editor in the Chemistry Department, University of California, Berkeley. Assistant Editor of *San Francisco Theatre Magazine,* and free-lance theatre and film critic. **Essay:** Ray Lawler.

BRISSENDEN, Alan. Senior Lecturer in English, University of Adelaide, Australia; Joint General Editor, Tudor and Stuart Text series. Author of *Rolf Boldrewood,* 1972. Editor of *A Chaste Maid in Cheapside* by Thomas Middleton, 1968, *Shakespeare and Some Others,* 1976, and *The Portable Boldrewood,* 1978. **Essay:** Rolf Boldrewood.

BROWN, Lloyd W. Member of the Department of Comparative Literature, University of Southern California, Los Angeles. **Essays:** Louise Bennett; Edward Brathwaite; Roger Mais.

CHAMBERS, D. D. C. Associate Professor of English, Trinity College, Toronto. **Essay:** James Reaney.

CLUCAS, Garth. Free-lance writer, currently engaged in research at Linacre College, Oxford. **Essay:** Geoffrey Dutton.

COPLAND, R. A. Former Member of the Department of English, University of Canterbury, Christchurch, New Zealand. **Essay:** James Courage.

DAVISON, Dennis. Senior Lecturer in English, Monash University, Melbourne. Author of *The Poetry of Andrew Marvell,* 1964, *Dryden,* 1968, and *W. H. Auden,* 1970. Editor of *Selected Poetry and Prose,* by Marvell, 1952, *Restoration Comedies,* 1970, and *The Penguin Book of Eighteenth-Century Verse,* 1973. **Essay:** Guy Butler.

DOYLE, Charles. Professor of English, and Director of the Division of American and Commonwealth Literature, University of Victoria, British Columbia. Author (as Mike Doyle) of several books of poetry, the most recent being *Going On,* 1974, and of critical studies of New Zealand poetry, R. A. K. Mason, and James K. Baxter. Editor of *Recent Poetry in New Zealand,* 1965. **Essays:** James K. Baxter; R. A. K. Mason; Al Purdy.

DUTTON, Geoffrey. See his own entry. **Essay:** Patrick White.

NOTES ON CONTRIBUTORS

ELLIOTT, Brian. Reader in Australian Literary Studies, University of Adelaide. Author of *Leviathan's Inch* (novel), 1946; *Singing to the Cattle and Other Australian Essays*, 1947; *Marcus Clarke*, 1958; *The Landscape of Australian Poetry*, 1967. Editor of *Coast to Coast: Australian Stories 1948*, 1949, and *Bards in the Wilderness: Australian Poetry to 1920* (with Adrian Mitchell), 1970. **Essays:** Martin Boyd; Charles Harpur; Xavier Herbert; Andrew Barton Paterson; Steele Rudd.

EVANS, Patrick. Lecturer in English and American Studies, University of Canterbury, Christchurch, New Zealand. **Essay:** Janet Frame.

FLETCHER, Ian. Reader in English Literature, University of Reading, Berkshire. Author of plays and verse, and of *Walter Pater*, 1959 (revised, 1970); *A Catalogue of Imagist Poets*, 1966; *Beaumont and Fletcher*, 1967; *Meredith Now*, 1971; *Swinburne*, 1972. Editor of anthologies of verse and drama, and of works by Lionel Johnson, Victor Plarr, and John Gray. **Essay:** Shaw Neilson.

FOSTER, John Wilson. Associate Professor of English, University of British Columbia, Vancouver; Book Review Editor of *The Canadian Journal of Irish Studies*. Author of *Forces and Themes in Ulster Fiction*, 1974. **Essay:** Margaret Atwood.

FRENCH, Warren. Professor of English and Director of the Center for American Studies, Indiana University-Purdue University, Indianapolis; Member of the Editorial Board, *American Literature* and *Twentieth-Century Literature;* series editor for Twayne publishers. Author of *John Steinbeck*, 1961; *Frank Norris*, 1962; *J. D. Salinger*, 1963; *A Companion to "The Grapes of Wrath,"* 1963; *The Social Novel at the End of an Era*, 1966; and a series on American fiction, poetry, and drama, *The Thirties*, 1967, *The Forties*, 1968, *The Fifties*, 1971, and *The Twenties*, 1975. **Essays:** Edgar Mittelholzer; Khushwant Singh.

GLASRUD, Clarence A. Professor of English Emeritus, Moorhead State University, Minnesota; Advisory Editor, *Studies in American Fiction;* Member of the Board of Publications, Norwegian-American Historical Association. Author of *Hjalmar Hjorth Boyesen: A Biographical and Critical Study*, 1963. Editor of *The Age of Anxiety*, 1960. **Essay:** Mazo de la Roche.

GORDON, Ian A. Professor of English, University of Wellington, 1936–74. Has taught at the University of Leeds and the University of Edinburgh. Author of *John Skelton*, 1943; *The Teaching of English*, 1947; *Katherine Mansfield*, 1954; *The Movement of English Prose*, 1966; *John Galt*, 1972. Editor of *English Prose Technique*, 1948, and of works by William Shenstone, John Galt, and Katherine Mansfield. **Essay:** Katherine Mansfield.

GREEN, Dorothy. Member of the Faculty, Humanities Research Centre, Australian National University, Canberra. Author of books of verse, including *The Dolphin*, 1967, and of articles on Australian literature. **Essays:** Christopher Brennan; Rosemary Dobson; Robert D. FitzGerald; Mary Gilmore; Henry Handel Richardson; Henry Kendall; Kenneth Mackenzie; Kenneth Slessor; Christina Stead; Douglas Stewart; Francis Webb.

GURR, Andrew. Professor of English Language and Literature, University of Reading, Berkshire. Author of *The Shakespearean Stage*, 1970. Editor of several plays by Beaumont and Fletcher. **Essays:** Allen Curnow; Amos Tutuola.

JONES, Lawrence. Associate Professor of English, University of Otago, Dunedin, New Zealand. Author of articles on Maurice Shadbolt and Thomas Hardy in *Landfall, Studies in the Novel, Journal of English Literary History*, and other periodicals, and of the introduction to *Roads from Home* by Dan Davin, 1976. **Essays:** Dan Davin; Maurice Duggan; Maurice Shadbolt.

JOYNER, Nancy C. Member of the Department of English, Western Carolina University, Cullowhee, North Carolina. **Essay:** Ngaio Marsh.

KELLNER, Bruce. Associate Professor of English, Millersville State College, Pennsylvania. Author of *Carl Van Vechten and the Irreverent Decades*, 1968; *The Wormwood Poems of Thomas Kinsella*, 1972; *The Poet as Translator*, 1973; *Alfred Kazin's Exquisites: An Excavation*, 1975. Editor of *Selected Writings of Van Vechten about Negro Arts and Letters*, 1978. **Essay:** Robert Service.

KIERNAN, Brian. Senior Lecturer in English, University of Sydney. Author of *Images of Society and Nature* (on the Australian novel), 1971; *Criticism*, 1974; "Patrick White," in *The Literature of Australia*, edited by Geoffrey Dutton, 1976; *Considerations: New Essays on Slessor, White, Stewart*, 1977. Editor of *The Portable Henry Lawson*, 1976, and *The Most Beautiful Lies* (anthology), 1978. **Essays:** Joseph Furphy; Henry Lawson.

LIVESAY, Dorothy. See her own entry. **Essay:** Isabella Valancy Crawford.

MAES-JELINEK, Hena. Chargé de Cours, University of Liège, Belgium. Author of *Criticism of Society in the English Novel Between the Wars*, 1970, *The Naked Design*, 1976, and articles on Peter Abrahams, V. S. Naipaul, Patrick White, and Wilson Harris. Editor of *Commonwealth Literature and the Modern World*, 1975. **Essay:** Wilson Harris.

MAHON, Derek. Writer-in-Residence, New University of Ulster, Coleraine. Author of seven books of verse, including *Night-Crossing*, 1968, *Lives*, 1972, and *The Snow Party*, 1975. Editor of *Modern Irish Poetry*, 1972. **Essay:** Brian Moore.

MARRS, Suzanne. Assistant Professor of English, State University of New York, Oswego. **Essay:** Thomas Chandler Haliburton.

McKAY, F. M. Member of the Department of English, Victoria University of Wellington, New Zealand. Author of *New Zealand Poetry: An Introduction*, 1970. Editor of *Poetry New Zealand*, 1971. **Essays:** Alistair Campbell; Eileen Duggan; C. K. Stead.

McNAUGHTON, Howard. Senior Lecturer in English, University of Canterbury, Christchurch, New Zealand; Theatre Critic, *The Press* since 1968; Advisory Editor, *Act* since 1976. Author of *New Zealand Drama: A Bibliographical Guide*, 1974, and *Bruce Mason*, 1976. Editor of *Contemporary New Zealand Plays*, 1976. **Essays:** Jane Mander; Bruce Mason.

MIRZA, Gail. Free-lance Writer and Translator; Joint Editor of the *Journal of Humanistic and Interdisciplinary Studies*. Author of a work on Juan Ramón Jiménez, Tagore, and Yeats. **Essay** (with H. A. Mirza): Sir Rabindranath Tagore.

MIRZA, H. A. Teacher of Literature and Interdisciplinary Studies, University of Connecticut, Storrs: Joint Editor of the *Journal of Humanistic and Interdisciplinary Studies*. Author of articles on literature, philosophy, psychology, and East-West studies. **Essay** (with Gail Mirza): Sir Rabindranath Tagore.

MORPURGO, J. E. Professor of American Literature, University of Leeds. Author and editor of many books, including the *Pelican History of the United States*, 1955 (third edition, 1970), and volumes on Cooper, Lamb, Trelawny, Barnes Wallis, and on Venice, Athens, and rugby football. **Essays:** Robertson Davies; Hugh MacLennan.

MUIRHEAD, John. Lecturer in English, Massey University, Palmerston North, New Zealand. **Essay:** Roderick Finlayson.

NESBITT, Bruce. Member of the Department of English, Simon Fraser University, Burnaby, British Columbia. Author of *Earle Birney,* 1975. **Essays:** Frederick Philip Grove; Archibald Lampman; Margaret Laurence; Dorothy Livesay; E. J. Pratt; F. R. Scott.

NIVEN, Alastair. Member of the Department of English Studies, University of Stirling, Scotland. Author of *D. H. Lawrence: The Novels,* 1978. **Essays:** Gabriel Okara; Raja Rao; Mordecai Richler; Wole Soyinka.

PETERSEN, Kirsten Holst. Member of the Commonwealth Literature Division of the English Department, University of Aarhus, Denmark; reviewer for *Danida.* Editor of *Enigma of Values* (with Anna Rutherford), 1975. **Essays:** John Pepper Clark; Cyprian Ekwensi; Athol Fugard; George Lamming; Alan Paton; Laurens van der Post.

POLLARD, Arthur. Professor of English, University of Hull, Yorkshire. Author of *Mrs. Gaskell, Novelist and Biographer,* 1965, and *Anthony Trollope,* 1978. Editor of *The Letters of Mrs. Gaskell* (with J. A. V. Chapple), 1966; *The Victorians* (Sphere History of Literature in English), 1970; *Crabbe: The Critical Heritage,* 1972; *Thackeray: Vanity Fair* (casebook), 1978. **Essays:** Thomas Keneally; James McAuley; Judith Wright.

RAWLINSON, Gloria. Free-lance Writer. Author of two books of verse, *The Island Where I Was Born,* 1955, and *Of Clouds and Pebbles,* 1963. Editor of *Houses by the Sea,* 1952, and *The Godwits Fly,* 1970, both by Robin Hyde. **Essay:** Robin Hyde.

REDEKOP, E. H. Associate Professor of English, University of Western Ontario, London. Author of *Margaret Avison,* 1970. **Essay:** Margaret Avison.

REID, Ian. Senior Lecturer in English, Adelaide University, Australia; Editorial Consultant, *Meanjin.* Author of *The Short Story,* 1977, and *Fiction and the Depression in Australia and New Zealand,* 1978. **Essays:** John Mulgan; Frank Sargeson; Kylie Tennant.

RUTHERFORD, Anna. Head of the Commonwealth Literature Division, University of Aarhus, Denmark. Editor of *Kunapipi,* and Chairman of the European branch of the Commonwealth Literature and Language Association. Editor of *Commonwealth Short Stories* (with Donald Hannah), 1971, *Commonwealth* (essays), 1972, and *Enigma of Values* (with Kirsten Holst Petersen), 1975. **Essays:** Peter Abrahams; Mulk Raj Anand; Ruth Prawer Jhabvala; John Lee; Hal Porter; Katharine Susannah Prichard; Vic Reid; Henry Savery; Samuel Selvon; Price Warung.

SIMPSON, Peter. Member of the Department of English, University of Canterbury, Christchurch, New Zealand. **Essays:** Mary Ursula Bethell; A. R. D. Fairburn; William Pember Reeves.

SIVARAMAKRISHNA, M. Reader in the Department of English, Osmania University, Hyderabad; Editor of *Tenor* magazine. Author of many articles on English and American literature. **Essays:** Dom Moraes; Sarojini Naidu.

SMITH, A. J. M. See his own entry. **Essay:** Ralph Gustafson.

SMITH, Rowland. Chairman of the Department of English, Dalhousie University, Halifax, Nova Scotia. Author of *Lyric and Polemic: The Literary Personality of Roy Campbell,* 1972. Editor of *Exile and Tradition: Studies in African and Caribbean Literature,* 1976. **Essay:** Nadine Gordimer.

STOUCK, David. Associate Professor of English, Simon Fraser University, Burnaby, British Columbia. Author of *Willa Cather's Imagination*, 1975, and of articles in *American Literary Scholarship*. **Essays:** Sinclair Ross; Ethel Wilson.

SWEETSER, Wesley D. Professor of English, State University of New York, Oswego. Author of *Arthur Machen*, 1964; *A Bibliography of Machen* (with A. Goldstone), 1965, and *Ralph Hodgson: A Bibliography*, 1974. **Essays:** Marcus Clarke; Alfred Domett.

THOMAS, Ned. Lecturer in English, University College of Wales, Aberystwyth; Founding Editor of *Planet* magazine. Author of *George Orwell*, 1965, and *The Welsh Extremist: Essays on Modern Welsh Literature and Society*, 1971. **Essay:** Derek Walcott.

THOMSON, Peter. Professor of Drama, University of Exeter, Devon. Author of *Ideas in Action*, 1977. Editor of *Julius Caesar* by Shakespeare, 1970; *Essays on Nineteenth-Century British Theatre* (with Kenneth Richards), 1971; *The Eighteenth-Century English Stage*, 1973; *Lord Byron's Family*, 1975. **Essay:** Stephen Leacock.

TIBBLE, Anne. Free-lance Writer. Author of *African Literature*, 1964, *The Story of English Literature*, 1970, *The God Spigo* (novel), 1976, two volumes of autobiography, and books on Helen Keller, Gertrude Bell, Gordon, and John Clare. Editor of works by Clare. **Essays:** Christopher Okigbo; Okot p'Bitek.

WALSH, George. Publisher and Free-lance Writer. **Essay:** Manmohan Ghose.

WALSH, William. Professor of Commonwealth Literature and Chairman of the School of English, University of Leeds. Author of *Use of Imagination*, 1958; *A Human Idiom*, 1964; *Coleridge*, 1967; *A Manifold Voice*, 1970; *R. K. Narayan*, 1972; *V. S. Naipaul*, 1973; *Patrick White's Fiction*, 1978. **Essays:** Earle Birney; A. D. Hope; A. M. Klein; V. S. Naipaul; Anne Wilkinson.

WINNIFRITH, T. J. Member of the Department of English, University of Warwick, Coventry. Author of *The Brontës and Their Background: Romance and Reality*, 1973. **Essays:** Chinua Achebe; Olive Schreiner.

WOODCOCK, George. Free-lance Writer, Lecturer, and Editor. Author of verse (*Selected Poems*, 1967), plays, travel books, biographies, and works on history and politics; critical works include *William Godwin*, 1946, *The Incomparable Aphra*, 1948, *The Paradox of Oscar Wilde*, 1949, *The Crystal Spirit* (on Orwell), 1966, *Hugh MacLennan*, 1969, *Odysseus Ever Returning: Canadian Writers and Writing*, 1970, *Mordecai Richler*, 1970, *Dawn and the Darkest Hour* (on Aldous Huxley), 1972, *Herbert Read*, 1972, and *Thomas Merton*, 1978. Editor of anthologies, and of works by Charles Lamb, Malcolm Lowry, Wyndham Lewis, and others. **Essays:** Morley Callaghan; Bliss Carman; Irving Layton; Malcolm Lowry; Charles Mair; R. K. Narayan; P. K. Page; Charles G. D. Roberts; Duncan Campbell Scott; A. J. M. Smith; Raymond Souster.